PRACTICAL WORK EXPERIENCE IN ACCOUNTING

Step by step practical guide using Sage 50 Cloud

Sterling Libs

Practical Work Experience in Accounting

www.sterlinglibs.com

STERLING LIBS

London, United Kingdom

ISBN: 978-1-911037-18-7

DEDICATION

"Yours, ADONAI is the greatness, the power, the glory, the victory and majesty; for everything in heaven and on earth is yours. The kingdom is yours, ADONAI; and you are exalted as head over all. Riches and honour come from you, you rule everything, in your hand is power and strength, you have the capacity to make great and give strength to all.
Therefore, our God, we thank you and praise your glorious name"
King David (1 Chronicles 29:11-13)

Table of Contents

NOTE TO THE READER

This step by step guide is designed to provide practical information on Work Experience in Accounting using Sage 50 Cloud.

Every effort has been made to make this book as complete and accurate as possible. However, no assurance is given that the information is comprehensive in its coverage or that it is suitable for dealing with your particular situation. Accordingly, the information provided should not be relied upon as a substitute for independent research. It is sold with the understanding that the publisher and author are not engaged in rendering any accounting, legal, or other professional advice nor do they have any responsibility for updating or revising any information presented herein.

No representation or warranty (express or implied) is given as to the accuracy or completeness of the information contained in this book, and, to the extent permitted by law, the Author/publisher, its members, employees and agents do not accept or assume any liability, responsibility or duty of care for any consequences of you or anyone else acting, or refraining to act, in reliance on the information contained in this book or for any decision based on it.
If legal or other expert assistance is required, the services of a competent professional should be sought.

The author and publisher cannot warrant that the material contained herein will continue to be accurate nor that it is completely free of errors when published. Readers should verify statements before relying on them.

Purpose

This book is information only and has been prepared for general guidance for those who are interested in learning how to work as an Accountant using Sage 50 Cloud accounting software.

INTRODUCTION

If you are struggling to get an accounting job due to lack of work experience, and if you are quite unsure of how to do some accounting tasks using Sage 50 cloud or if you want to understand how to do month end and yearend tasks, then this book is for you.

I distil for you in this book my many years of experience practising as an accountant and training many accounting students and graduates.

I show and guide you step by step to do accounting tasks right from scratch to year end and by the time you are done with all the tasks, you will feel confident and competent enough to work as an accounts assistant, bookkeeper and financial accountant.

Let's begin.

Sterling Libs FCCA,

London United Kingdom.

"If one concentrates on one thing and does not get away from it ... he will have strong moving power"
Cheng Yi

TASK 1: GETTING STARTED – 18 QUESTIONS & ANSWERS

Question 1: Under what legal entities can businesses operate in the UK?

Answer: *Sole Trader, Partnership, Company Limited by Shares (LTD), Company Limited by guarantee (Charity), Community Interest Company (CIC), Limited Liability Partnership (LLP) Designated Activity Company, Public Listed Company (PLC)*

Question 2: What is a tax year and what is a financial year?

Answer: *A tax year in the UK is from the 6th of April the current year to the following 5th April next year.*
A financial year is a 12-month period commencing from the date the business starts trading or gets registered with Companies House (UK)

Question 3: What are the three key stages of the accounting cycle?

Answer: *Analysis stage, Recording stage and Reporting stage*

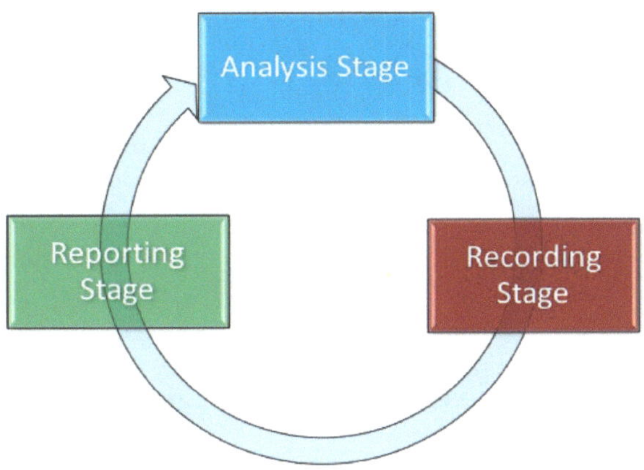

Question 4: Briefly describe what you should do at each of the three stages listed above.

Answer:

a. *Analysis Stage*
   - *Classification of financial documents*
   - *checking that the correct values are reflected in the financial documents*
   - *Making sure that the documents are within the financial year date to which they relate to.*

b. *Recording stage*
   - *It is mostly about data entry*
   - *Using double-entry bookkeeping principles*

c. *Reporting stage*
   - *Checking for any errors in the nominal accounts*
   - *Making yearend/period end adjustments*
   - *Producing yearend/period end reports and statements for filing with government agencies (Companies House & HMRC in the UK)*

Question 5: What are the key steps in the sales ledger (Accounts Receivable process)

Answer:

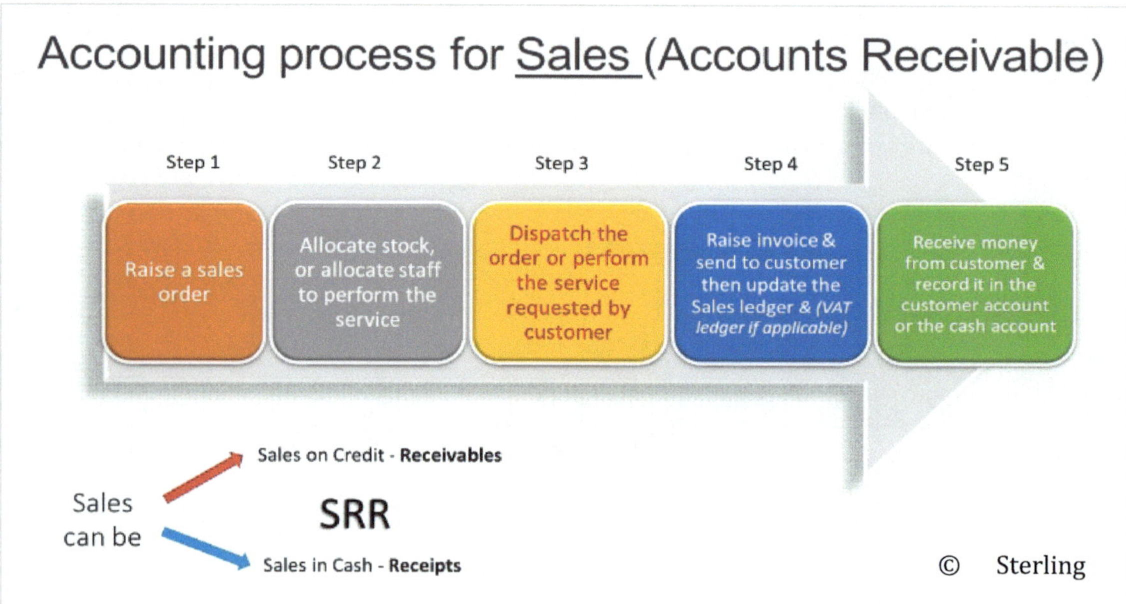

Fig. 1

Question 6: What are the key steps in the purchase ledger (Accounts payable) process

Answer:

See next page...

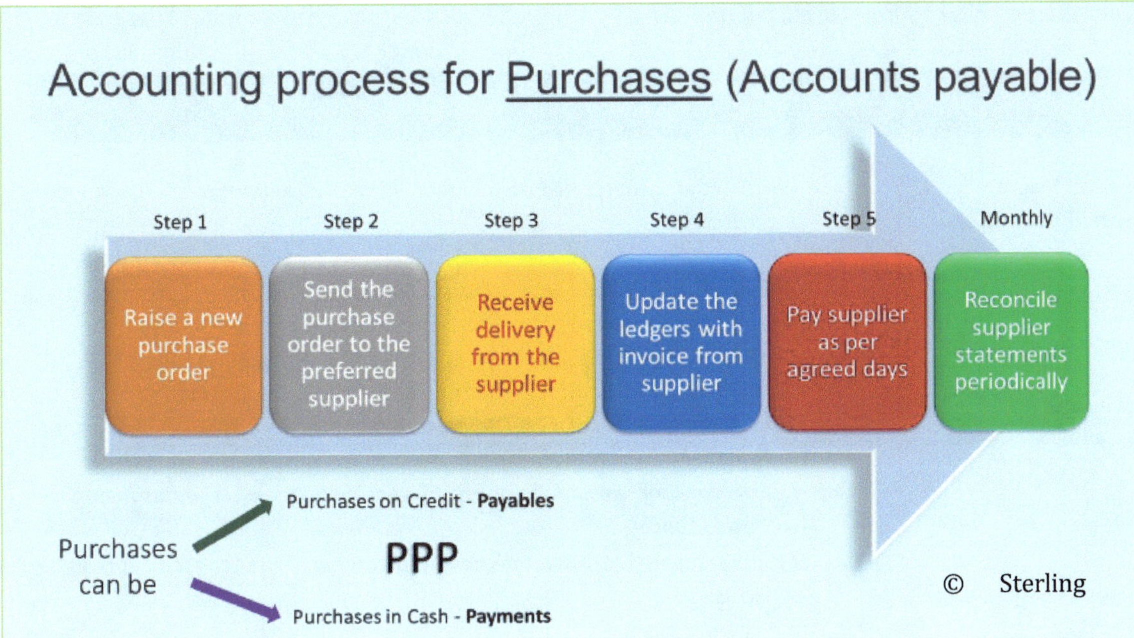

Fig. 2

Question 7: When does a business need to register for PAYE in the UK?

Answer: *When it starts employing people or becomes an employer*

Question 8: When does a business have to register for VAT?

Answer: *Compulsory* ***registration****. You must* ***register for VAT*** *if: your* ***VAT*** *taxable turnover is more than £85,000 (the 'threshold') in a 12-month period or if you expect to go over the threshold in a single 30-day period.*

Question 9: What is the current standard rate of VAT in the UK

Answer: *20%*

Question 10: What is the current rate of corporation tax in the UK?

Answer: *19% for tax year 2017/2018*

Question 11: What is normally done at the month end close process

See next page...

Answer: *Three key steps are usually performed to manage the end-of-the-month accounting process successfully. They are:*

Description of the key steps	*What to do at each stage (the tasks)*
Key step 1: Checking the general ledger accounts for errors & making the necessary corrections	• *Correct the general ledger account errors including mispostings and inaccuracies.*
Key step 2: Doing Adjustments and Reconciliations	• *Financial adjustments, e.g. interest payments adjustments, prepayments, accruals and depreciation* • *Control account reconciliations: Debtors' control account, Creditors' control account, VAT control account, Bank account, Wages account etc.* • *Balance sheet reconciliation (Reconciliation of the Assets, Liabilities, Equity & Reserves)* • *Calculations of closing balances of the accounts after adjustments & reconciliations*
Key step 3: Reporting to senior management	• *Producing a profit & Loss statement and other various management reports if necessary.*

Question 12: Why is it important to do bank reconciliation?

Answer:
A bank reconciliation is used to compare your records to those of your bank, to see if there are any differences between these two sets of records for your cash transactions. The ending balance of your version of the cash records is known as the book balance, while the bank's version is called the bank balance. It is extremely common for there to be differences between the two balances, which you should track down and adjust in your own records. If you were to ignore these differences, there would eventually be substantial variances between the amount of cash that you think you have and the amount the bank says you actually have in an account. The result could be an overdrawn bank account, bounced checks, and overdraft fees. In some cases, the bank may even elect to shut down your bank account.

It is also useful to complete a bank reconciliation to see if any customer checks have bounced, or if any checks you issued were altered or even stolen and cashed without your knowledge. Thus, fraud detection is a key reason for completing a bank reconciliation. When there is an ongoing search for fraudulent transactions, it may be necessary to reconcile a bank account on a daily basis, in order to obtain early warning of a problem.

Question 13: Which government agencies do businesses in the UK need to submit accounts and returns to?

Answer:
Her Majesty's Revenue and Customs (HMRC) and Companies House.

Question 14: Which reports usually are submitted to the government agencies you have stated above?

Answer:

a) HMRC – *Tax returns, VAT Returns,*
b) Companies House - *Statutory annual accounts and annual returns*

Question 15: And who is legally responsible for submitting the reports you've stated above?

Answer: *The Director(s) of the company*

Question 16: What key competencies will help you work effectively as an accountant?

Answer:

a. Attention to detail
b. Analytical skills
c. Numerical skills
d. Communication skills and teamwork
e. Accounting software skills
f. Speed and accuracy

Question 17: What code of ethics are accountants expected to abide by?

Answer:

a. Integrity
b. Objectivity
c. Confidentiality
d. Professional competence and due care
e. Adopting professional behaviour

Question 18: If you were invited to a job interview and were asked why you should be hired over someone else or if you have an accounting job already, but you want a promotion and you were asked why you should be promoted over someone else, how would you answer that question?

Answer:
There is no straightforward answer to this question.
What you need to consider is your skill set together with your experience (if any) and how that helps you add value to the organisation.

You should also be very articulate and confident when answering these kinds of questions and give concrete examples of how you will be the perfect fit for the role. Make sure you have done thorough research on the role and the company and be very prepared to answer any questions that may arise related to the role and your competencies for it.

"When you like your work, every day is a holiday"

Francis Bacon

"Of all kinds of knowledge that we can ever obtain, the knowledge of God and the knowledge of ourselves are the most important"

Jonathan Edwards

TASK 2 – SETTING UP

Task 2a – How to set up a company on Sage 50 Accounts

If you already have Sage 50 Cloud or Sage 50 Accounts installed on your computer, go straight to figure 3 and start there. Otherwise, you will need to download a copy of the software first to your computer (windows only).

To download the software, you need visit the following link for a 30 day free trial https://www.sage.com/en-gb/shop/sage50c/freetrial/

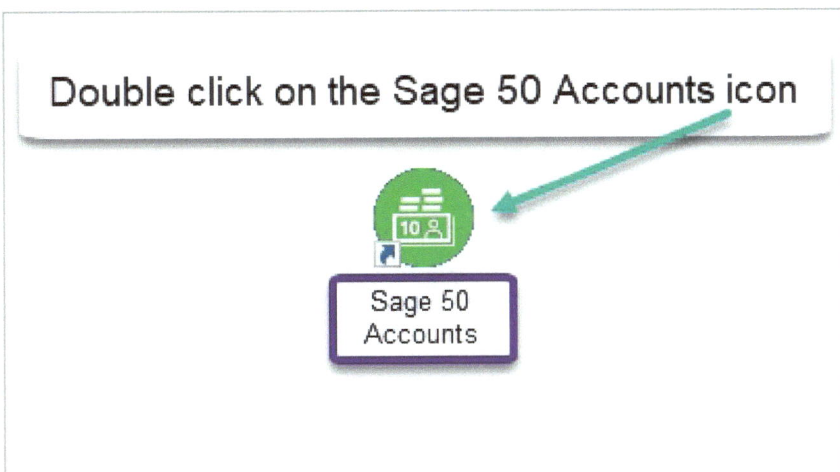

Fig. 3

After double clicking on the Sage 50 Accounts icon on your desktop, you will see a window similar to the figure below. Follow the inset instruction as shown in the figure below.

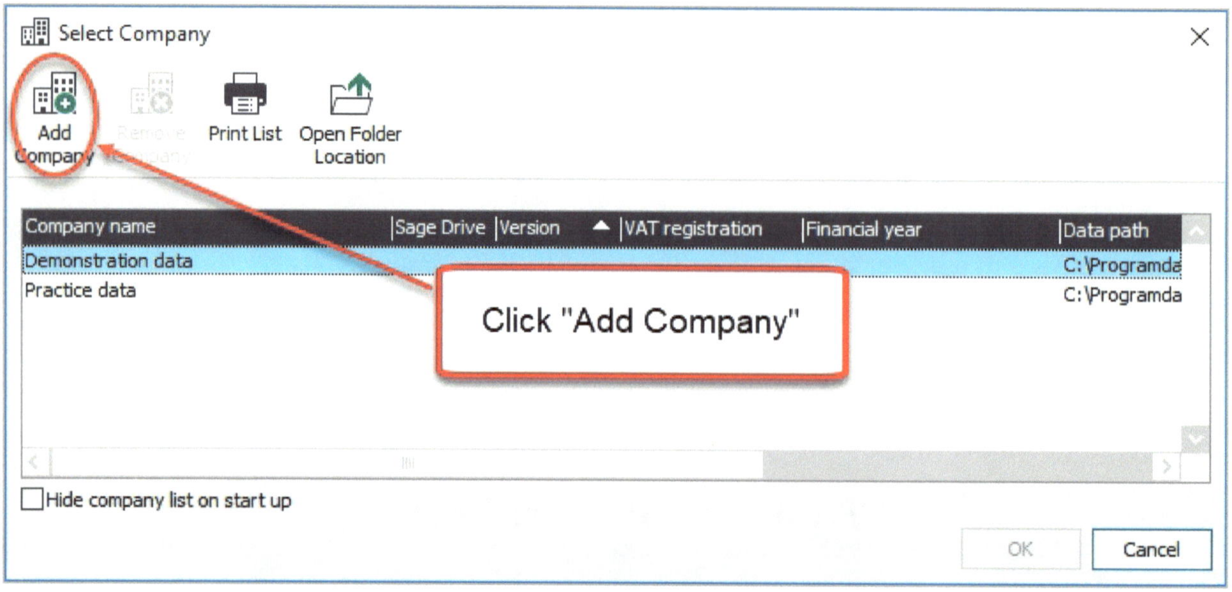

Fig. 4

Once you click Add Company as shown in the figure above, you will see a window similar to the figure on the next page.

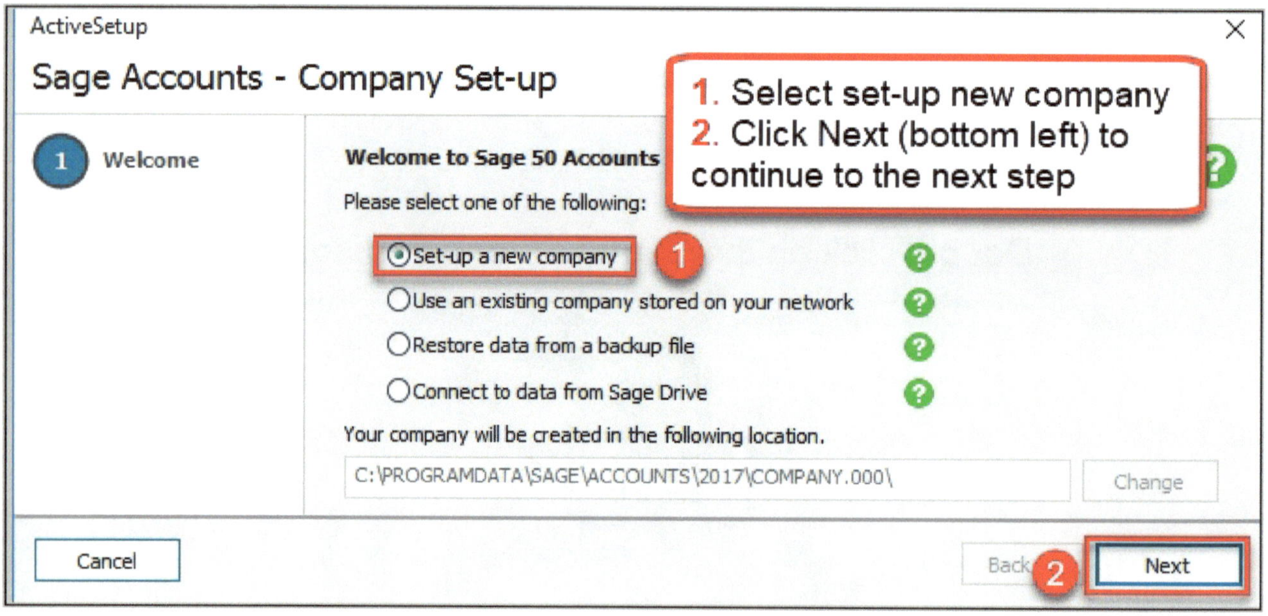

Fig. 5

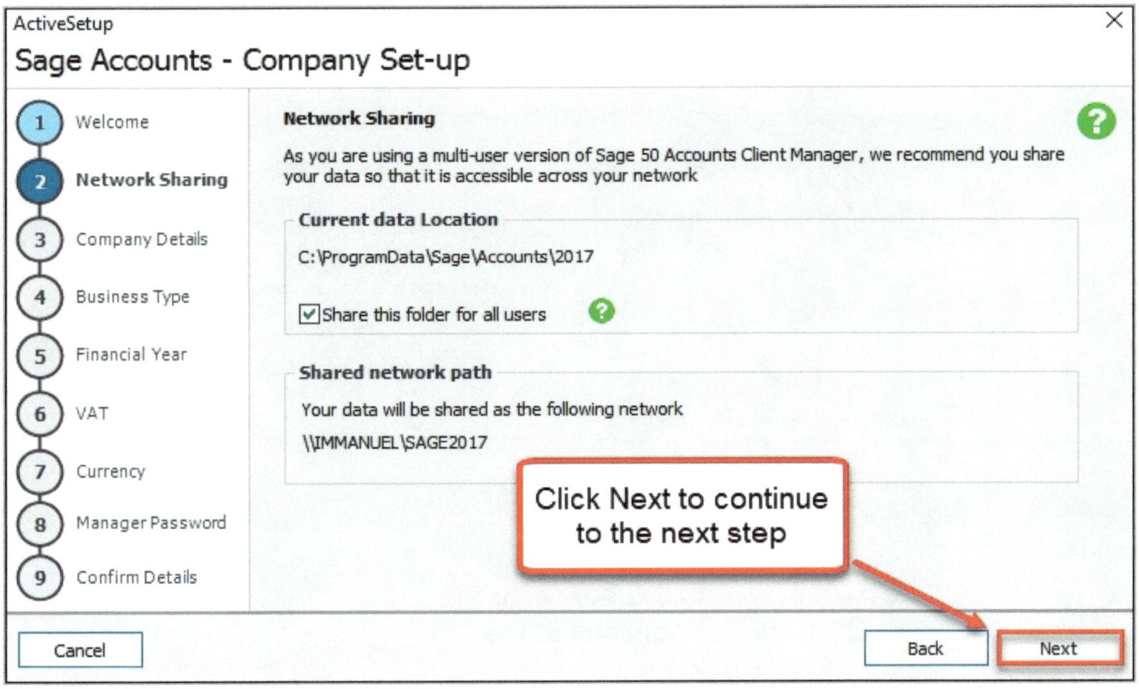
ActiveSetup
Sage Accounts - Company Set-up
1 Welcome
2 Network Sharing
3 Company Details
4 Business Type
5 Financial Year
6 VAT
7 Currency
8 Manager Password
9 Confirm Details
Network Sharing
As you are using a multi-user version of Sage 50 Accounts Client Manager, we recommend you share your data so that it is accessible across your network
Current data Location
C:\ProgramData\Sage\Accounts\2017
Share this folder for all users
Shared network path
Your data will be shared as the following network
\\IMMANUEL\SAGE2017
Click Next to continue to the next step
Cancel
Back
Next

Fig. 6

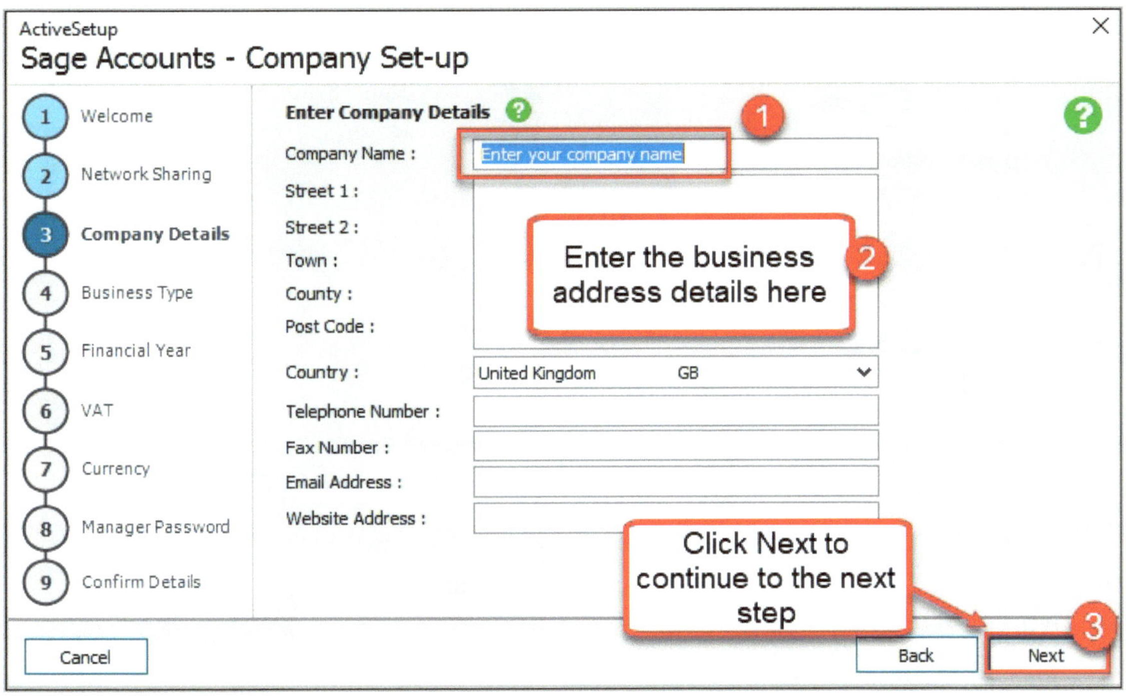
ActiveSetup
Sage Accounts - Company Set-up
1 Welcome
2 Network Sharing
3 Company Details
4 Business Type
5 Financial Year
6 VAT
7 Currency
8 Manager Password
9 Confirm Details
Enter Company Details
Company Name :
Enter your company name
Street 1 :
Street 2 :
Town :
County :
Post Code :
Enter the business address details here
Country :
United Kingdom GB
Telephone Number :
Fax Number :
Email Address :
Website Address :
Click Next to continue to the next step
1
2
3
Cancel
Back
Next

Fig. 7

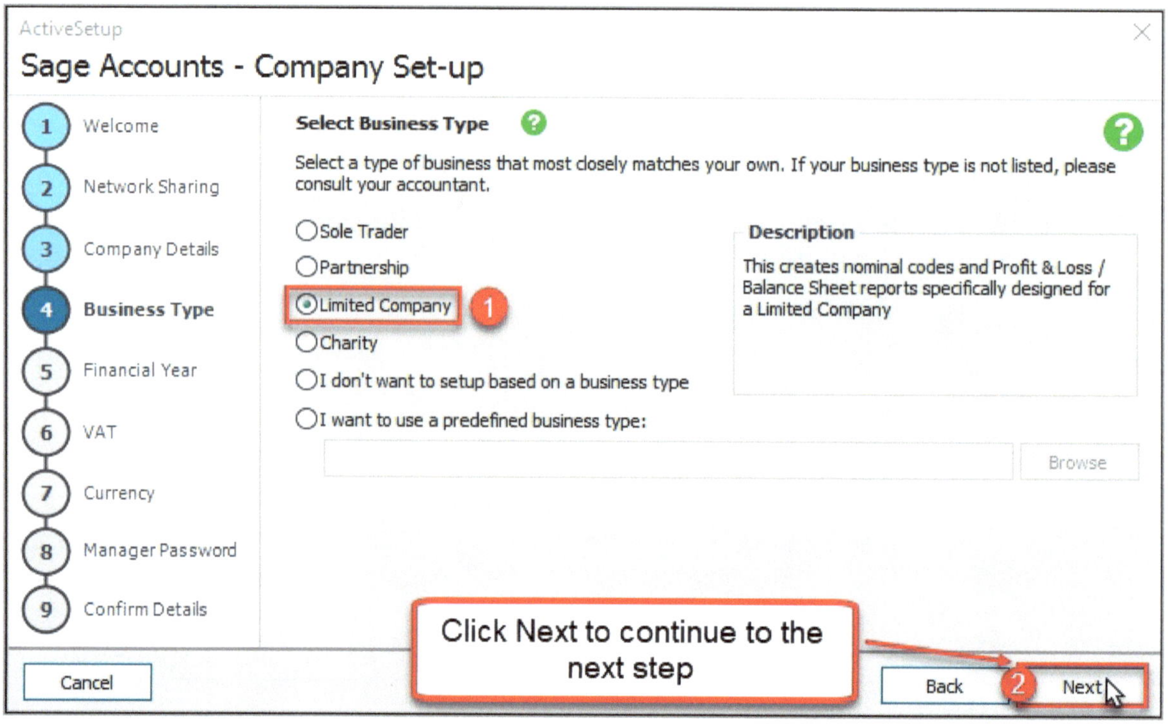
ActiveSetup
Sage Accounts - Company Set-up
1 Welcome
2 Network Sharing
3 Company Details
4 Business Type
5 Financial Year
6 VAT
7 Currency
8 Manager Password
9 Confirm Details
Select Business Type
Select a type of business that most closely matches your own. If your business type is not listed, please consult your accountant.
Sole Trader
Partnership
Limited Company
Charity
I don't want to setup based on a business type
I want to use a predefined business type:
Browse
Description
This creates nominal codes and Profit & Loss / Balance Sheet reports specifically designed for a Limited Company
Click Next to continue to the next step
Cancel
Back
Next

Fig. 8

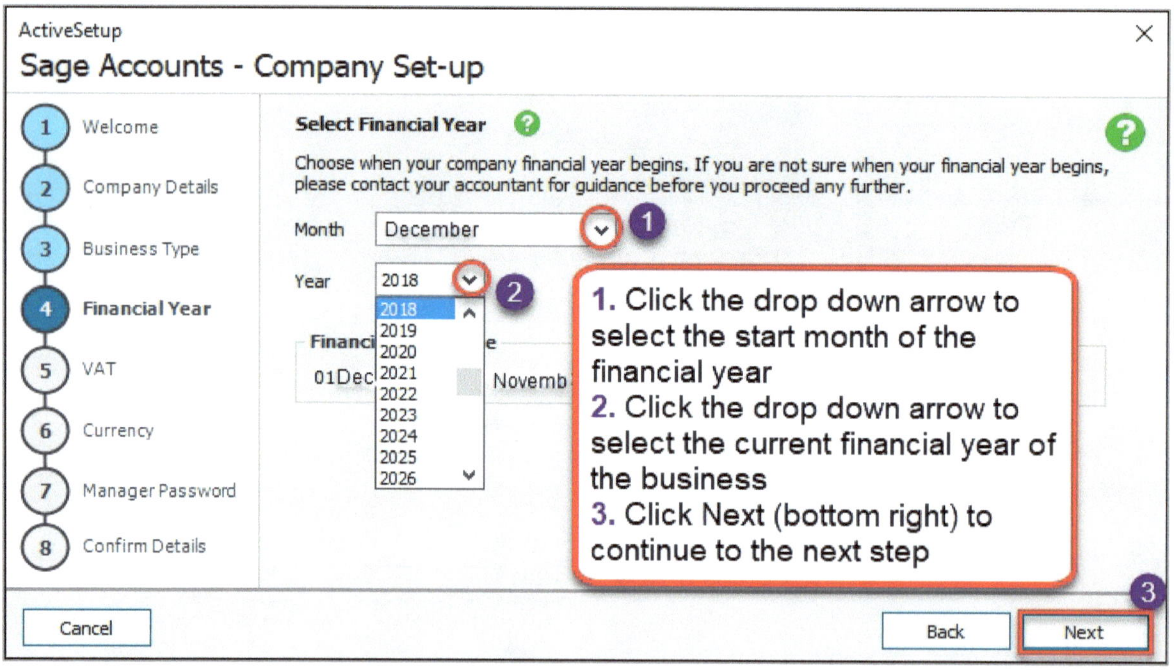
ActiveSetup
Sage Accounts - Company Set-up
1 Welcome
2 Company Details
3 Business Type
4 Financial Year
5 VAT
6 Currency
7 Manager Password
8 Confirm Details
Select Financial Year
Choose when your company financial year begins. If you are not sure when your financial year begins, please contact your accountant for guidance before you proceed any further.
Month December
Year 2018
2018
2019
2020
2021
2022
2023
2024
2025
2026
1. Click the drop down arrow to select the start month of the financial year
2. Click the drop down arrow to select the current financial year of the business
3. Click Next (bottom right) to continue to the next step
Cancel
Back
Next

Fig. 9

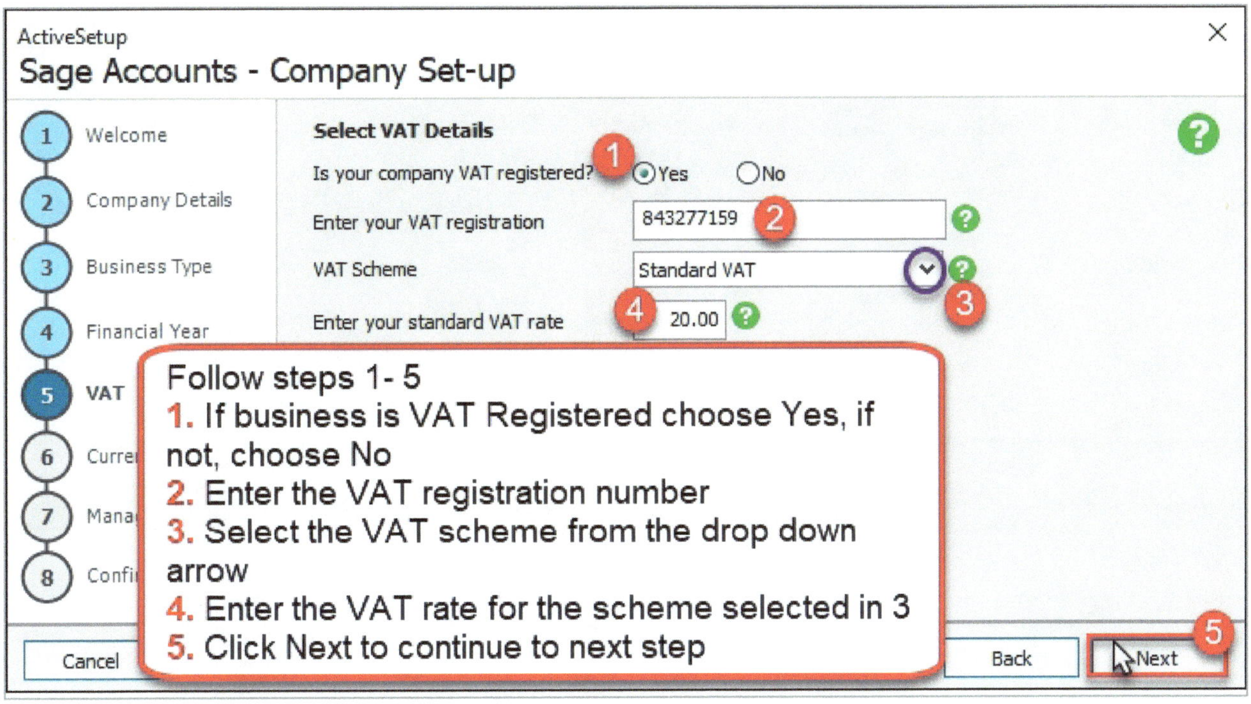
ActiveSetup
Sage Accounts - Company Set-up
1 Welcome
2 Company Details
3 Business Type
4 Financial Year
5 VAT
Select VAT Details
Is your company VAT registered?
Yes
No
Enter your VAT registration
843277159
VAT Scheme
Standard VAT
Enter your standard VAT rate
20.00
Follow steps 1- 5
1. If business is VAT Registered choose Yes, if not, choose No
2. Enter the VAT registration number
3. Select the VAT scheme from the drop down arrow
4. Enter the VAT rate for the scheme selected in 3
5. Click Next to continue to next step
Cancel
Back
Next

Fig. 10

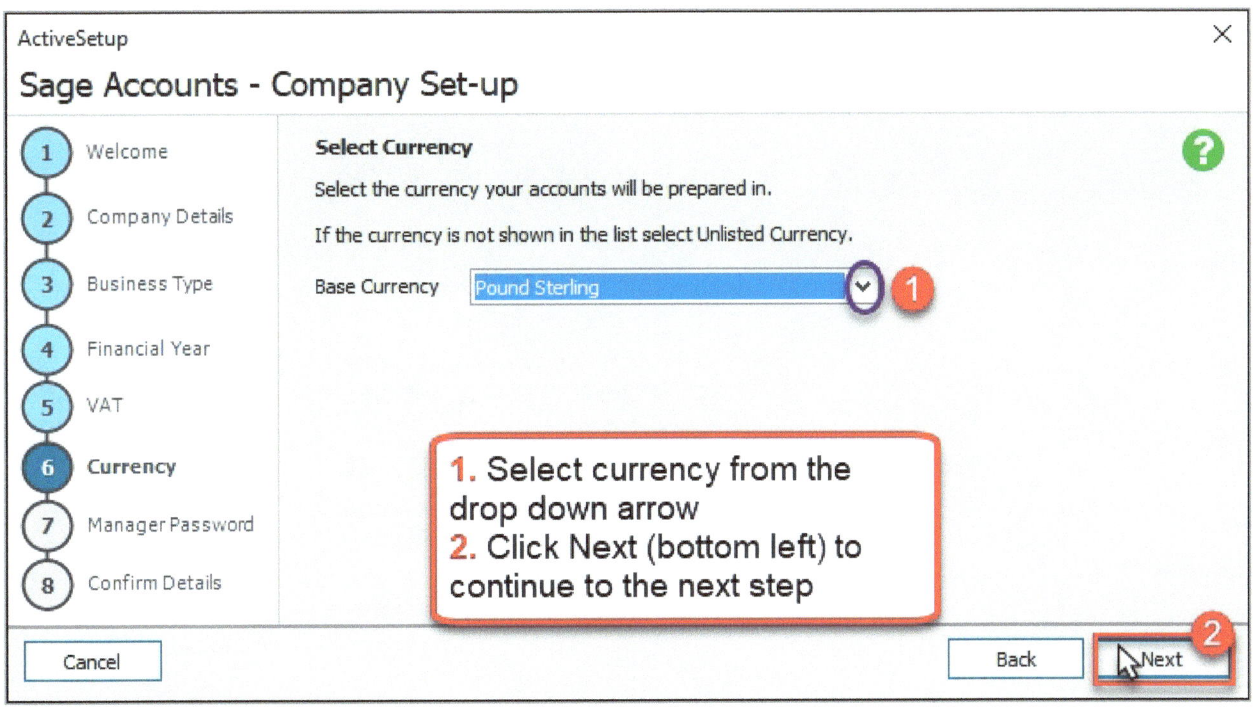
ActiveSetup
Sage Accounts - Company Set-up
1 Welcome
2 Company Details
3 Business Type
4 Financial Year
5 VAT
6 Currency
7 Manager Password
8 Confirm Details
Select Currency
Select the currency your accounts will be prepared in.
If the currency is not shown in the list select Unlisted Currency.
Base Currency
Pound Sterling
1. Select currency from the drop down arrow
2. Click Next (bottom left) to continue to the next step
Cancel
Back
Next

Fig. 11

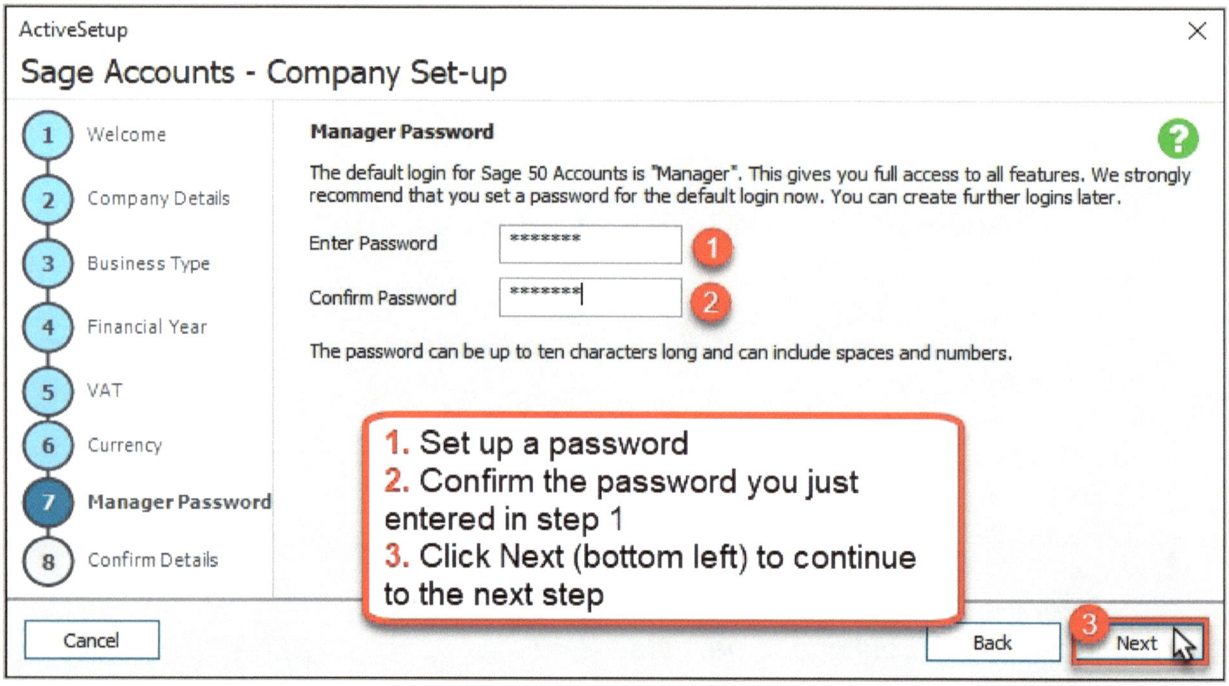
ActiveSetup
Sage Accounts - Company Set-up
1 Welcome
2 Company Details
3 Business Type
4 Financial Year
5 VAT
6 Currency
7 Manager Password
8 Confirm Details
Manager Password
The default login for Sage 50 Accounts is "Manager". This gives you full access to all features. We strongly recommend that you set a password for the default login now. You can create further logins later.
Enter Password
Confirm Password
The password can be up to ten characters long and can include spaces and numbers.
1. Set up a password
2. Confirm the password you just entered in step 1
3. Click Next (bottom left) to continue to the next step
Cancel
Back
Next

Fig. 12

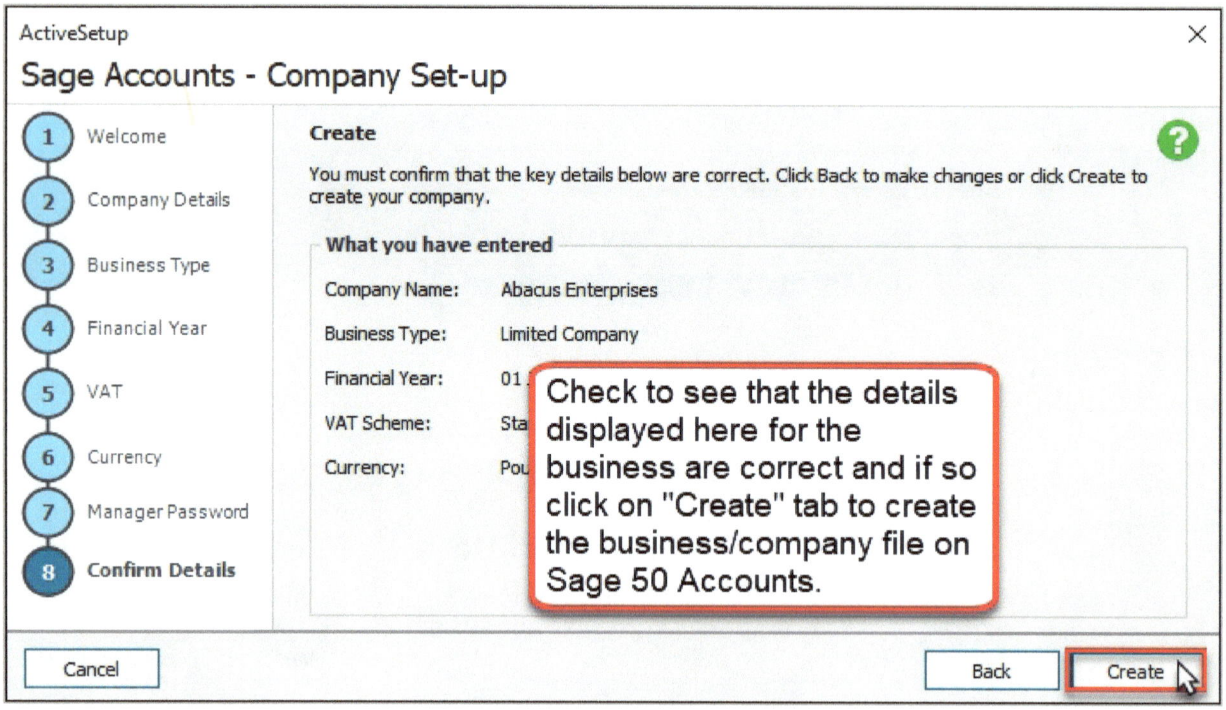
ActiveSetup
Sage Accounts - Company Set-up
1 Welcome
2 Company Details
3 Business Type
4 Financial Year
5 VAT
6 Currency
7 Manager Password
8 Confirm Details
Create
You must confirm that the key details below are correct. Click Back to make changes or click Create to create your company.
What you have entered
Company Name: Abacus Enterprises
Business Type: Limited Company
Financial Year:
VAT Scheme:
Currency:
Check to see that the details displayed here for the business are correct and if so click on "Create" tab to create the business/company file on Sage 50 Accounts.
Cancel
Back
Create

Fig. 13

Once you've clicked create as illustrated in the figure above, a progress window similar to the figure below will appear.

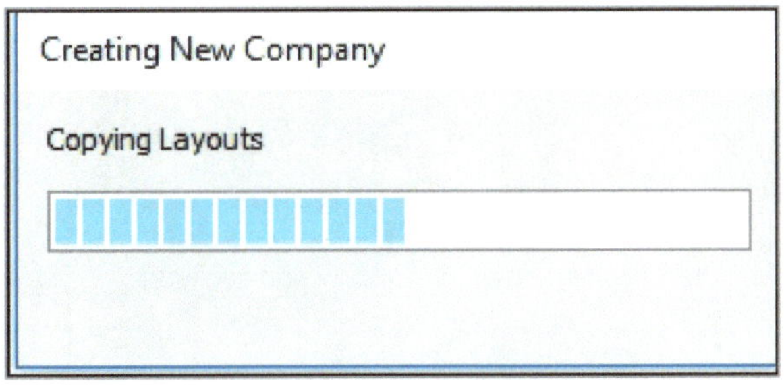

Fig. 14

Wait for this process to finish and a login window similar to the figure below will appear.

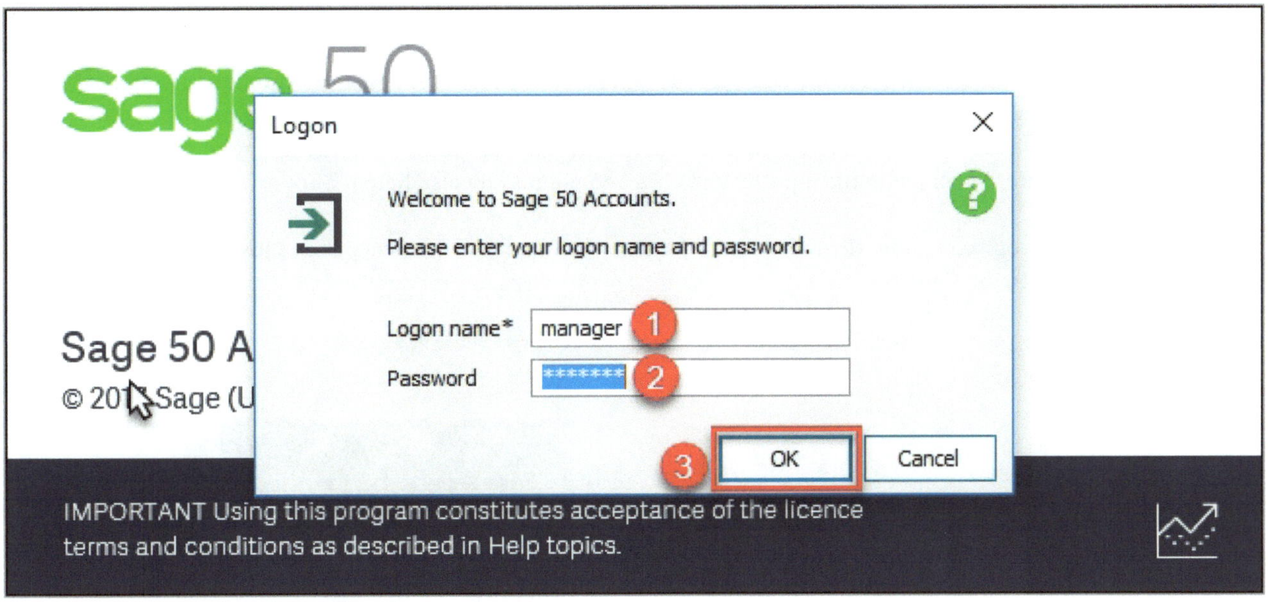

Fig. 15

1. The default manager logon ID in Sage 50 Accounts is manager (it is not case sensitive)
2. Remember the password you created? Refer to fig. 12
3. Click okay to complete login in, and you will see a window similar to figure 16 on the next page.

This space is for notes

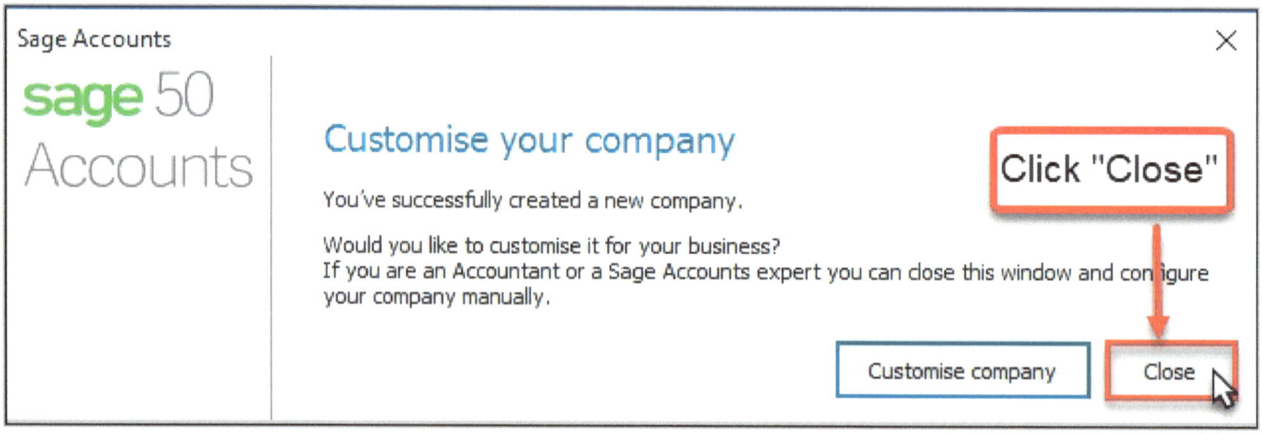

Fig. 16

In the figure above, clicking customise company will basically open a new window to guide you through setting up defaults for customers & sales, suppliers & purchases, banking, products, transactions, services, automatic enrolment. The whole point of the customisation is to set some defaults within Sage 50 Accounts specific to your company or business type and thus help you save time later when doing the inputting of data and potentially also help reduce errors.

If you wish to customise your company, then click on "customise company" otherwise, click **Close** to continue and you will see a window similar to the figure below.

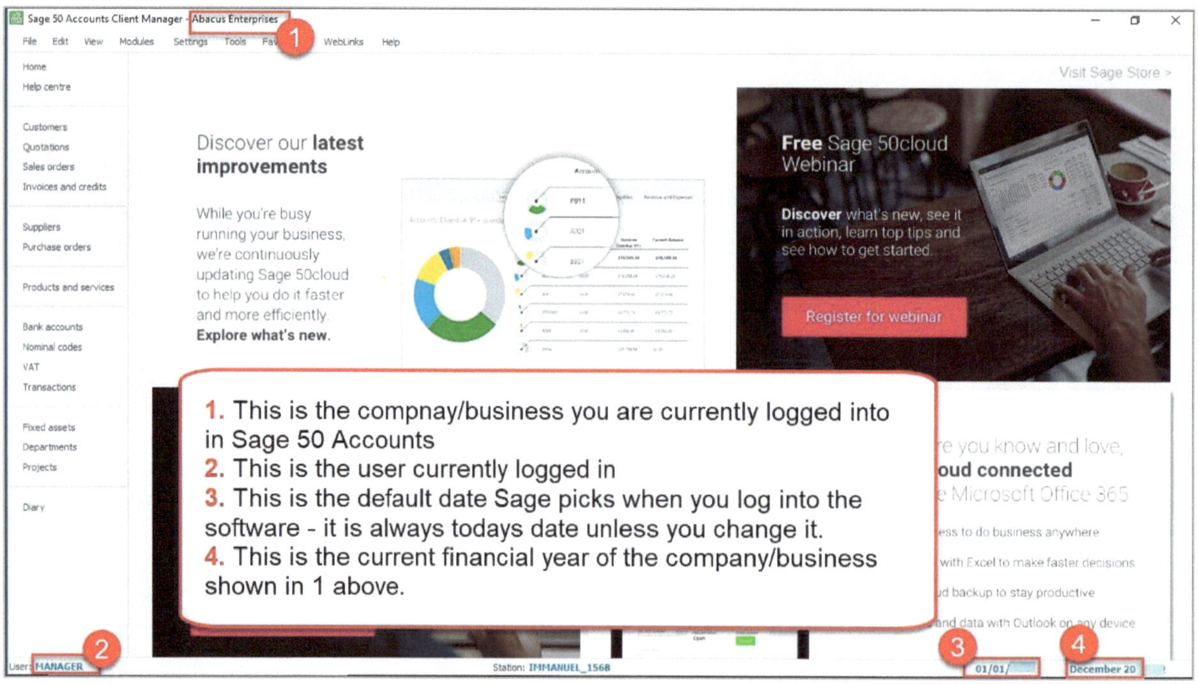

Fig. 17

Let's change the default date that picked by Sage from whatever date it is right now to the 1st of January this year because we will be entering some opening balances for this company as of the 1st January.

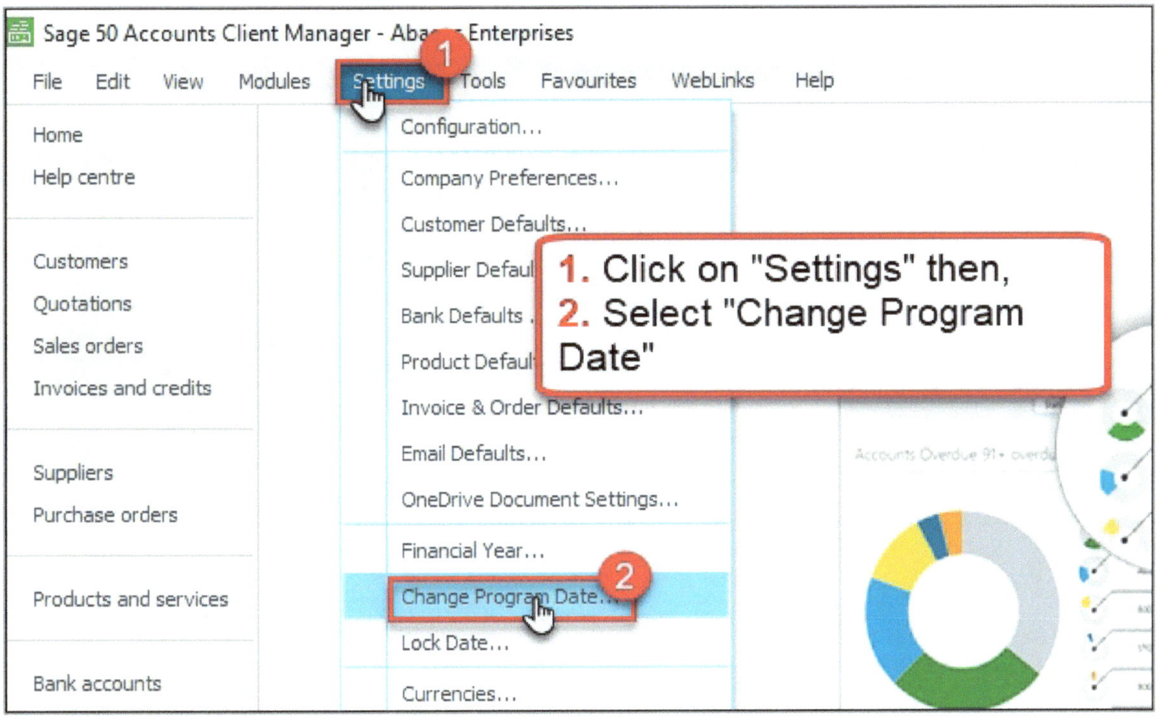

Fig. 18

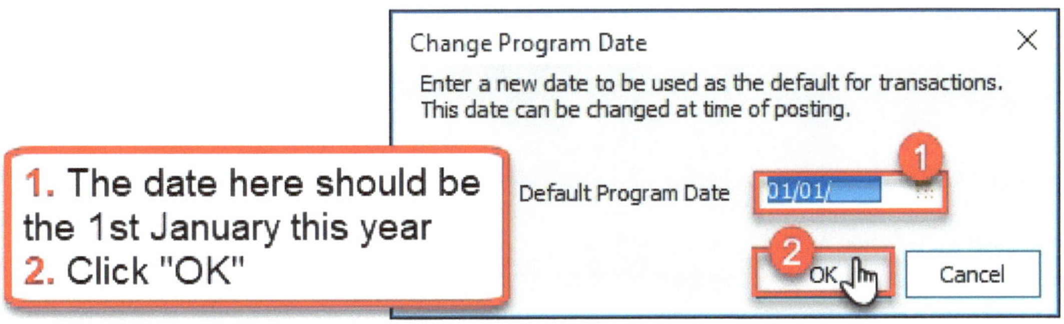

Fig. 19

Next, we are going to customise some of the Sage 50 Accounts nominal codes for our business use. In particular, we will customise some of the Sales and Purchase nominal codes.

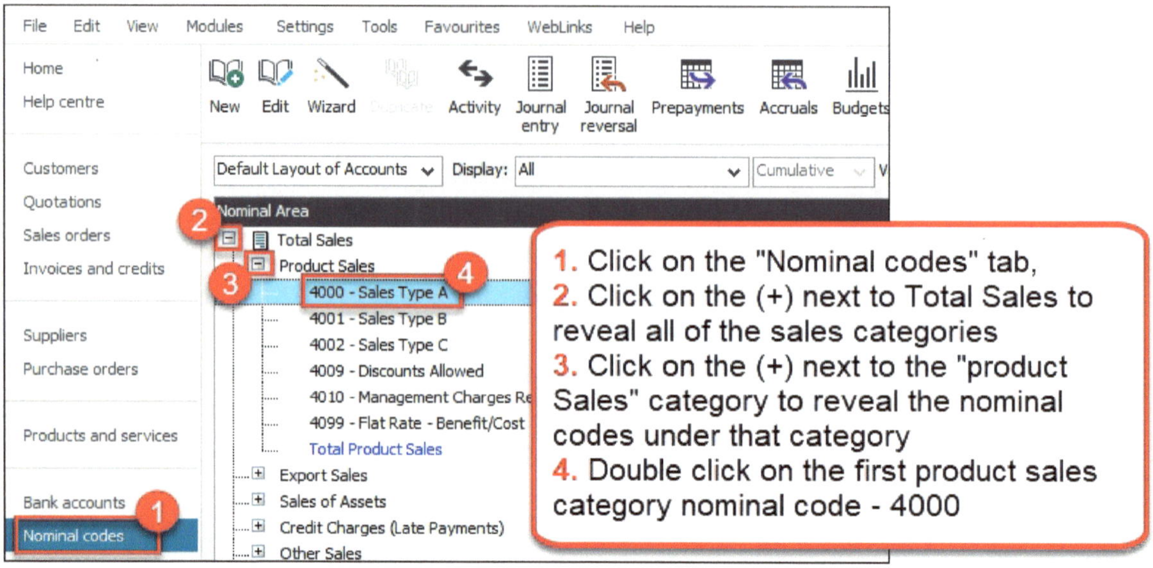
1. Click on the "Nominal codes" tab,
2. Click on the (+) next to Total Sales to reveal all of the sales categories
3. Click on the (+) next to the "product Sales" category to reveal the nominal codes under that category
4. Double click on the first product sales category nominal code - 4000

Fig. 20

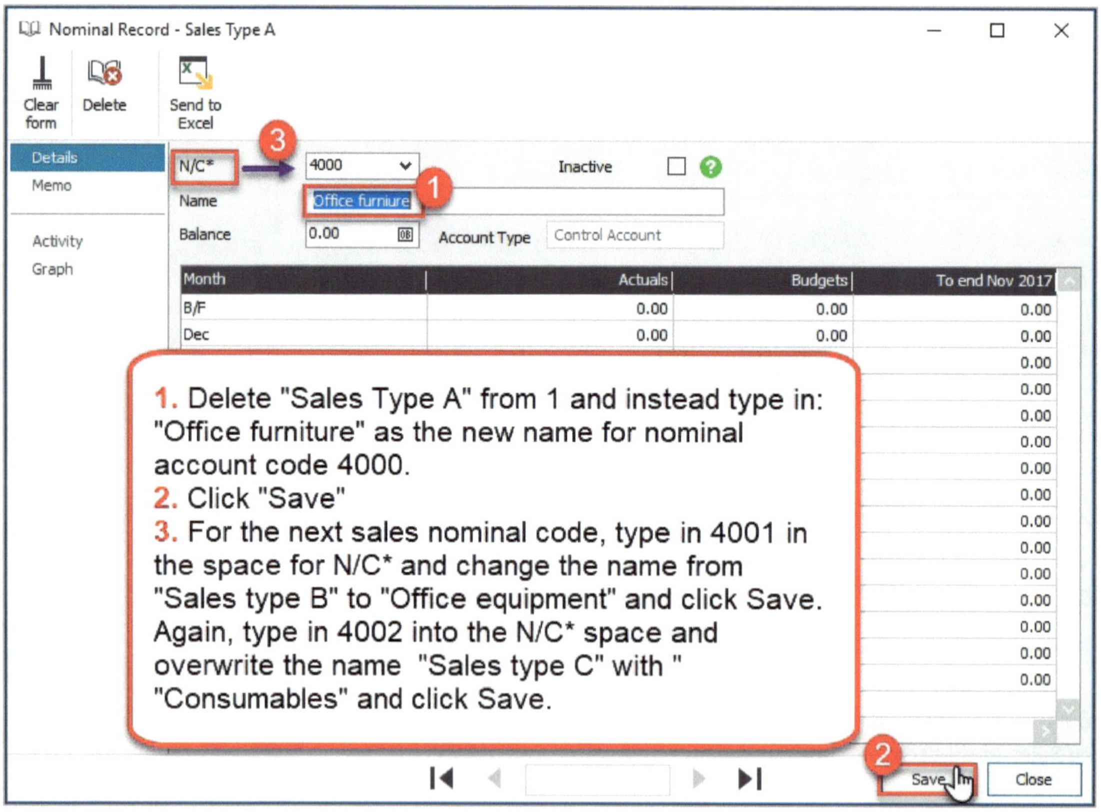
1. Delete "Sales Type A" from 1 and instead type in: "Office furniture" as the new name for nominal account code 4000.
2. Click "Save"
3. For the next sales nominal code, type in 4001 in the space for N/C* and change the name from "Sales type B" to "Office equipment" and click Save. Again, type in 4002 into the N/C* space and overwrite the name "Sales type C" with " "Consumables" and click Save.

Fig. 21

Likewise, update the purchase nominal codes as follows – see figure below

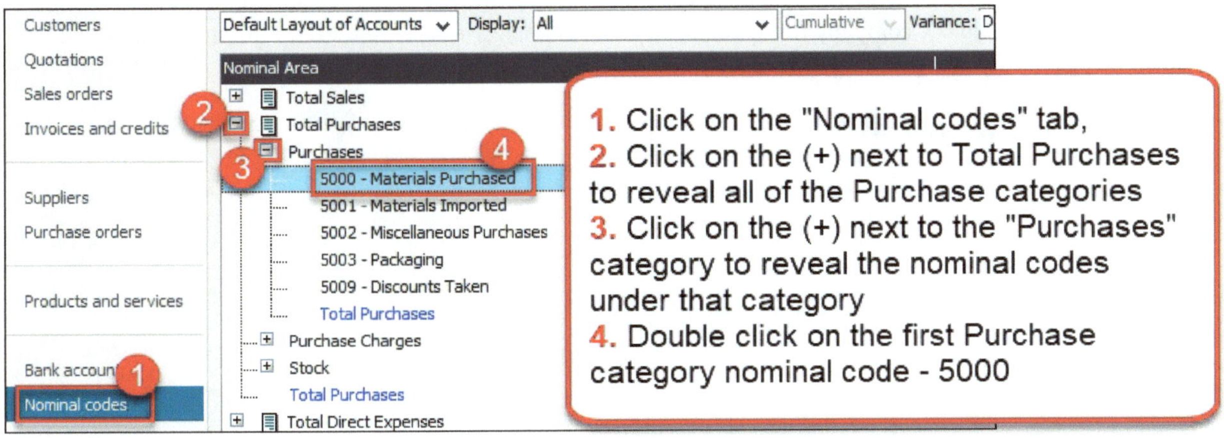

Fig. 22

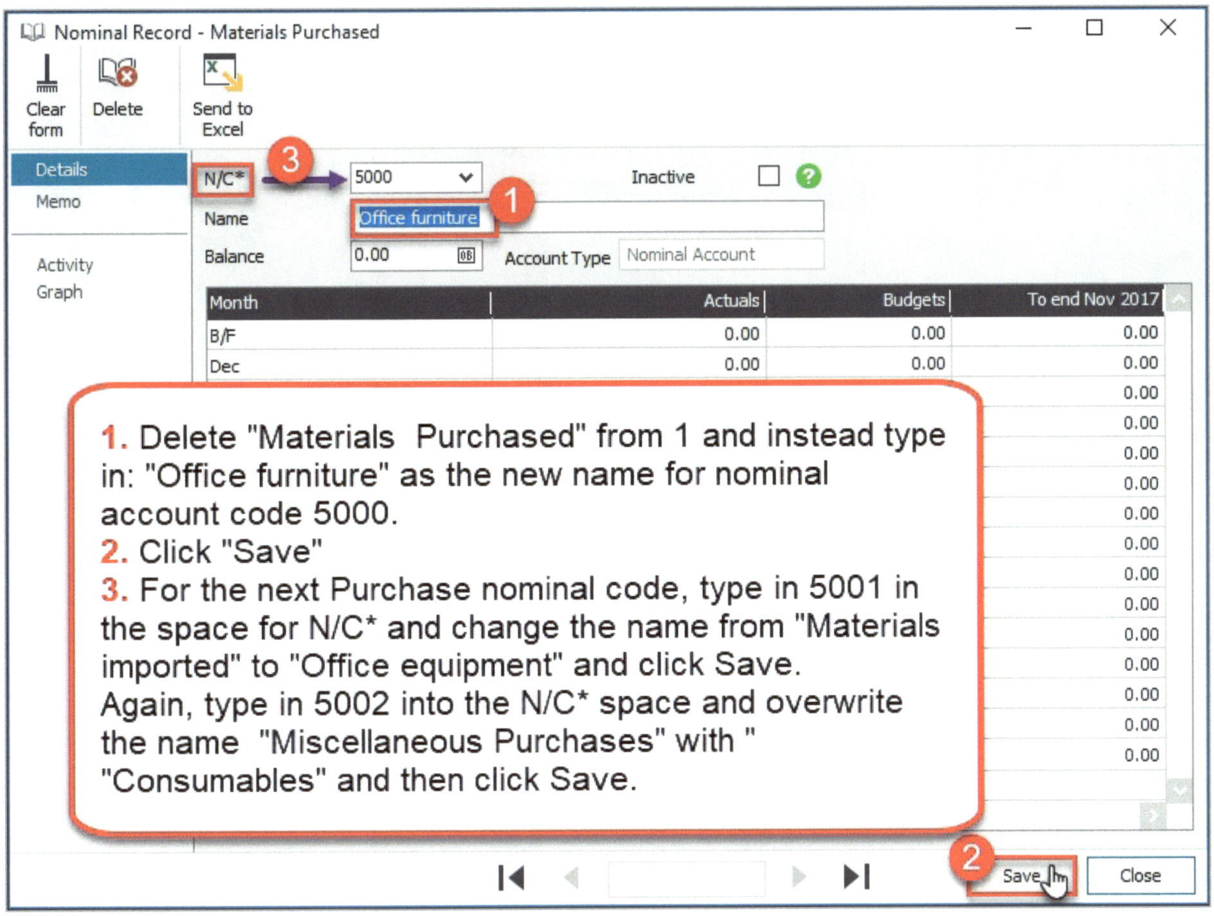

Fig. 23

Many small businesses are managed by their owners (shareholders/Directors) and many of them have lots of transactions with the business. That is, they lend money to the business and also buy things for the business using their own funds while at the same time they also use company funds for their own personal use. We are therefor going to create a special "bank" account in Sage to cater for this kind of transactions.

Click on Bank>arrow under New/Edit>Wizard – See figure below.

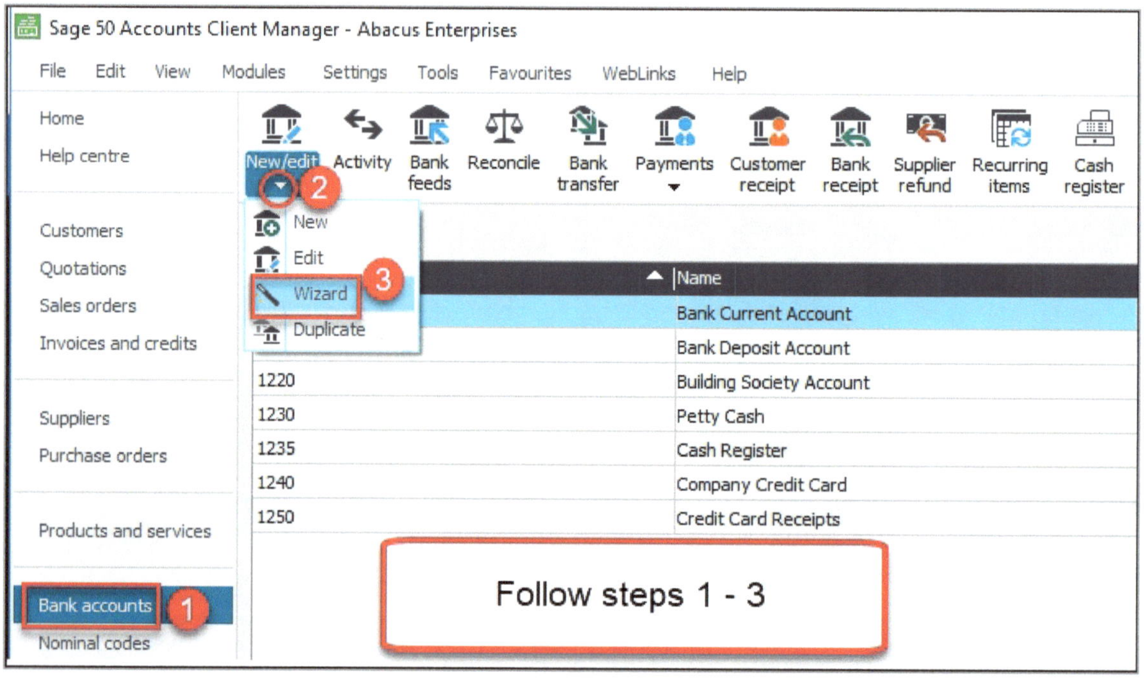

Fig. 24

This space is for notes

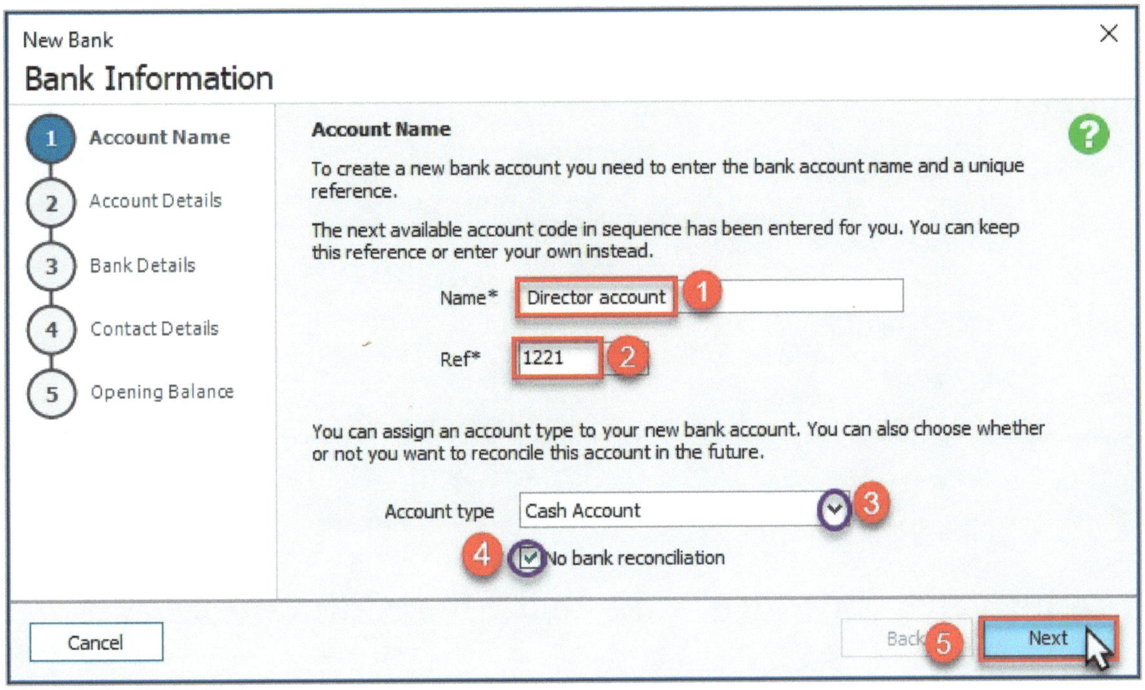

Fig. 25.

The steps as illustrated in the figure above:

1. Enter the new "bank" account name as Director account
2. Next, enter the account nominal account reference number. Please note that this number has to be within 1200 and 1250 but excluding those reference numbers already taken by other bank accounts. If it is under 1200 and over 1250; that will mean that that code is outside the range of chart of accounts for bank accounts in Sage 50 Accounts and as such it will not be reflected in your balance sheet reports. Therefore, in this case, let's use, say for example, code 1221.
3. From the drop-down list of account types, assign this account to be a cash account.
4. Tick this check box to signify that you do not want to reconcile this account in the future. If you want to be able to reconcile it later, then leave it unticked
5. Click next to continue with the setup.

Directors current account

The directors current account (DCA) (also known as simply directors account) is a notional balance between a company and its directors. It is not a real bank account and is not represented by real monies. It records:

- Monies drawn by the director, on account of salary, dividends, expenses, etc. (if not attributed to salary/dividend at the time of drawing)
- Other drawings by the director – e.g. personal bills paid by the company.
- Net amounts of salary and dividend due.
- Expense re-reimbursements due

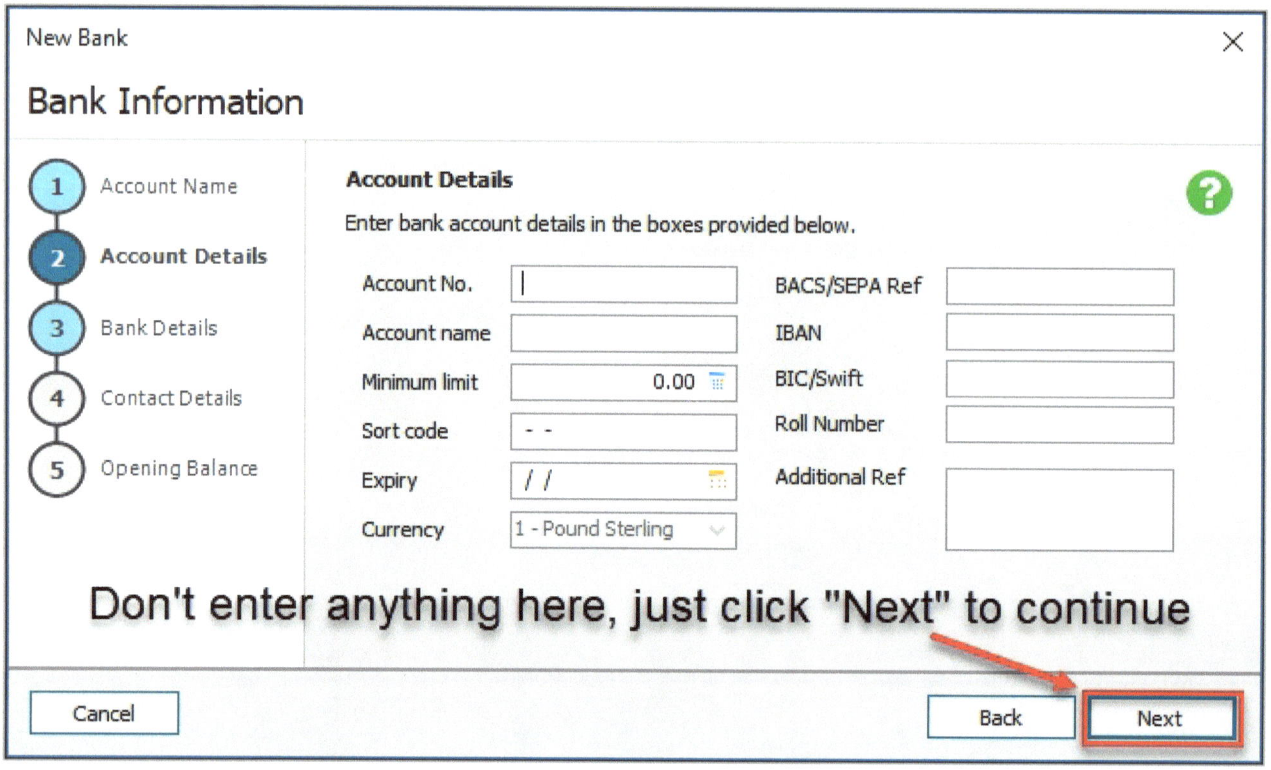
New Bank
Bank Information
1 Account Name
2 Account Details
3 Bank Details
4 Contact Details
5 Opening Balance
Account Details
Enter bank account details in the boxes provided below.
Account No.
Account name
Minimum limit
0.00
Sort code
Expiry
Currency
1 - Pound Sterling
BACS/SEPA Ref
IBAN
BIC/Swift
Roll Number
Additional Ref
Don't enter anything here, just click "Next" to continue
Cancel
Back
Next

Fig. 26

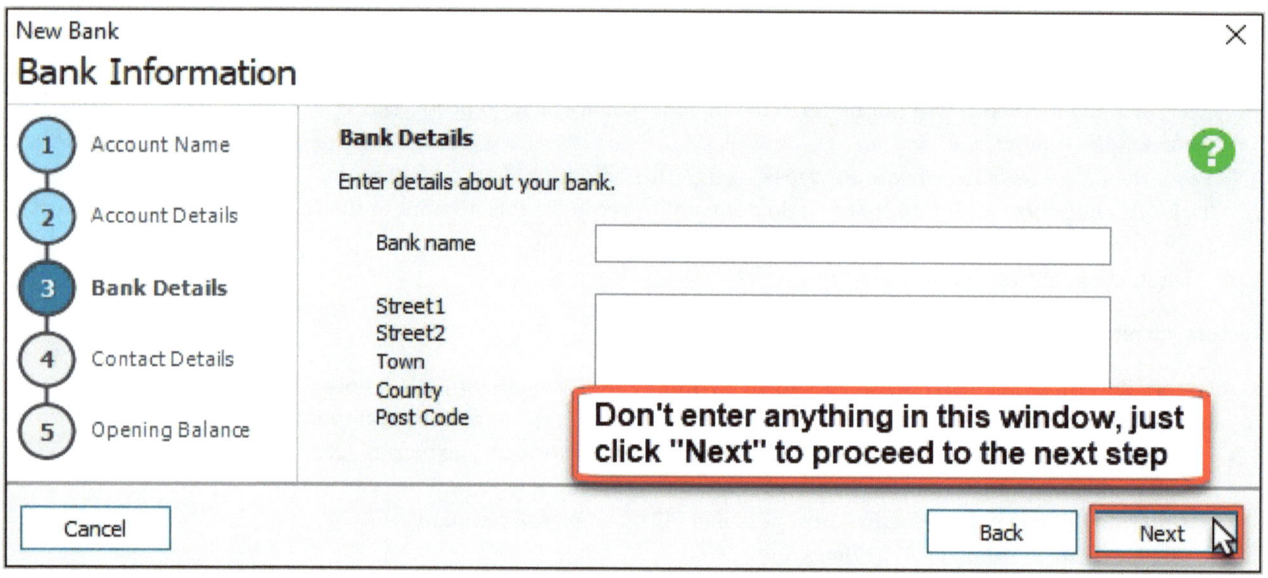
New Bank
Bank Information
1 Account Name
2 Account Details
3 Bank Details
4 Contact Details
5 Opening Balance
Bank Details
Enter details about your bank.
Bank name
Street1
Street2
Town
County
Post Code
Don't enter anything in this window, just click "Next" to proceed to the next step
Cancel
Back
Next

Fig. 27

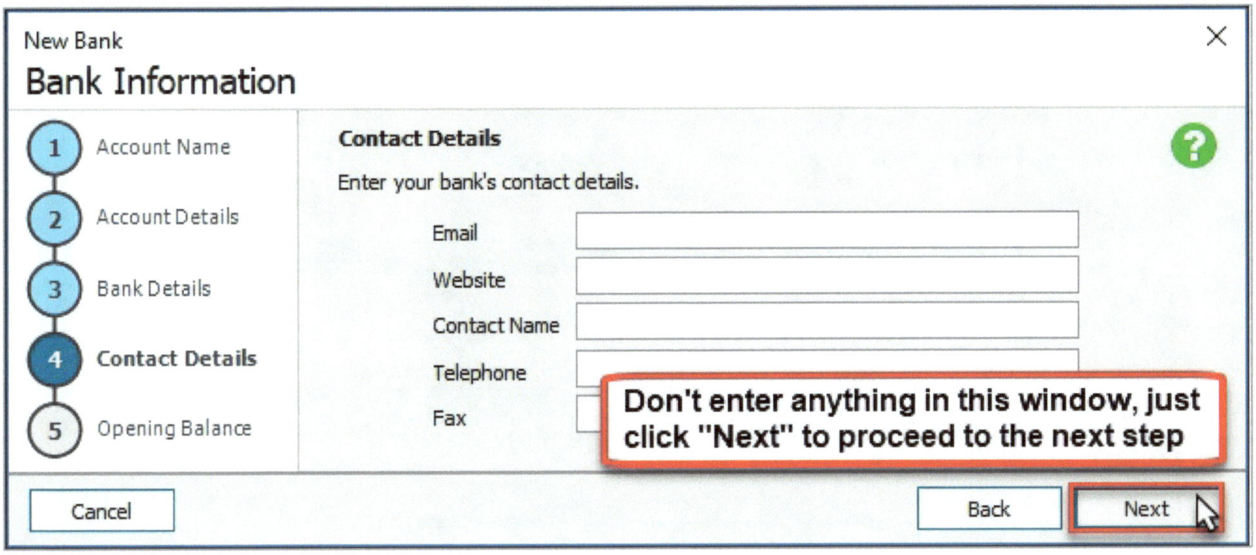

Fig. 28

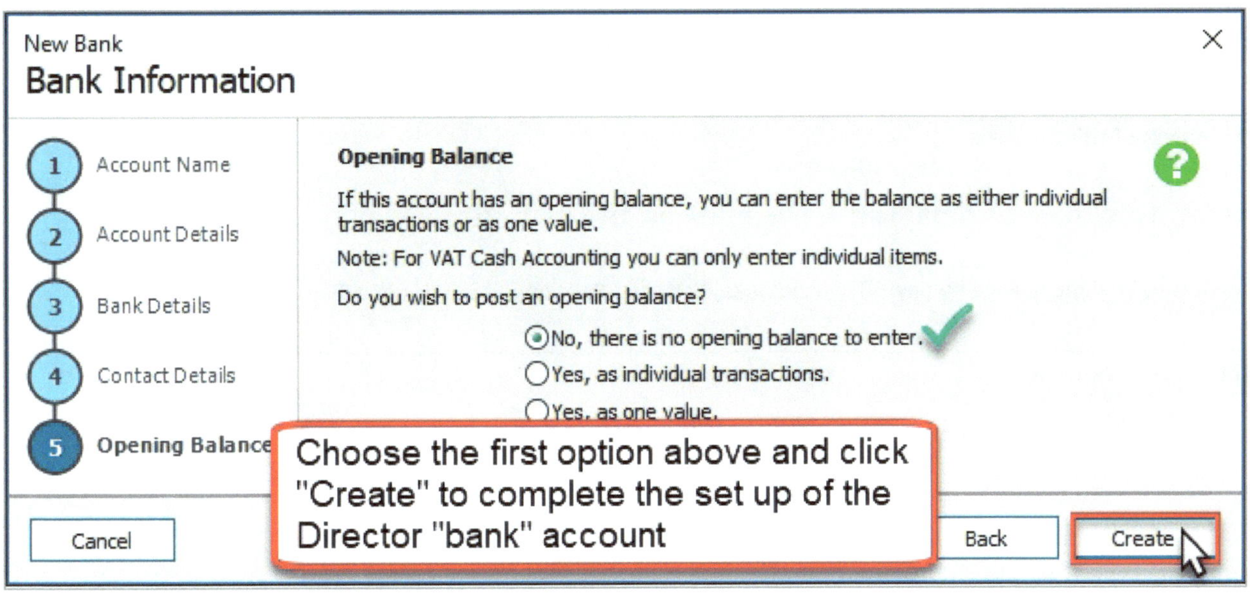

Fig. 29

Here is your new bank account (Director account) in the list of bank accounts – see figure on the next page.

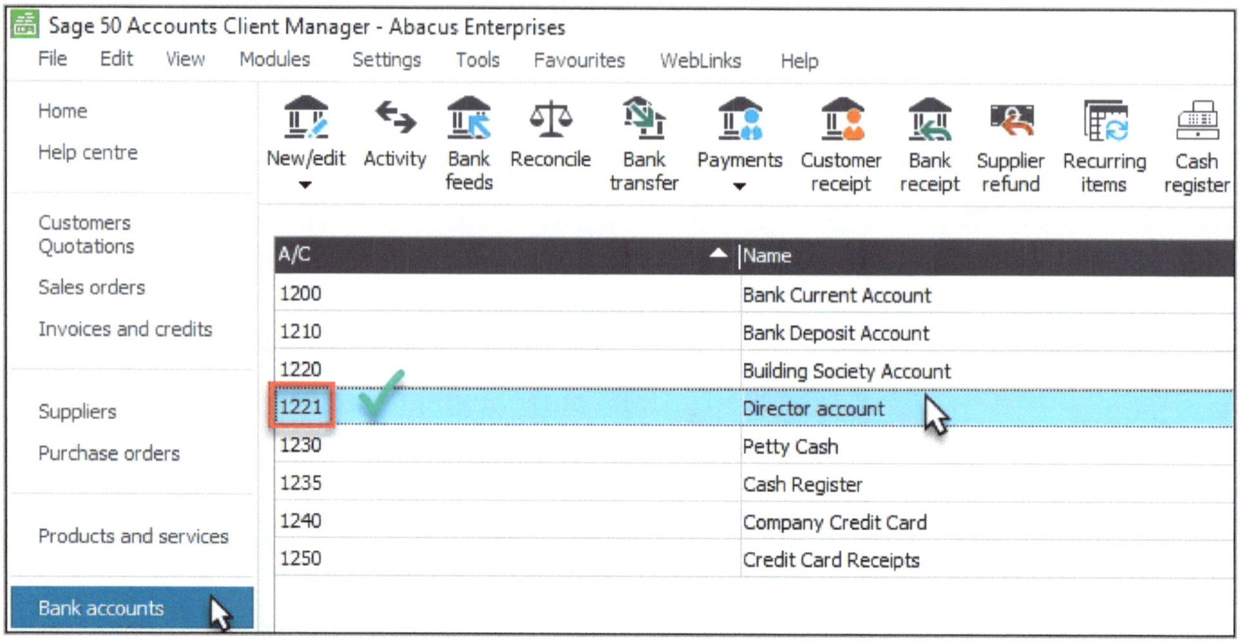

Fig. 30

The setup of your company/business on Sage 50 Accounts is now complete. Let's move on to the next task of setting up the customers of this business.

Task 2b: How to set up payroll & the staff on the payroll

This task is to be done in Sage 50 payroll, QuickBooks, Xero and Sage one, it not done in Sage 50 Accounts

This space is for notes

Task 2c: How to set up customers and corresponding opening balances

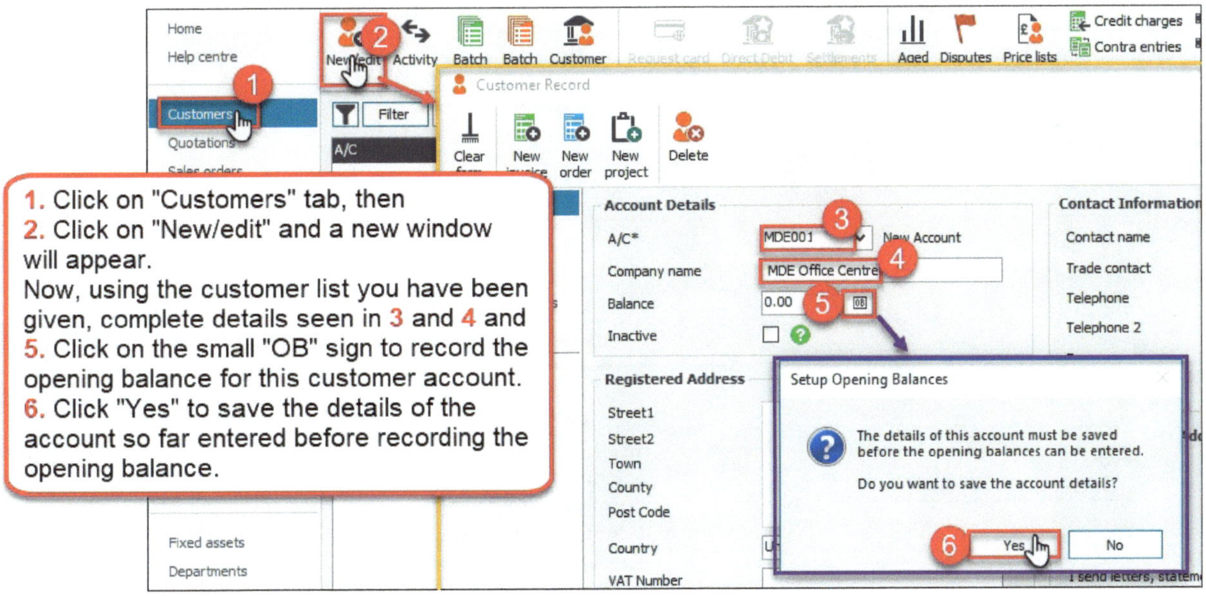

Fig. 31

Once you click "Yes" you will see a window similar to the figure below;

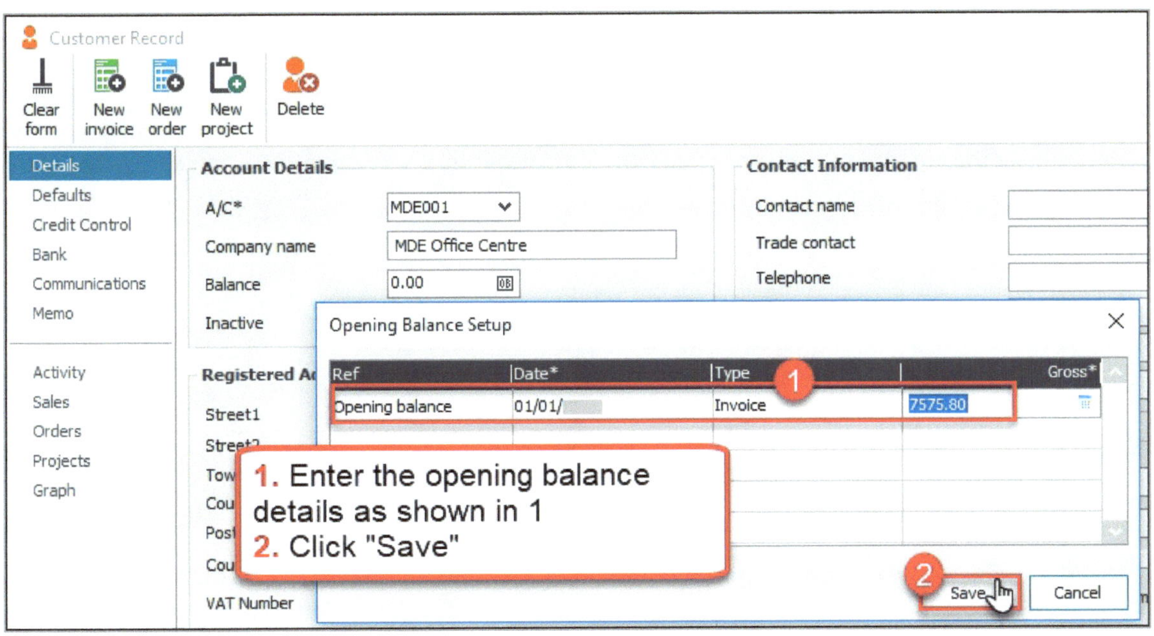

Fig. 32

Next, enter the rest of the details like the address and then click on the "Credit control" tab and complete the details as shown in the figure below.

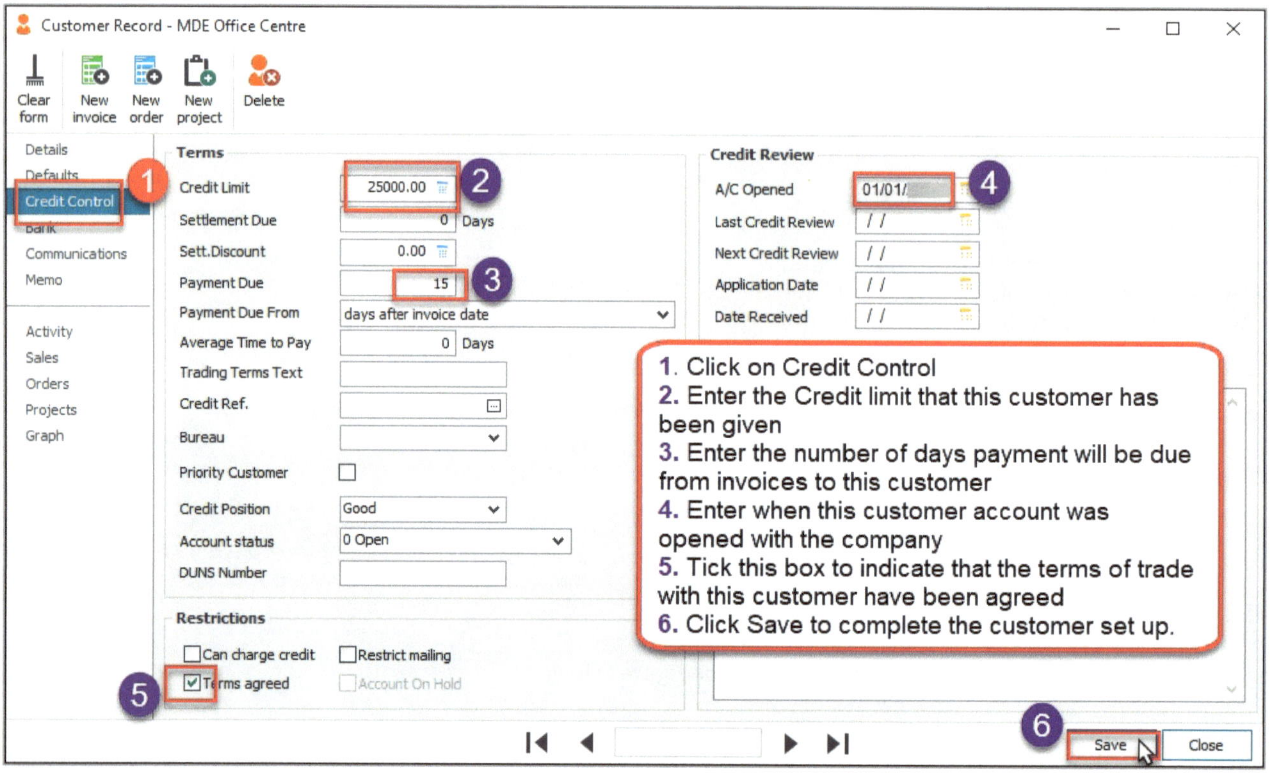

Fig. 33

Now, go ahead and set up all the other remaining customers and you should finally see something similar to the figure below – All of your customers set up.

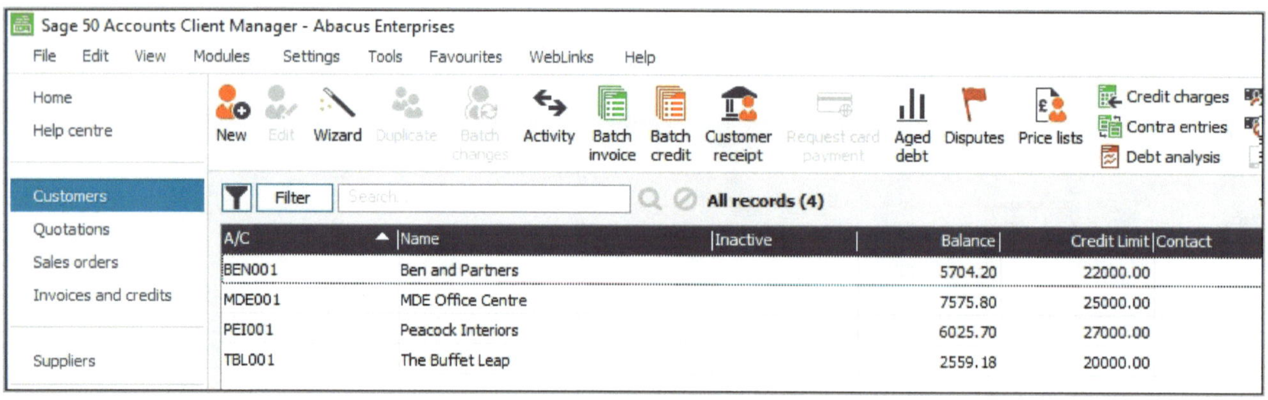

Fig 34

Let's now set up the suppliers for this company/business.

Task 2d: How to set up suppliers and corresponding opening balances

Setting up the suppliers is done in precisely the same way as for customers. What you have to do at the start is to select the supplier tab and the rest of the setup is almost identical to the one for setting up the customers.

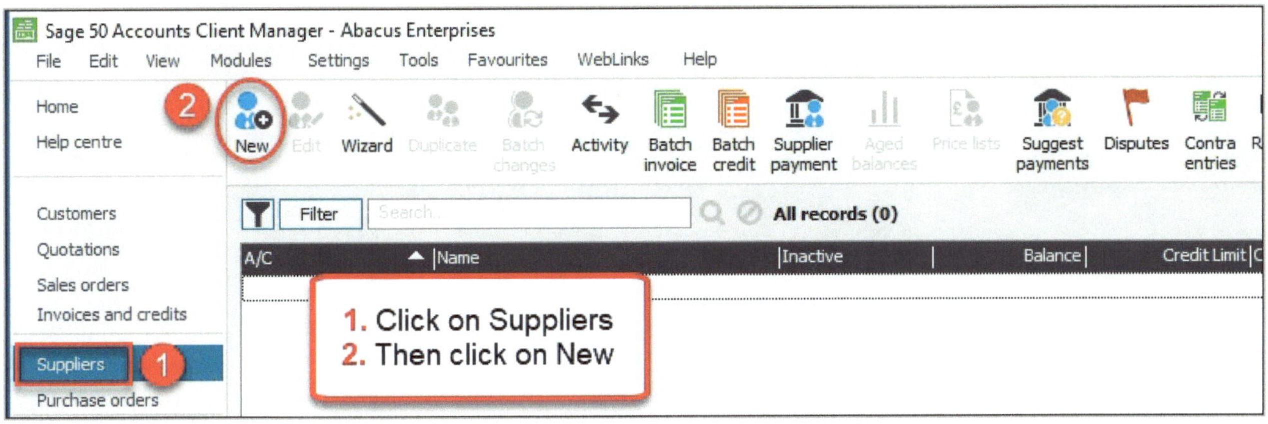

Fig. 35

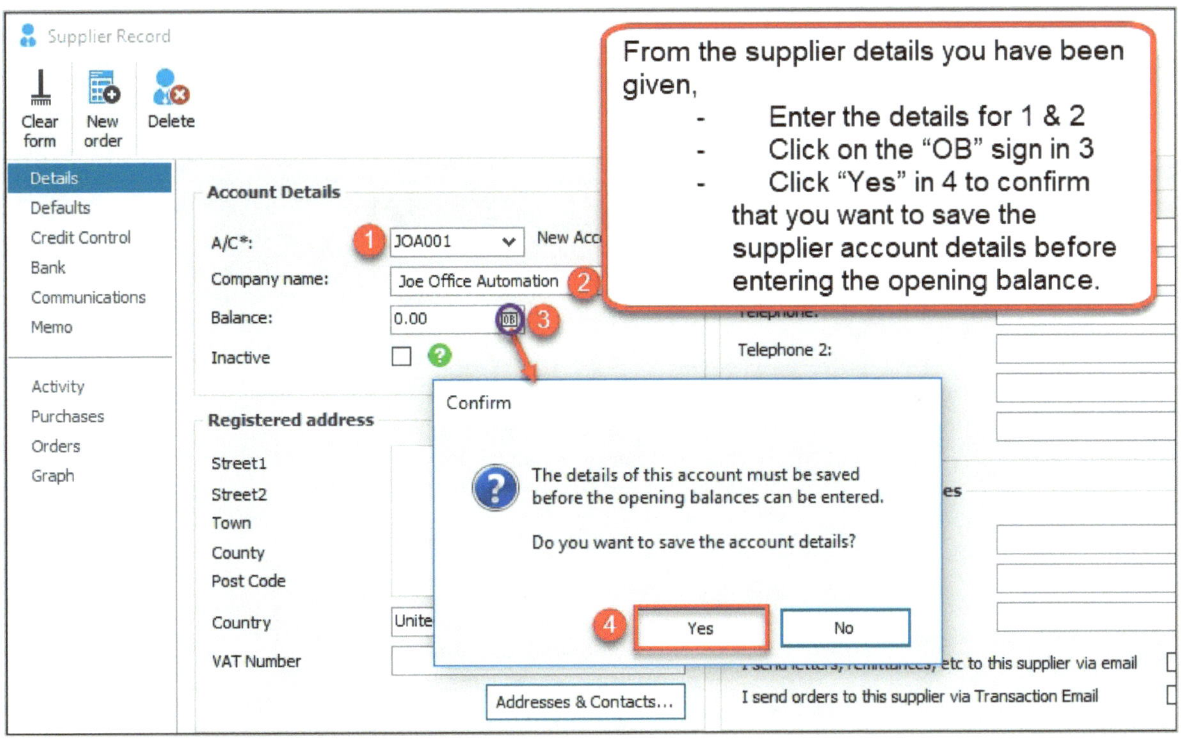

Fig. 36

Once you click "Yes" in 4 – figure above, a window similar to the figure below will appear.

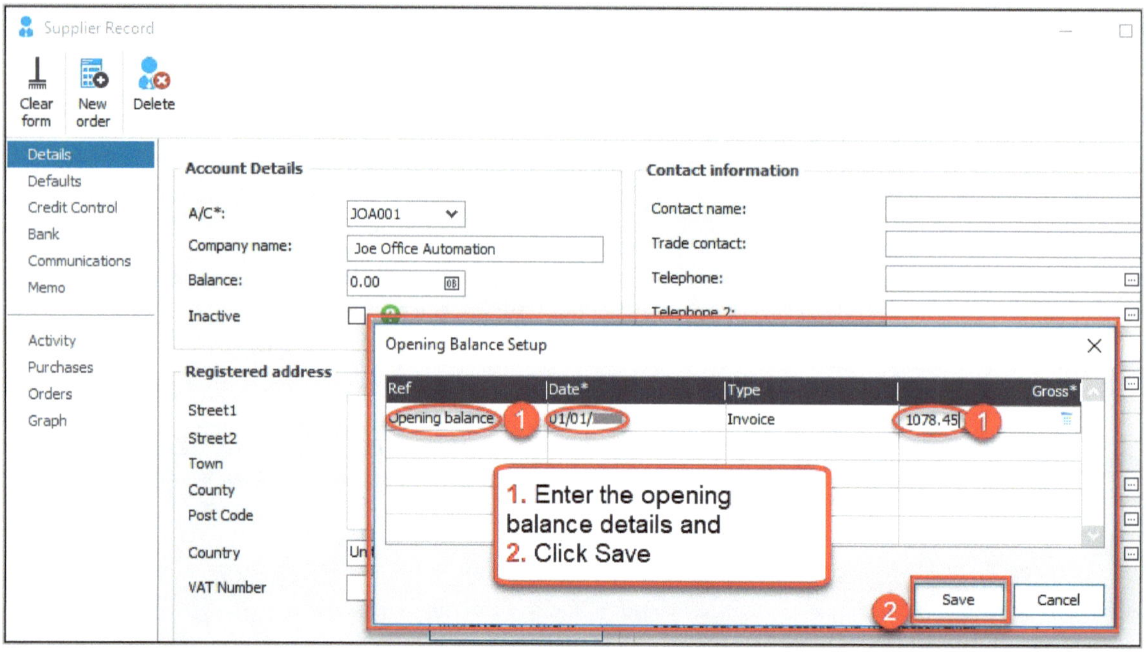

Fig. 37

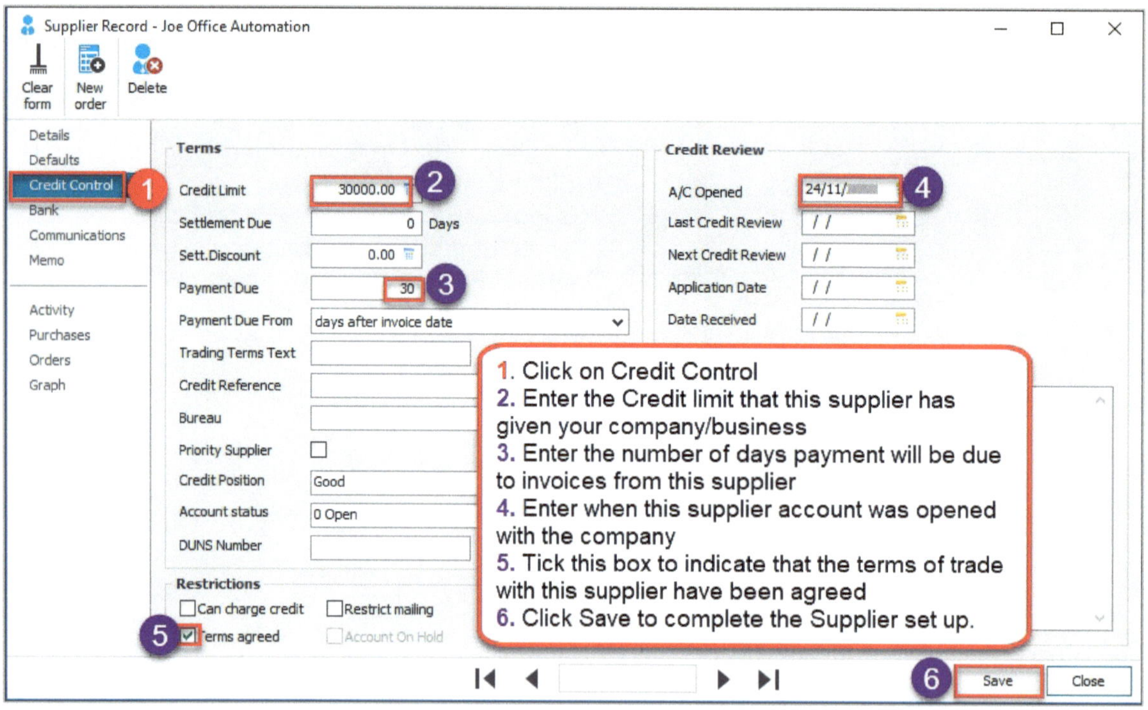

Fig. 38

Now, go ahead and set up all the other remaining suppliers and you should finally see something similar to the figure below.

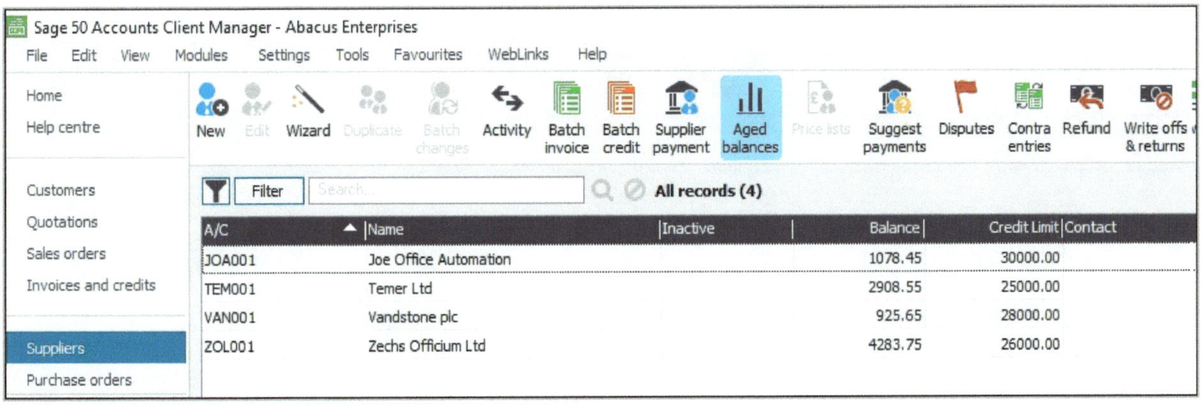

Fig. 39

Let's now move on and set up the products and or services that this company/business buys and sells.

Task 2e – How to set up products and opening stock values

Let's begin by setting up some of the product categories that the company buys and sells.

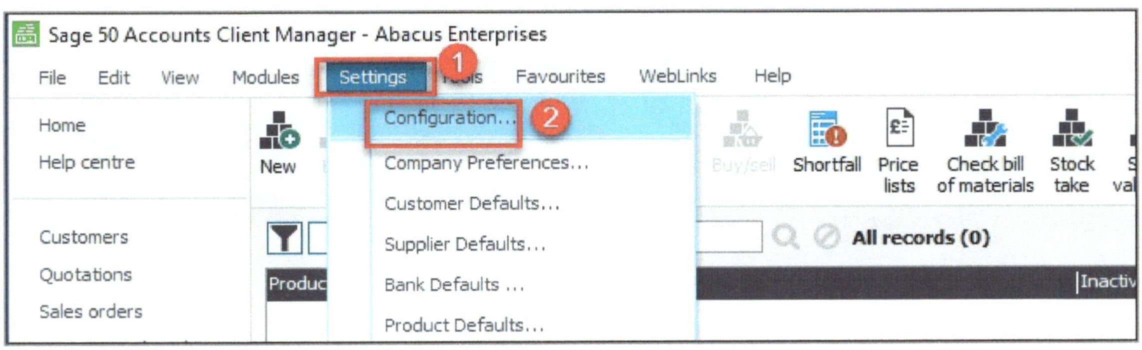

Fig. 40

1. Click on settings
2. Then click on configuration and a window similar to the figure below will appear.

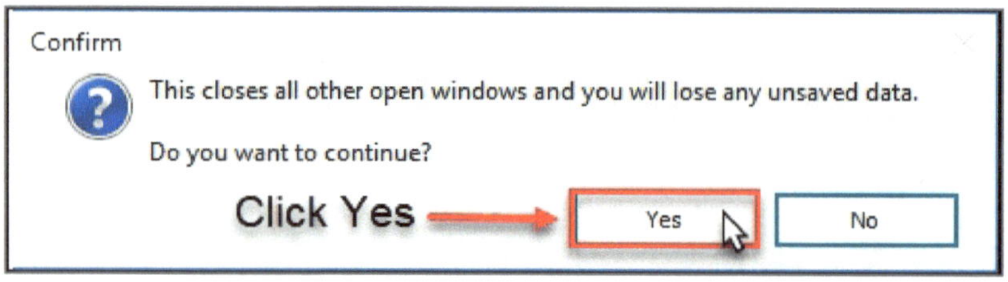

Fig. 41

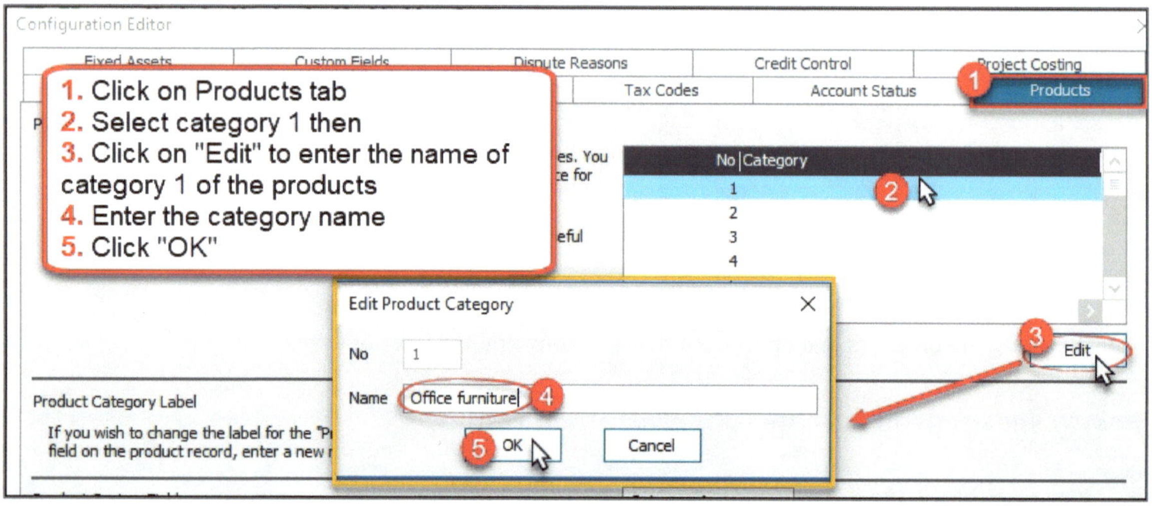

Fig. 42

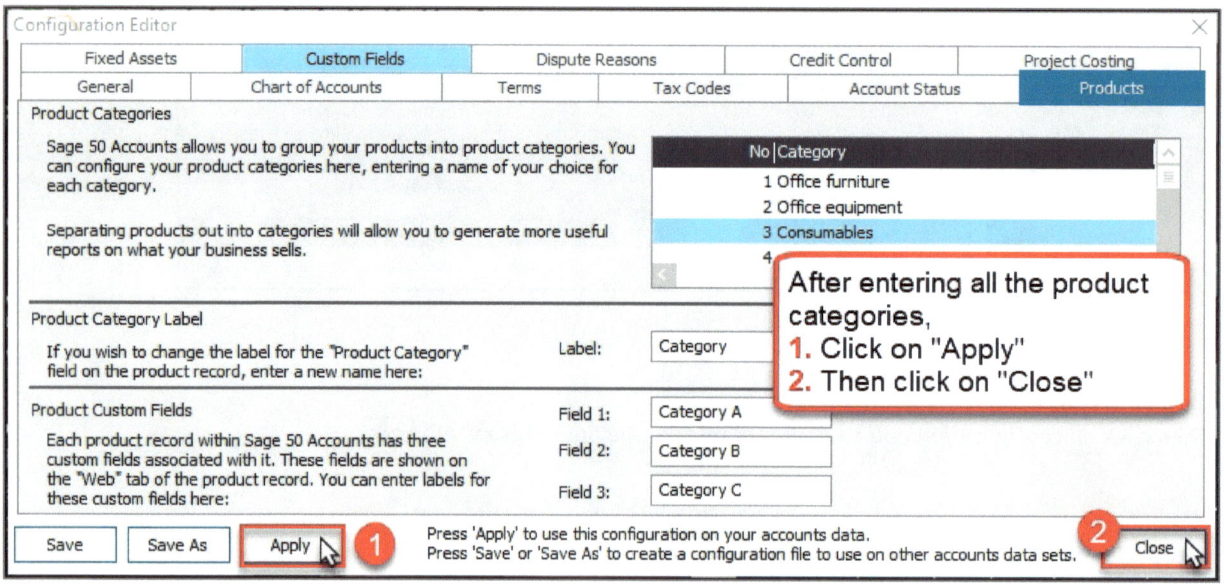

Fig. 42

Having set up the product categories, you can now go ahead and enter the product details. See the figures on the next page.

*Click on: **Products and services** tab then click on **New***

A window similar to the figure below will appear.

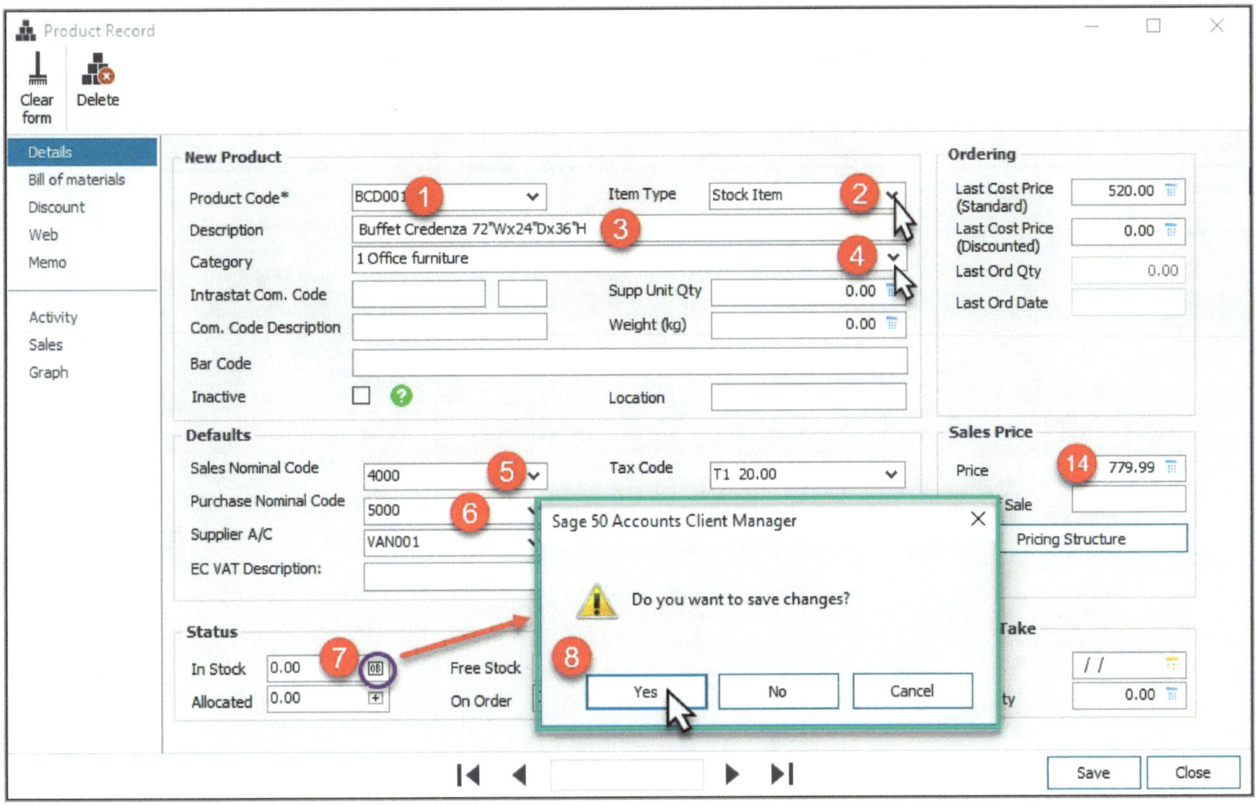

Fig. 43

From the product details, you have been given,

1. Enter the product code here
2. From the drop-down menu, select – Stock item
3. Enter in here the product description
4. Select the category this product belongs to (use drop down arrow to select) from the list of categories already entered in earlier steps.
5. Select the Sales nominal code for this product
6. Select the purchase nominal code for this product
7. If there is any opening stock for this product, click on the "OB" letters. A warning window appears asking whether you want to save changes so far before entering the opening stock values.

Click "Yes" to accept. Once you click "Yes" a window similar to figure 44 on the next page will appear.

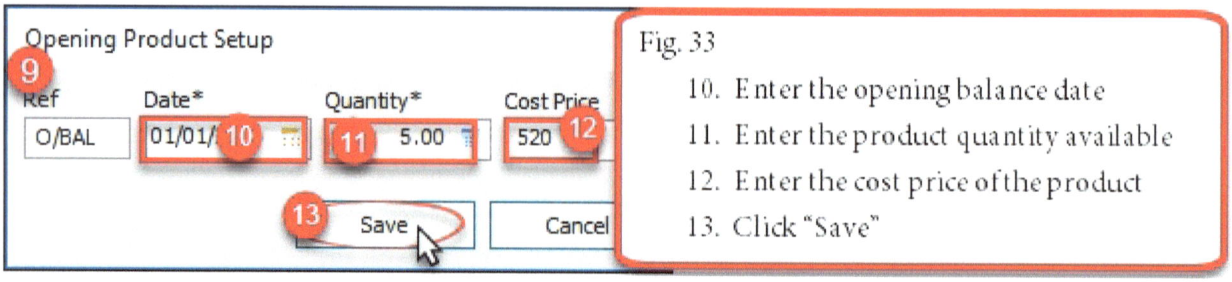

Fig. 44

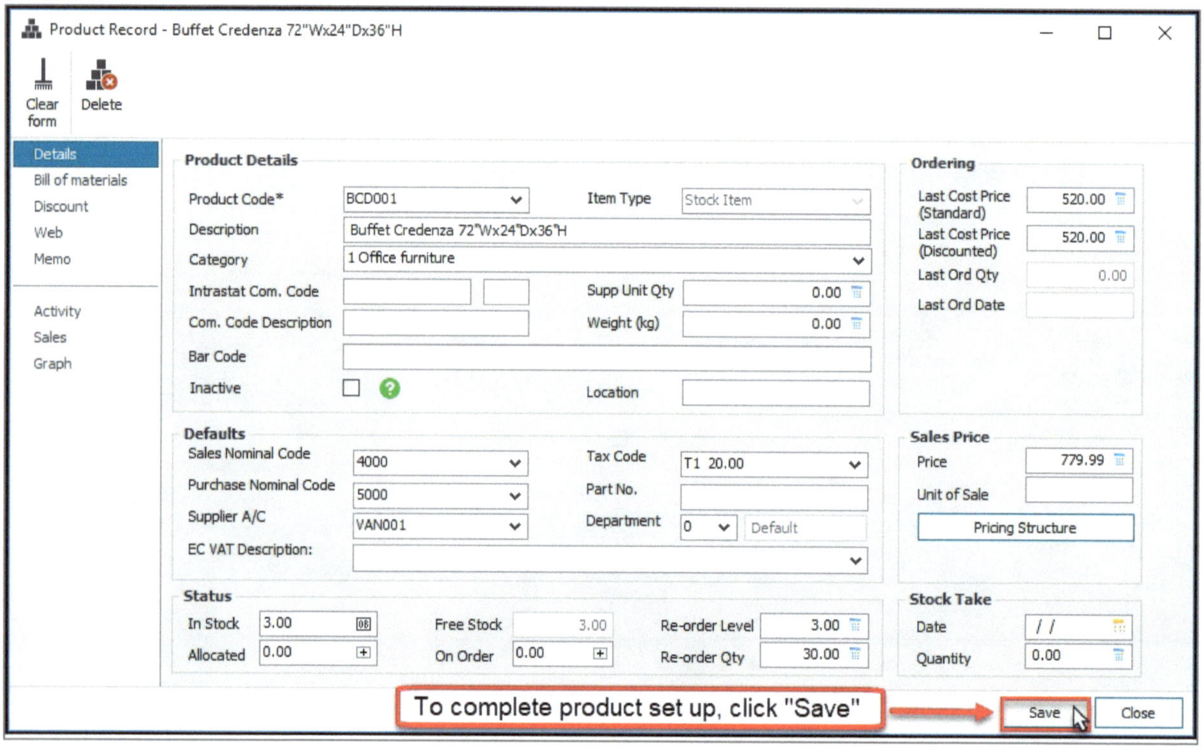

Fig. 45

After you set up all the products, here is how your products and services window will look like – see figure 46 on the next page.

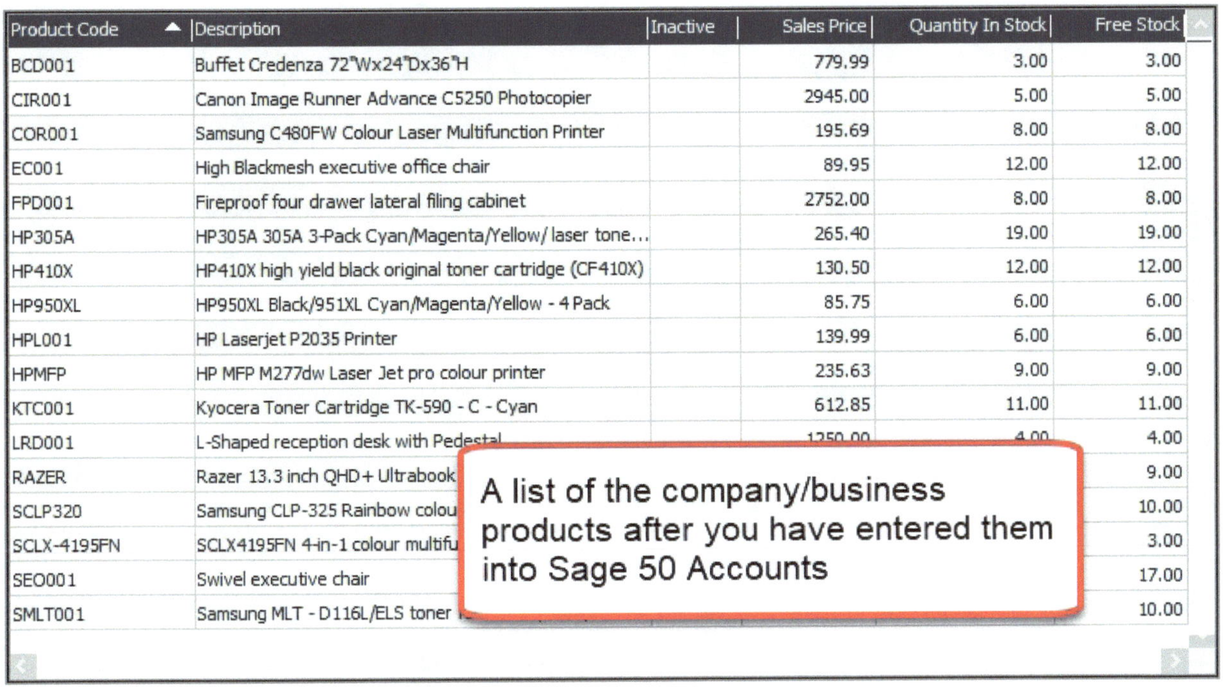

Product Code	Description	Inactive	Sales Price	Quantity In Stock	Free Stock
BCD001	Buffet Credenza 72"Wx24"Dx36"H		779.99	3.00	3.00
CIR001	Canon Image Runner Advance C5250 Photocopier		2945.00	5.00	5.00
COR001	Samsung C480FW Colour Laser Multifunction Printer		195.69	8.00	8.00
EC001	High Blackmesh executive office chair		89.95	12.00	12.00
FPD001	Fireproof four drawer lateral filing cabinet		2752.00	8.00	8.00
HP305A	HP305A 305A 3-Pack Cyan/Magenta/Yellow/ laser tone...		265.40	19.00	19.00
HP410X	HP410X high yield black original toner cartridge (CF410X)		130.50	12.00	12.00
HP950XL	HP950XL Black/951XL Cyan/Magenta/Yellow - 4 Pack		85.75	6.00	6.00
HPL001	HP Laserjet P2035 Printer		139.99	6.00	6.00
HPMFP	HP MFP M277dw Laser Jet pro colour printer		235.63	9.00	9.00
KTC001	Kyocera Toner Cartridge TK-590 - C - Cyan		612.85	11.00	11.00
LRD001	L-Shaped reception desk with Pedestal		1250.00	4.00	4.00
RAZER	Razer 13.3 inch QHD+ Ultrabook				9.00
SCLP320	Samsung CLP-325 Rainbow colou				10.00
SCLX-4195FN	SCLX4195FN 4-in-1 colour multifu				3.00
SEO001	Swivel executive chair				17.00
SMLT001	Samsung MLT - D116L/ELS toner				10.00

Fig. 46

Having set up the company, the customers and suppliers of the company and the products that the company buys and sells, it's now time to set up some opening balances.

Task 2f: How to set up Trial balance opening balances

Here is a brief review of what opening balances are:

The opening balance is the balance that is brought forward from the end of one accounting period to the beginning of a new accounting period.

The funds in a company's/business accounts at the start of a new financial period are called the opening balances. ***The opening balance is the first entry in a company's accounts, either when they are first starting up or at the start of a new financial year or when changing accounting systems.***

In the case of a new company, the opening balances usually are just two: one is the cash on hand and the other is the capital contributed by the company's founders or loan from investors.

Opening balances are entered into the accounting system using the double entry accounting principles.

Okay, I hope that brief introduction to opening balances was sufficient. Now, from the Trial balance you have been given, could you please enter the opening balances for the items listed on the trial balance.

Step 1.

Click on Nominal codes tab and a window similar to the figure below will appear

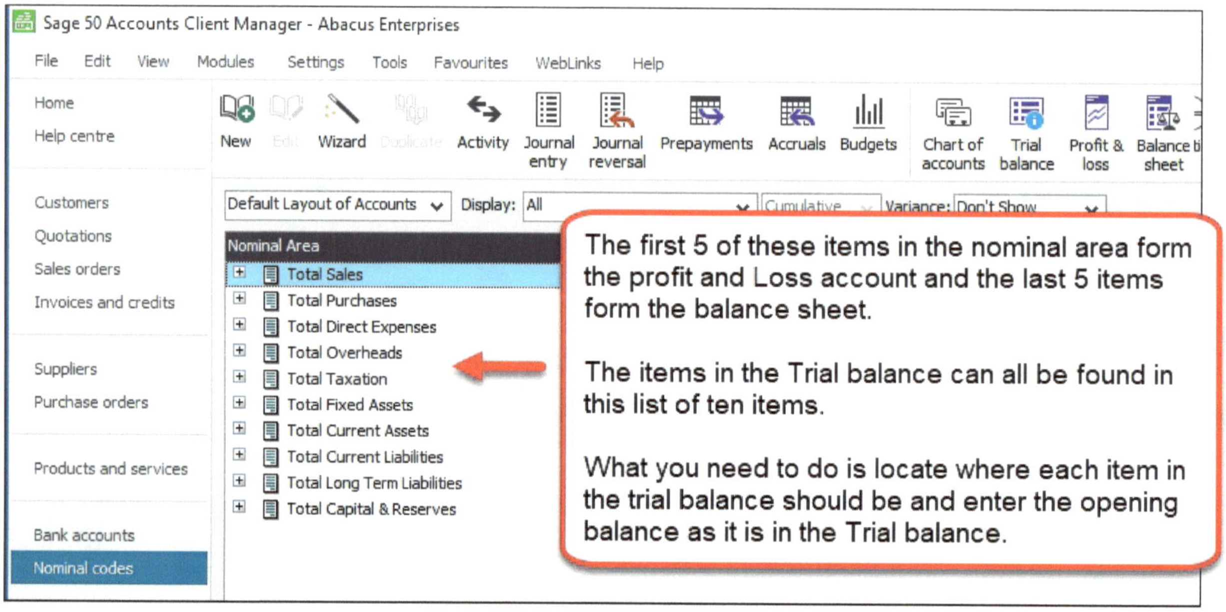

Fig. 47

Let's begin by entering the opening balance for motor vehicles.

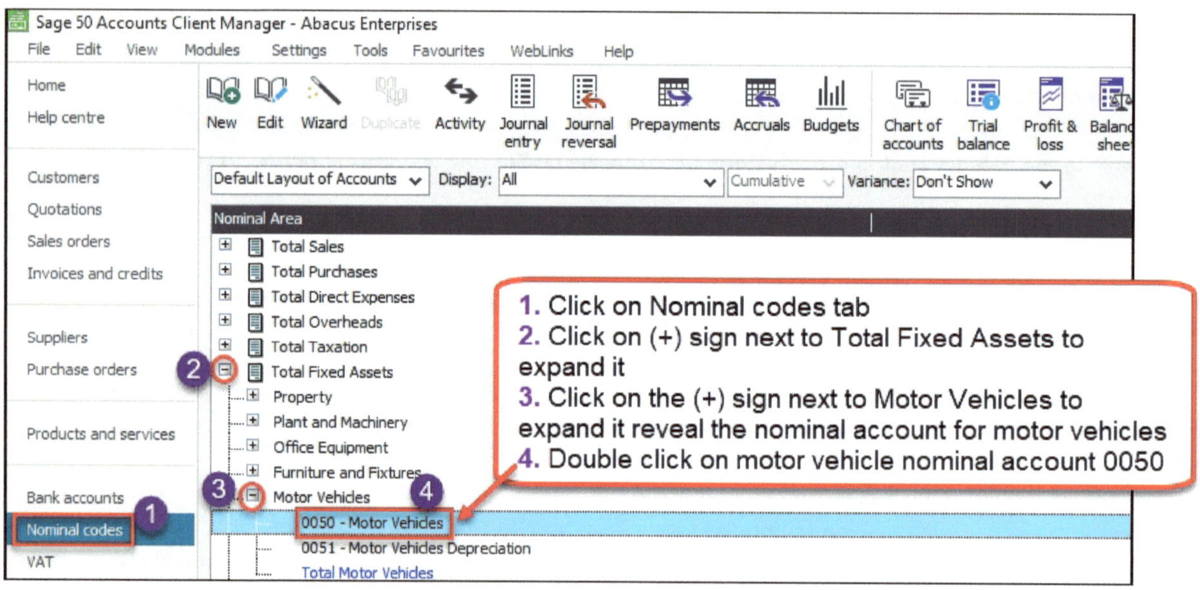

Fig. 48

Once you double-click on the motor vehicle nominal account 0050, a window similar to the figure below will appear. See figure below.

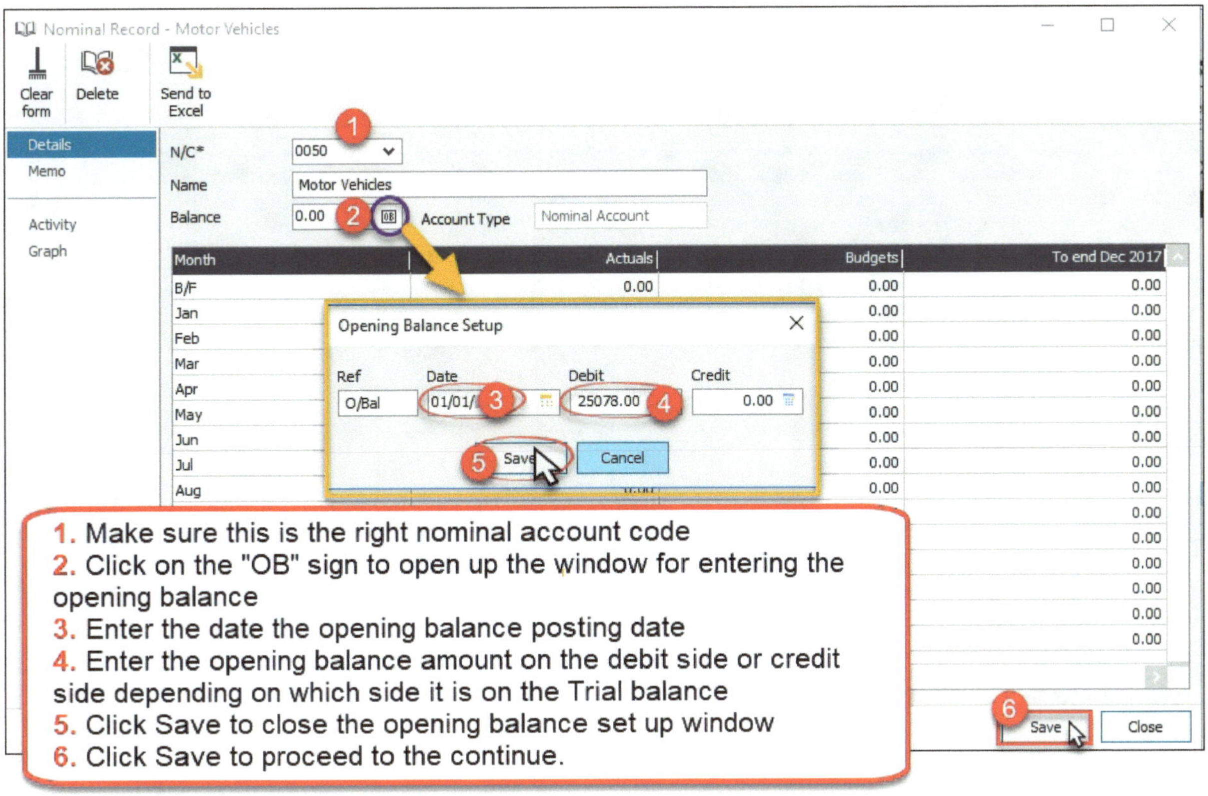

Fig. 49

Having successfully entered that first opening balance from your Trial balance, you can now proceed to enter the rest of the opening balances from the Trial balance items using the steps similar to the ones illustrated in figure 37 & 38

After you have entered all the opening balances from the Trial balance, produce the trial balance from Sage and compare it with the Trial balance you used to enter the opening balances.

Here is how to do it:

First, click on the nominal codes tab and then click on Trial balance tab. See figure 50 on the next page

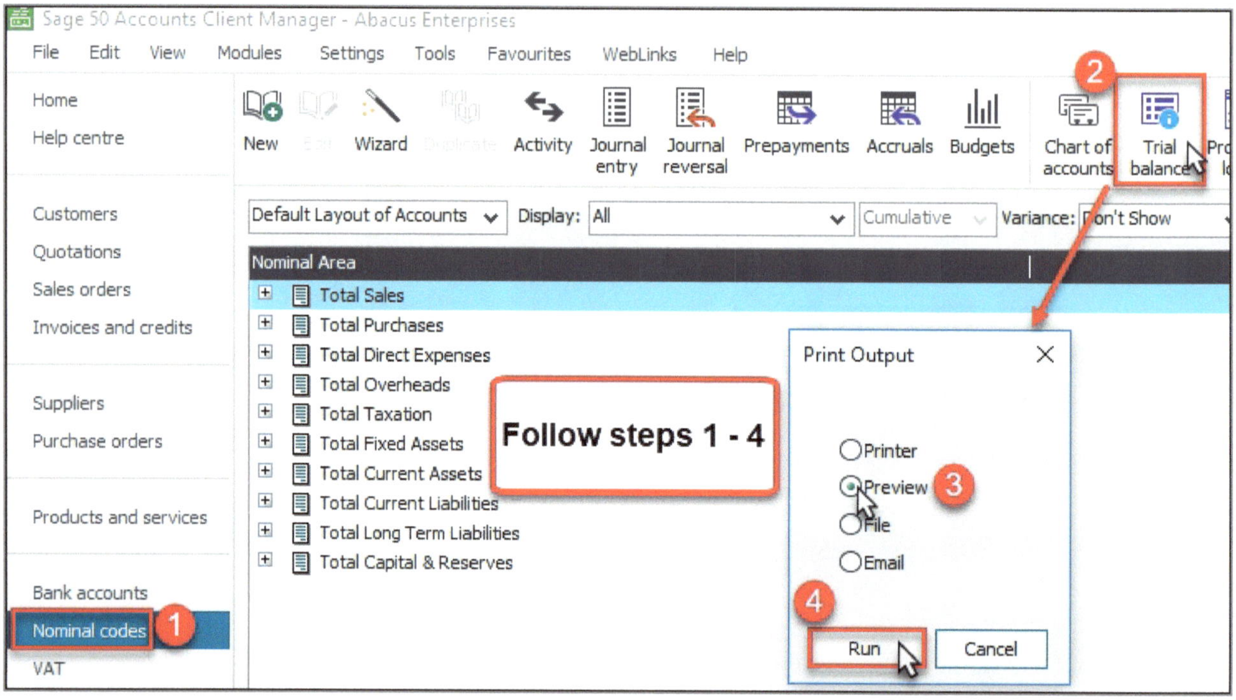

Fig. 50

Once you click “Run” as illustrated in the figure above, a window similar to the figure below will appear.

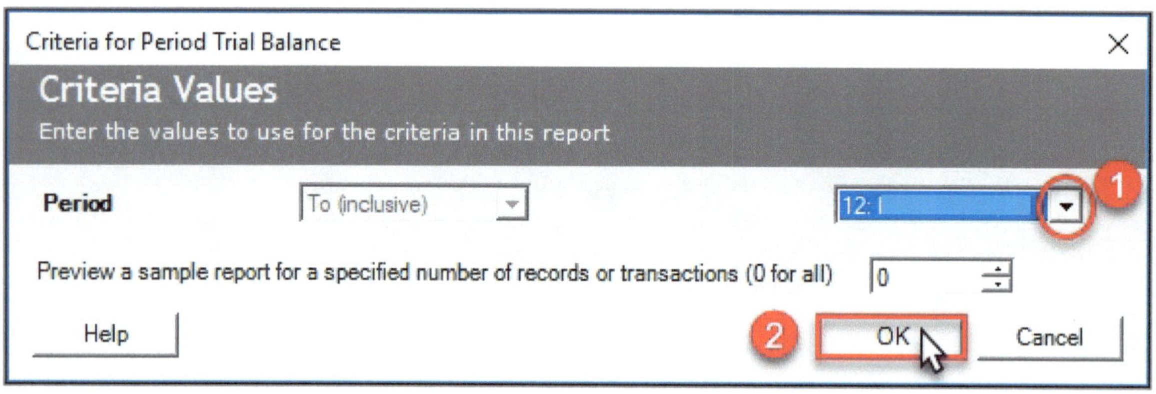

Fig. 51

1. Select month 12 from the drop-down list (you can select any month you want depending on the reporting period you want)
2. Click “OK” to proceed and a Trial balance report will be displayed. See figure 52 on the next page.

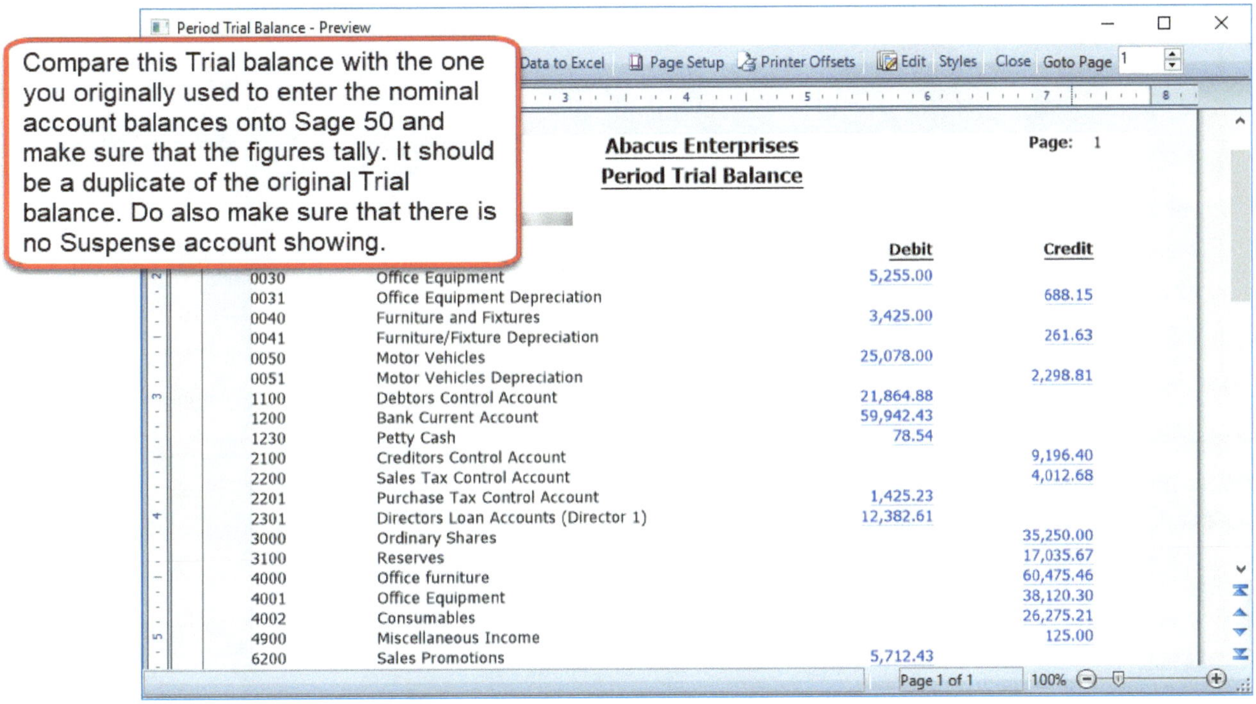

Abacus Enterprises
Period Trial Balance
Page: 1

		Debit	Credit
0030	Office Equipment	5,255.00	
0031	Office Equipment Depreciation		688.15
0040	Furniture and Fixtures	3,425.00	
0041	Furniture/Fixture Depreciation		261.63
0050	Motor Vehicles	25,078.00	
0051	Motor Vehicles Depreciation		2,298.81
1100	Debtors Control Account	21,864.88	
1200	Bank Current Account	59,942.43	
1230	Petty Cash	78.54	
2100	Creditors Control Account		9,196.40
2200	Sales Tax Control Account		4,012.68
2201	Purchase Tax Control Account	1,425.23	
2301	Directors Loan Accounts (Director 1)	12,382.61	
3000	Ordinary Shares		35,250.00
3100	Reserves		17,035.67
4000	Office furniture		60,475.46
4001	Office Equipment		38,120.30
4002	Consumables		26,275.21
4900	Miscellaneous Income		125.00
6200	Sales Promotions	5,712.43	

Fig. 52

Task 2g: How to set up a fixed asset register

The next task is to set up the fixed asset register. See how in figures 53 & 54 on the next page.

> *Fixed assets are any assets that cannot be easily converted to cash. They are typically tangible, physical things that have an economic life of longer than a year. These include buildings, vehicles, furniture and office equipment. Fixed assets normally don't include intangible things like royalties and brand names.*
>
> *Fixed assets are also known as non-current and long-term assets. They may also be referred to as property, plant and equipment. They are assets intended to be used within the business, not sold or converted to cash.*

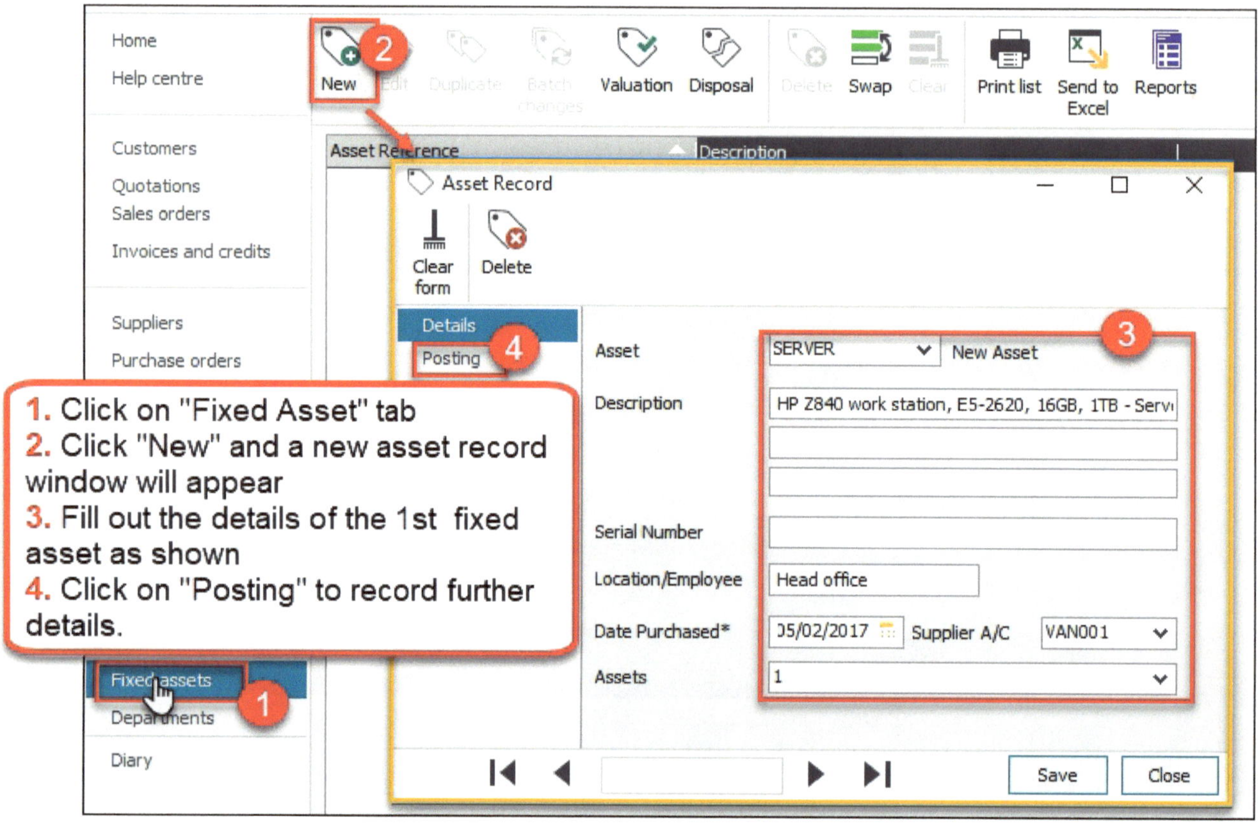

Fig. 53

After step 4 as illustrated in figure 42, the posting details window appears – see figure below.

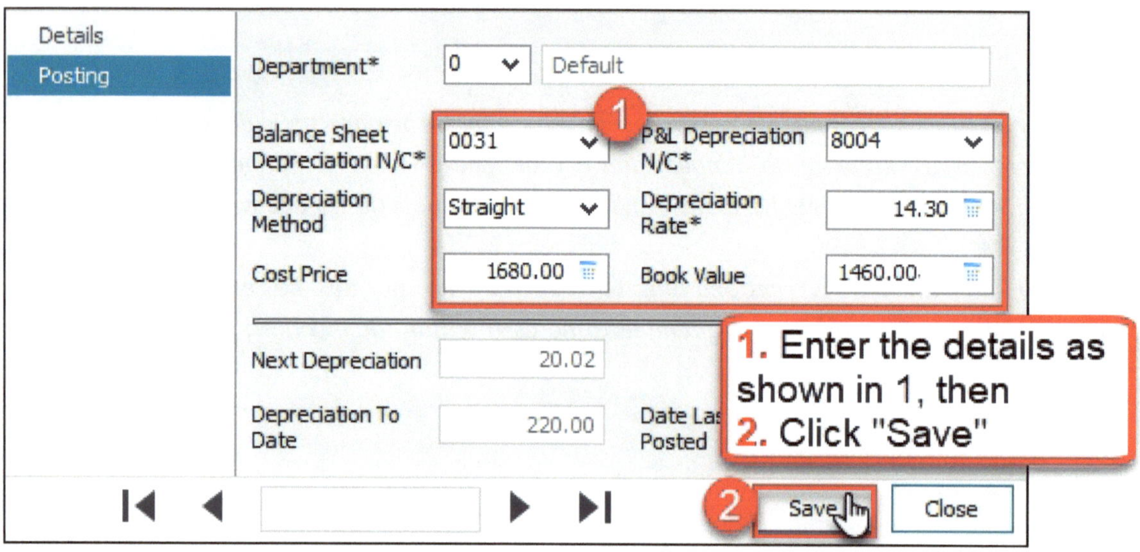

Fig. 54

Next: Record the rest of the fixed assets in the register as per the steps illustrated in figure 54 in the previous page. Here is a list of the complete list of fixed assets for Abacus set up on Sage 50 Accounts:

Asset Reference	Description	Cost Price	Depreciation To Date	Book Value
BMW316SI	BMW 316si	16078.00	1406.31	14671.69
IMAC1	Apple iMac 27" Retina 5K Display intel core i5, 8GB	1700.00	222.62	1477.38
IMAC2	Apple iMac 27" 5K Display intel core i5, 8GB RAM, 1TB Fusion	1700.00	222.62	1477.38
OFFICEF	Office furniture	2225.00	169.96	2055.04
PEUGEOT1	Peugeot hatchback	9000.00	892.50	8107.50
PRINTER1	Samsung CLP -680ND - A4 Colour laser printer	175.00	22.91	152.09
RECEP	Showroom reception desk and chairs	1200.00	91.67	1108.33
SERVER	HP Z840 work station, E5-2620, 16GB, 1TB - Server Comp...	1680.00	220.00	1460.00

Fig. 55

Congratulations!

You have so far completed the setup process of the company, customers & suppliers, products, opening balances from the Trial balance and Fixed asset register.

Task 2h: How to prepare a budget for a 3-month period in Sage 50 accounts

We are now going to prepare a 3-month budget for Abacus Enterprises.

In Sage Accounts you can monitor how your business is performing by entering budgets. You can compare your actual figures against the budgets for each month and for the whole year, to see if your business is on track.

This space is for notes

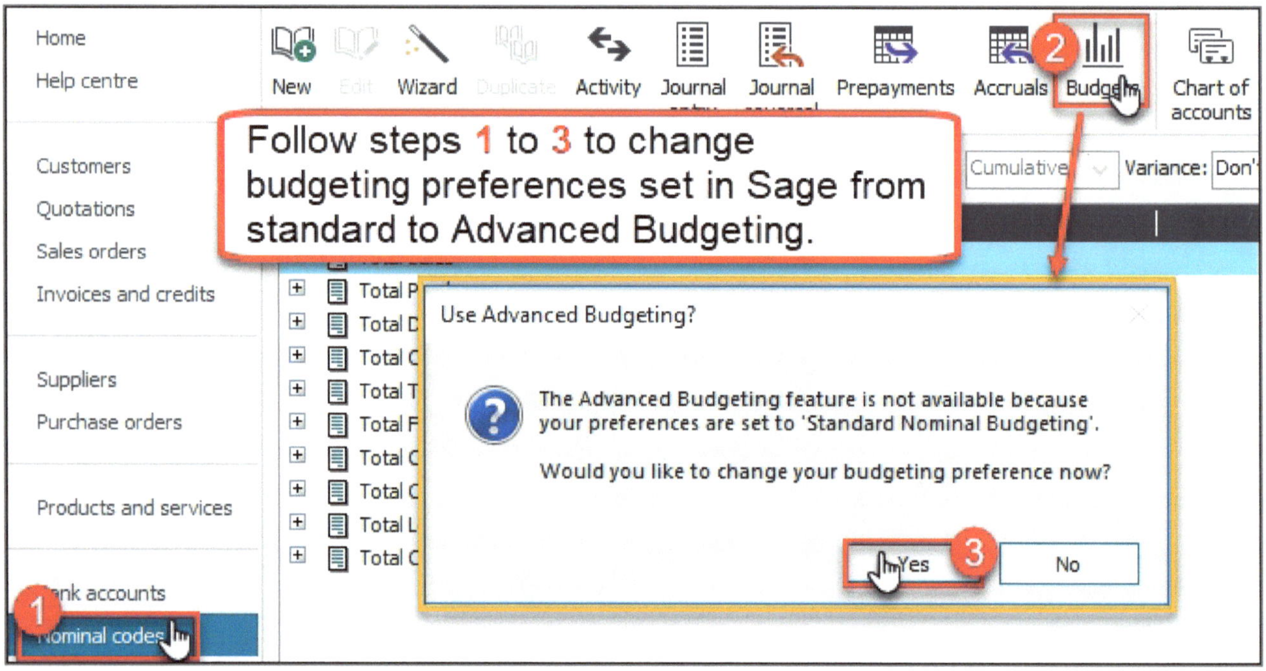

Fig. 56

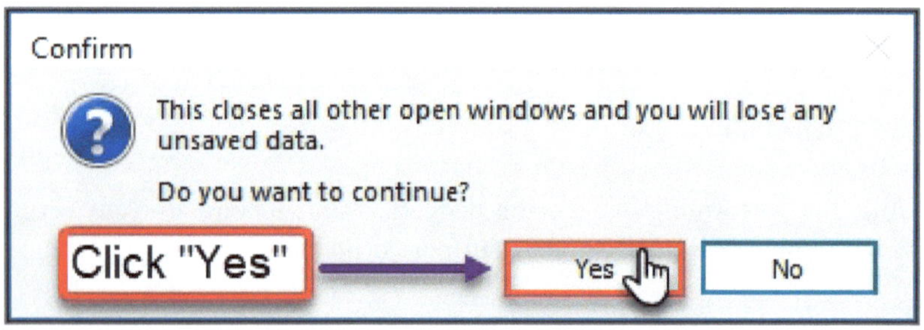

Fig. 57

Next,

Fig. 58

Next, set the budget preferences as shown in figure 59 on the next page.

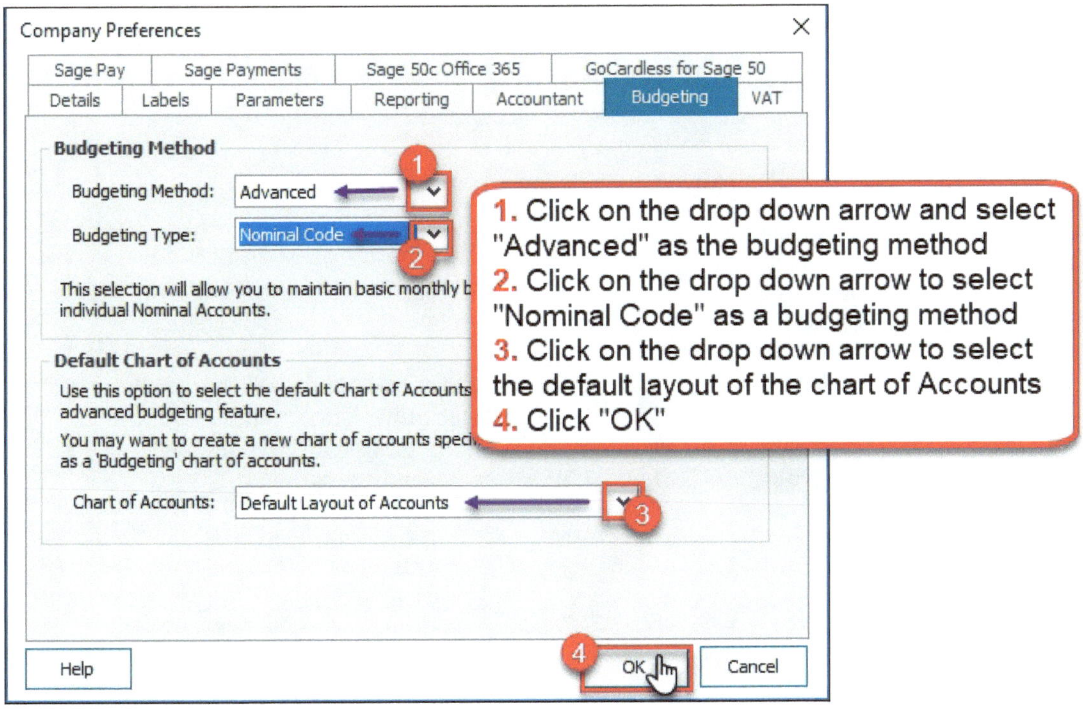
Company Preferences
Sage Pay
Sage Payments
Sage 50c Office 365
GoCardless for Sage 50
Details
Labels
Parameters
Reporting
Accountant
Budgeting
VAT
Budgeting Method
Budgeting Method: Advanced
Budgeting Type: Nominal Code
This selection will allow you to maintain basic monthly b
individual Nominal Accounts.
Default Chart of Accounts
Use this option to select the default Chart of Accounts
advanced budgeting feature.
You may want to create a new chart of accounts speci
as a 'Budgeting' chart of accounts.
Chart of Accounts: Default Layout of Accounts
Help
OK
Cancel
1. Click on the drop down arrow and select "Advanced" as the budgeting method
2. Click on the drop down arrow to select "Nominal Code" as a budgeting method
3. Click on the drop down arrow to select the default layout of the chart of Accounts
4. Click "OK"

Fig. 59

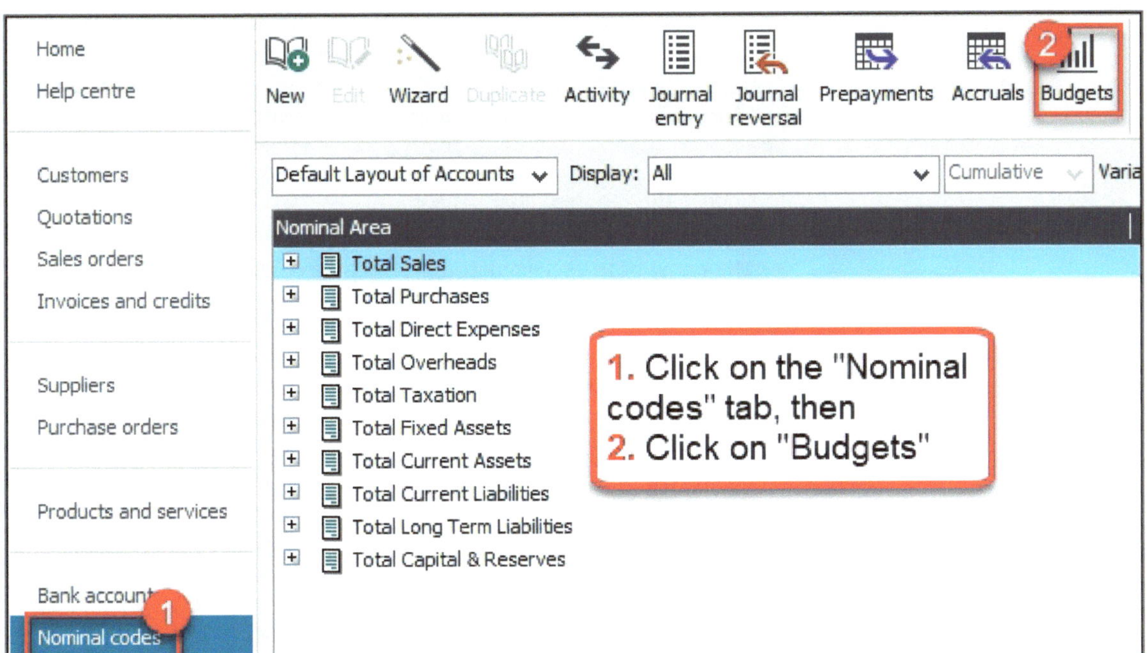
Home
Help centre
Customers
Quotations
Sales orders
Invoices and credits
Suppliers
Purchase orders
Products and services
Bank accounts
Nominal codes
New
Edit
Wizard
Duplicate
Activity
Journal entry
Journal reversal
Prepayments
Accruals
Budgets
Default Layout of Accounts
Display: All
Cumulative
Varia
Nominal Area
Total Sales
Total Purchases
Total Direct Expenses
Total Overheads
Total Taxation
Total Fixed Assets
Total Current Assets
Total Current Liabilities
Total Long Term Liabilities
Total Capital & Reserves
1. Click on the "Nominal codes" tab, then
2. Click on "Budgets"

Fig.60

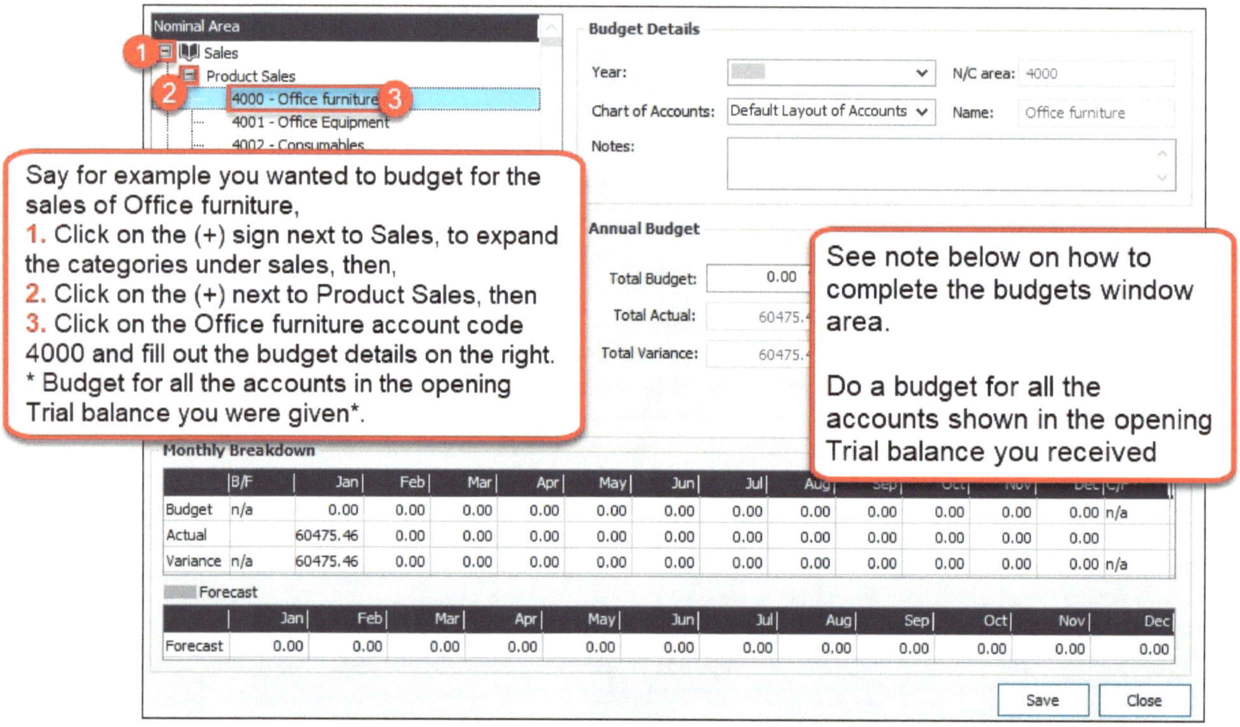

Fig. 61

After steps 1 to 3 in the figure above, complete the rest of the Budgets window as follows:

Budget Details	**Year**	Choose the financial year that you want to enter the budgets for.
	Nominal	The selected nominal code appears here.
	Chart of Accounts	Choose the required chart of accounts. If you choose a different Chart of Accounts, the Nominal box resets.
	Name	The name of the selected nominal code appears here.
	Notes	If required, enter some notes for the budget. Maximum 1023 characters.
Annual Budget	**Total Budget**	If required, you can enter the total budget in this box. When you tab out of this box, a message appears asking if you want to apportion the value across 12 months. To apportion the total budget equally across the 12 months, click Yes.
	Total Actual	The total value of all transactions for the selected nominal code and financial year appears here.
	Total Variance	Total Actual - Total Budget.
Monthly Breakdown	**Budget**	Enter the monthly budgets in the relevant boxes.

		To copy the first budget, you enter to the remaining months, click Copy Values. If required, you can increment the values by an amount or a percentage.
	Actual	The total value of all transactions for the selected nominal code and relevant months appear here.
	Variance	Actual minus Budget.
	Forecast	If required, enter forecast values for the following financial year in the relevant boxes.

Click Save > Close after filing out the budget details.

This space is for notes

The next task is to all about doing the purchase ledger process (Accounts payable tasks)

"If you are patient in one moment of anger, you will escape a hundred days of sorrow"

Chinese Proverb

"The end of something is better than its beginning, so the patient are better than the proud"
Ecclesiastes 7:8

TASK 3: ACCOUNTS PAYABLE (AP) – PURCHASE LEDGER

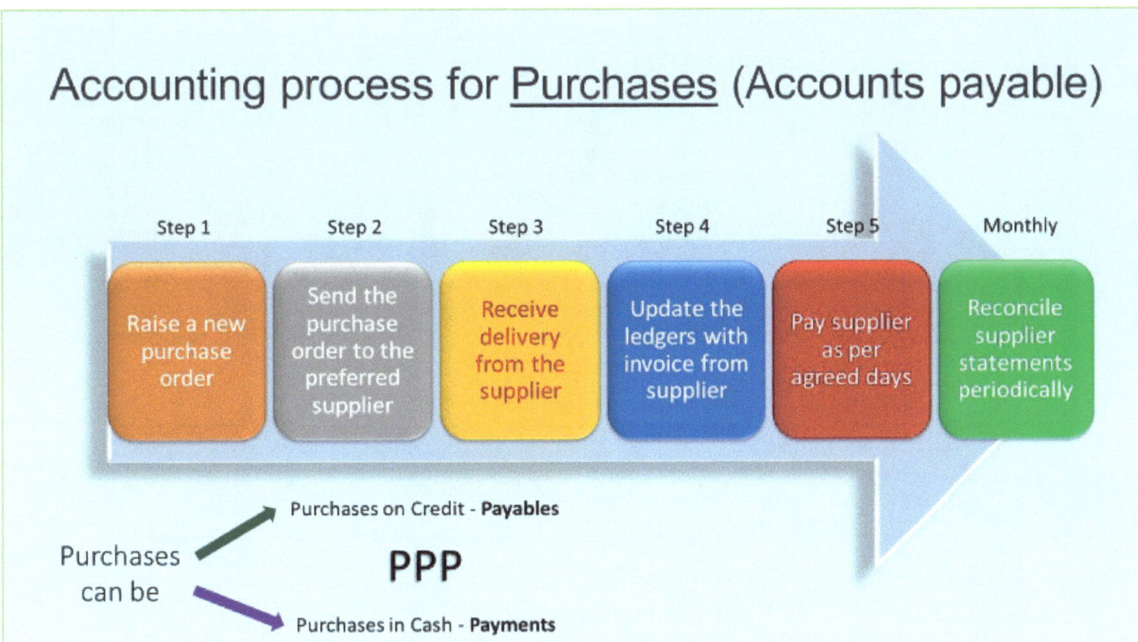

Fig. 62

A Note

When a company orders and receives goods (or services) in advance of paying for them, we say that the company is purchasing the goods *on account* or *on credit*. The supplier (or vendor) of the goods on credit is also referred to as a creditor. If the company receiving the goods does not sign a promissory note, the vendor's bill or invoice will be recorded by the company in its liability account Accounts Payable (or Trade Payables).

Accounts Payable will normally have a credit balance. Hence, when a Supplier/vendor invoice is recorded, Accounts Payable will be credited and another account must be debited (as required by double-entry accounting). When an account payable is paid, Accounts Payable will be debited and Cash will be credited. Therefore, the credit balance in Accounts Payable should be equal to the amount of vendor invoices that have been recorded but have not yet been paid.

Under the *accrual method of accounting*, the company receiving goods or services on credit must report the liability no later than the date they were received. The same date is used to record the debit entry to an expense or asset account as appropriate. Hence, accountants say that under the accrual method of accounting expenses are

Task 3a: How to raise purchase orders and converting them into invoices

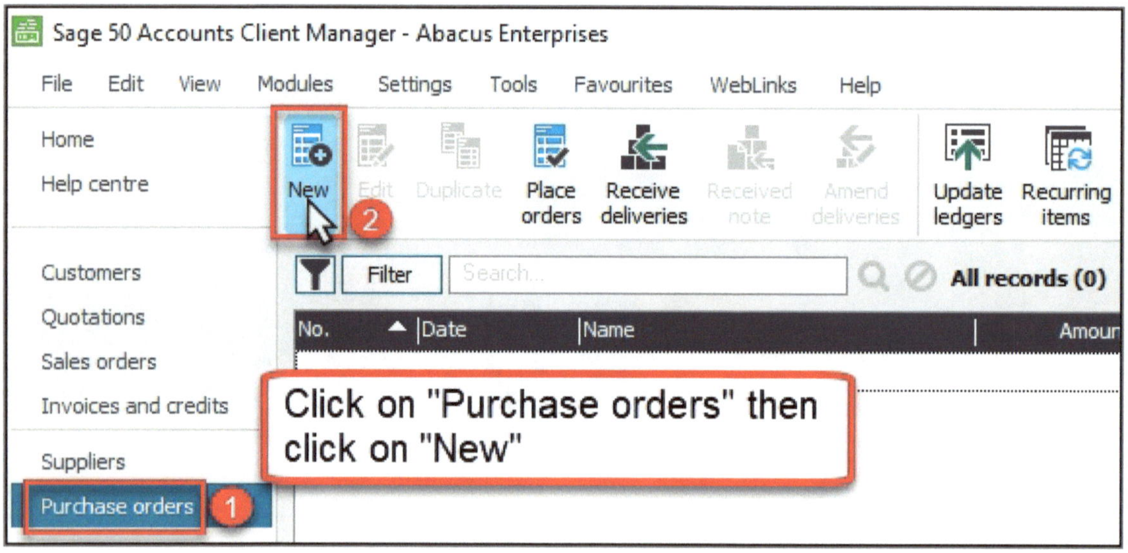

Fig. 63

Once you click "New" as illustrated in the above, a window similar to figure 64 on the next page will appear.

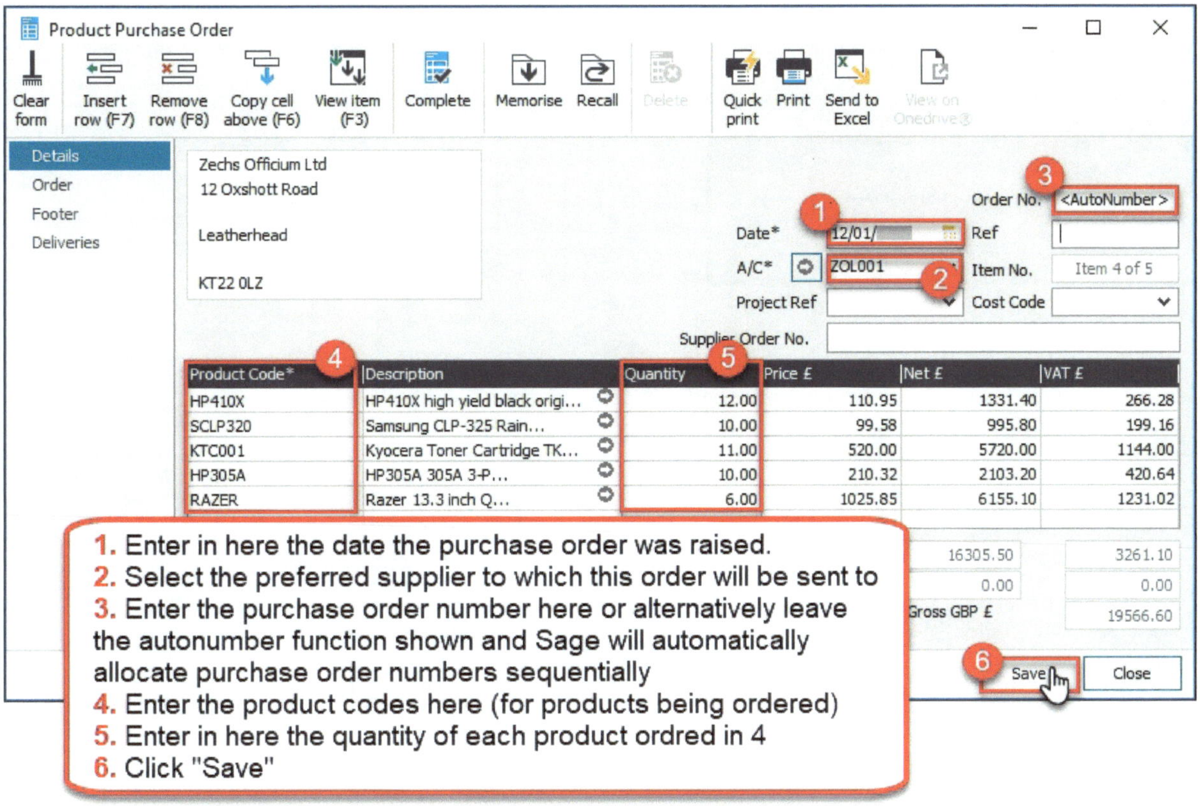

Fig. 64

Once you click "Save" as illustrated in the figure above, a pop-up window similar to the figure below will appear. Click "Order Now" to place the order on Order now.

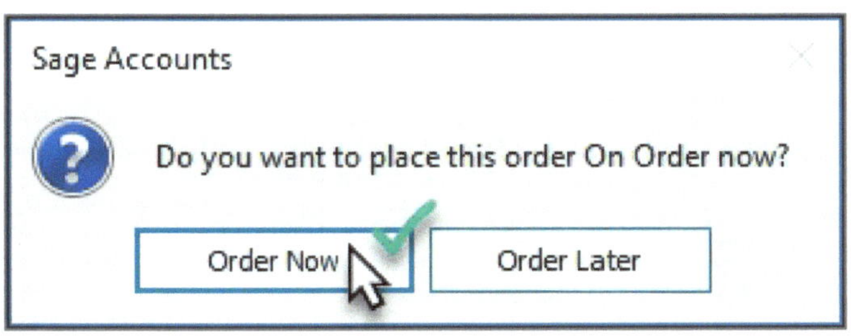

Fig. 65

Once you click "Order Now" a popup window similar to figure 66 on the next page will appear. If you want to order the goods/products right away, click "Yes", if you would like to do so later, click "No"

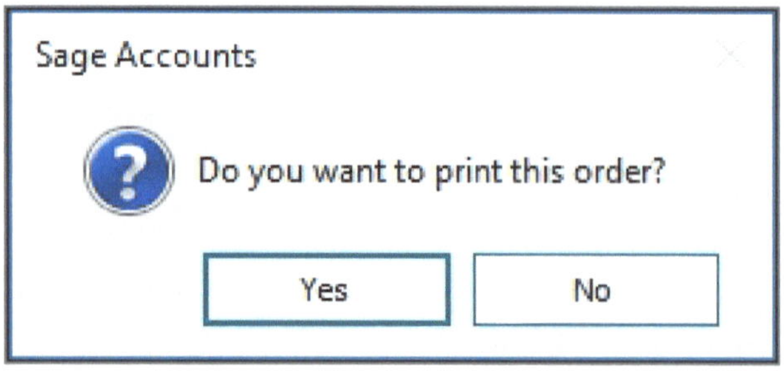

Fig. 66

In this situation, click “Yes” because we are going to send this order by post. See figure below.

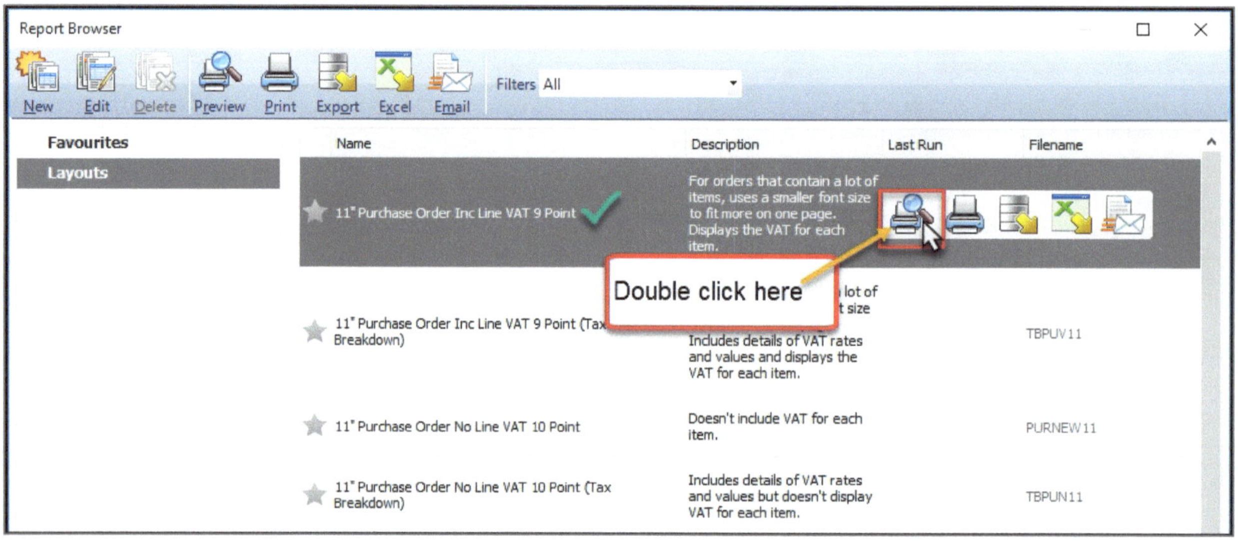

Fig. 67

After taking the step illustrated in the figure above, your purchase order to be printed will look like this – see figure 68 on the next page.

This space is for notes

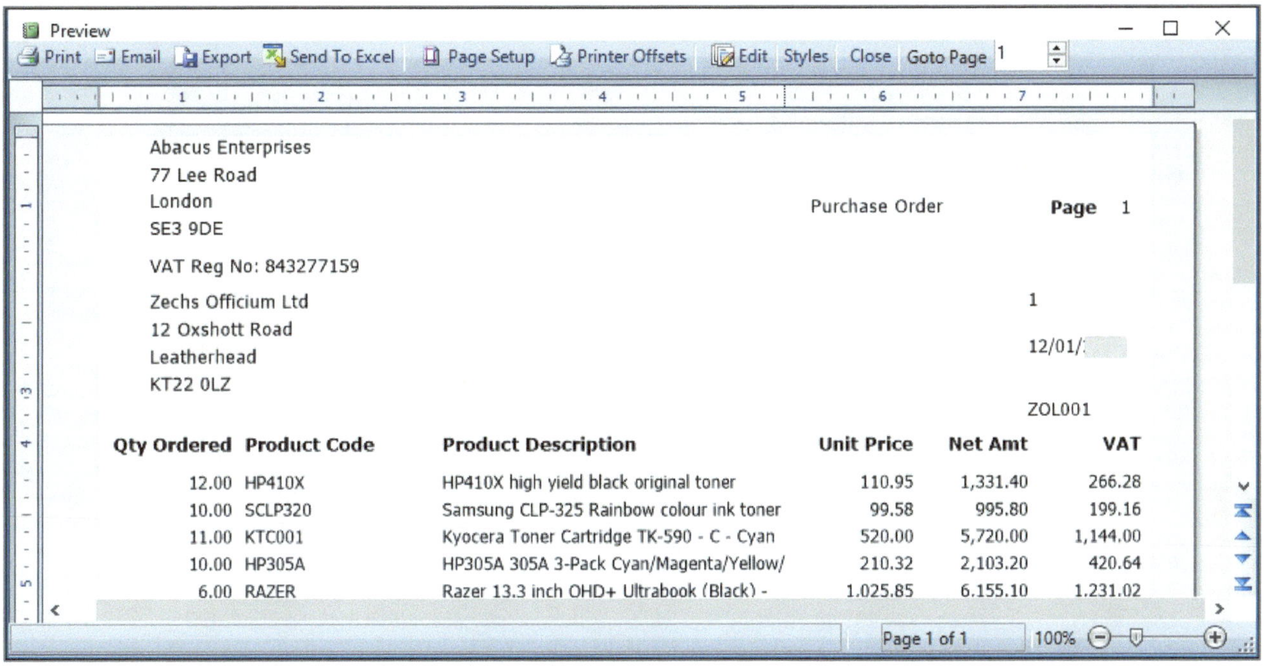

Fig. 68

Once the supplier receives your order if he has the goods/products they will send them over to you. So, you will need to record receipt of those goods/products in your system. See figure below.

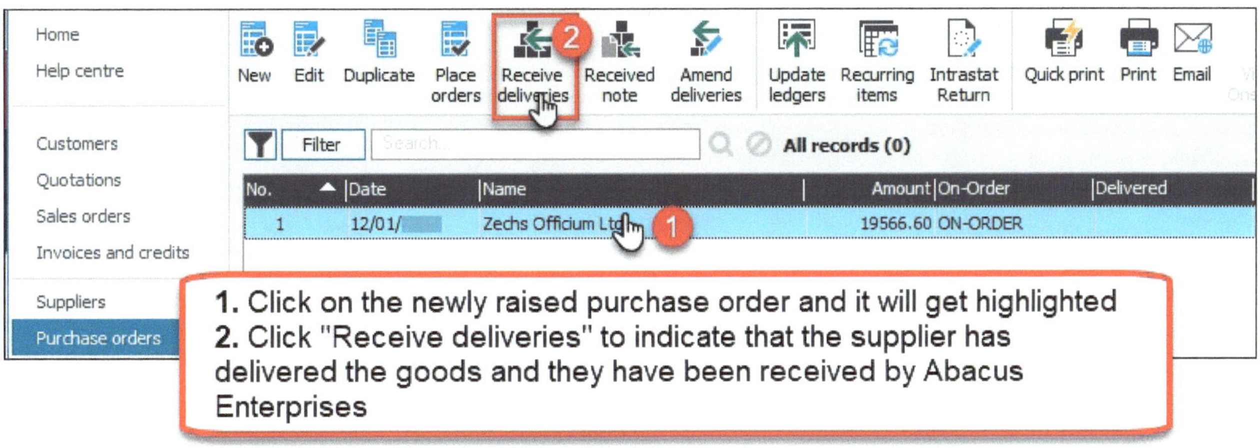

Fig. 69

Once you click on the "Receive deliveries" tab as illustrated in the figure above, a popup window similar to the figure 70 on the next page will appear.

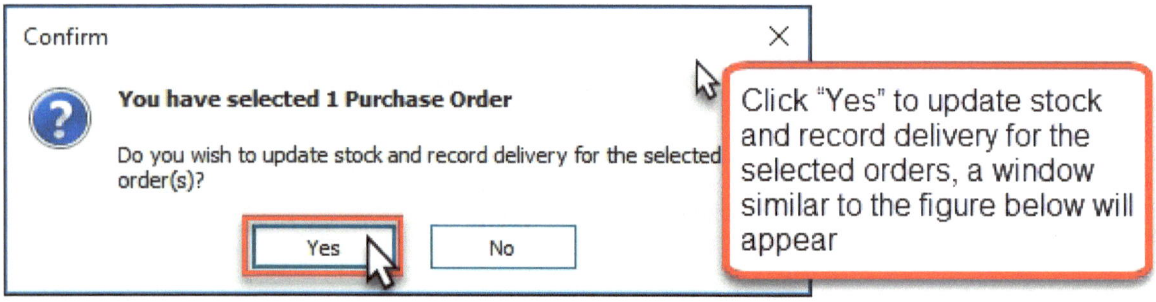

Fig. 70

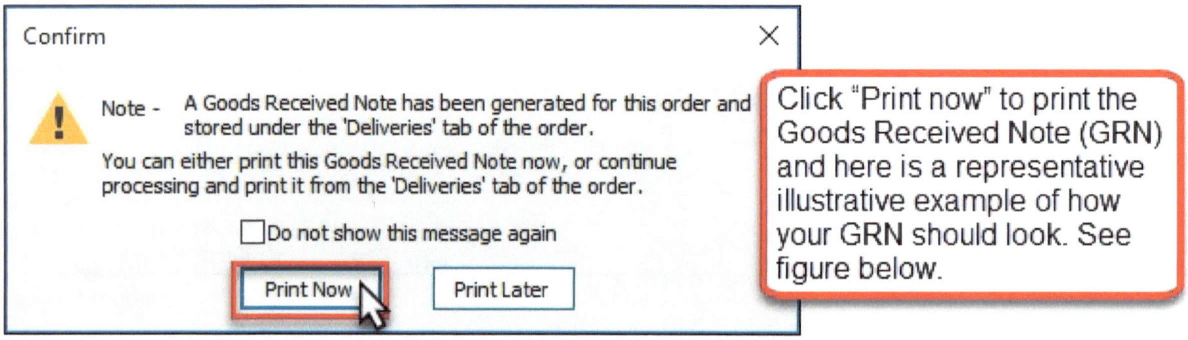

Fig. 71

Here is how a goods received note (GNR) from Sage 50 Accounts looks like.

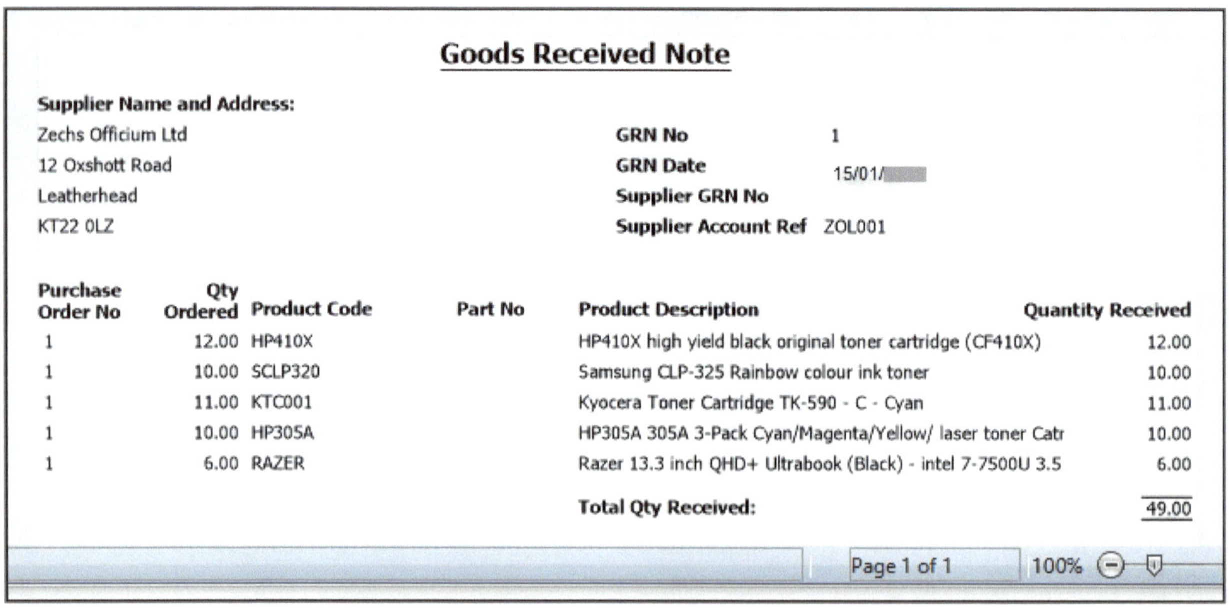

Goods Received Note

Supplier Name and Address:
Zechs Officium Ltd
12 Oxshott Road
Leatherhead
KT22 0LZ

GRN No 1
GRN Date 15/01/
Supplier GRN No
Supplier Account Ref ZOL001

Purchase Order No	Qty Ordered	Product Code	Part No	Product Description	Quantity Received
1	12.00	HP410X		HP410X high yield black original toner cartridge (CF410X)	12.00
1	10.00	SCLP320		Samsung CLP-325 Rainbow colour ink toner	10.00
1	11.00	KTC001		Kyocera Toner Cartridge TK-590 - C - Cyan	11.00
1	10.00	HP305A		HP305A 305A 3-Pack Cyan/Magenta/Yellow/ laser toner Catr	10.00
1	6.00	RAZER		Razer 13.3 inch QHD+ Ultrabook (Black) - intel 7-7500U 3.5	6.00
				Total Qty Received:	49.00

Page 1 of 1 100%

Fig. 72

You will now need to process the invoice received from the supplier.

To do so, highlight the order you raised and click update ledgers. See the figure below.

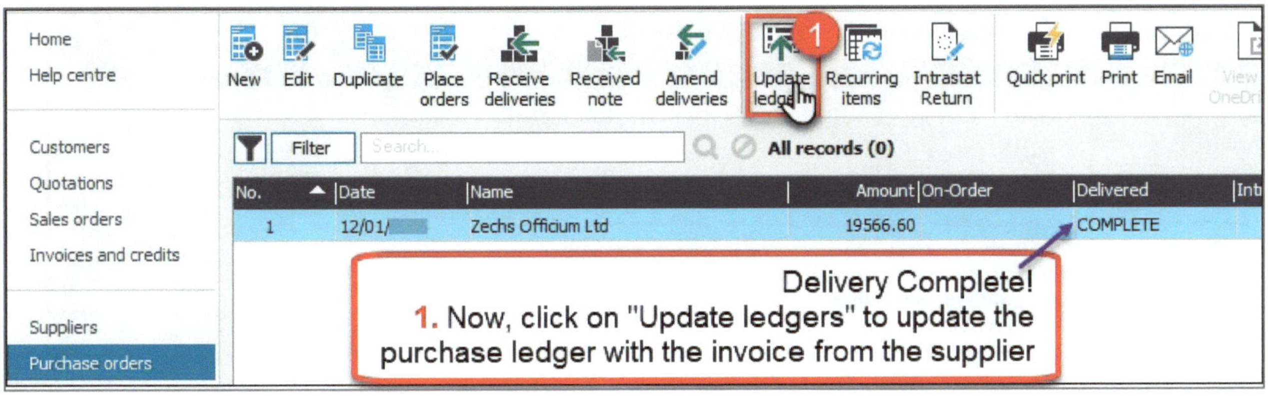

Fig. 73

Once you click "Update ledgers" as illustrated in the figure above, a window similar to the figure below will appear.

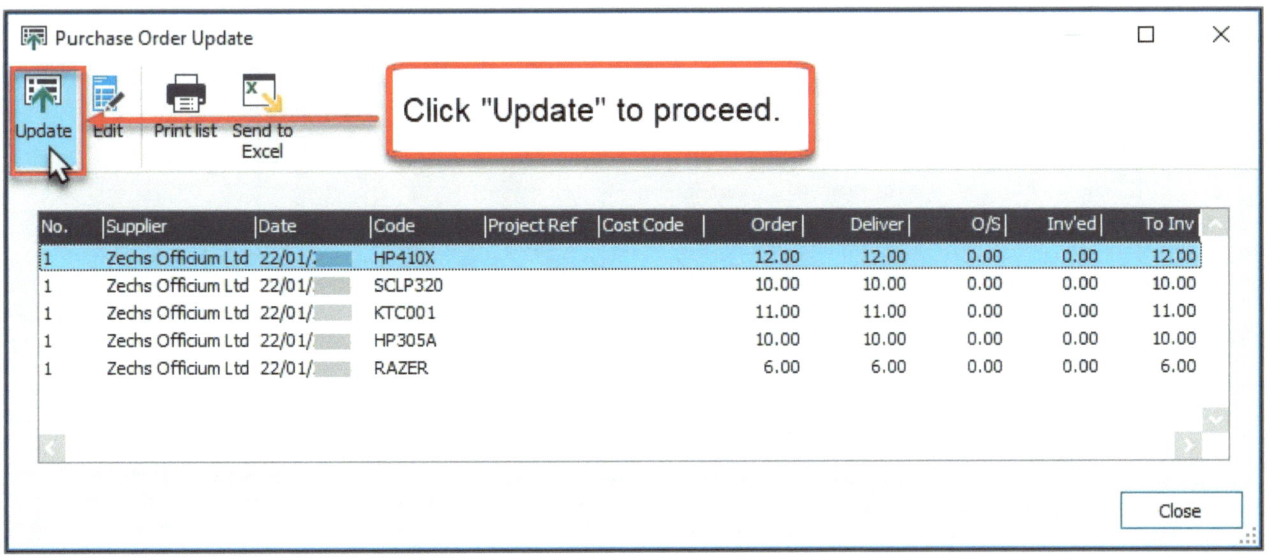

Fig. 74

Once you click on "Update" as illustrated in the figure above, "Batch supplier invoice" window will appear similar to the figure 75 on the next page.

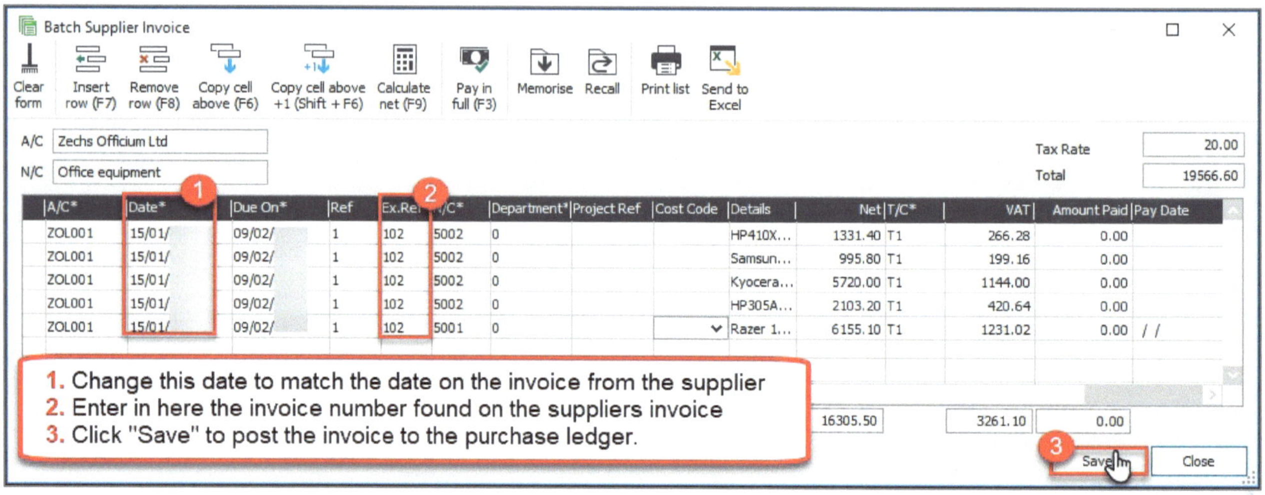

Fig. 75

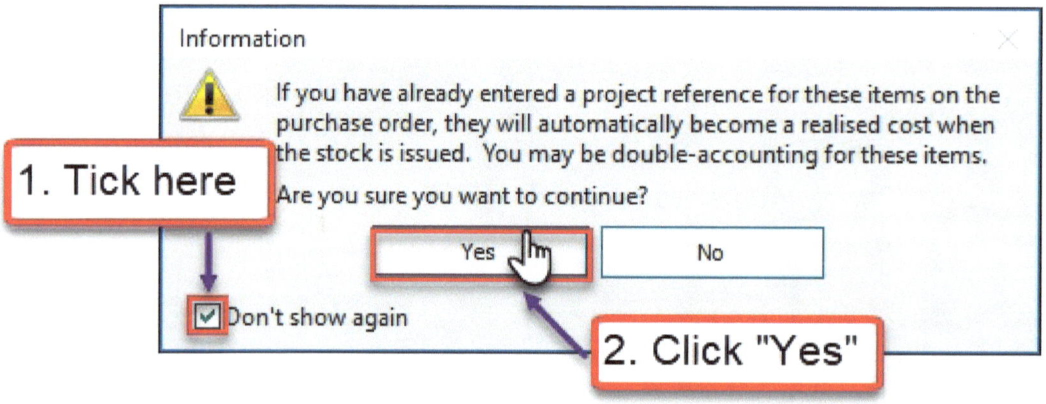

Fig. 76

There is one more purchase order and invoice to update, for Vandstone, please raise the purchase order and update the ledgers just as has been illustrated in the task you have just done for Zechs Officium Ltd. ***Do this now before proceeding to the next task.***

Let's move on and look at how we record a credit note we received from the supplier since we returned some goods/products back.

Task 3b: How to raise a purchase credit note

From the "Suppliers" tab, click on "Batch credit" tab as illustrated in the figure below.

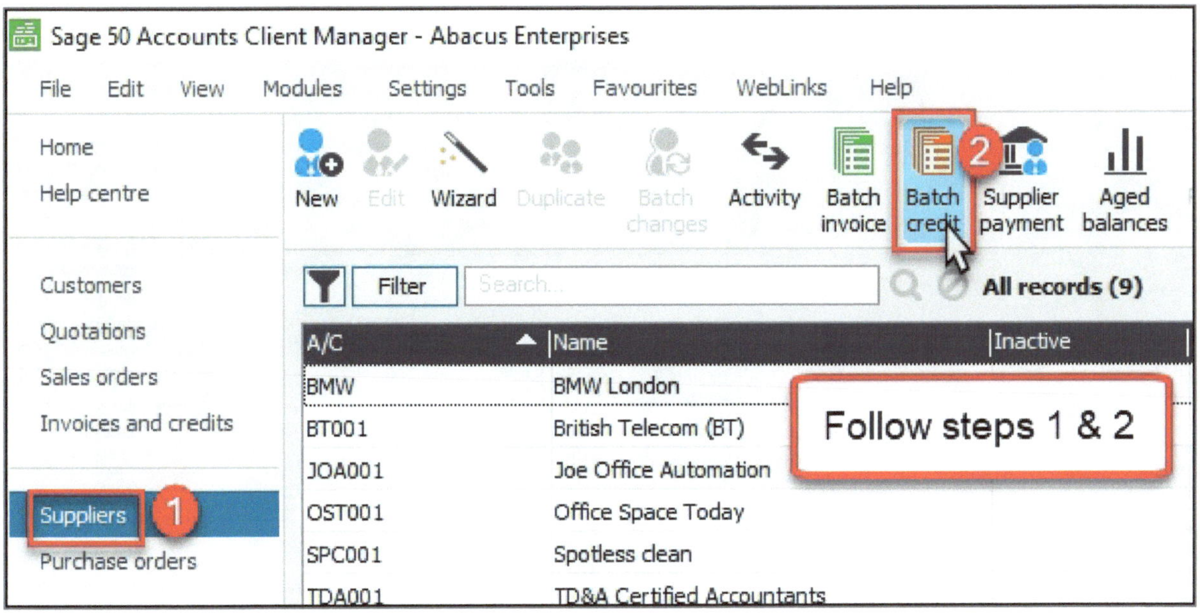

Fig. 77

After step 2 as illustrated in the figure above, you will see a "Batch supplier credit note" window similar to the figure below. Fill it out as illustrated in the inset numbered instructions.

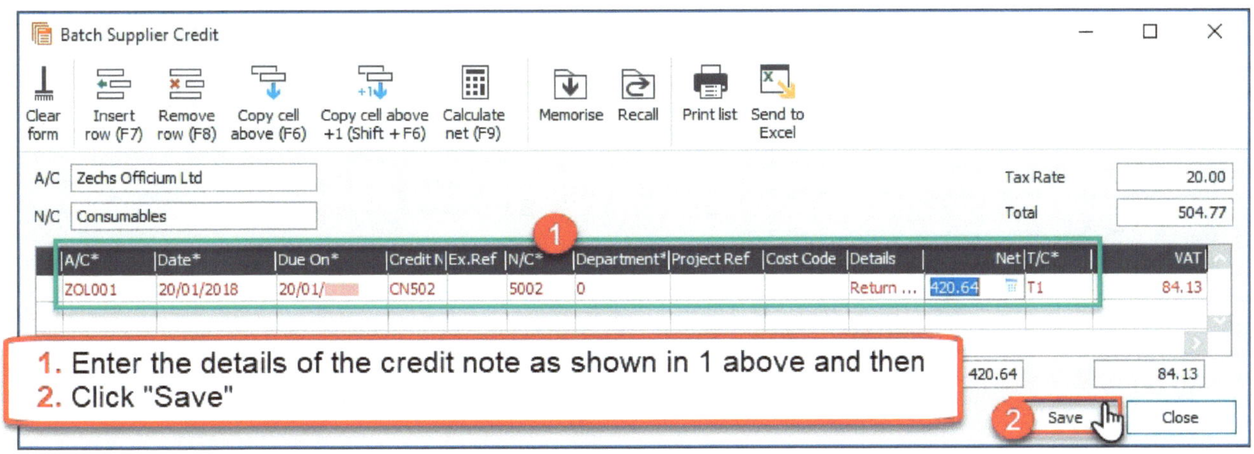

Fig. 77

Having processed the credit note from the supplier, you will now need to adjust the stock with the details of the returned goods/products

You do so by first clicking on the "Products and services" tab, then clicking on "Returns" tab. See figure 78 on the next page.

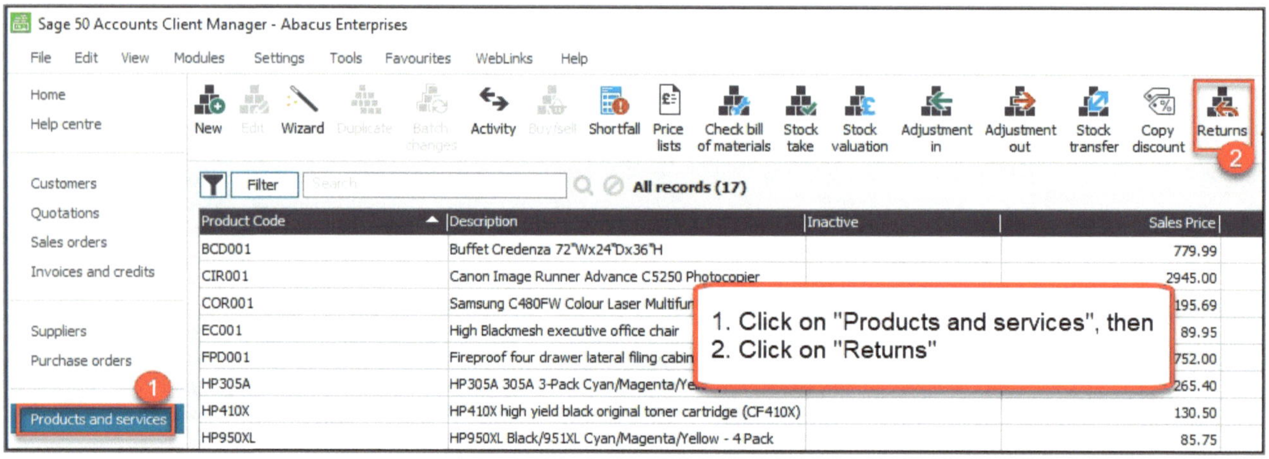

Fig. 78

After step 2 as illustrated in the figure above, a goods returns window appears – see figure below.

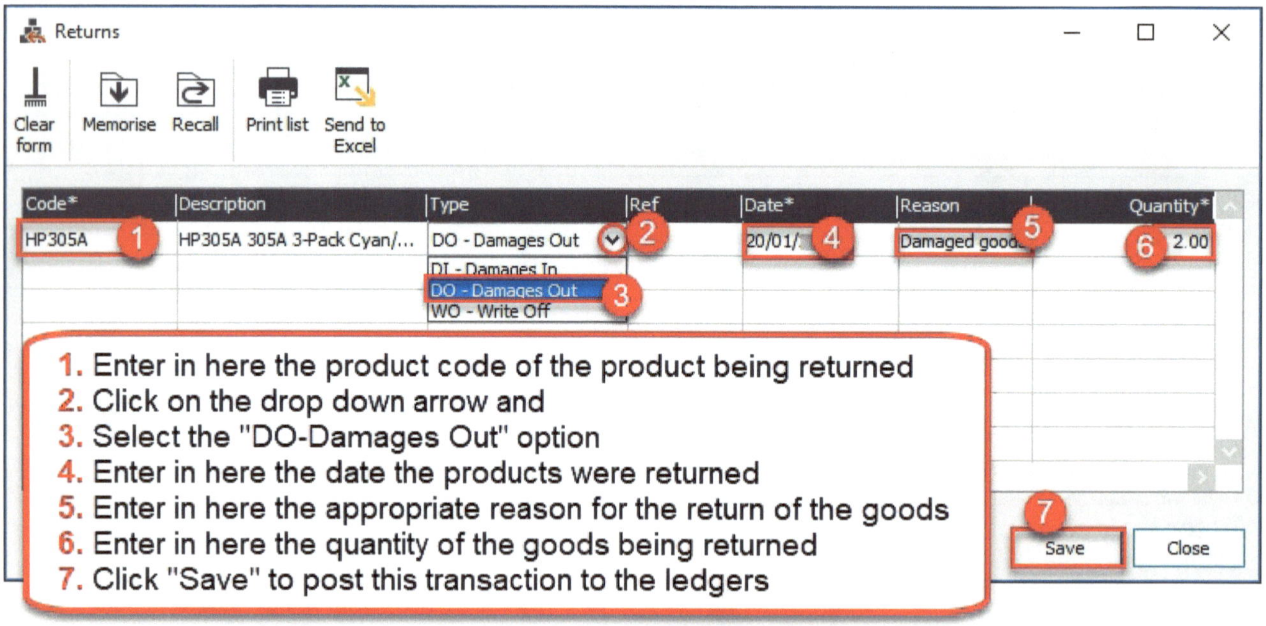

Fig. 79

Task 3c: How to process service purchase invoices

The next task is all about recording supplier service invoices.

First, you will need to create more supplier accounts before you can batch these invoices. Supplier accounts for TD&A Certified Accountants, Office Space Today and Spotless Clean.

To do so, refer to figures; 35 to 38 on pages 25 & 26 and create these supplier accounts.

After you have created the required supplier accounts, you can then proceed to record the supplier invoices via a batch. See illustration in the next page.

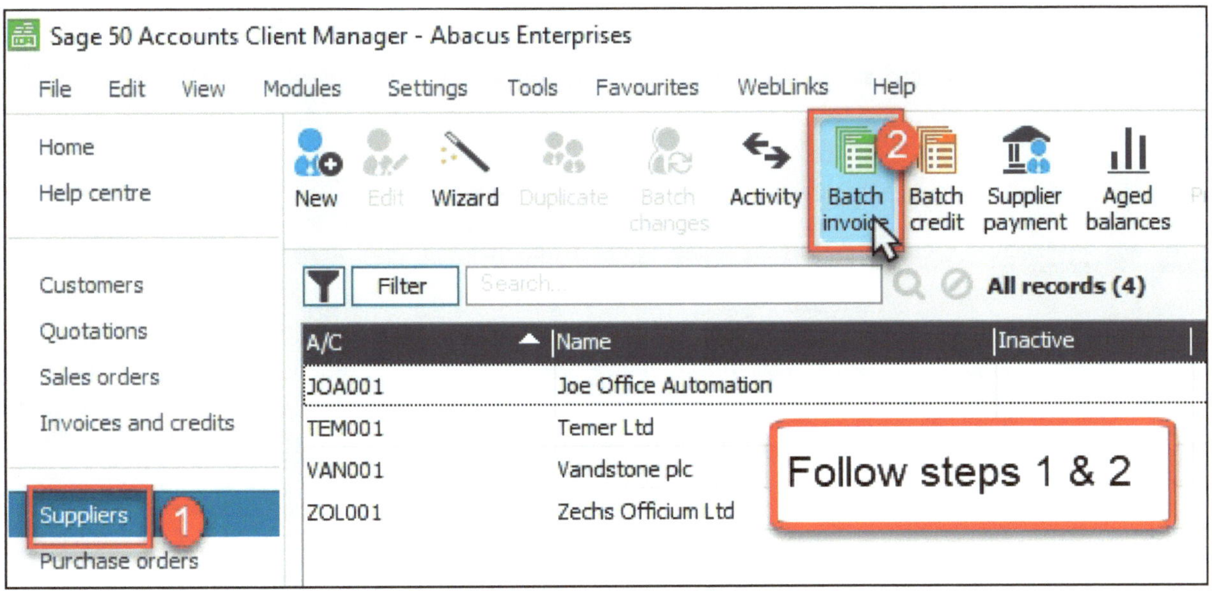

Fig. 80

After you click on "Batch suppliers" tab as illustrated in the figure above, a batch supplier window will appear. Record it with the details from the invoices and the final batch should look like the window in figure 81 on the next page.

This space is for notes

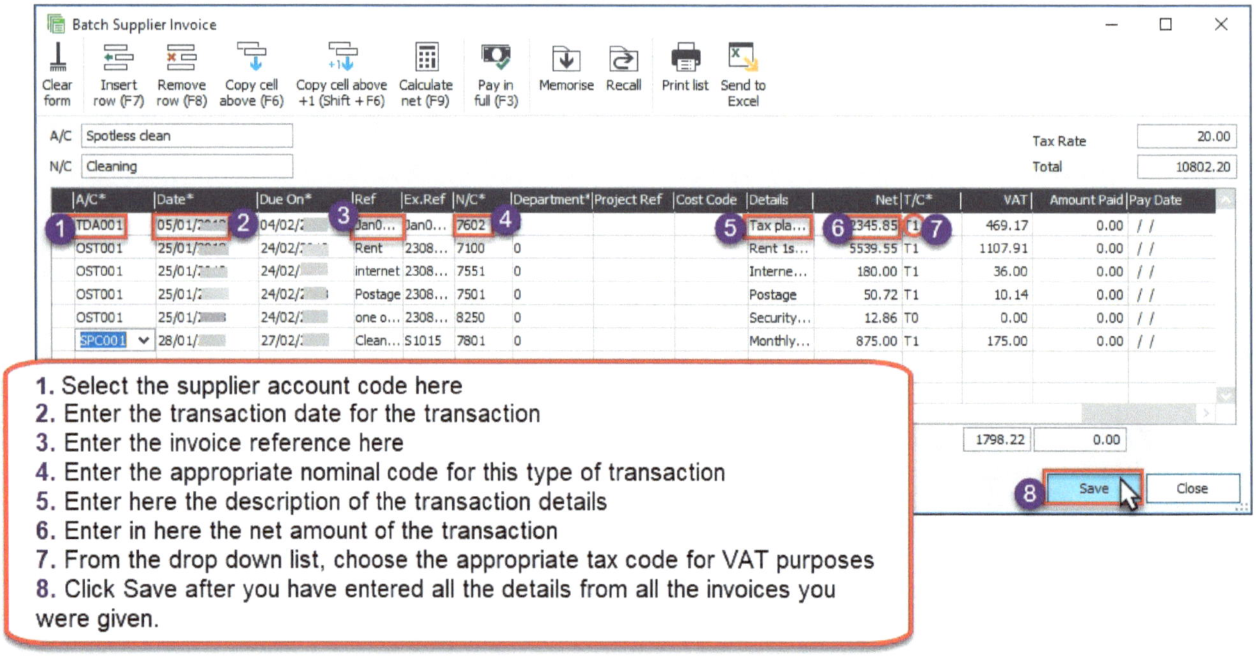

A/C*	Date*	Due On*	Ref	Ex.Ref	N/C*	Department*	Project Ref	Cost Code	Details	Net	T/C*	VAT	Amount Paid	Pay Date
TDA001	05/01/	04/02/	Jan0...	Jan0...	7602				Tax pla...	2345.85	T1	469.17	0.00	/ /
OST001	25/01/	24/02/	Rent	2308...	7100	0			Rent 1s...	5539.55	T1	1107.91	0.00	/ /
OST001	25/01/	24/02/	internet	2308...	7551	0			Interne...	180.00	T1	36.00	0.00	/ /
OST001	25/01/	24/02/	Postage	2308...	7501	0			Postage	50.72	T1	10.14	0.00	/ /
OST001	25/01/	24/02/	one o...	2308...	8250	0			Security...	12.86	T0	0.00	0.00	/ /
SPC001	28/01/	27/02/	Clean...	S1015	7801	0			Monthly...	875.00	T1	175.00	0.00	/ /

Fig. 81

This space is for notes

"A gentle response deflects fury, but a harsh word makes tempers rise". Proverbs 15:1 CJB

TASK 4: ACCOUNTS RECEIVABLE (AR) – SALES LEDGER

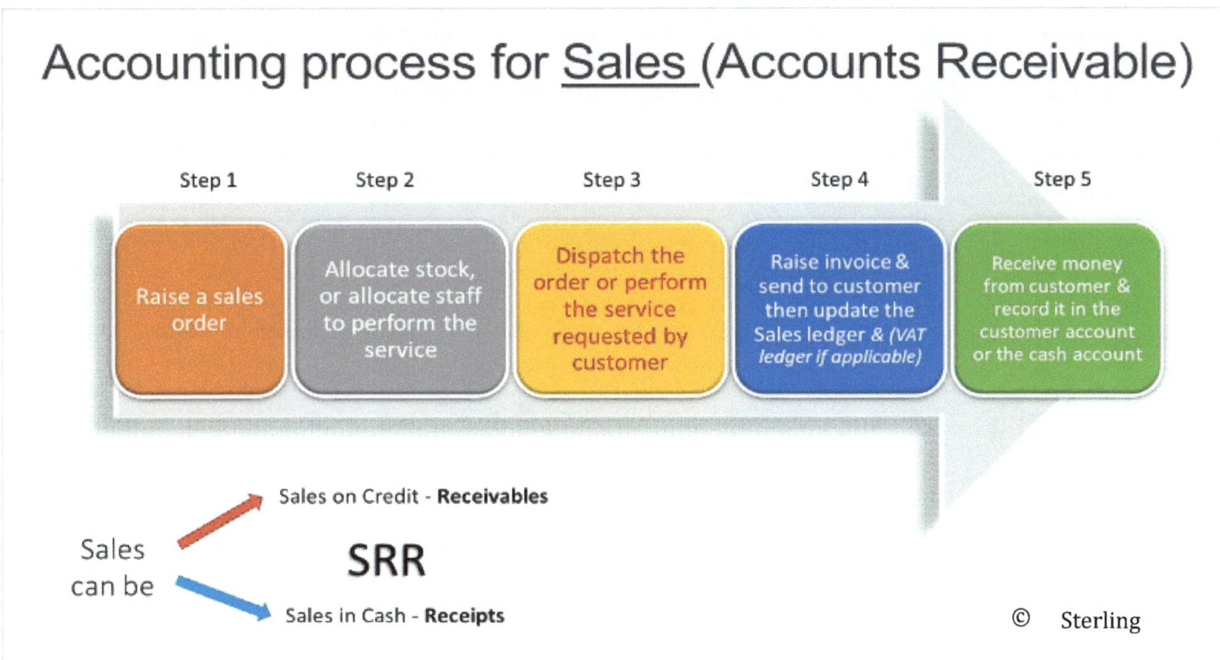

Fig. 82

Task 4a: How to record a cash sale paid by cash & bank transfer

Let's first begin by creating a customer called Cash Sale. This is to be able to record all those cash sales happening in the business on this account especially when we are going to be selling items from our stock. This will make it easier later when doing stock control.

To create a new customer account, follow the steps as illustrated in figure 83 below.

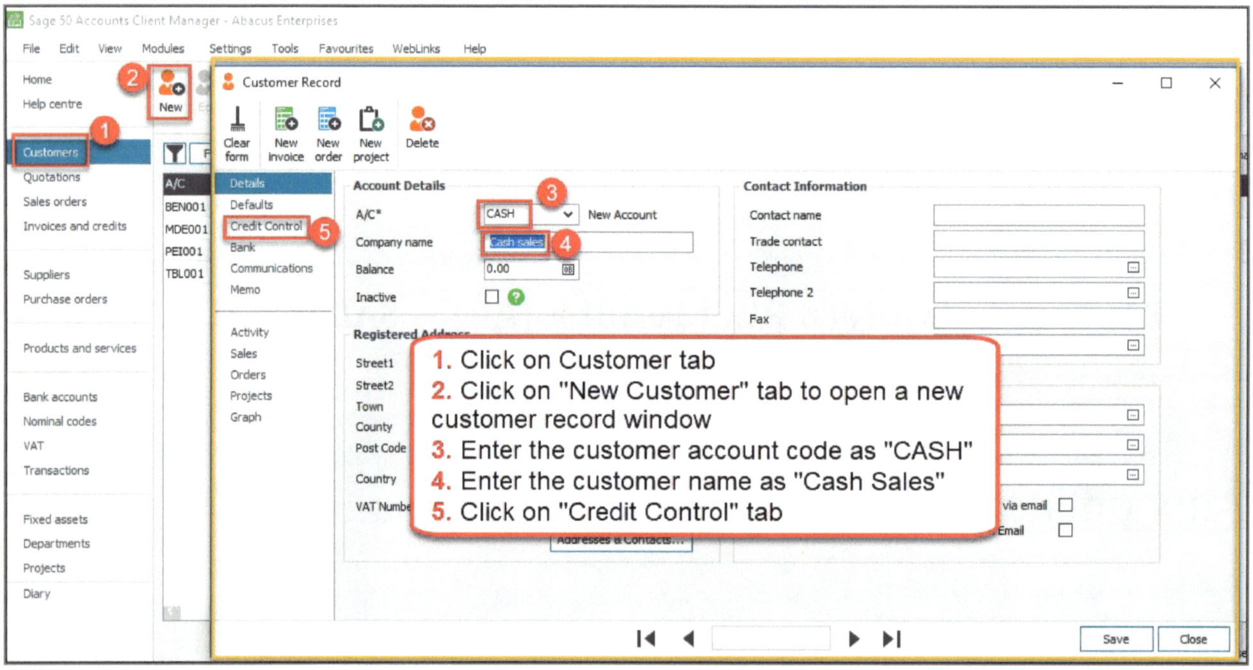

Fig. 83

Upon clicking the credit "Credit control" tab, a window similar to the figure 84 on the next page will appear.

This space is for notes

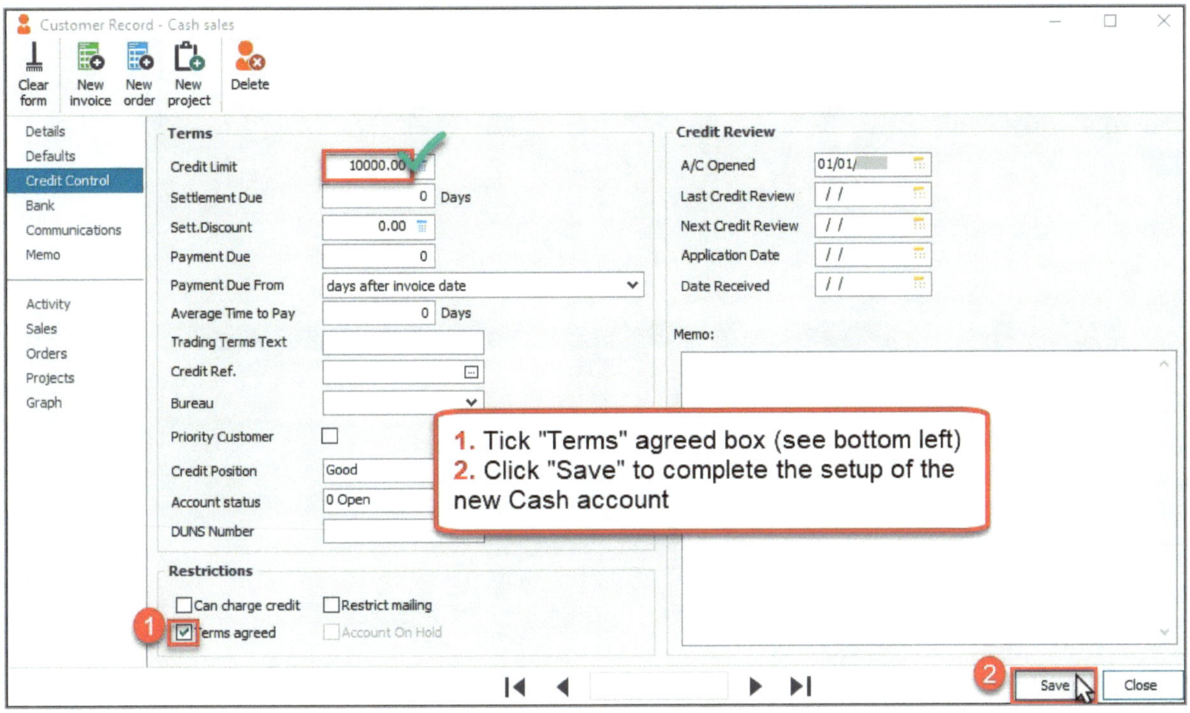

Fig. 84

Once the cash account is setup, you can now record the cash sale.

First, change the program/system date to the date of the cash sale (This is important for VAT purposes because Sage will update the sales ledger with this transaction based on the system/program date)
Click Settings>select change program date from the drop-down list that appears>change date to 7th January current year (date of the cash sale). After that, click on "Invoices and credits" tab and select "New invoice" – see below.

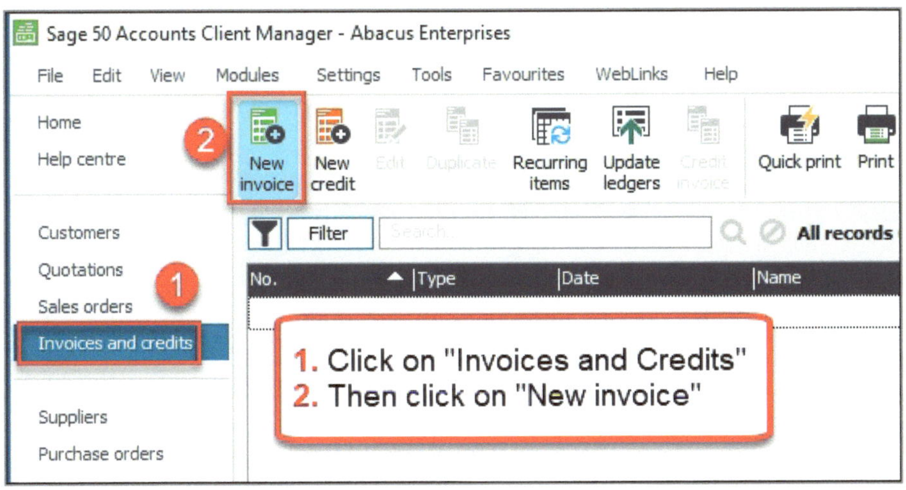

Fig. 85

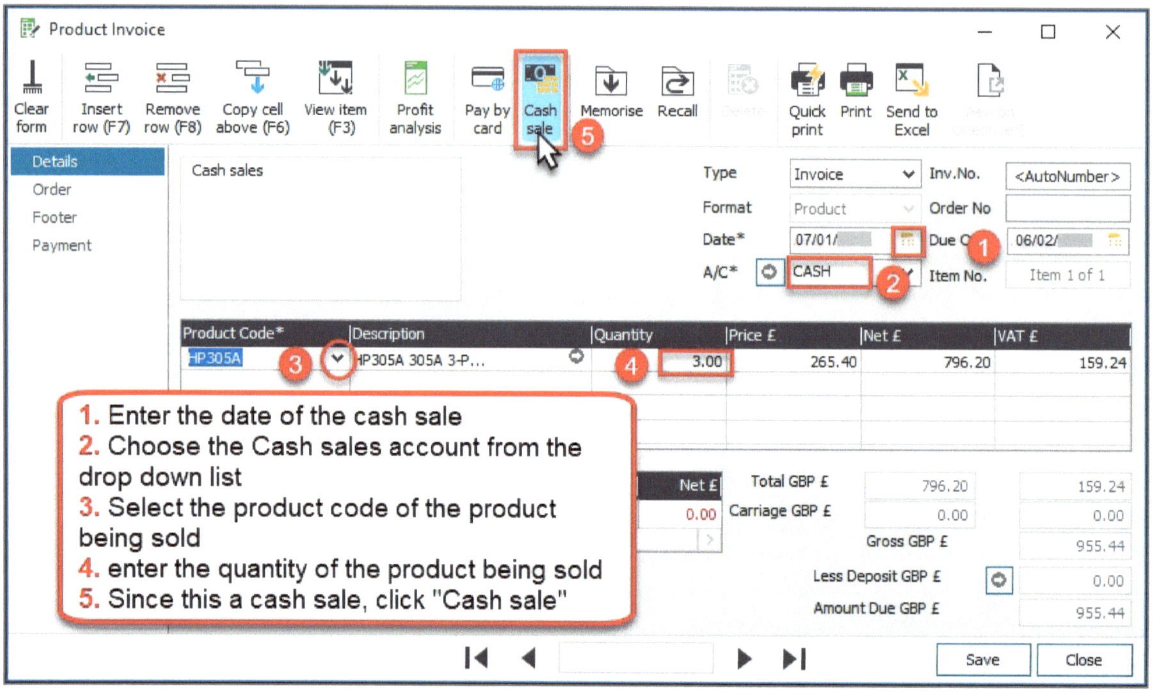

Fig. 86

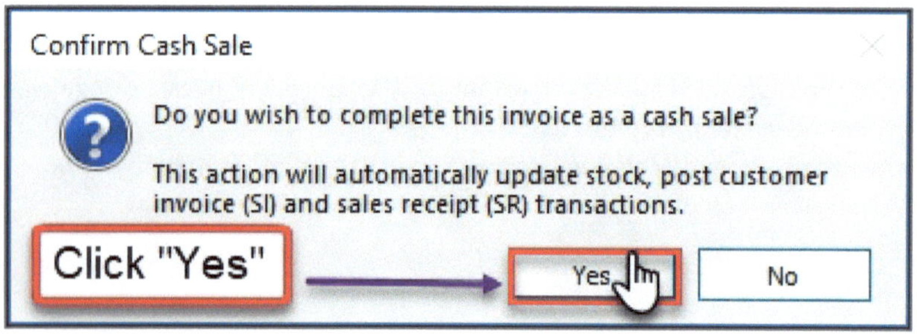

Fig. 87

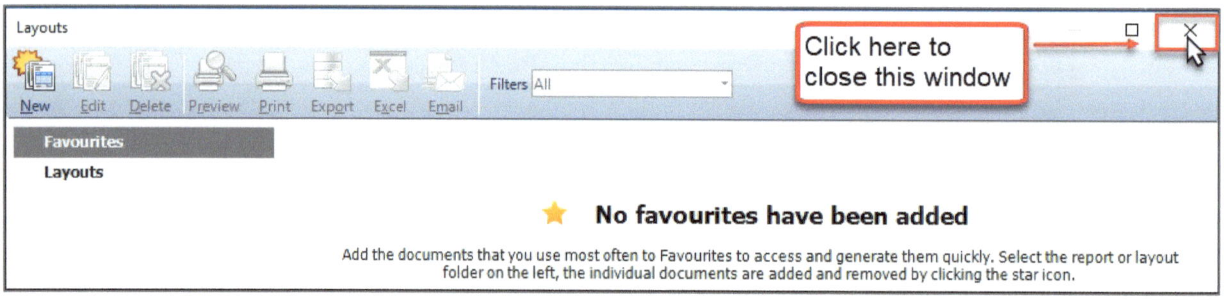

Fig. 88

Task 4b: How to record a credit sale and returns in

- Change the program/system date to 12th January current year (the date for the credit sale transaction).
- Click on Invoice and credits tab and then click "New invoice" and a product invoice window will appear.

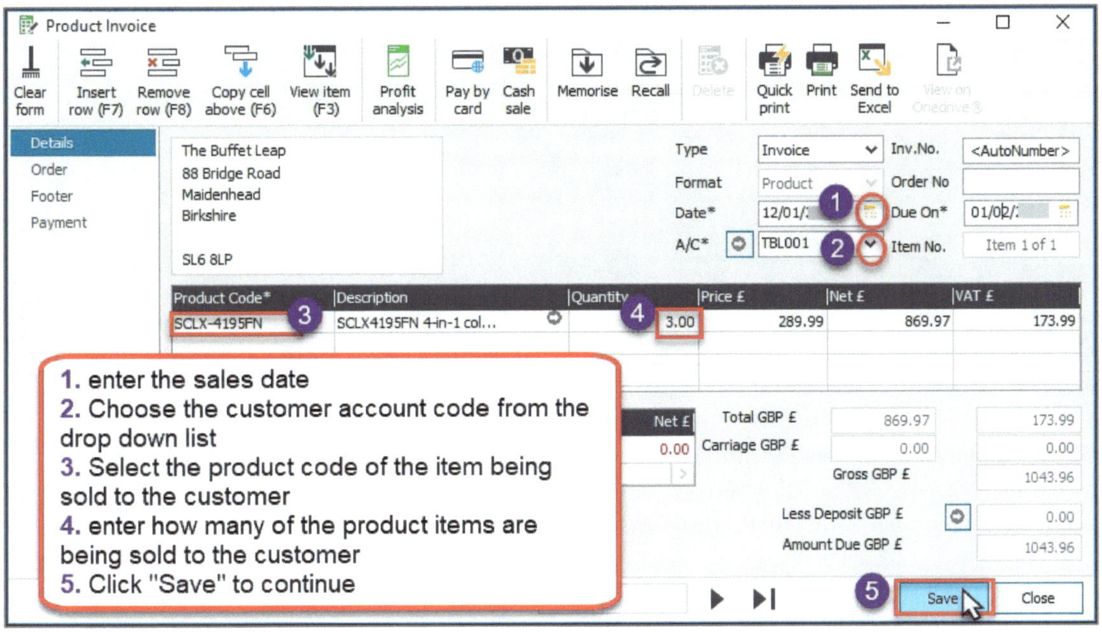

Fig. 89

After step 5 as shown in the figure above, the cash sale would have been recorded in Sage 50 Accounts, however, the sales ledger and VAT (sales) need to be updated. See figure below;

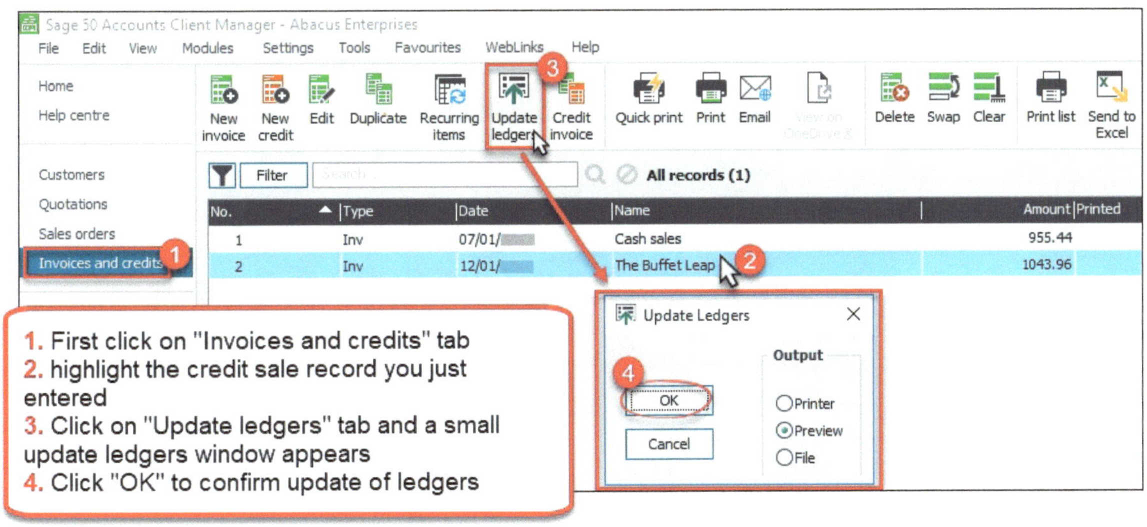

Fig. 90

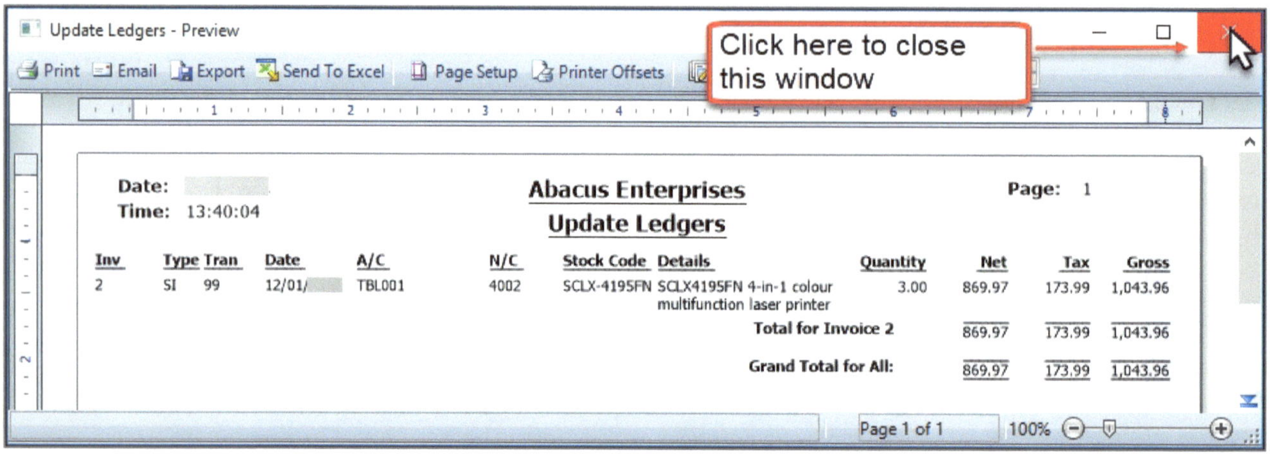

Fig. 91

Raising a customer credit note.

You are told that three days later one of the laser printers was returned still in good condition/unused.

Here is how you should record the return of this item – see figure below.

Steps: First change the system/program date to the date the credit note is being raised, then click on "Invoices and credits" tab, then click on the Buffet Leap invoice you raised on the 12th January and then click on "Credit invoice."

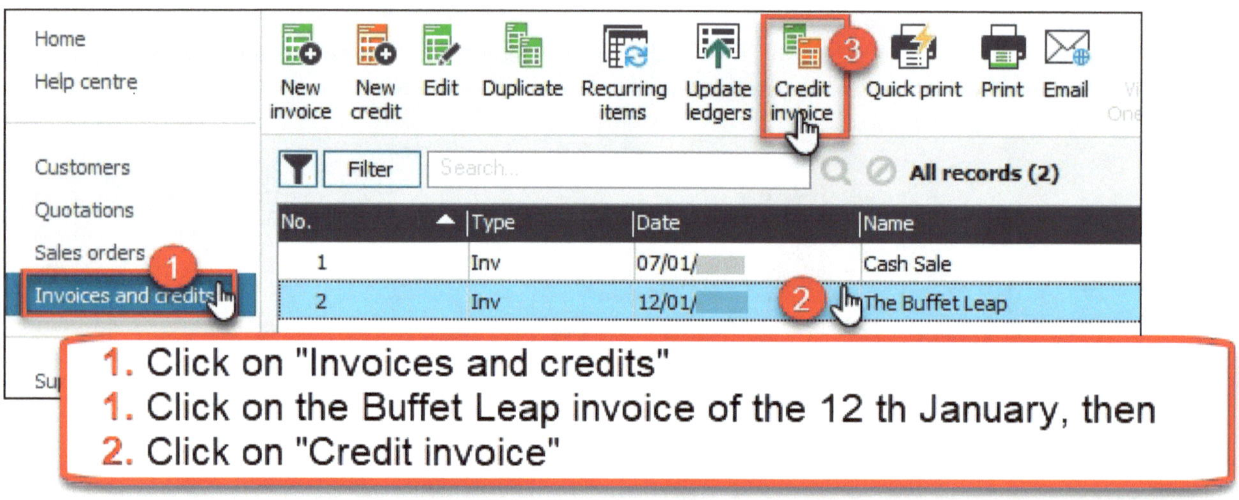

Fig. 92

Next, fill out the product credit window as illustrated in figure 93 on the next page.

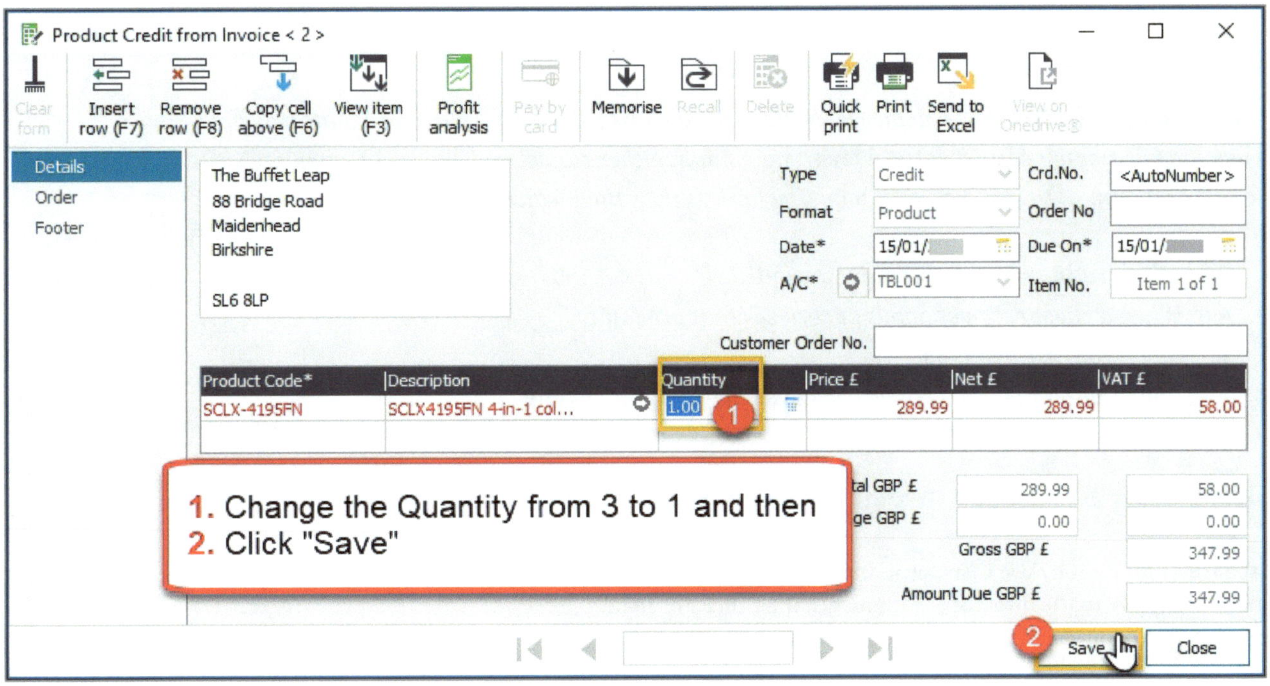

Fig. 93

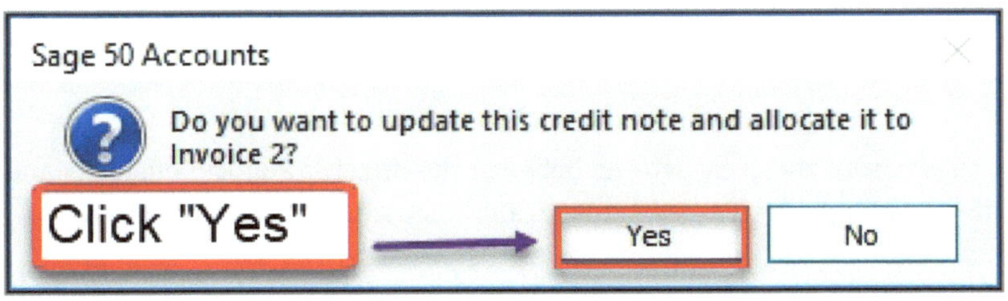

Fig. 94

Fig. 95

What is a credit note?

A credit note is effectively a negative invoice - it's a way of showing a customer that they don't have to pay the full amount of an invoice. A credit note might either cancel an invoice out completely if it's for the same amount as the invoice, or it might be for less than the invoice.

Typically, credit notes are usually issued:

- *When a client receives goods or services that are faulty*
- *Any errors in the billing*
- *Any disputes there may have been over the invoiced amount*

Task 4c: How to record company money spent by the Director for personal benefit

A purchase of an item by the director using company money for his or his relatives benefit is counted as a loan from the business/company to the director – famously called Director loan.
Here is how you can record it in Sage 50 Accounts.

If there are or will be lots of transactions between the director and the business, then it is better to set up a bank account and call it Director account and have all transactions between the director and the business recorded here (***we have already done so in the setup process***). If this account is overdrawn, then it means the business owes the director money by the overdrawn amount if the account is in a positive balance, then it means the director owes the business that positive balance amount.

Having set up the Director bank account, we can now record the transactions between the director and the business and the first of those transactions is one where the director bought an iPad as a gift for his son using company money.

This space is for notes

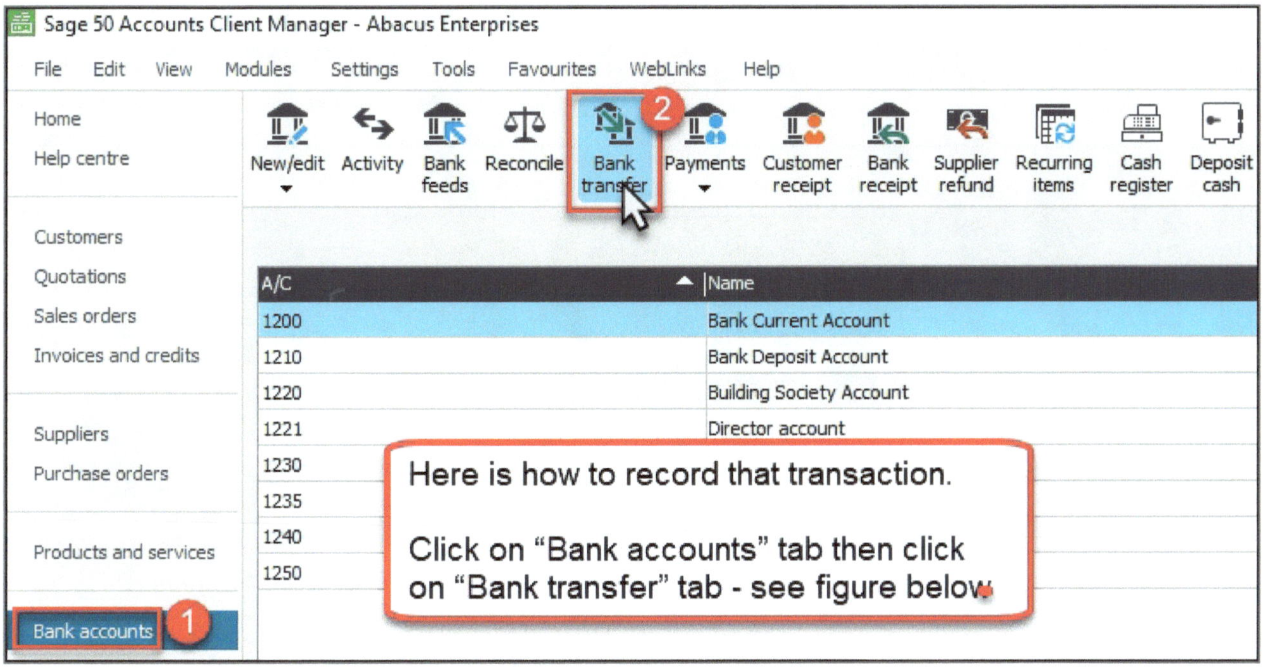

Fig. 96

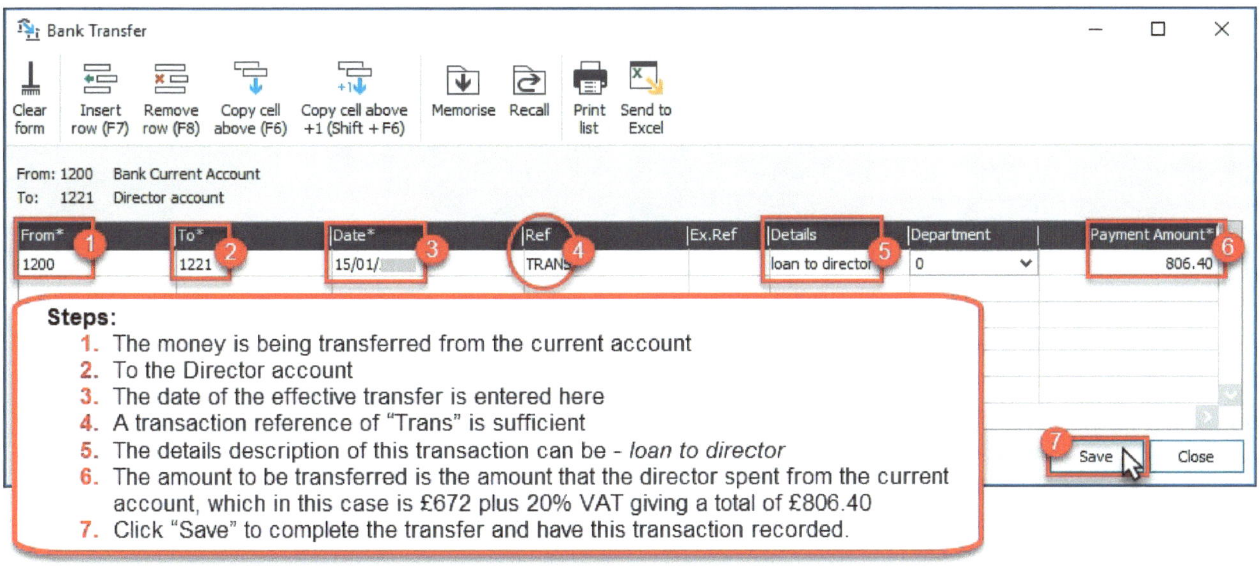

Fig. 97

If the transactions between the director and the business are a few odd ones here and there, there is no need to create a separate bank account for the director; you can just record the transaction directly to the director loan account code already provided in the Sage nominal account codes; nominal account number 2301.

To record the transaction stated here in this way, first click on "Bank accounts>select the current account-1200>>then ***click on the drop-down arrow under "Payments"> and select "Bank payments" > and record the transaction as shown below.*** **Don't do this step; it is just for illustration purpose only**

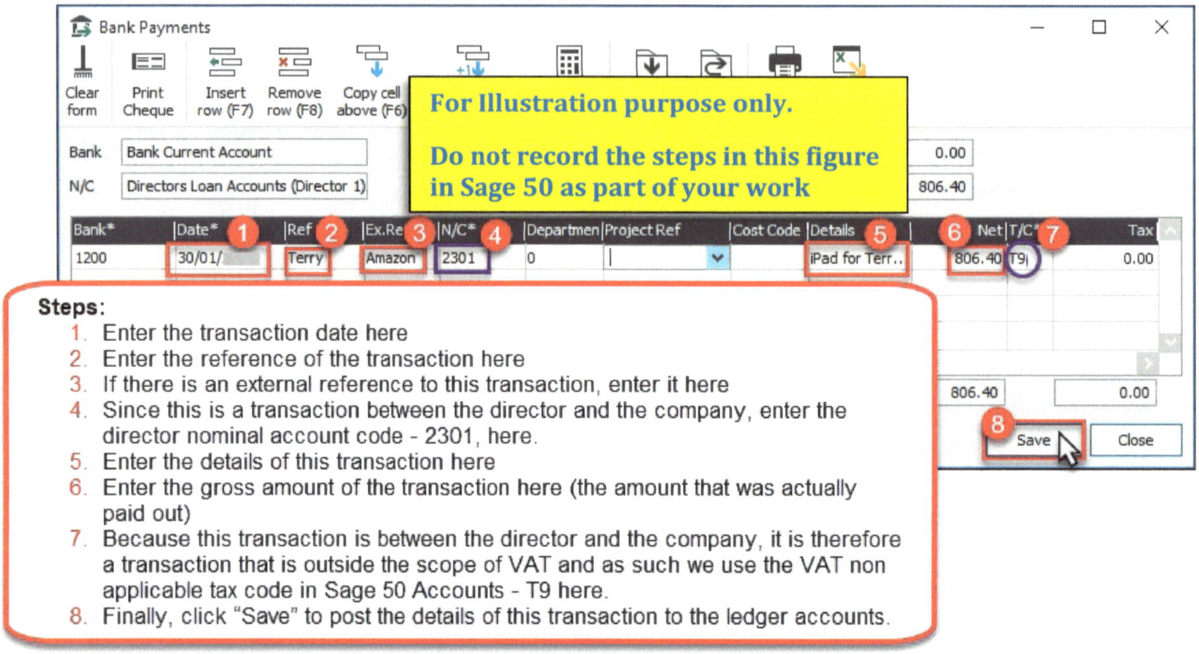

Fig. 98

Task 4d: How to record the Directors money spent on behalf of the business.

A purchase of an item for the business by the director using his own money for is counted as a loan from the director to the business.

If this kind of transaction regularly happens in the business – where the director pays for business expenses using his own funds, then use the director "bank" account that was set up for such transactions – see figure 99 on the next page.

This space is for notes

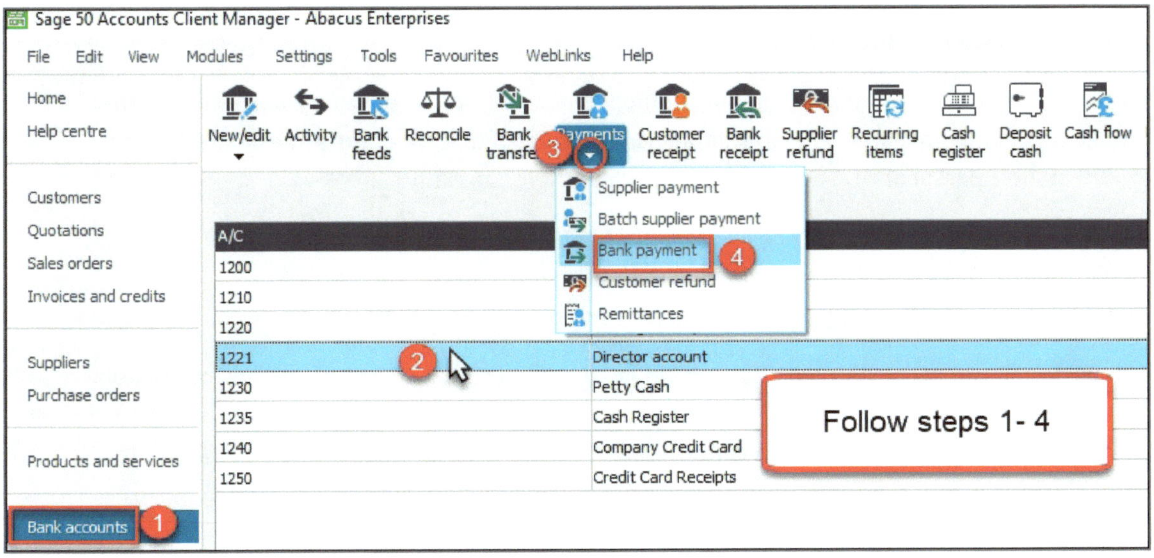

Fig. 99

After step 4 as illustrated in the figure above, a window similar to the figure below will appear.

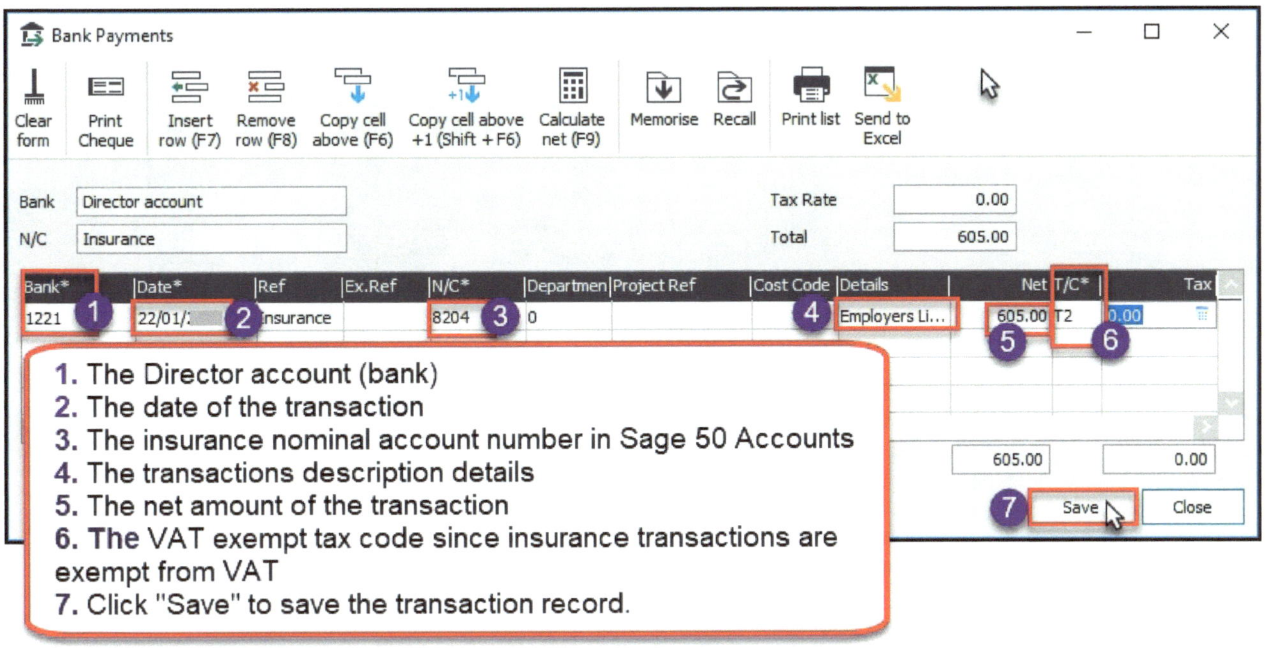

Fig. 100

What is a Director Loan Account (DLA)?

Any funds a director takes out from their company, which is not a dividend or salary and exceeds the amount they have personally invested as a shareholder, is classified as a **director's loan**. The amount **must** be recorded in their personal DLA and then paid back to their company.

Items you should record in the DLA are:

- ✓ Any cash withdrawals from the company that they have made as a director
- ✓ Personal expenses which were paid with company money

HMRC defines personal expenses as anything which is not wholly, exclusively and necessary for conducting your business.

You need to ensure that the DLA provides a comprehensive record of all transactions involving the director's personal finances, and the company's, to ensure it will stand up to scrutiny by HMRC.

If you have not set up a Director "Bank account" for transactions between the director and the company, you can use the default director loan account set up in Sage 50 for this purpose by using journal entries. The only thing is that you wouldn't be able to directly record a payment of supplier invoices in Sage 50 Accounts by the director's own funds) via a journal entry.

To record transactions between the director and the company using journals, first click on "Nominal codes" tab, then click on the "Journal entry"– see figure 101 below.

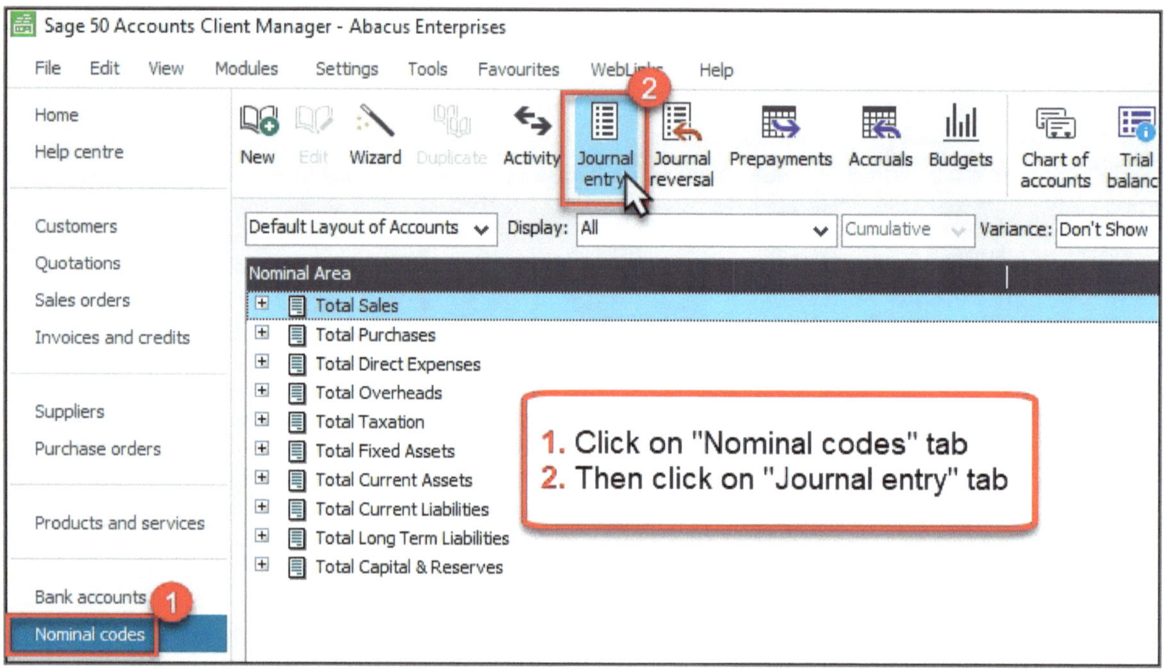

Fig. 101

Once you click the "Journal entry" tab a window similar to the figure below will appear. See inset for what steps to take to enter the details of the transaction.

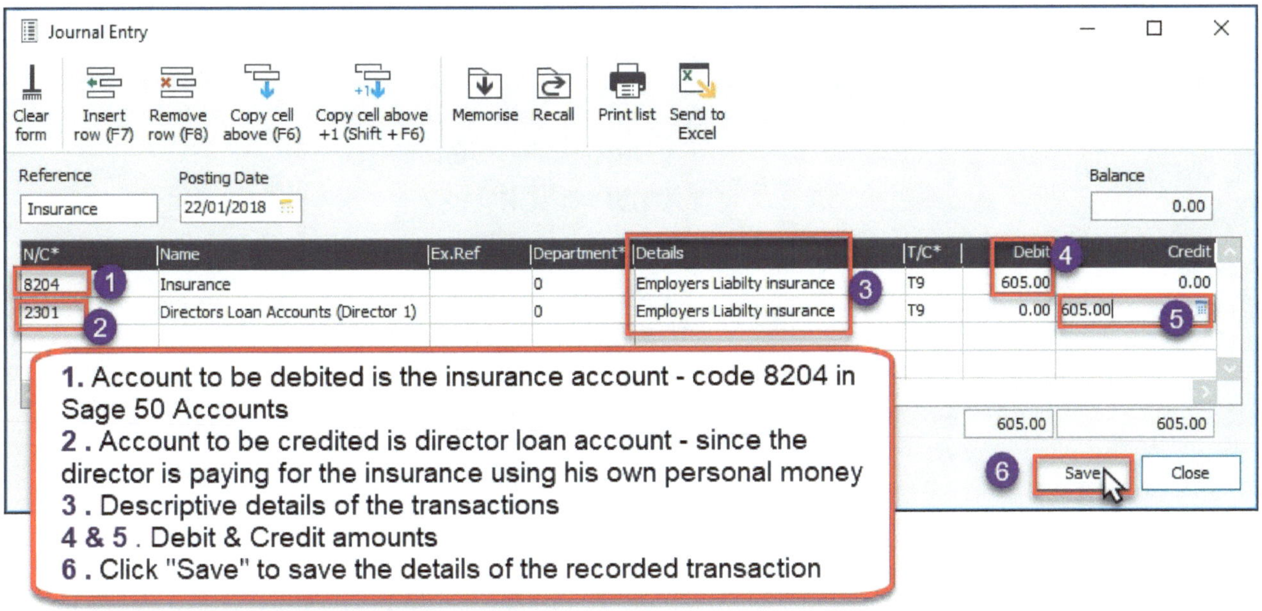

Fig. 102

Task 4e: How to raise sales orders and sales invoices

The sales manager has been working really hard and has secured some orders from customers. It's over to you now to process those sales orders and make sure that the customers get what they have ordered for and not forgetting to invoice them and collect the money.

Let's get this done in Sage 50 Accounts!

We begin by changing the system date to today's date (date we are invoicing for the product/service). This is because this will be the default date Sage will use to update the ledgers with the Sales invoice details.

So, let's do that first – change the system/program date.

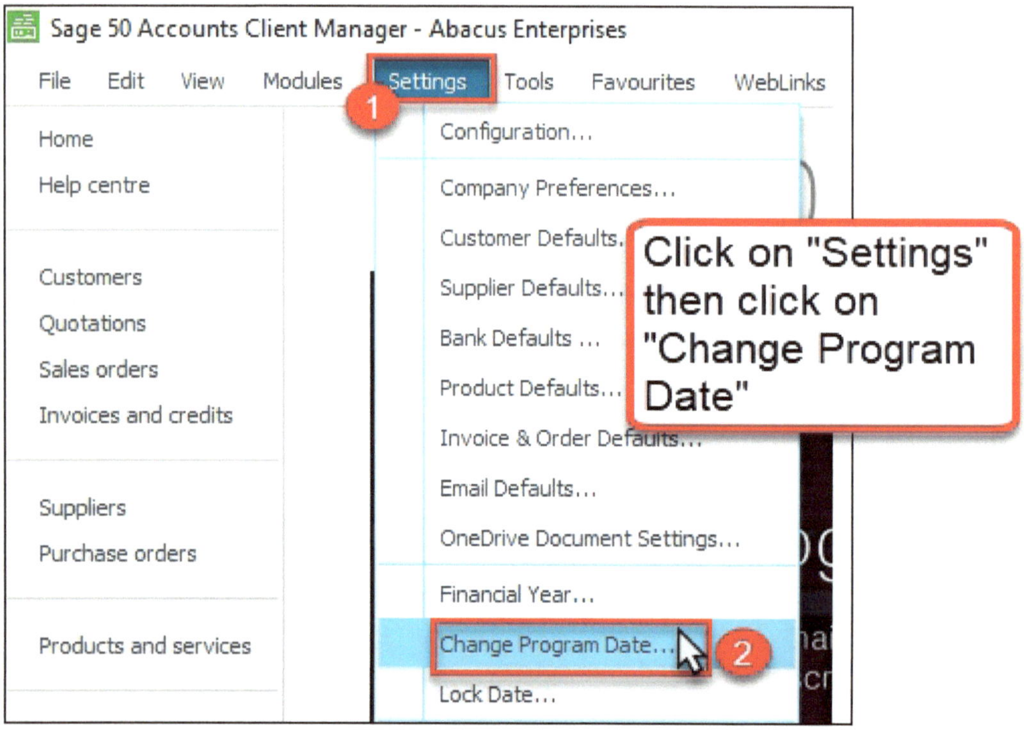

Fig. 103

After step 2 as illustrated in the figure above, a change program date window appears. Enter the date the invoice was raised or is to be raised here -see figure 104 below.

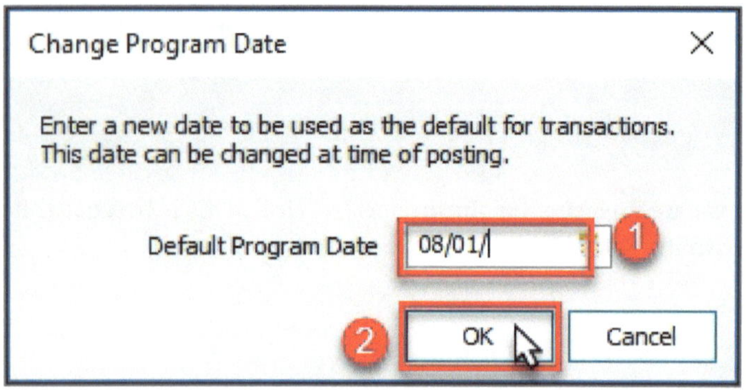

Fig. 104

Let's begin by raising the sales order. To do so, click on "Sales orders" tab then click on "New" – see figure 105 on the next page.

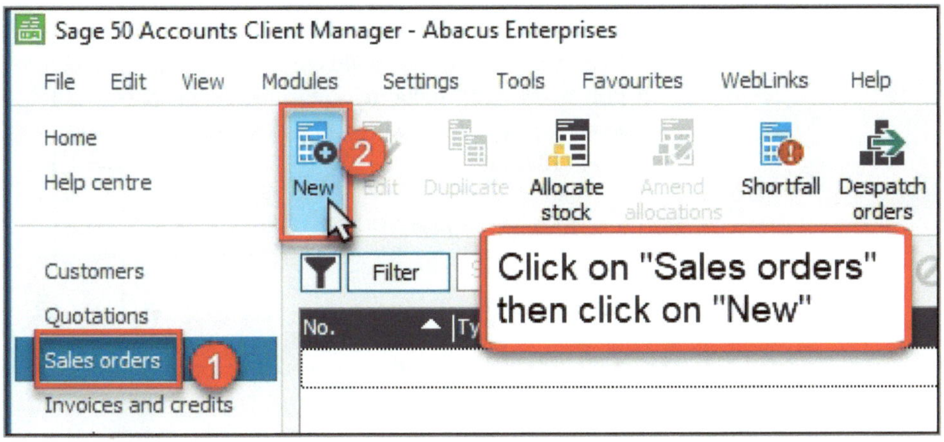

Fig. 105

A product sales order window similar to the figure on the next page. Fill it out as illustrated in the inset steps.

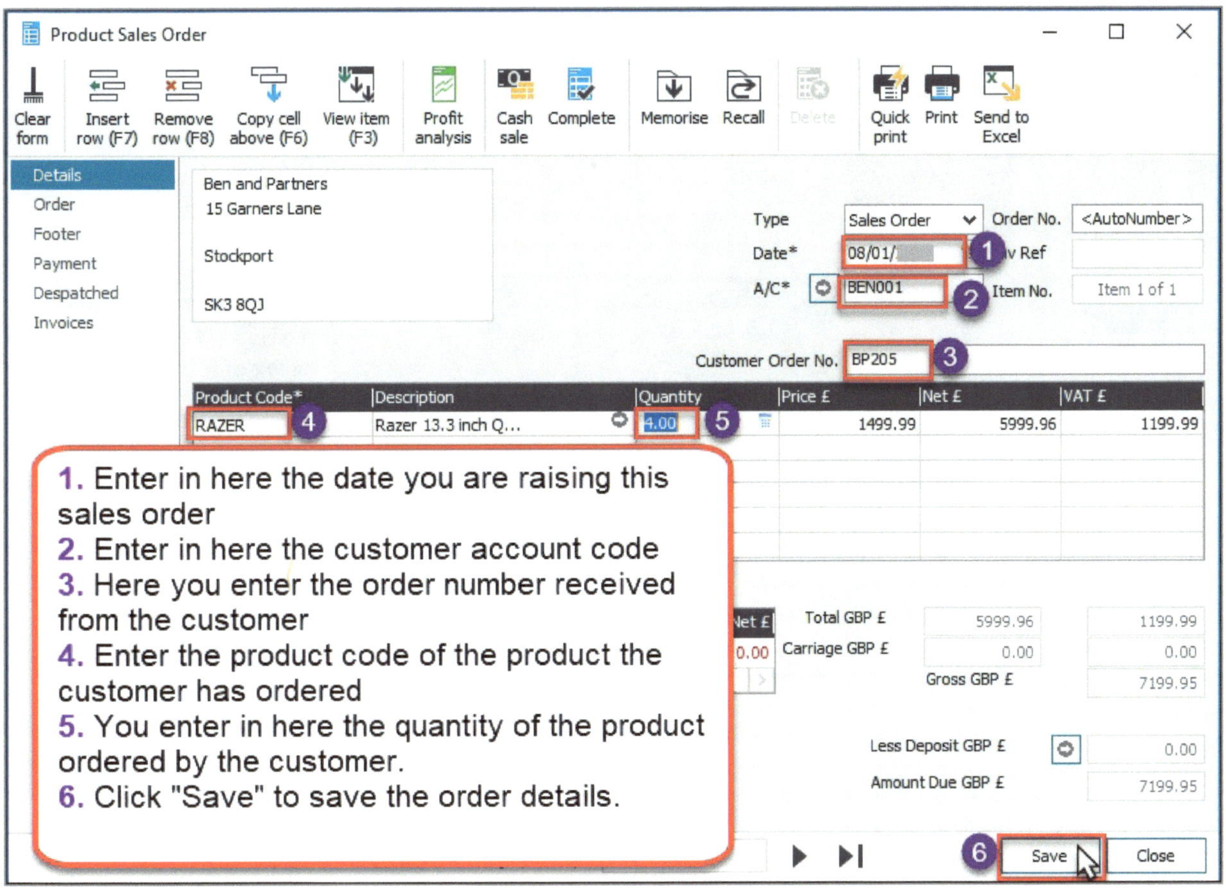

Fig. 106

After step 6 in the figure above, the system will ask whether you want to allocate stock to the sales order right away (to make it unavailable for sale by someone else) or you would like to allocate the stock to the order late.

Click, "Allocate Now"

Fig. 107

Once the sales order is raised and the stock allocated to it, the goods/products should be delivered/shipped to the customer.
Once the goods/products are shipped/dispatched to the customer, you will need to update the sales order status accordingly.

To do so, close the product sales order window that is currently on your screen, then select the order to be dispatched by clicking on it once, then click on "Dispatch orders" tab. See figure 108 below.

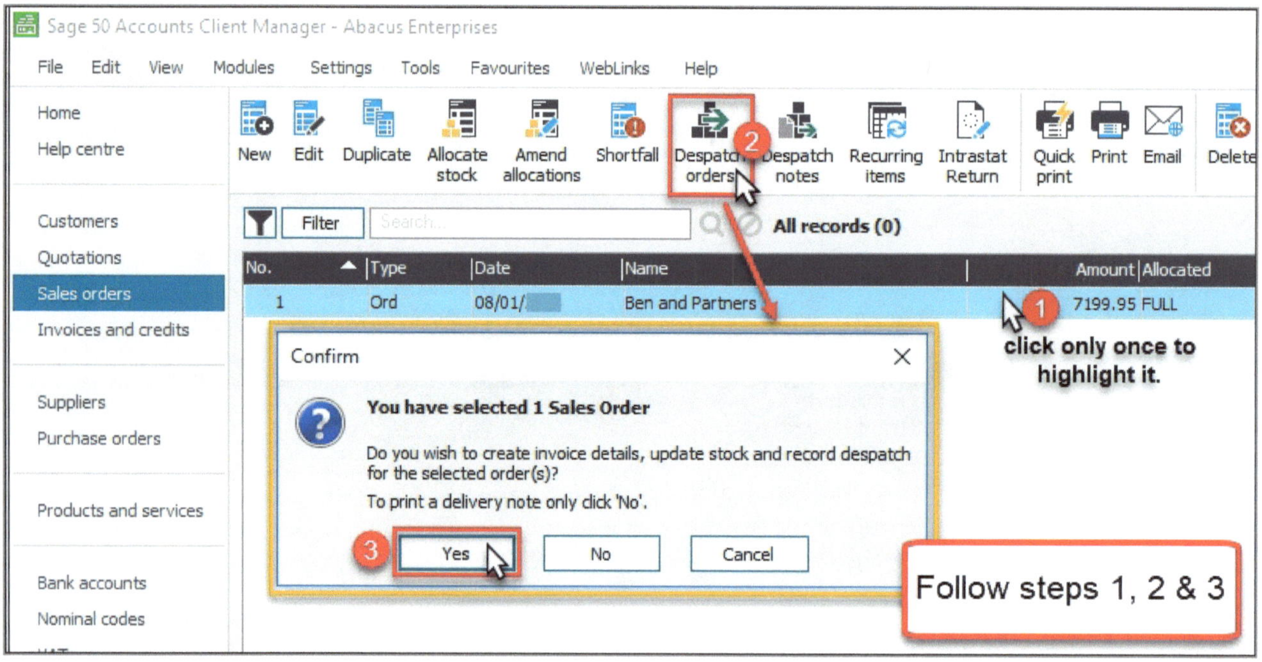

Fig. 108

After step 3 as illustrated in the figure above, a goods despatch note (delivery note) would be automatically generated for the order that was selected for despatch.

Since you want confirmation for the receipt of the goods/products by the customer, print the goods despatch note. See how in figure 109 on the next page.

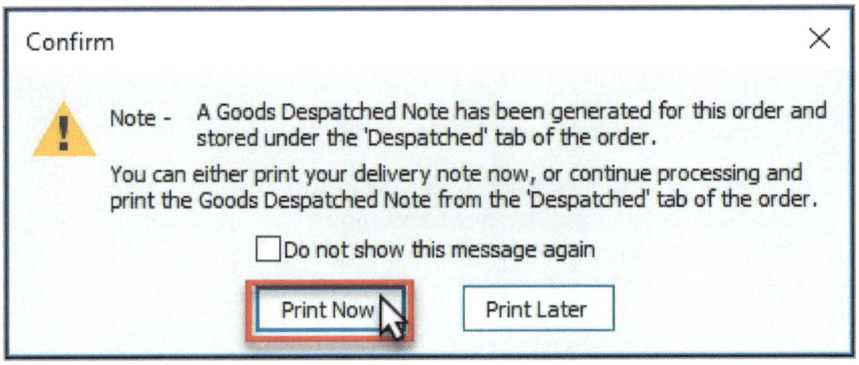

Fig. 109

Once you click "Print Now" as illustrated in the figure above, a despatch order layout window similar to the figure 110 below will appear. Follow the inset illustrative steps to proceed to the next step.

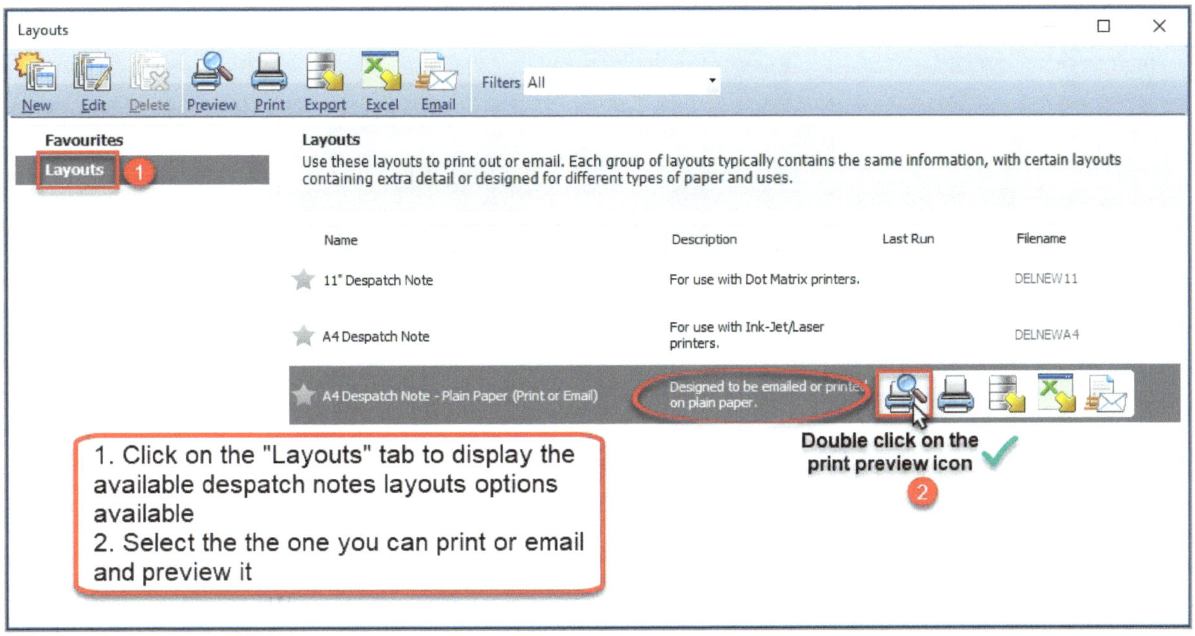

Fig. 110

After step 2 as illustrated in the figure above, here is an illustrative example of the despatch/delivery note. See figure 111 on the next page.

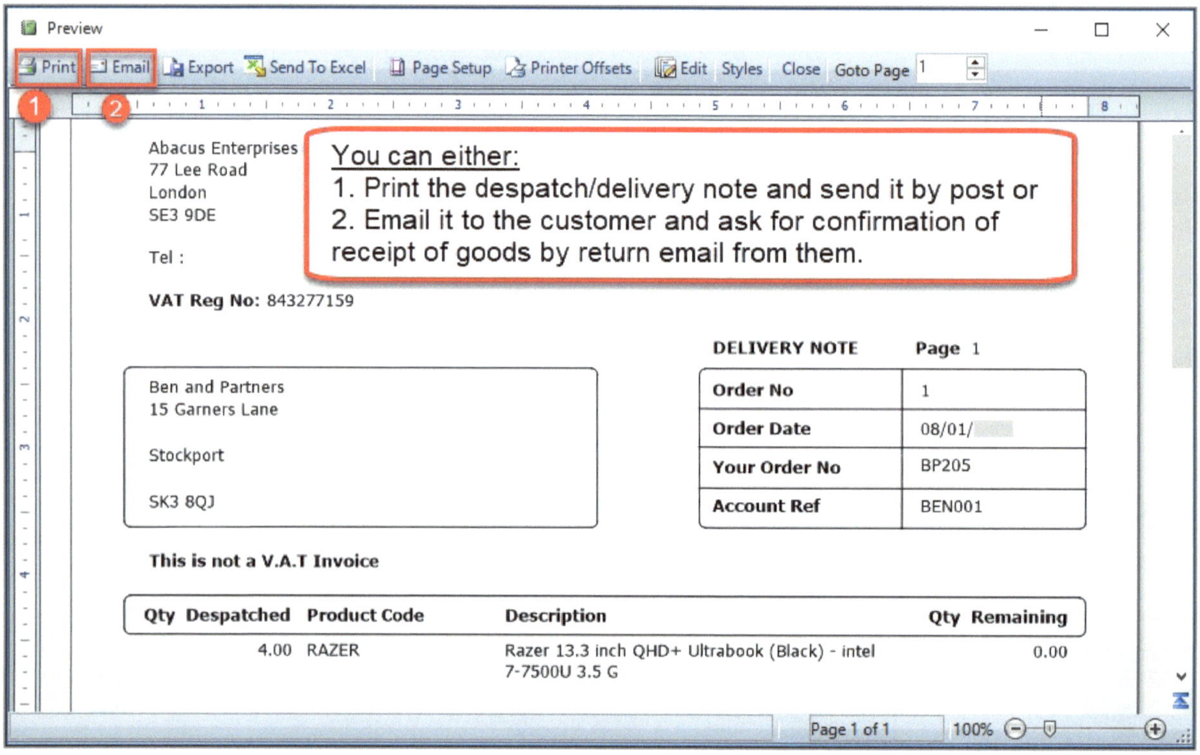

Fig. 111

Okay. The other thing now left to do is to raise an invoice and update the sales ledger and (VAT- sales) ledger. The good news is that in Sage 50 Accounts, these two steps are almost done simultaneously. See figure below.

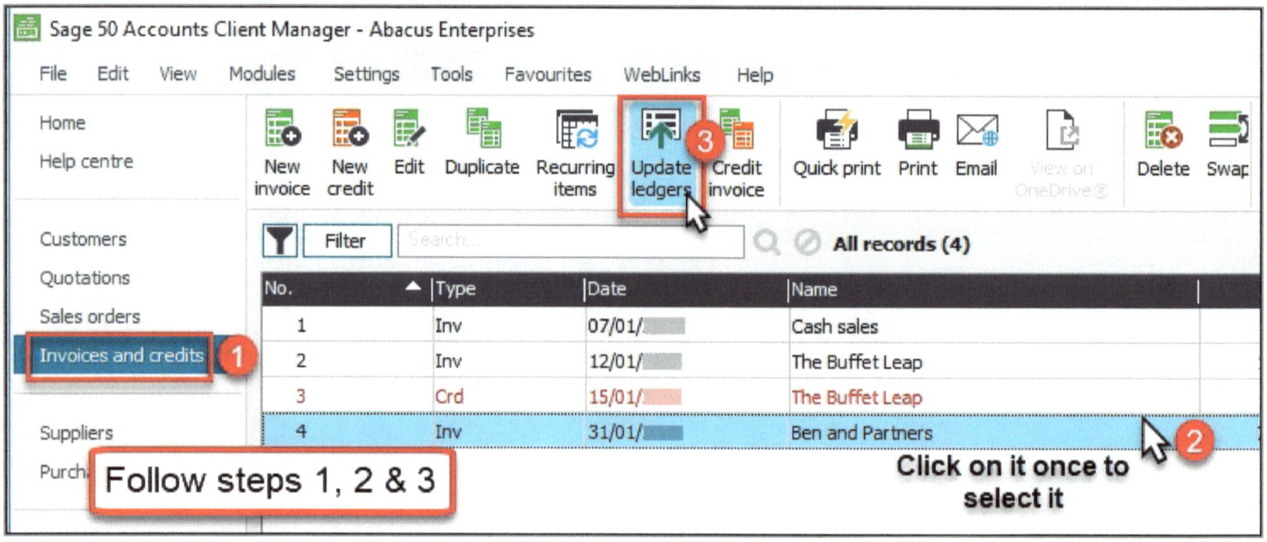

Fig. 112

After step 3 as illustrated in figure 112 in the previous page, a window similar to the figure below will appear.

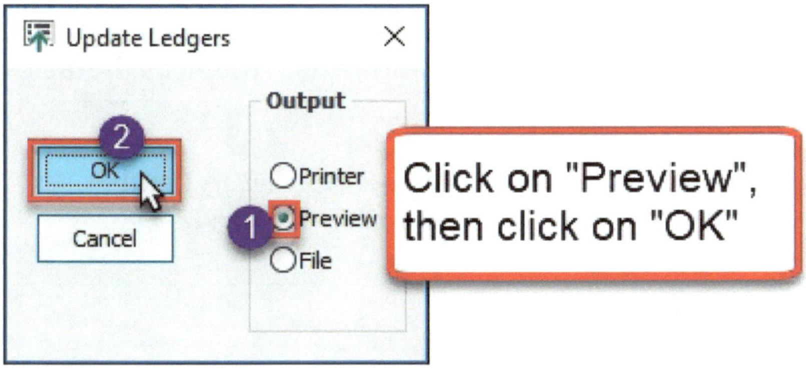

Fig. 113

After step 2 as illustrated in the figure above, an update ledgers preview window will appear – see figure 114 below for an illustrative example.

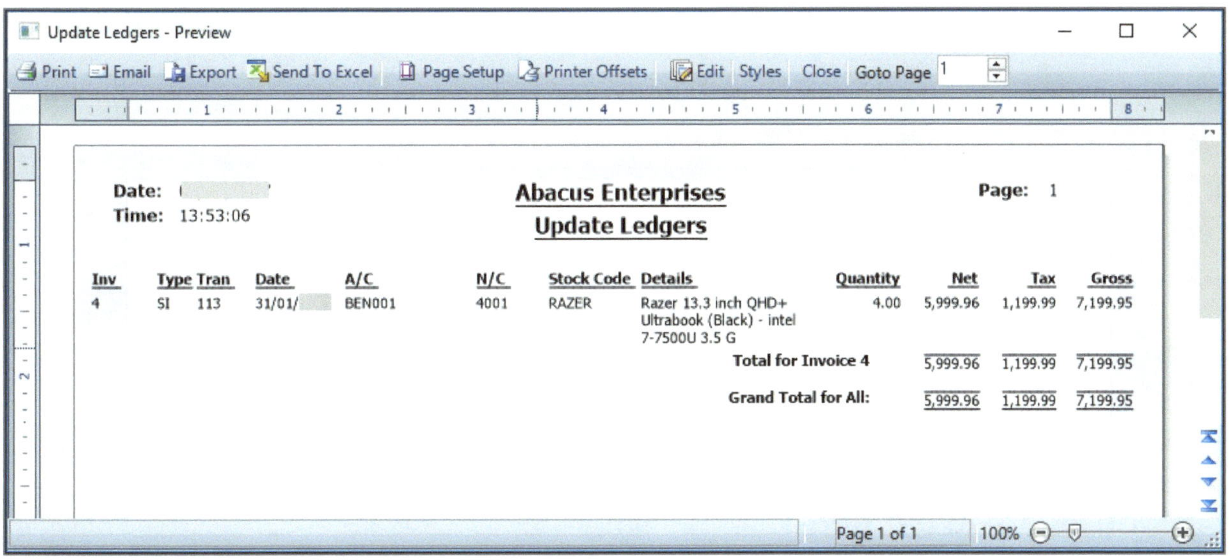

Fig. 114

Close the preview window.

That's it! You have done it! You raised the sales order, you then allocated stock to that order, you made sure that the goods/products were despatched/delivered to the customer and you got confirmation from the customer for the same, you then raised an invoice, sent it to the customer and updated your sales and VAT ledgers.

Now be sure to chase the customer and ensure that they pay on time. You don't want them taking forever to pay, cash flow issues may arise, and you might lose your job if there is no money to pay you.

Okay, it is over to you now to process the rest of the sales order and corresponding invoices.

*** **Continue with the rest of the other sales orders and raise invoices before proceeding to the next task*****
Process the sales orders of:
- **MDE Office Centre (*remember to change program/system date to 22nd January*) and**
- **Peacock Interiors (*remember to change program/system date to 28th January*)**

Do not proceed to the next task before completing this task!!!

Task 4f: How to raise a sales credit note

Hey, you can't always have everything "honki dori" and on this occasion, one of your customers just returned some of the products they bought/ordered from you. Stuff like that happens.

Now that Ben & Partners returned the computer and it is perfectly alright, this computer can be put back in stock for resale.
A credit note should be raised and allocated to the customer invoice. To do this look at the steps in figures 115 & 116.

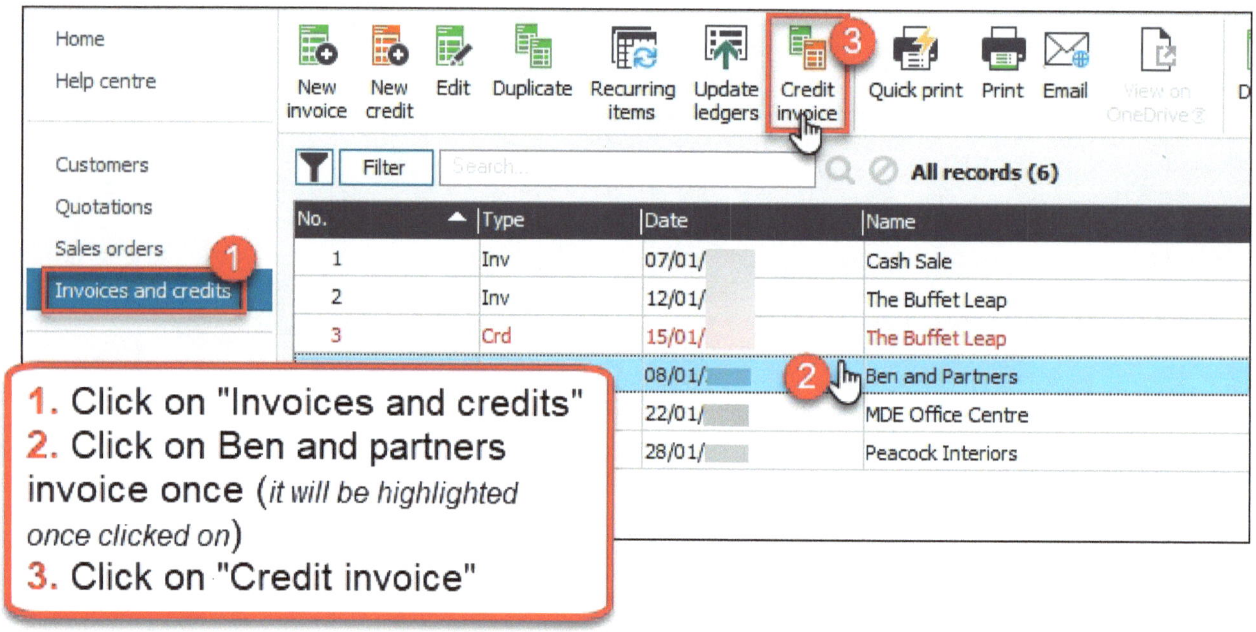

Fig. 115

After clicking Credit invoice as illustrated in the figure above, a product credit from invoice window will appear – see figure 116 on the next page for illustration.

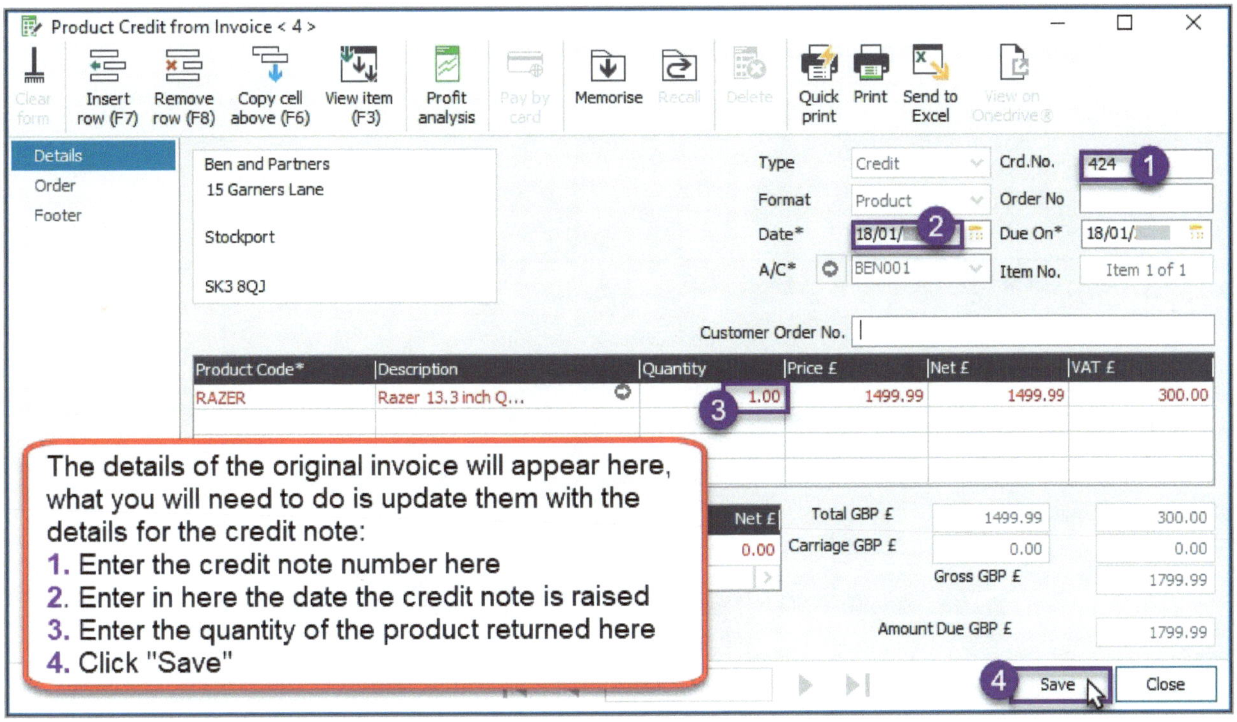

Fig. 116

Once you click Save as illustrated in step 4 in the figure above, the following message will appear:

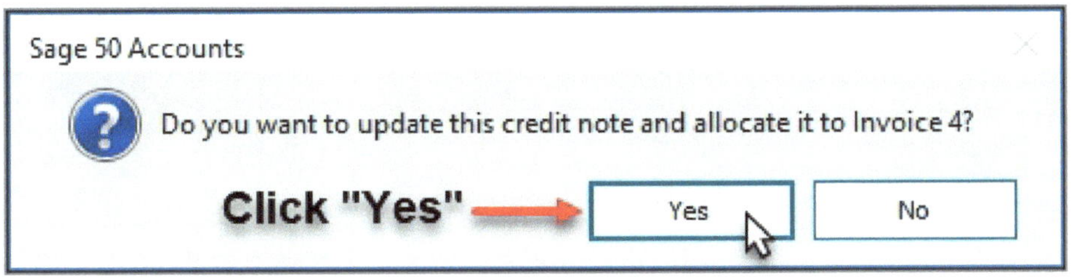

Fig. 117

To allocate the credit note to the invoice click **Yes** and the following message will then appear:

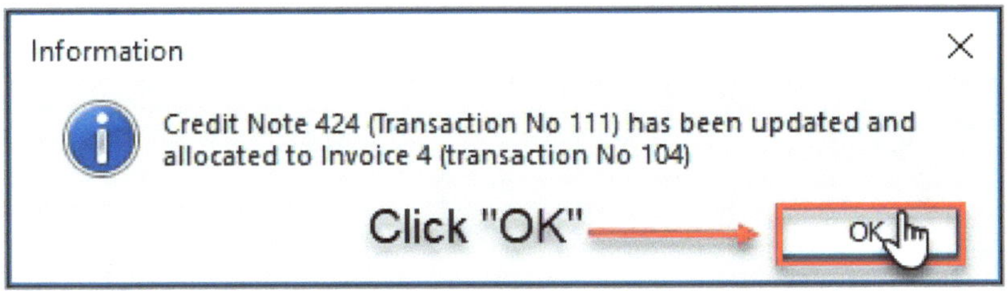

Fig. 118

Well done. You have so far sorted the main parts of the purchase ledger (accounts payable) and sales ledger (accounts receivable). Let's deal with receipts from customers and payments from suppliers next.

Task 4g: How to record a cash sale transaction via Batch invoice receipt option

Recording sales of walk-in customers.

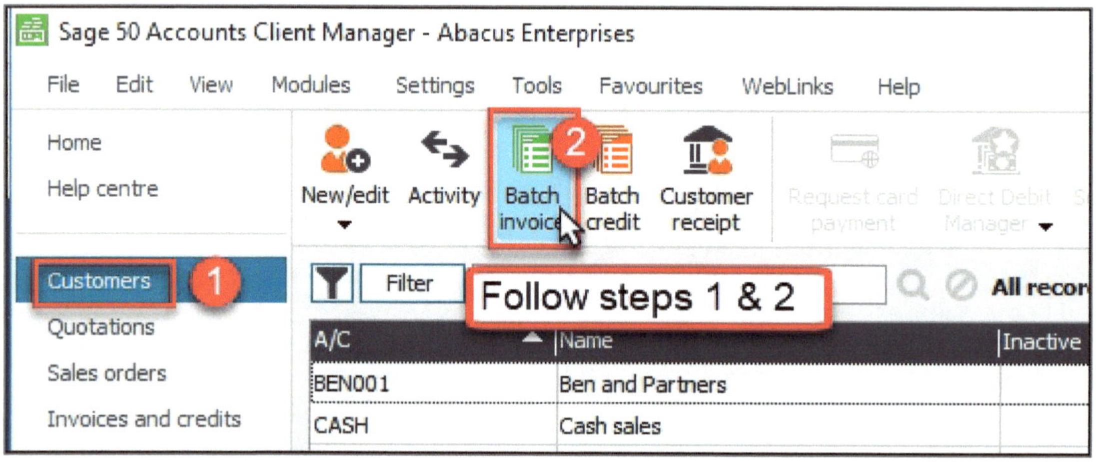

Fig. 119

A customer batch invoice window appears. Follow the illustrative inset steps.

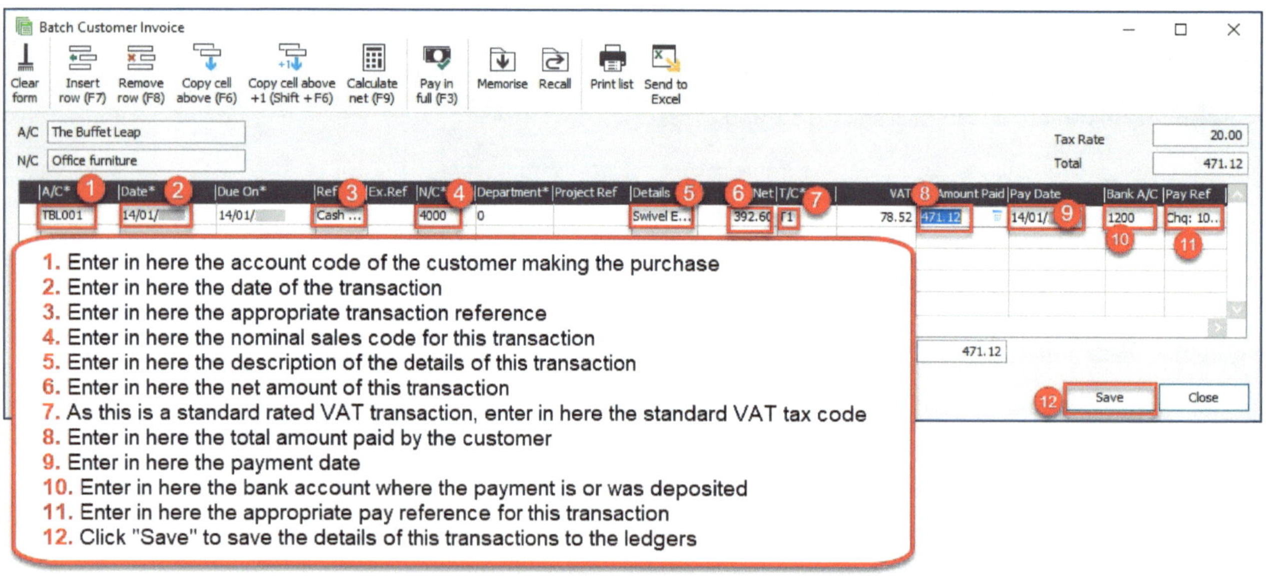

Fig. 120

You now need to adjust the stock to reflect this cash sale. This is because any sale that is not recorded via the "Invoice and credits" tab does not automatically get the stock adjusted, you have to manually adjust the stock.
Here is how to do it – see figure 121 below.

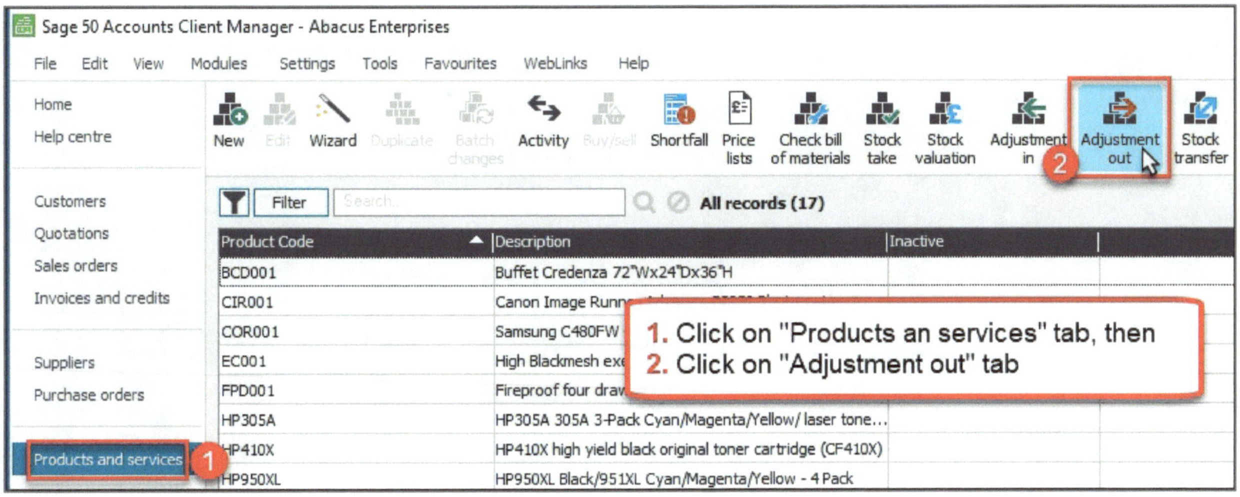

Fig. 121

After step 2 as illustrated in the figure above, an adjustment out window appears. Follow the inset steps to complete it.

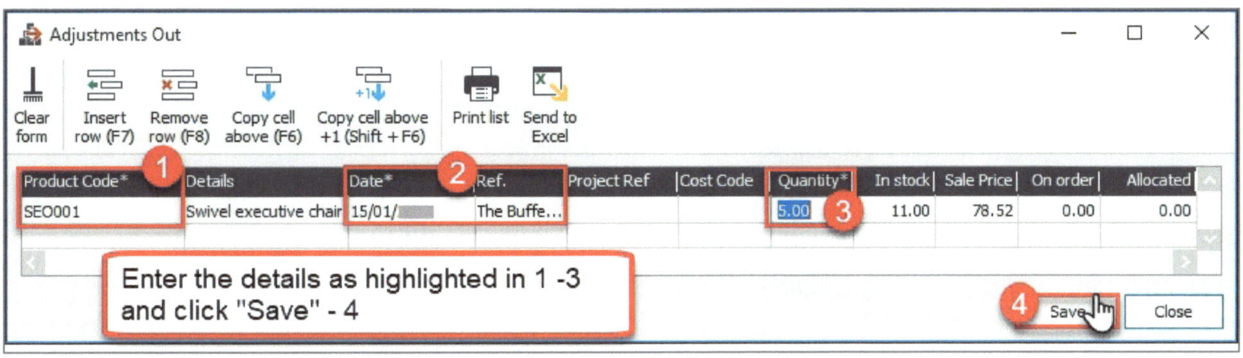

Fig. 122

A note on batch invoice

If you need to record a sale quickly without printing an invoice or updating stock. You can post a batch invoice.

To create a printable invoice for your customer you must create a product invoice or service invoice instead of a batch invoice.
If you enter more than one invoice with the same account, date, reference and net amount, an alert appears (a yellow triangle with an exclamation mark inside it) to indicate you've a potential duplicate entry. If you posted similar transactions previously, a box appears, listing the duplicate transactions.

Task 4h: How to record a cash sales transaction made to a non-regular customer

Four Kyocera toner cartridges have been sold to a walk-in "customer" and here is how to record this kind of transaction.

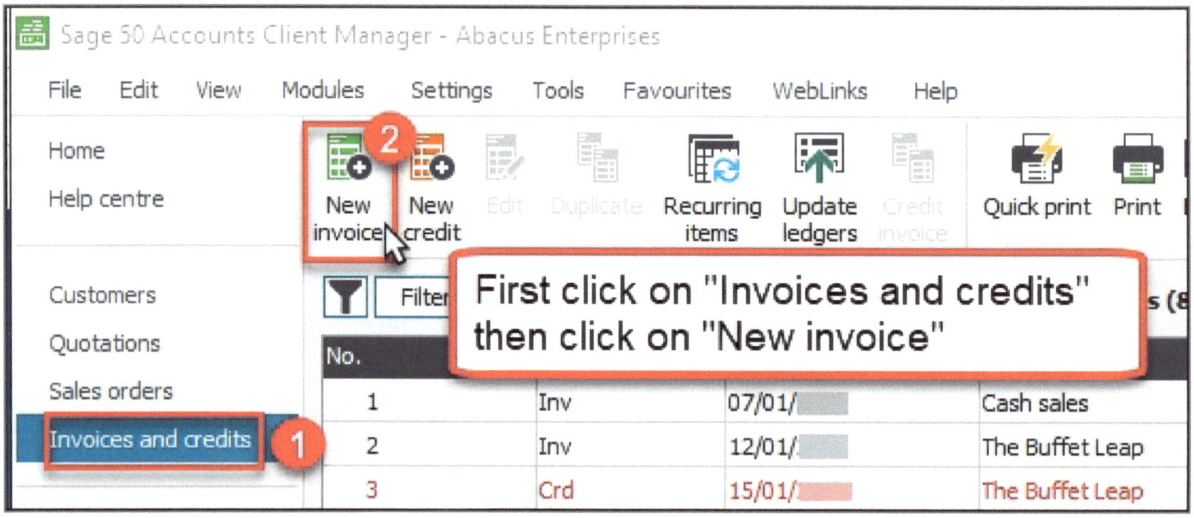

fig. 123

After step 2 as illustrated above, a product invoice window appears. Follow the illustrative inset steps to record the detail of the transaction.

A quick note

In Sage 50 Accounts you can raise invoices and credit notes to print and send to your customers. You can also quickly post the invoice to the ledgers, updating your stock levels and creating transactions.

Once created, you can print your invoice and, to make the transactions appear on your nominal ledger, you must update your ledger.

The transaction we are currently dealing with is a cash sale transaction - a walk-in customer who paid by cash. The good news is that we already have set up a "Cash customer" in our records to cater for all cash sales in the company and as such we will now use that "Cash customer" account to record this cash sale transaction.

This space is for notes

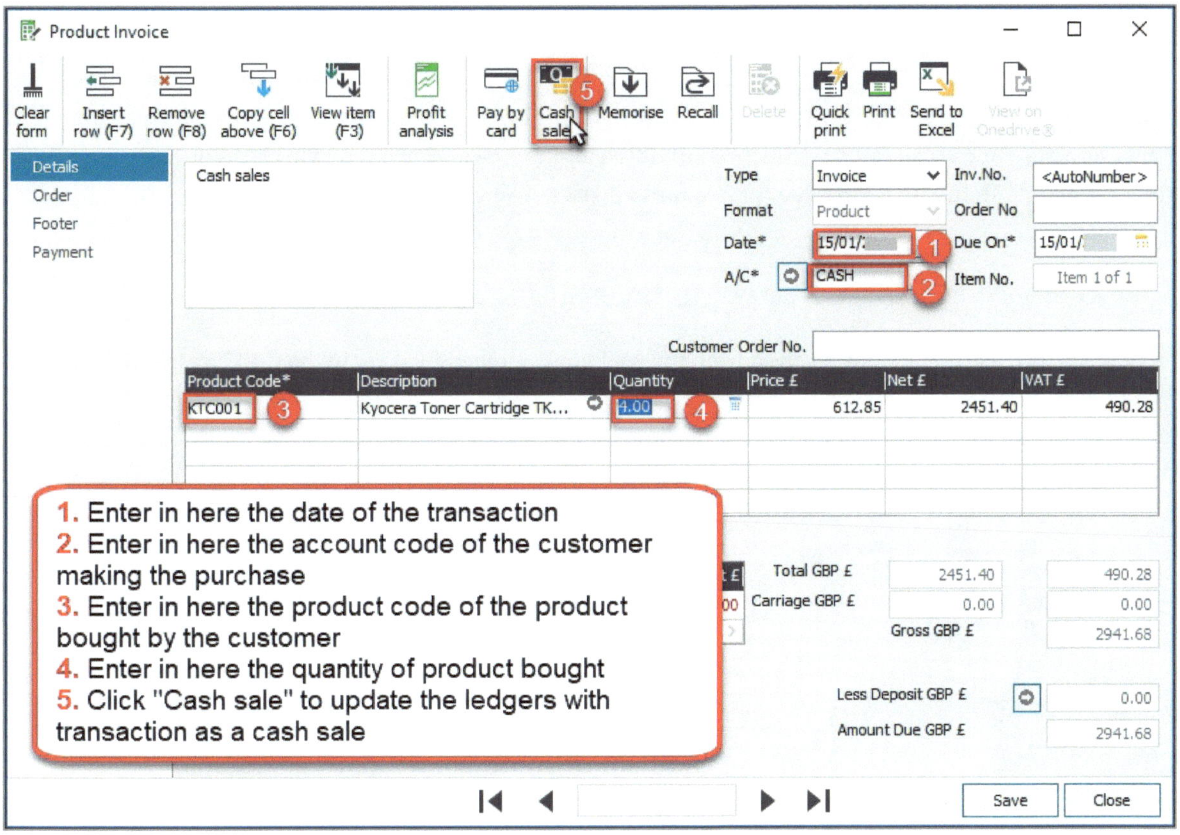

Fig. 124

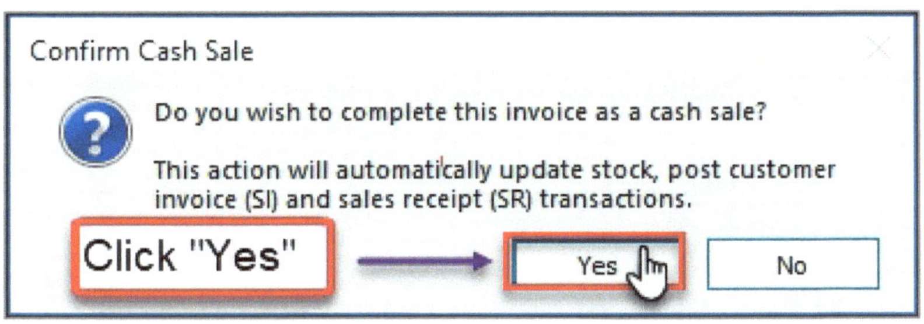

Fig. 125

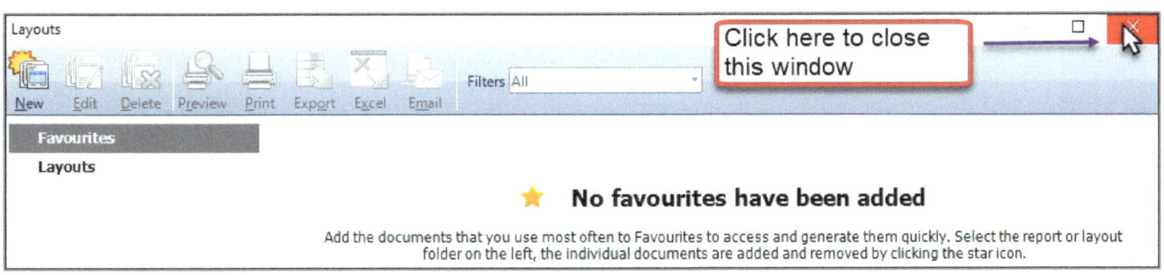

Fig. 126

The Cash Sales option

The Cash Sales option can be used to complete all the necessary transactions for a sale without having to make each posting individually. When you complete a sales order or invoice and use the Cash Sales option, Sage Accounts adjusts your stock out, creates then updates an invoice and posts a sales receipt. The Cash Sales option is available in Invoicing in Sage 50 Accounts 2013 (v19) and above.

Task 4i: How to record a cash sale through the cash register option.

In the task illustrated below, the money was received from the walk-in customer and kept in the till. Here is how we record such till receipts in Sage 50 Accounts.

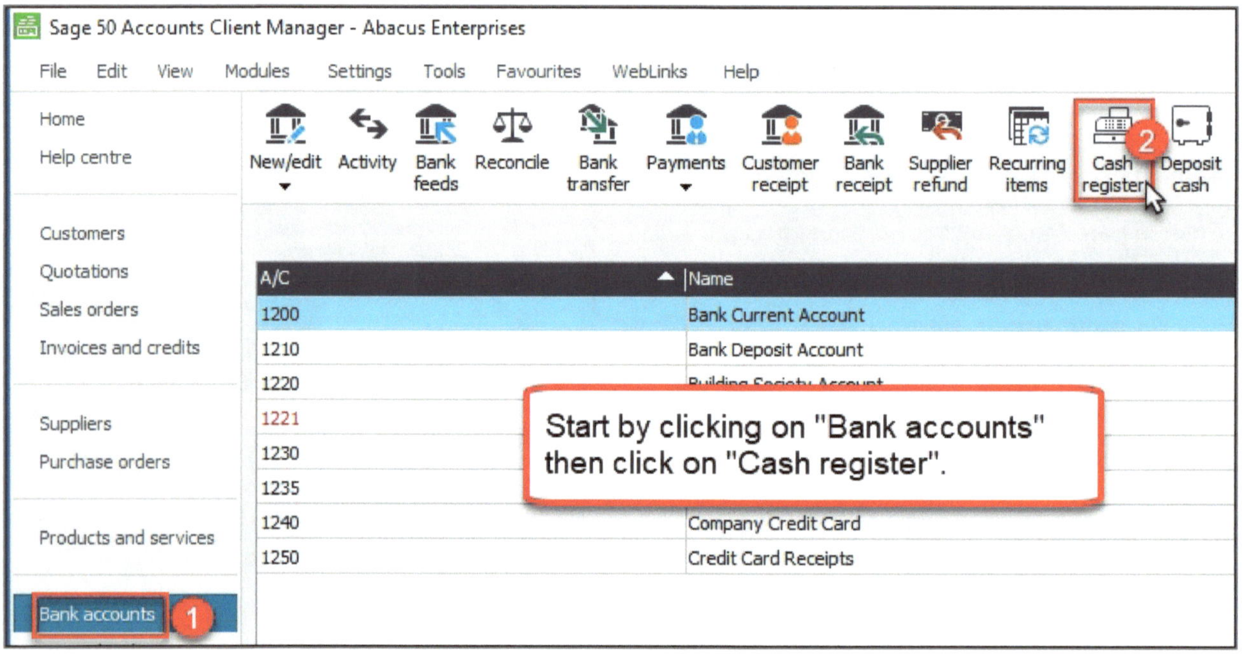

Fig. 127

When you click cash register as illustrated in step 2 in the figure above, a cash register window appears. See fig 128 on the next page.

The Cash register

If you use a cash register or till system for your sales, the Cash register option in Sage Accounts is a great tool for tracking your cash takings accurately until they're deposited at the bank. This helps you to avoid errors and gives you an audit trail for cash takings.

At the end of each day, you can enter the till takings you've recorded into the Cash register option. You can record discrepancies If there's a difference between your recorded takings and the actual cash in the till. Once you pay your till takings into the bank, you can record this using the Deposit cash feature.

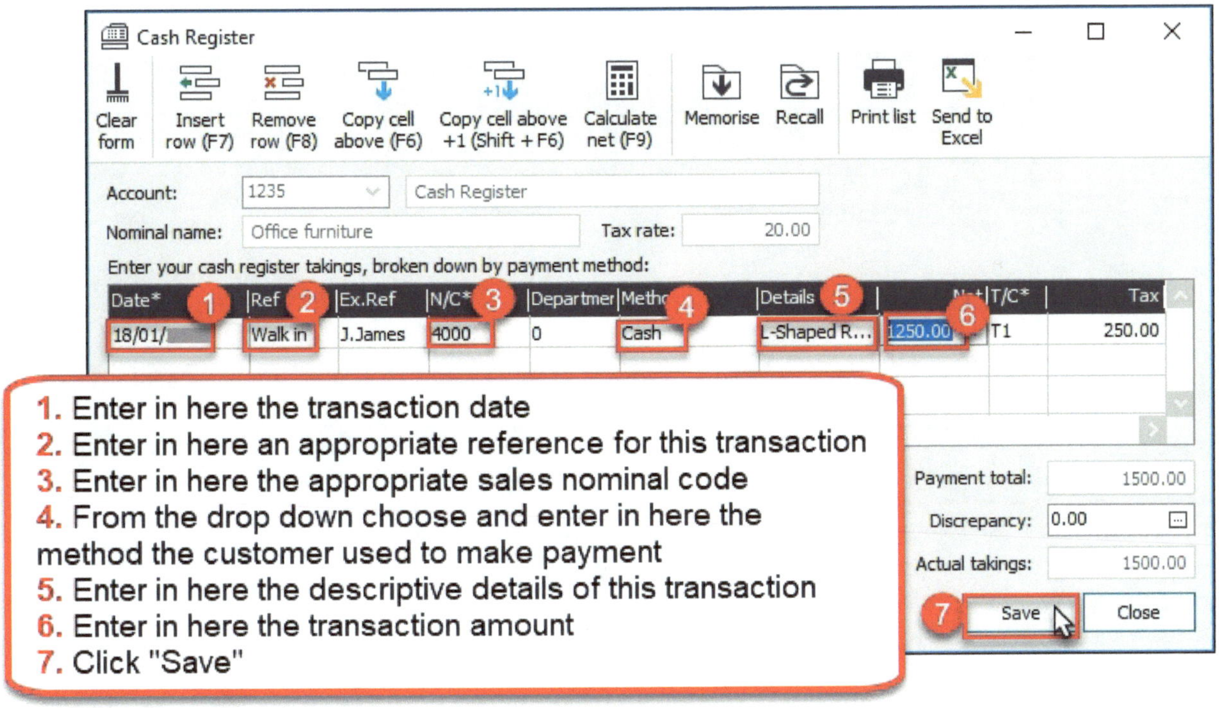

Fig. 128

Keeping such an amount of cash in the till is not that safe at all and as such, early the next day, the money was deposited to the bank account and now you have to update the accounting records with this transaction.

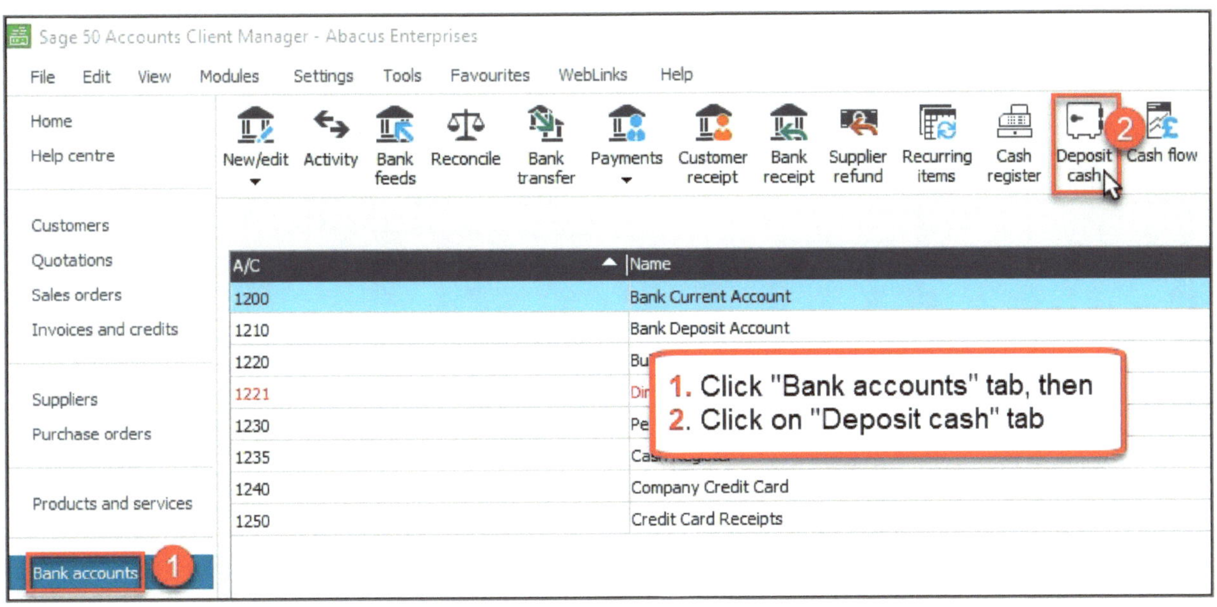

Fig. 129

After you click on "Deposit cash" tab as illustrated in step 2 in the figure above, a deposit cash window appears. See figure below and follow the illustrative inset steps.

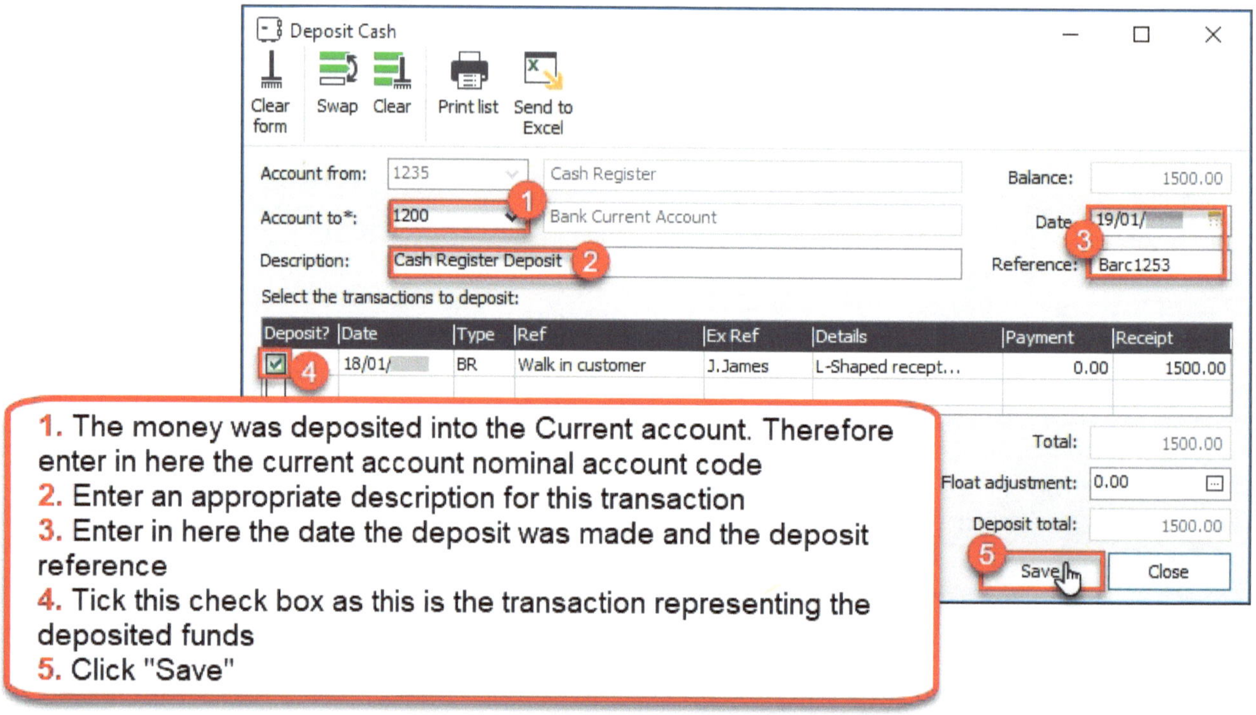

Fig. 130

This space is for notes

Task 4j: How to record customer receipts

Regardless whether it is customers making payments of their outstanding invoices or the company making payments to its suppliers, there basically three options available to do so:

1. Full payment of outstanding invoice
2. Part payment of outstanding invoice
3. Payment on account to reduce any outstanding balance (more like when you pay the minimum balance on your credit card)

See table below for a brief explanation of this a bit further

Payment option	What it means
1. Full payment	In this payment option, an outstanding invoice is paid in full. This payment method is specific in that there is a specific outstanding invoice which the customer is paying for when they send a remittance.
2. Part payment	This payment option is similar to a full payment option in that there is specificity as to what invoice is being paid, except on this occasion, not the full amount of the outstanding invoice is being paid but just part of it.
3. Payment on account	In this payment option, a customer will just make payment but will not specify which particular outstanding invoice he/she is paying for. It is then left to the accounts receivable department to allocate the payment to the customers outstanding invoices perhaps with the oldest ones cleared first. Think of the way most credit card bills are paid, most of those payments are payments on account – just to reduce the credit card bill amount each month. The credit card company then makes the payment allocations according to the terms they agreed with you when you signed up for the credit card.

Let's see how we can deal with this in Sage 50 Accounts.

So, peacock interiors have just paid you by BACS and have sent you a remittance advise to that effect. The money is in the bank and you now need to reflect in the books the fact that they have made payment.

> **A quick note**
>
> To help you keep track of money coming in and manage your cash flow it's important that you record your customer receipts.
>
> The Customer Receipt window helps you easily record receipts and allocate them to the relevant invoices. You can see what the oldest outstanding invoices are so that you can clear these invoices first or you can even spread the receipt value over multiple invoices.
>
> From here you can also allocate outstanding credit notes and outstanding payments on account to invoices.

Here is how we do it in Sage 50 Accounts: – see figures 131 & 132 below.

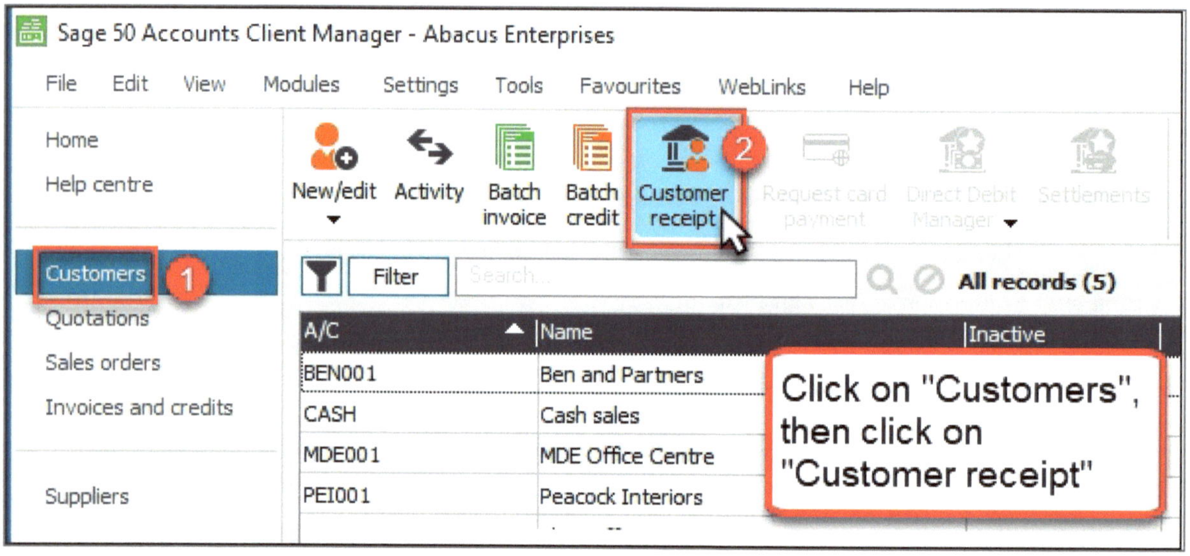

fig. 131

This is an illustrative example of a payment in full of an outstanding invoice.

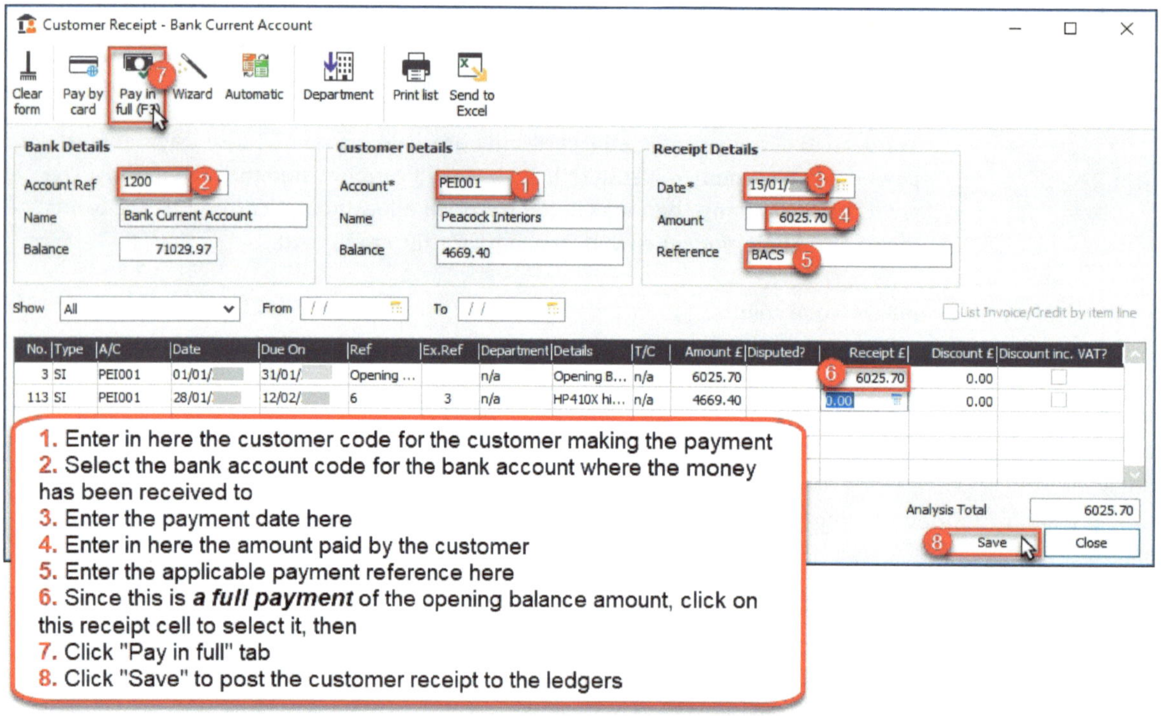

fig. 132

The next illustration is for a **part payment** – payment by Ben & Partners

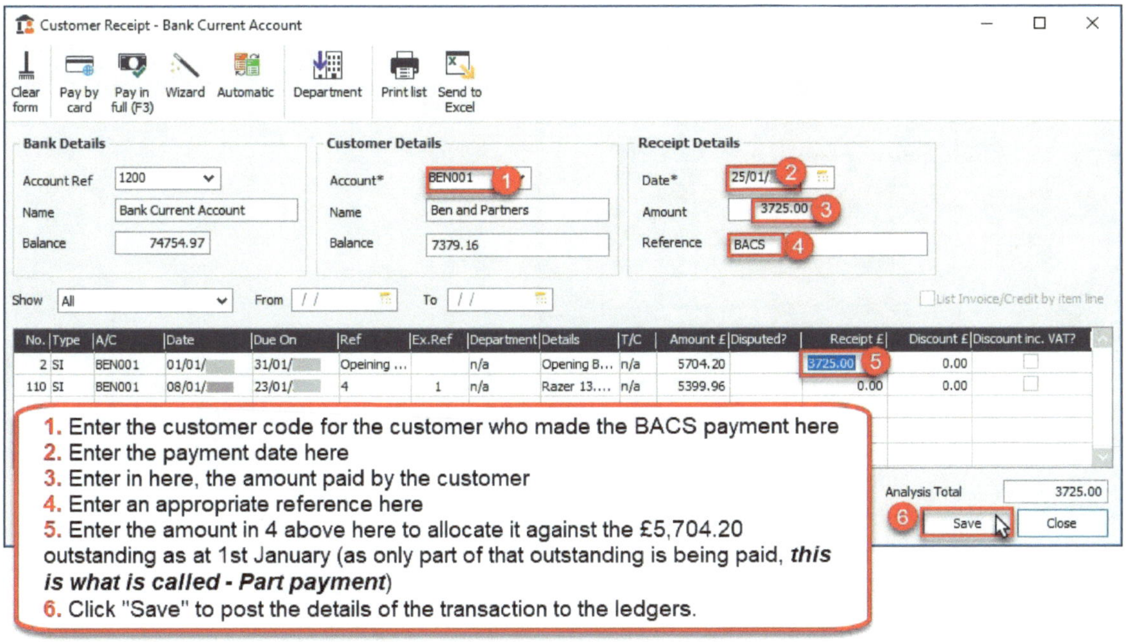

fig. 133

The next illustration is for payment on account. A payment is received from the customer, but it is not a payment for any specific outstanding invoice, just a payment to reduce the outstanding balance that the customer has with the company. See the figure below.

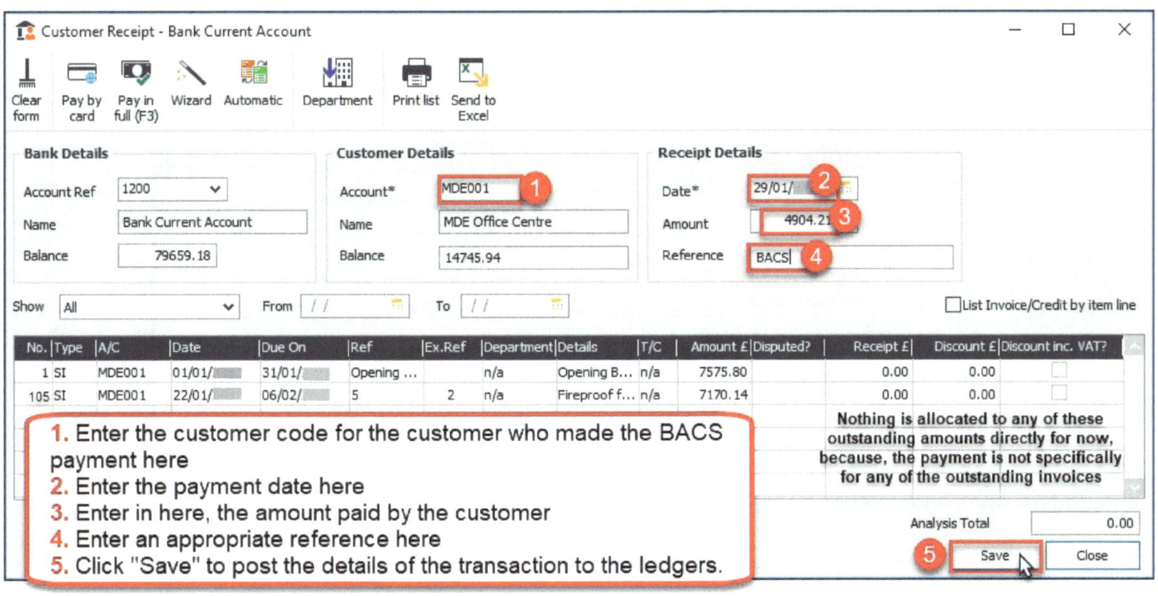

Fig. 134

After step 5 as illustrated in the figure above, a window similar to figure 135 below will appear, click "Yes" to confirm that it is a payment on account.

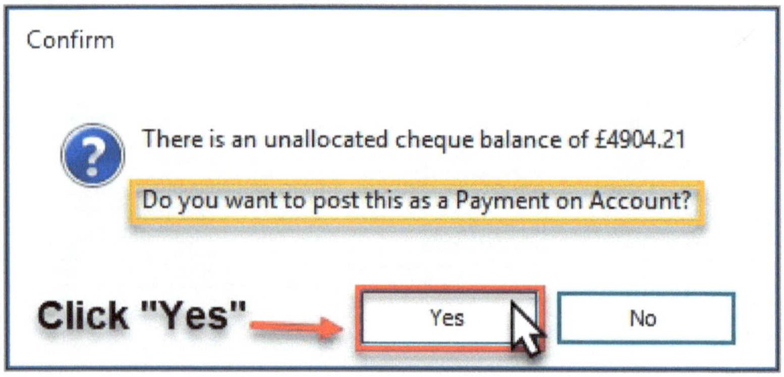

Fig 135

That's customer receipts done for now.

Task 4k: How to record a non - customer receipt

In the next task, you have received a refund from HMRC and it has to be registered in the books.

Well, HMRC is not really a customer as such to the company, and therefore we won't be using the customer receipt tab in Sage to record this transaction, instead, we will use the bank receipt tab to do so. See the figure below.

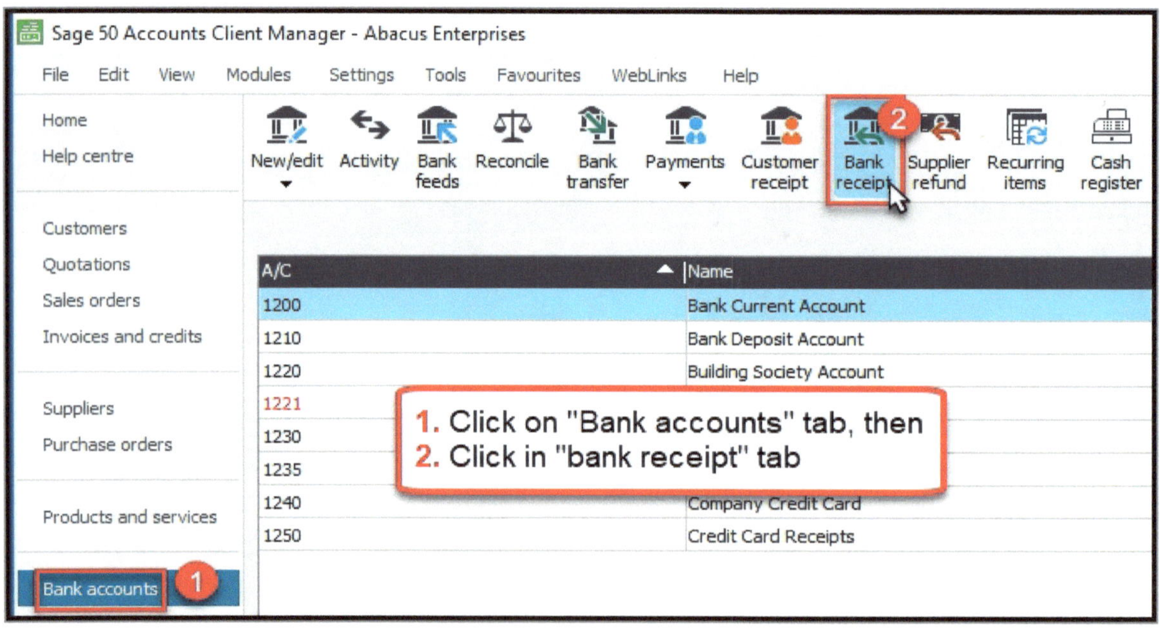

Fig. 136

After step 2 as illustrated in the figure in the previous page, a bank receipt window similar to the figure below will appear, follow the illustrative inset steps to record the details of the transaction.

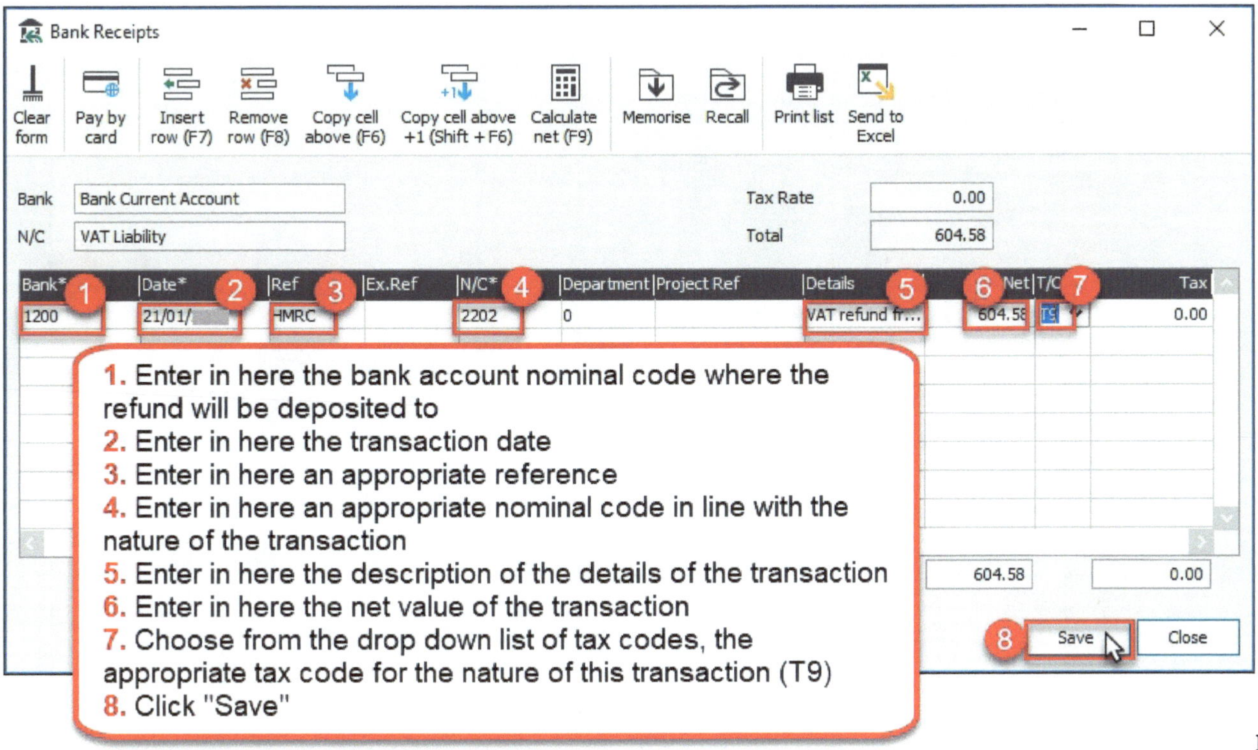

Fig. 137

A quick recap

You may need to record income that isn't linked to a particular customer record. Maybe a one-off sale, the banking of cash sales or bank interest received for the day. In these cases, you simply post a receipt to your bank account.

1. Click **Bank accounts**.
2. Click the bank account you want to receive the money into.
3. On the tool bar, click **Bank receipt**.
4. Complete the boxes as required.
5. Click **Save**

Task 4L: How to write off a transaction for a bounced cheque

The occasions where you will need to write off a transaction is when it becomes a bad debt (uncollectable debt) or when a cheque that has been already recorded as a receipt bounces (is not honoured by the bank).

The write off in the next task is about a cheque that has bounced.

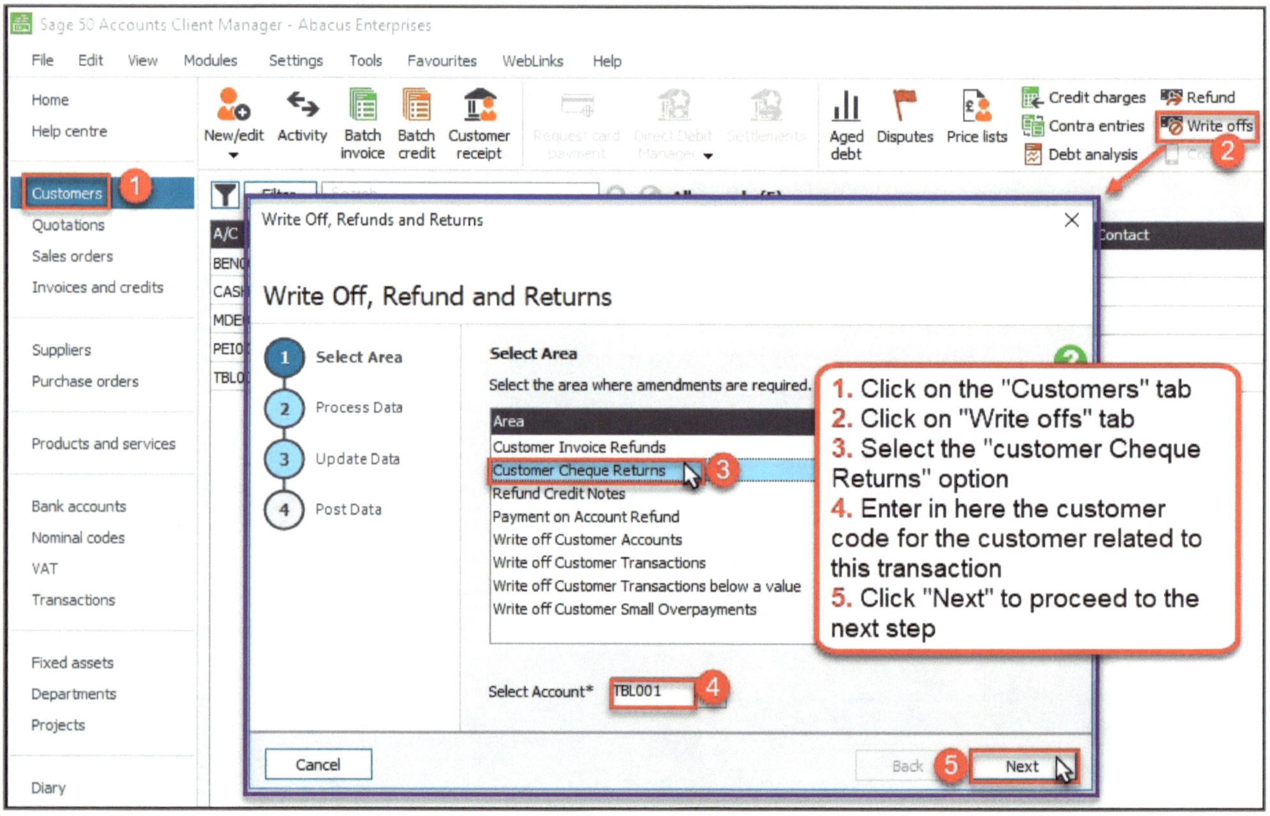

Fig. 138

After step 5 as illustrated in the figure above, complete the details in the next window accordingly, see figure 139 on the next page.

This space is for notes

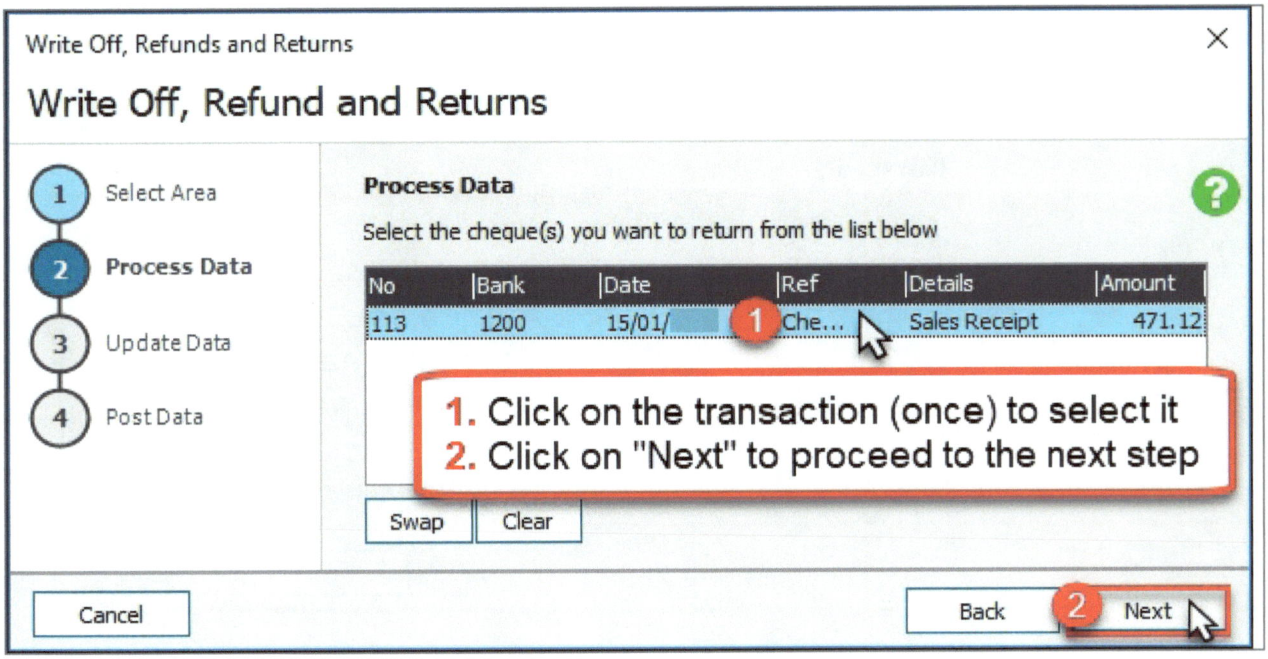

Fig. 139

After step 2 as illustrated in the figure above, the next step is to update your data. See figure below.

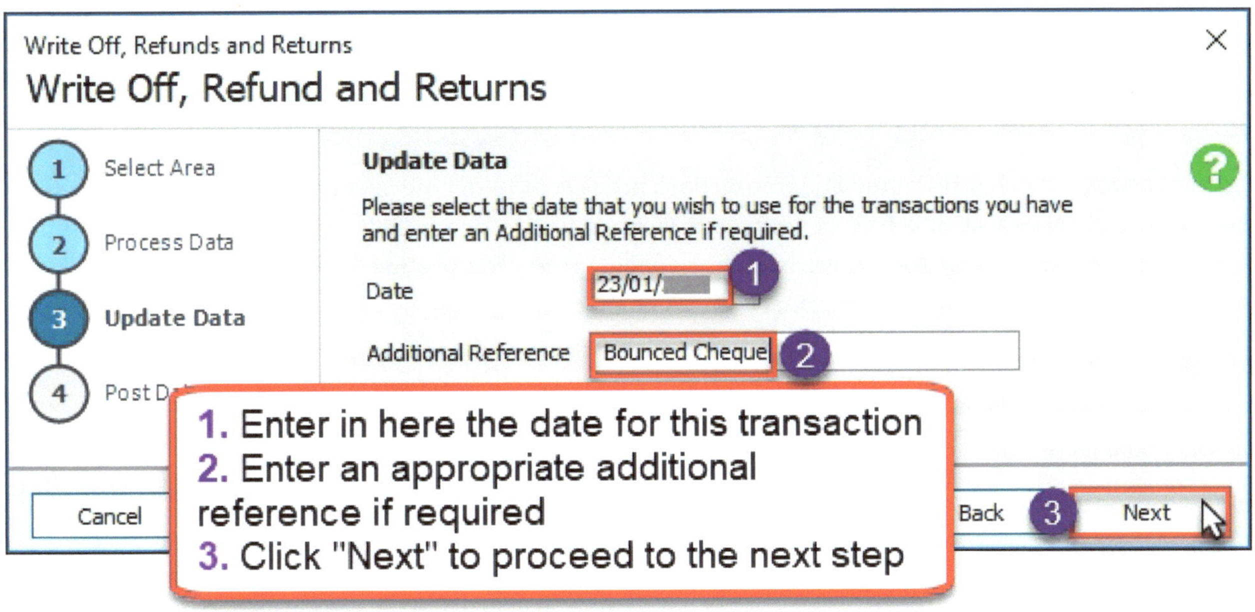

Fig. 140

After step 3 as illustrated in the figure above, the next step is to post your data. See figure 141 on the next page.

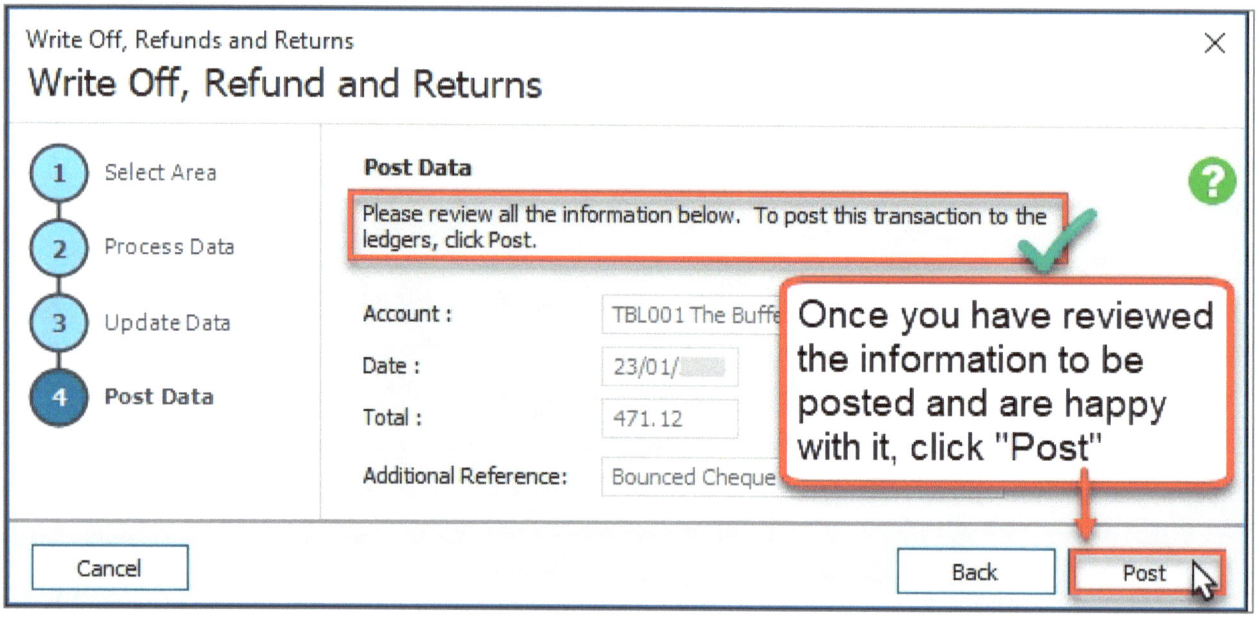

Fig. 141

Rules automatically applied when using the Write Off, Refunds and Returns wizard

VAT - When writing off a transaction, VAT is not accounted for, therefore all of the automatic transactions are posted with the non-vatable tax code, by default T9.

Dates - When using the wizard, you can specify a date for the automatic transactions.

Nominal codes - Many of the automatic transactions are posted to the mispostings account nominal code. This ensures they do not affect your profit and loss nominal codes. Where postings are made to the mispostings account nominal code, there is always a debit and a credit posting. This ensures that the overall balance on the mispostings account nominal code is not affected.

This space is for notes

Task 4m: How to process refunds for returned goods

Occasionally a customer buys goods/services from your business in cash and later returns it because they don't like or have changed their mind about wanting it. In this case, you have to refund them their cash. If they had bought it on credit, you would issue them a credit note, but for cash, you issue a refund. Some companies instead of issuing a refund give customers vouchers that they can use against any other purchase in their store/company.

In the next task, you are to issue a customer a refund for a cash purchase they made a few days ago. See below.

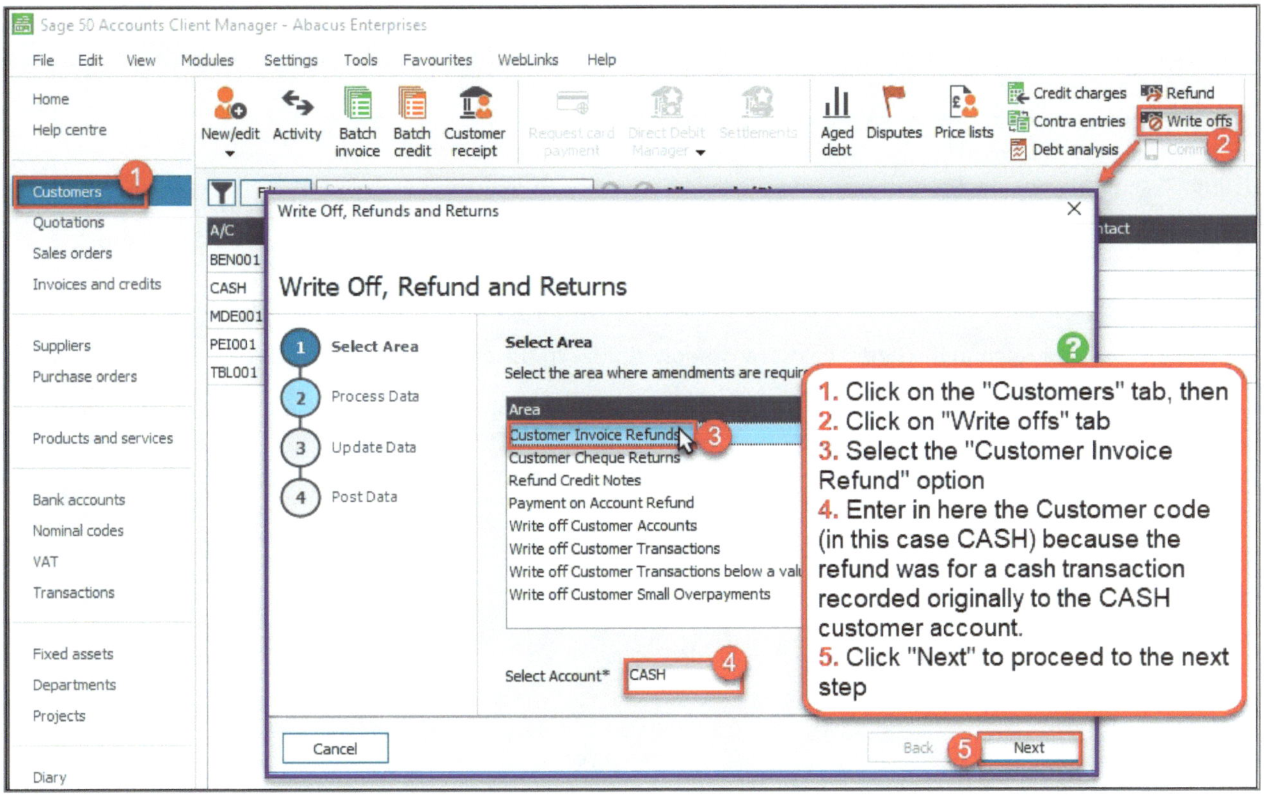

Fig. 142

Note about Online, mail and phone order sales

Online, mail and telephone order customers have the right to cancel their order for a limited time even if the goods aren't faulty. Sales of this kind are known as 'distance selling'.

You must offer a refund to customers if they've told you within 14 days of receiving their goods that they want to cancel. They have another 14 days to return the goods once they've told you.

You must refund the customer within 14 days of receiving the goods back. They don't have to provide a reason.

After step 5 as illustrated in the figure above, a window similar to figure 143 below will appear.

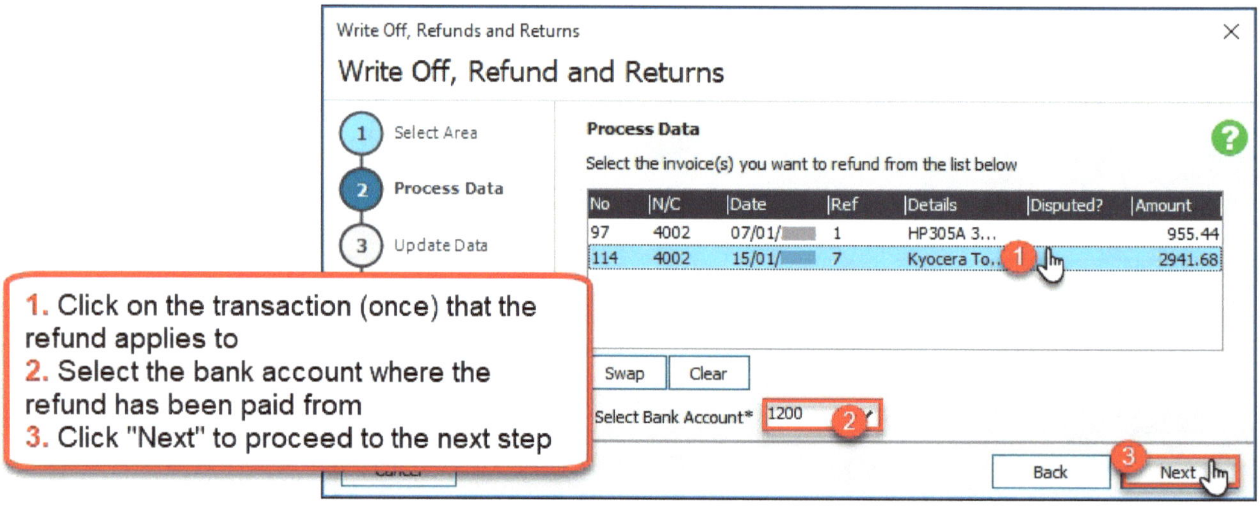

Fig. 143

Next, after step 3 as illustrated in the figure below, a window similar to the figure below will appear.

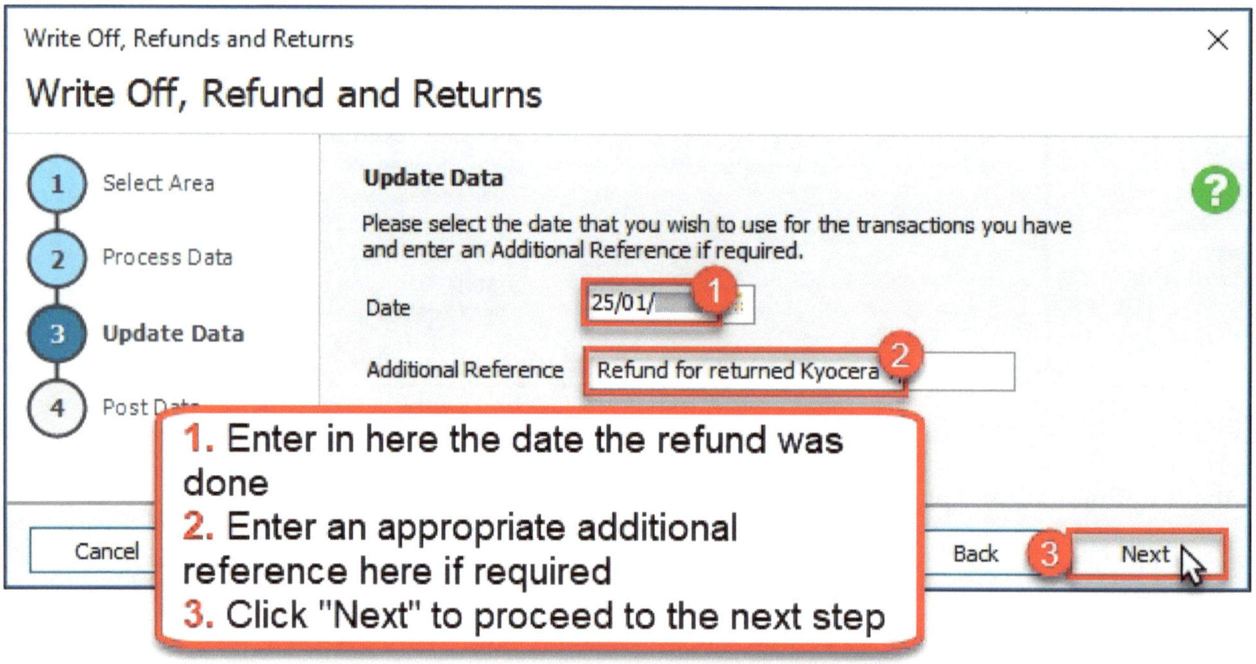

Fig. 144

When you click "Next" as illustrated in step 3 in the figure above, a window similar to the figure 145 on the next page will appear.

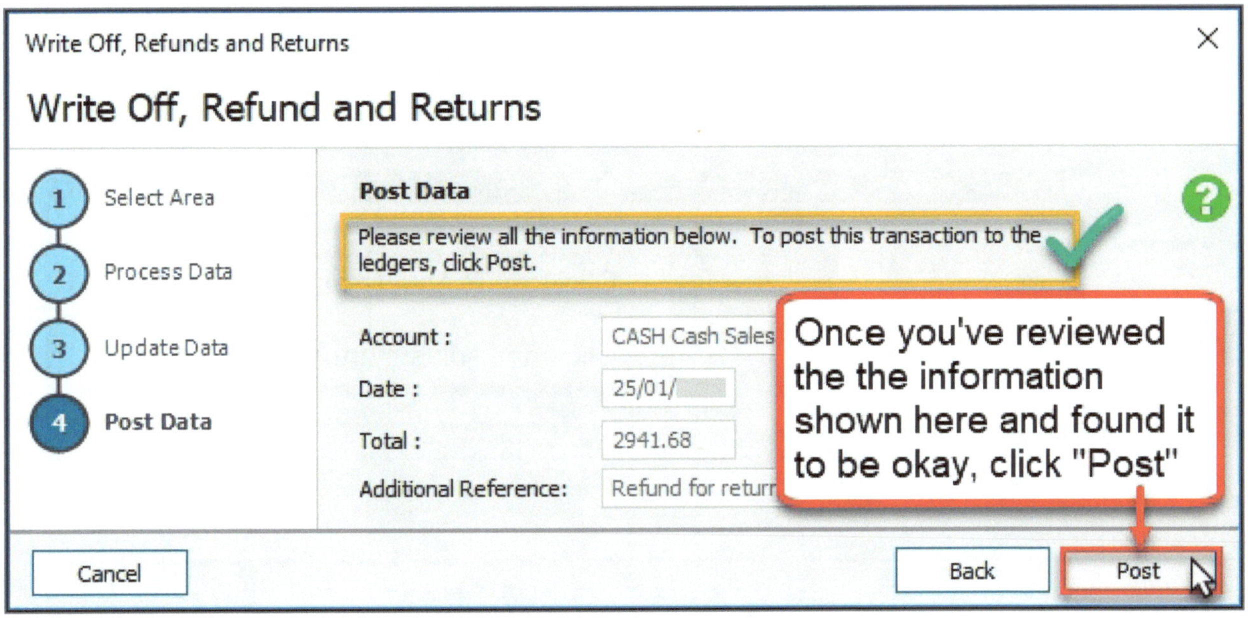

Fig. 145

What the law says about refunds - UK

You must offer a full refund if an item is faulty, not as described or doesn't do what it's supposed to. Under the Consumer Rights Act 2015, consumers may be entitled to a refund, replacement, repair and/or compensation where goods are faulty or not as described; they are also entitled to a refund and/or compensation where the seller had no legal right to sell the goods.

When you don't have to offer a refund

You don't have to refund a customer if they:

- knew an item was faulty when they bought it
- damaged an item by trying to repair it themselves or getting someone else to do it (though they may still have the right to a repair, replacement or partial refund)
- no longer want an item (e.g. because it's the wrong size or colour) unless they bought it without seeing it

You have to offer a refund for certain items only if they're faulty, such as:

- personalised items and custom-made items, e.g. curtains
- perishable items, e.g. frozen food or flowers
- newspapers and magazines
- unwrapped CDs, DVDs and computer software

Since the chairs and the toner were returned in a perfectly saleable condition, we will now need to adjust the stock to reflect the increase.

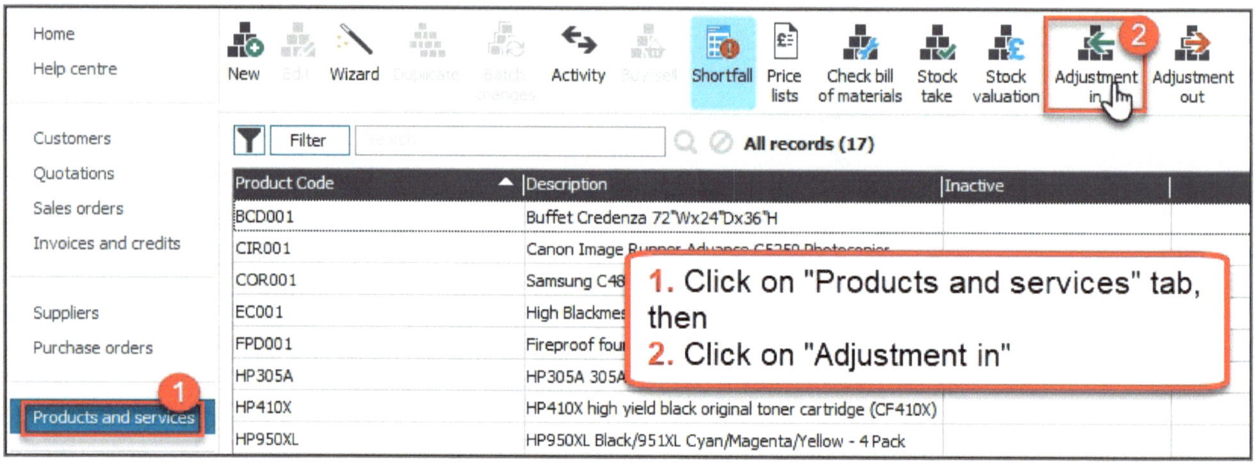

Fig. 146

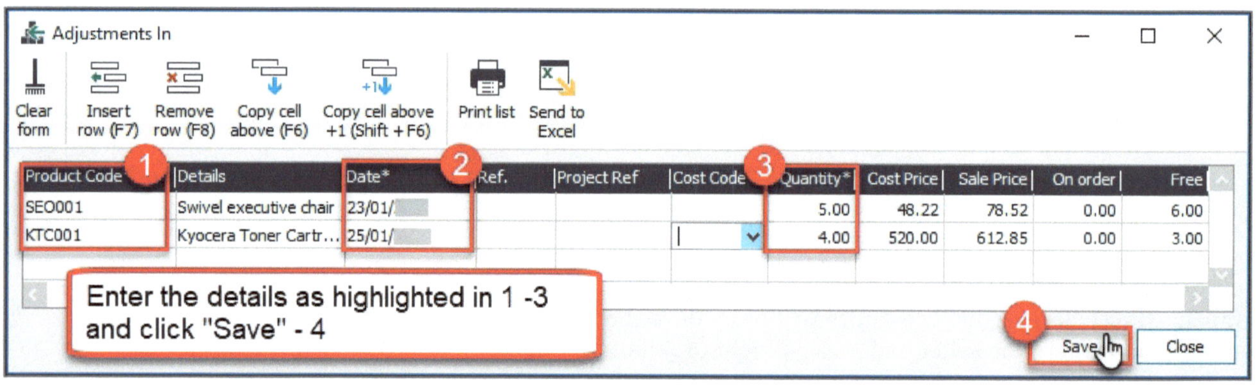

Fig. 147

This space is for notes

"Plan your work for today and every day, then work your plan."
Margaret Thatcher

TASK 5: HOW TO DO CREDIT CONTROL - COLLECTIONS

14 steps to take to collect outstanding debts from debtors

1. *Send the customer a current account statement or gentle reminder.*
2. *Five working days after sending the statement check to see whether the amount has been paid.*
3. *If the amount has not been paid, telephone the client and discuss the reason for non-payment, remind them of their credit terms, and agree on a payment date.*
4. *Write a letter to the client summarising the telephone conversation and noting the agreed payment date.*
5. *Make a note on the system of the date payment should be received. Use the communication tab on customer record window from Sage to make a note.*
6. *If payment is not received by the agreed date telephone the client and remind them of your previous discussion.*
7. *Agree on a date for payment (or direct debit/credit card if applicable).*
8. *Write a letter to the client summarising the telephone conversation and noting the agreed payment date.*
9. *Make a note on the system of the date payment should be received.*
10. *If payment is not received by the agreed date telephone the client.*
11. *Write a letter to the client summarising the telephone conversation and noting the date court proceedings will commence.*
12. *Make a note on the system of the date payment should be received.*
13. *If payment is not received within the specified time, then continue with the County Court procedure.*
14. *Make arrangements to attend court.*

Here is how to get a credit managers' report from Sage 50 Accounts to use to facilitate the credit control process of debt collection.

Click on the "Customers" tab, then click on the "Reports" tab. ***See figure 148 on the next page***

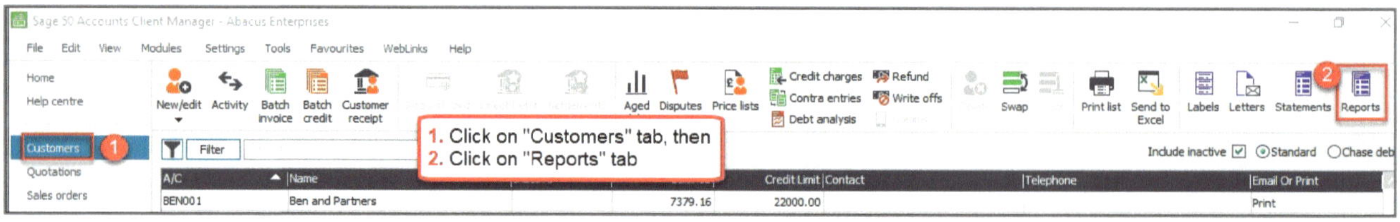

Fig. 148

After step 2 as illustrated in the figure above, a customer reports window appears.

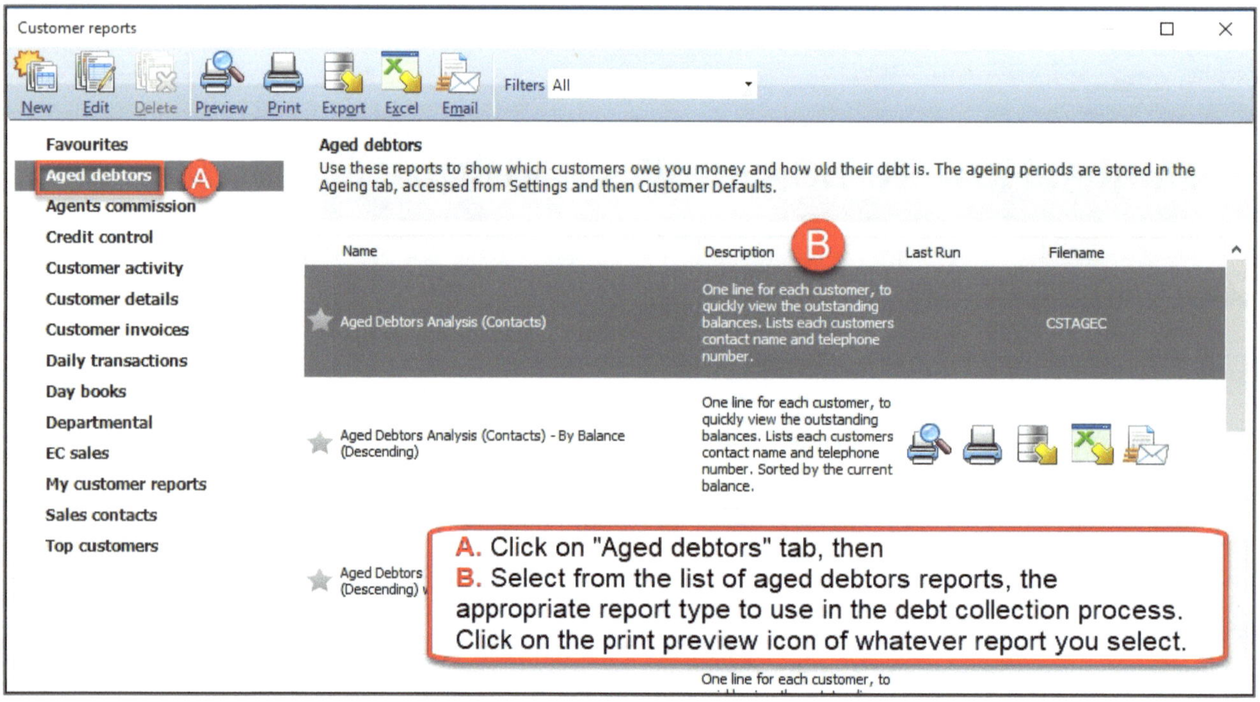

Fig. 149

Whichever report you select from B as illustrated in the figure above, a report criteria window will appear. Enter the appropriate criteria you want the report to display and click "OK" and your specified report will be generated.

This space is for notes

"Come to me, all of you who are struggling and burdened, and I will give you rest"
Matthew 11:28 CJB

TASK 6: HOW TO PROCESS SUPPLIER & NON SUPPLIER PAYMENTS

When recording payments to suppliers through Sage 50 Accounts, the same options of full payment, part payment and payment on account can be used.

Task 6a. How to process supplier payments

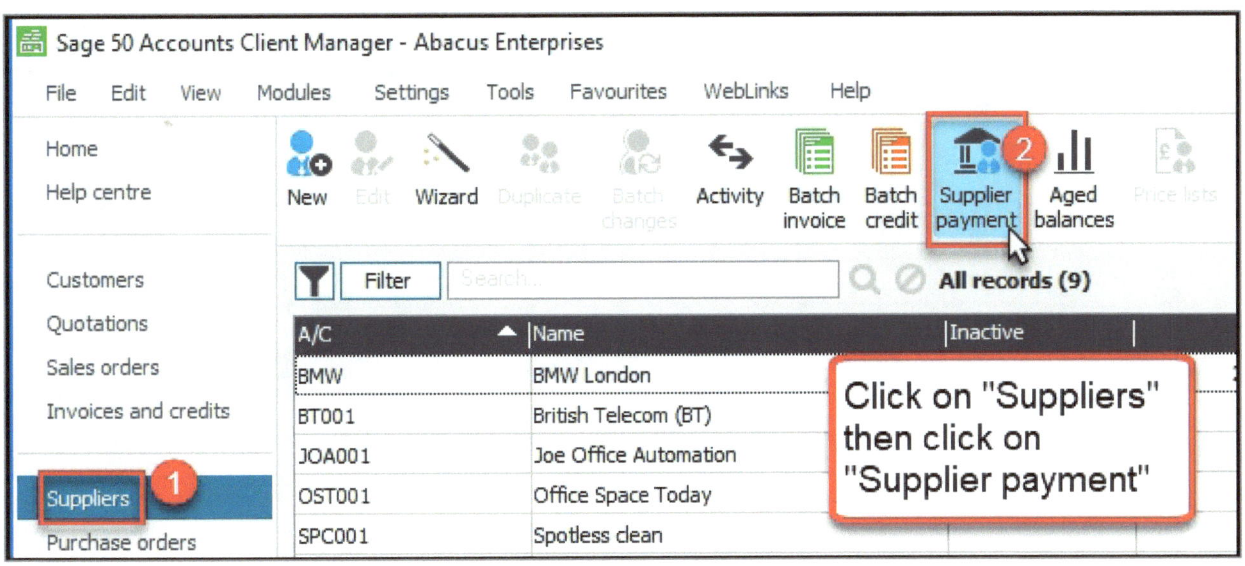

Fig. 150

After step 2 as illustrated in the figure 150 in the previous page, a supplier payment window will appear – see figure 151 in the next page.

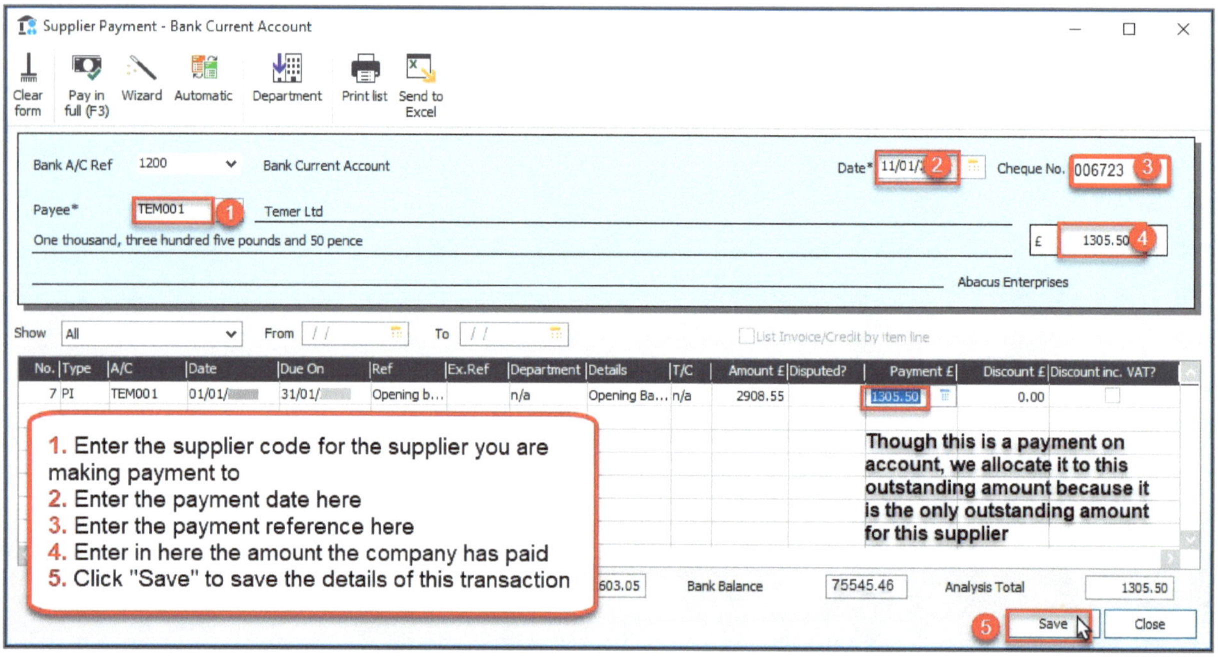

Fig. 151

The next supplier payment is a full payment of a specific supplier outstanding balance. See illustration in the figure below.

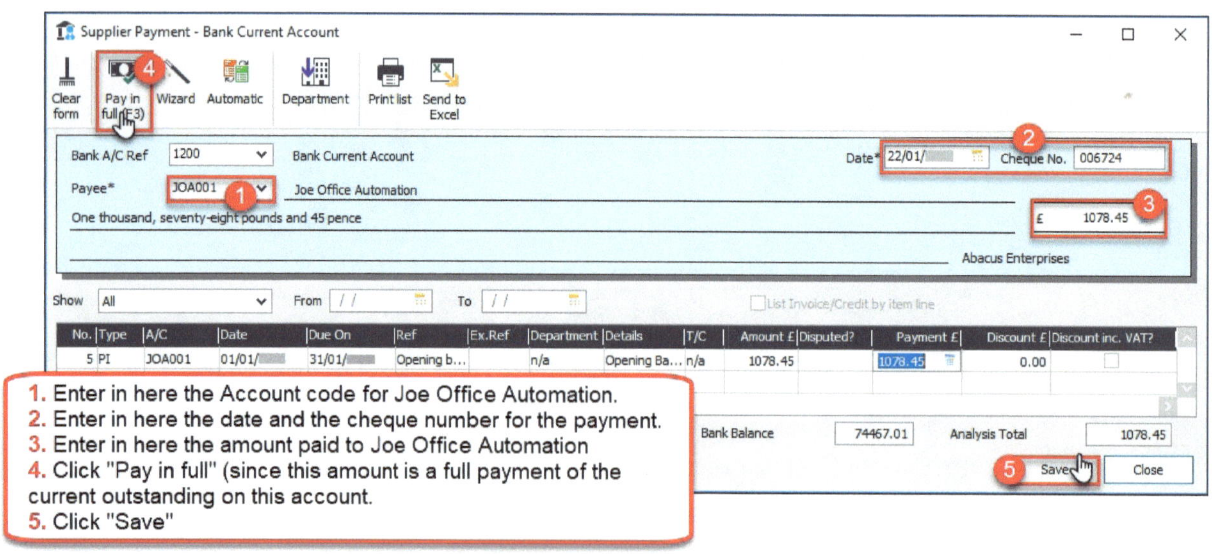

Fig. 152

The next payment is a full payment of the rent invoice, but this time it is paid by the Directors own funds. What you will need to do is select the supplier payment window as in previous occasions but this time around, the bank payment account will be the Director account – see an illustration in figure 153 below.

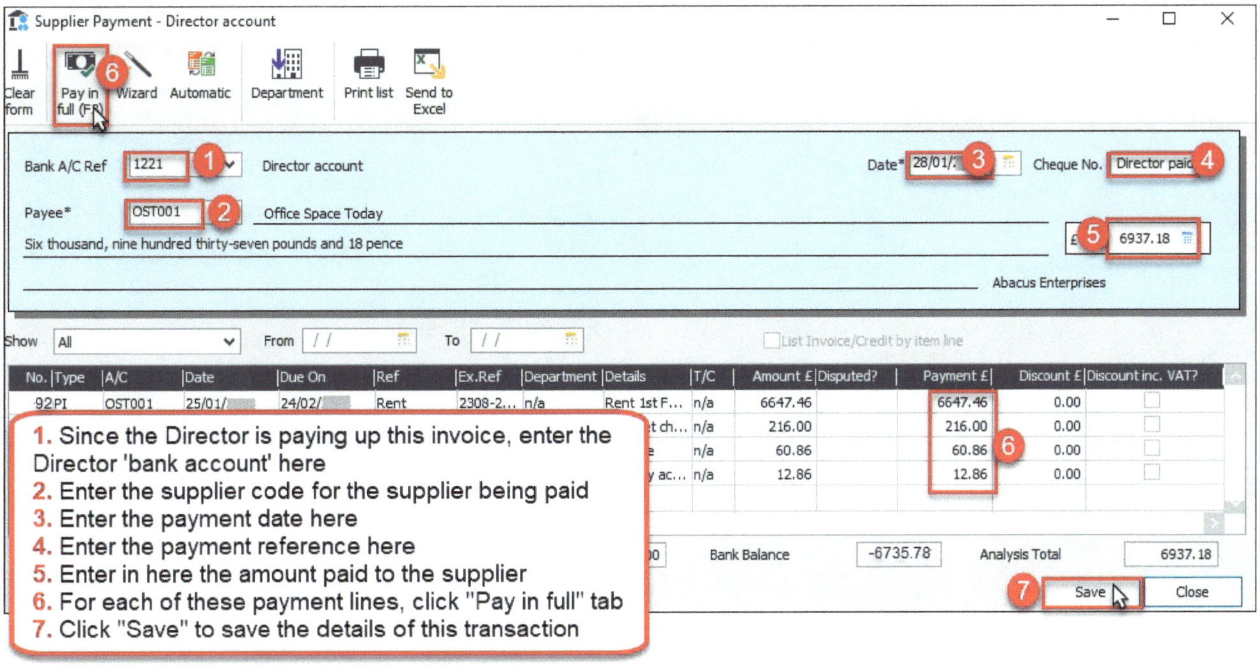

Fig. 153

Print remittance advise slip from Sage 50 Accounts software. See figure 154 on the next page.

> Quote
>
> *"Pay everyone what he is owed: if you owe the tax –collector, pay your taxes; if you owe the revenue-collector, pay revenue; if you owe someone respect, pay him respect; if you owe someone honour, pay him honour. Don't owe anyone anything – except to love one another; for whoever loves his fellow human being has fulfilled Torah"*
> Romans 13:7-8

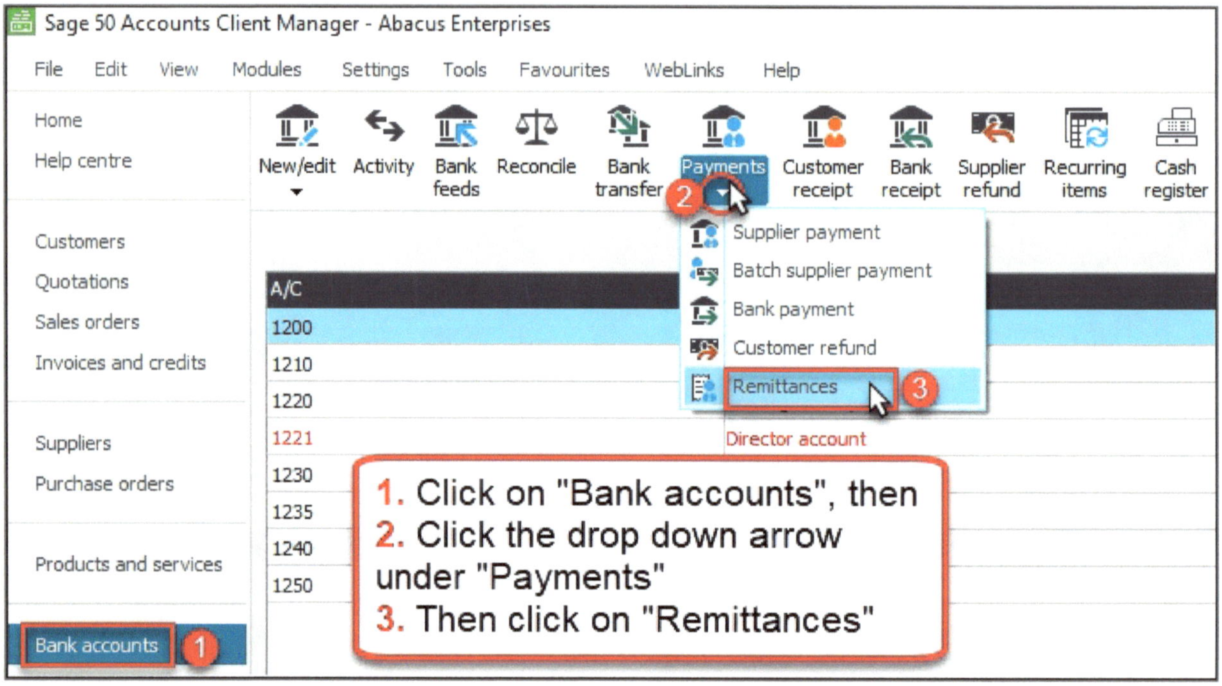

Fig. 154

After step 3 as illustrated in the figure above, the remittance window appears – see figure 155 below.

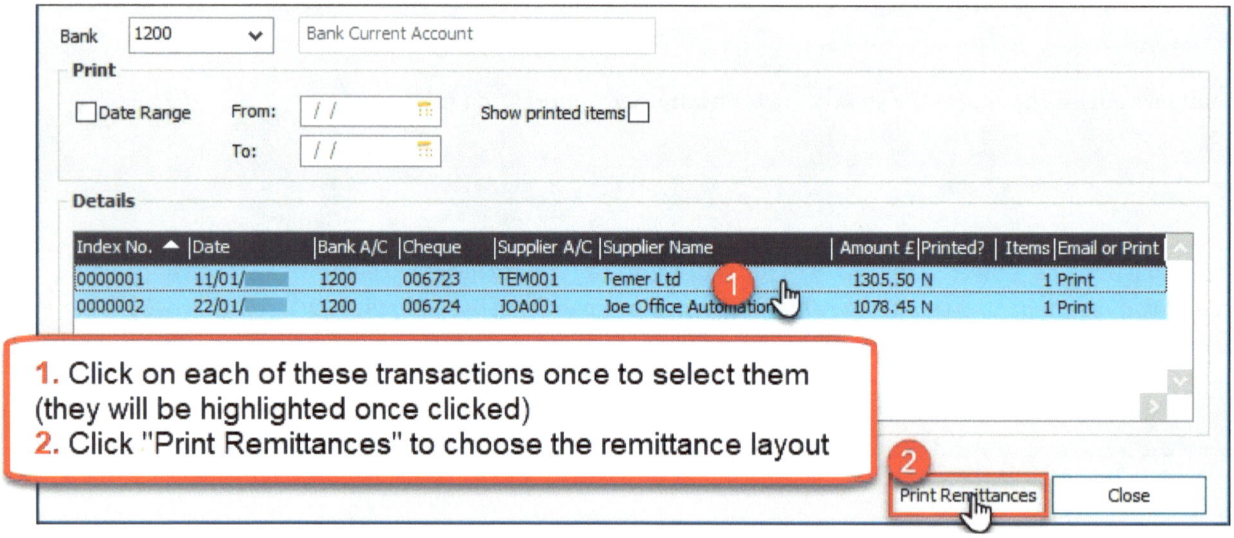

Fig. 155

After you click "Print Remittances" as illustrated in the figure above, a remittance advice printing window appears – see figure 156 on the next page.

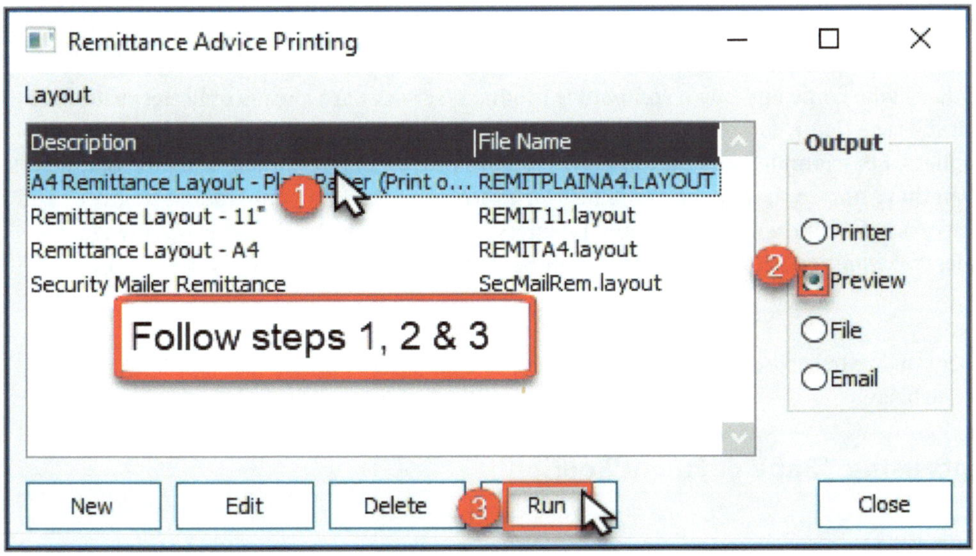

Fig. 156

After step 3 in the figure above, a remittance advice note similar to the figure 157 below will appear.

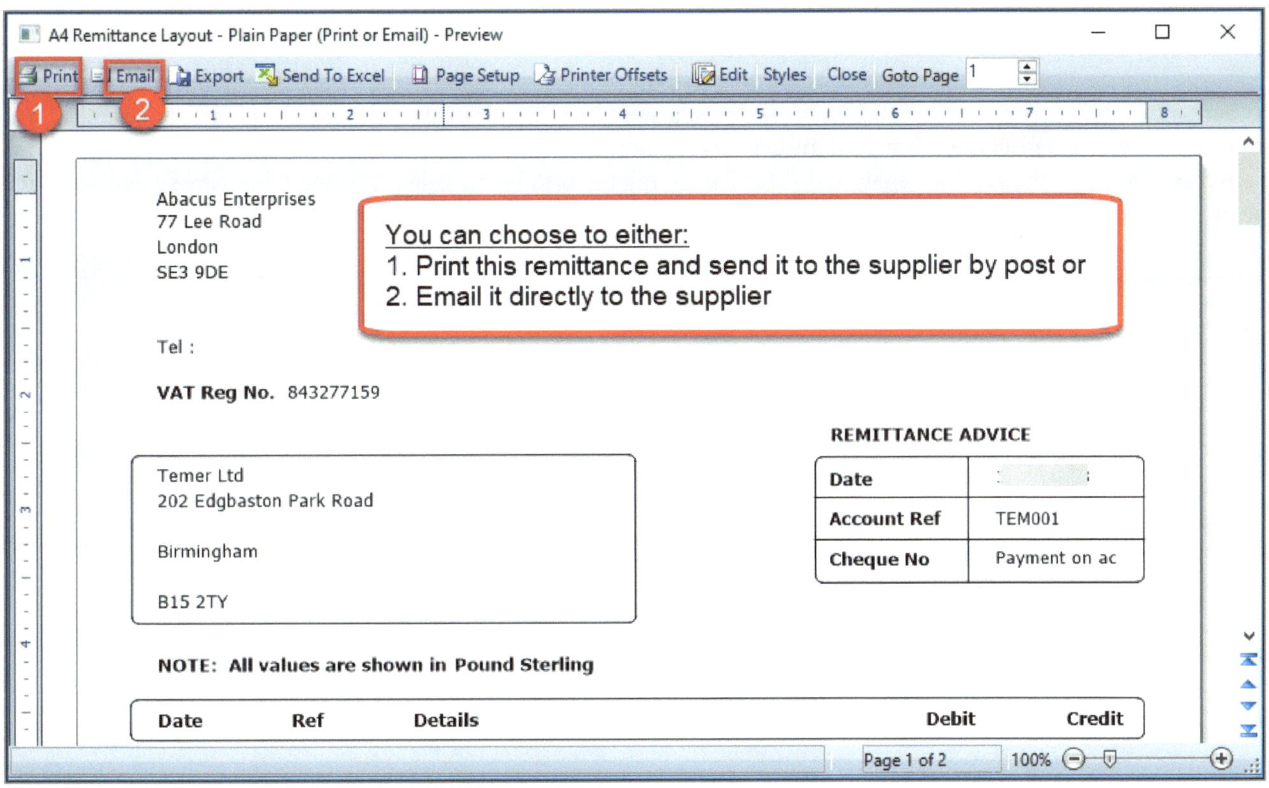

Fig. 157

Task 6b: How to process a non-supplier payment.

It is not always the case that all those who come and buy a company's products/services are always only the customers they have records for neither is it the case that a company will only spend money in buying products/goods only from those persons designated as suppliers. For example, when a company employs people and pays them a salary, employees can hardly be called suppliers! Can they? And so, is someone who just for example walks into your trading premises and buys a one-off item, you won't necessarily call them one of your customers– those in your books I mean, or when you receive a VAT refund, for example, you won't call HMRC your customer because they have given you some money, will you? Of course not.

So, in Sage 50 Accounts, whenever you are to record a payment other than to a supplier, you use the "Bank payment" option or use a journal option – see below.

Recording payment receipts using "Bank payment" option

First, begin by analysing all the receipts.

First receipt (from Sainsbury's), the Wasabi receipts and the receipt from Boots have not been recorded yet due to insufficient analytical information: We know the date of the transaction and what was bought in each receipt, but we do not know whether this were business transactions or not. The best thing to do is to keep these receipts aside and not record them until all the analytical information is received.

The other Sainsbury's receipt is a transaction for the purchase of fuel (diesel) using the company credit card, the Clintons and Specsavers receipt are transactions using company debit card receipt.
These receipts have all the relevant analytical information for them to be recorded. We know the cards being used for payment, the Items bought, the date of the transactions.

Let's record these transactions into the accounting software.

Click on "Bank accounts" tab, then click on arrow under bank payments and select "Bank payment" option.
A window similar to the figure below will appear.

See figure 158 & 159 on the next page for the steps to fill out the bank payment window (use the details in the receipts)

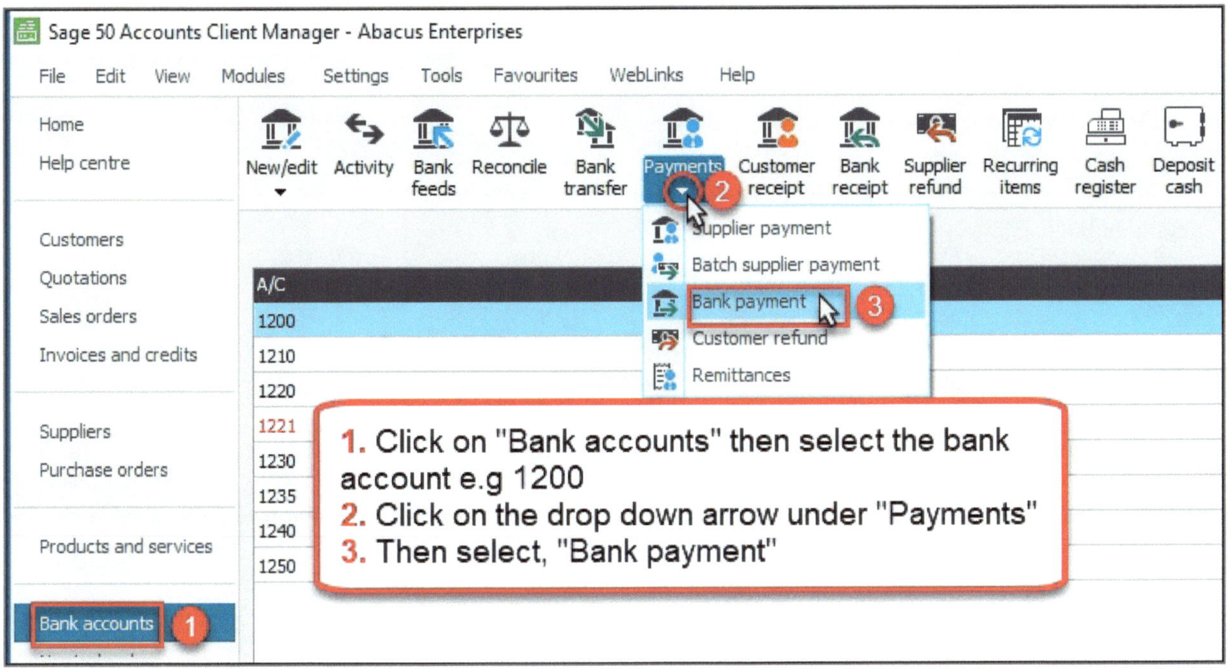

Fig. 158

After step 3 as illustrated in the figure above, a "bank payment" window will appear – see figure 159 below.

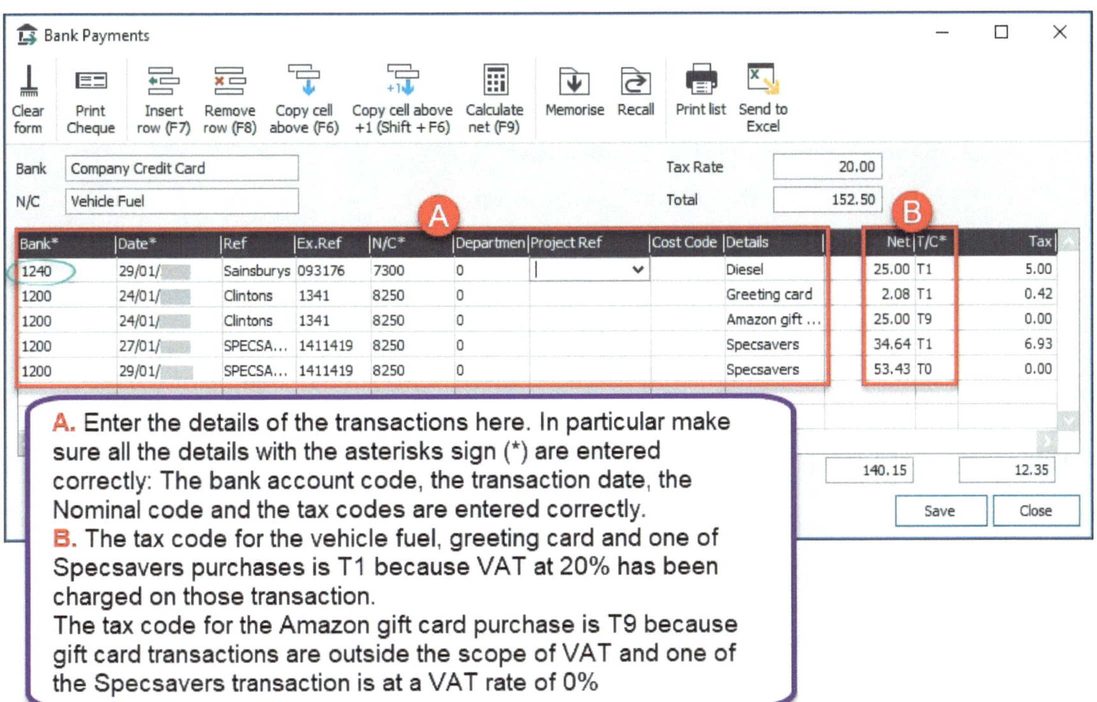

Fig. 159

A note on trade discounts and prompt payment discounts.

What are discounts?
There are two types of discount a business may offer to its customers:

A **trade discount** may be offered to a customer for a number of reasons, including:

- buying in bulk
- the total price of an order exceeding a certain amount
- loyalty
- to promote a certain product.

An example of a trade discount is, a customer receiving 10% off the trade price for placing an order of more than £500.

A **prompt payment** (or early settlement) discount may be offered to a customer to encourage them to pay more quickly.

An example of a prompt payment discount is a customer being offered a reduction in the amount payable of 3% if the payment is made within seven days.

How do I calculate VAT for trade discounts?

To calculate the VAT on a trade discount, deduct the discount from the net price before the VAT is calculated.
How do I calculate VAT for prompt payment (early settlement) discounts?
Calculating the VAT on a prompt payment discount is more complicated than the calculation for a trade discount.

With a prompt payment discount the VAT is based on the **actual amount received,** but you (the supplier) will need to account for the VAT and prepare the invoice before the amount is received.
To calculate VAT on a prompt payment discount:

- decide which of the options below your business wishes to follow
- calculate the VAT in the normal way, i.e. net x VAT rate.

Choose one of the following two options:

Option 1. Issue a credit note - If the customer pays the lower amount (i.e. takes advantage of the prompt payment discount offered), issue a credit note for the amount of the discount (plus VAT).

Option 2. Include further information on the original invoice - If you do not want to issue a credit note each time a customer takes advantage of a prompt payment discount, then further information must be included on the original invoice:

- a statement that the customer can only recover the VAT actually paid, and
- the terms of the prompt payment discount. HMRC recommends that we include the discounted price, the VAT on the discounted price and the total amount due if the prompt payment discount is taken up.

HMRC recommend the following standard wording: "A discount of X% of the full price applies if payment is made within Y days of the invoice date. No credit note will be issued. On payment, you may only recover the VAT actually paid".

Example: Calculating VAT on discounts
Calculating VAT on discounts can be done in one of the two ways. Extracts in the attached invoices contain discounts shown as follows:

Option 1: Issue an invoice

- An invoice is prepared for the full amount. In this example, the amount is £300.
- The rate of VAT is clearly shown (at 20%)
- The trade discount is calculated at 15% and deducted from the usual price (£300 - £45.00 = £255)
- The VAT is calculated on the net: £255 x 20% = £51
- The amount payable if the prompt payment discount is not taken is shown (£306), along with the terms of the prompt payment discount - 'A 3% discount applies if payment is made within seven days of the invoice date.'

Option 1 - Issue a credit note

The customer pays the reduced amount; therefore, a credit note is issued.

- The rate of VAT is clearly shown (at 20%)
- This is 3% of the net figure on the invoice: £255 x 3% = £7.65
- The VAT is calculated on the net: £7.65 x 20% = £1.53
- This is the amount by which the original invoice has been reduced. The customer paid £296.82 (£306.00 - £9.18).

Option 2: Include further information on the original invoice

The invoice is prepared for the full amount of £300 with additional information:

- The rate of VAT is clearly shown (at 20%)
- The trade discount is calculated at 15% and deducted from the usual price (£300 - £45 =£255)
- The VAT is calculated on the net. £255 x 20% = £51
- The amount payable if the prompt payment discount is not taken is shown (£306), along with the terms of the prompt payment discount - 'A 3% discount applies if payment is made within seven days of the invoice date. No credit note will be issued. On payment, you may only recover the VAT actually paid.'

This space is for notes

Task 6c: How to set up and process recurring entries or standing orders

In this next task, you are to set up a standing order to pay business rates to the council and Finance lease interest payments.

Let's go ahead now and set up the recurring entries.

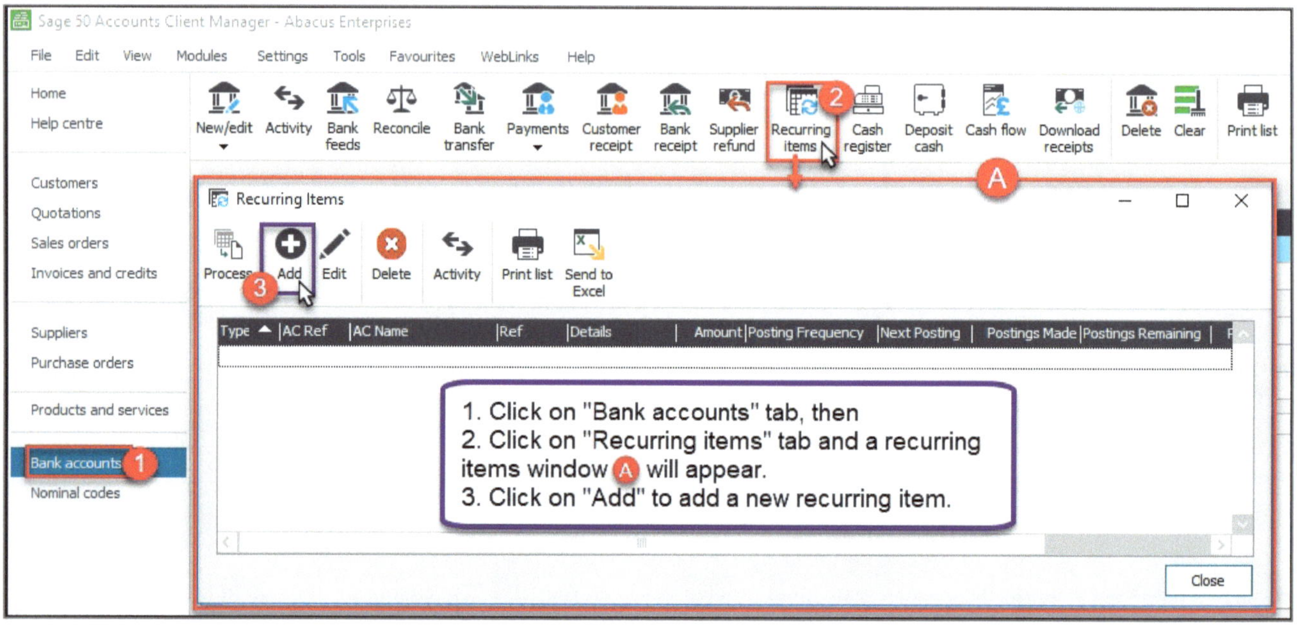

Fig. 160

After step 3 as illustrated in the figure above, a recurring item set up window will appear – see figure 161 on the next page.

This space is for notes

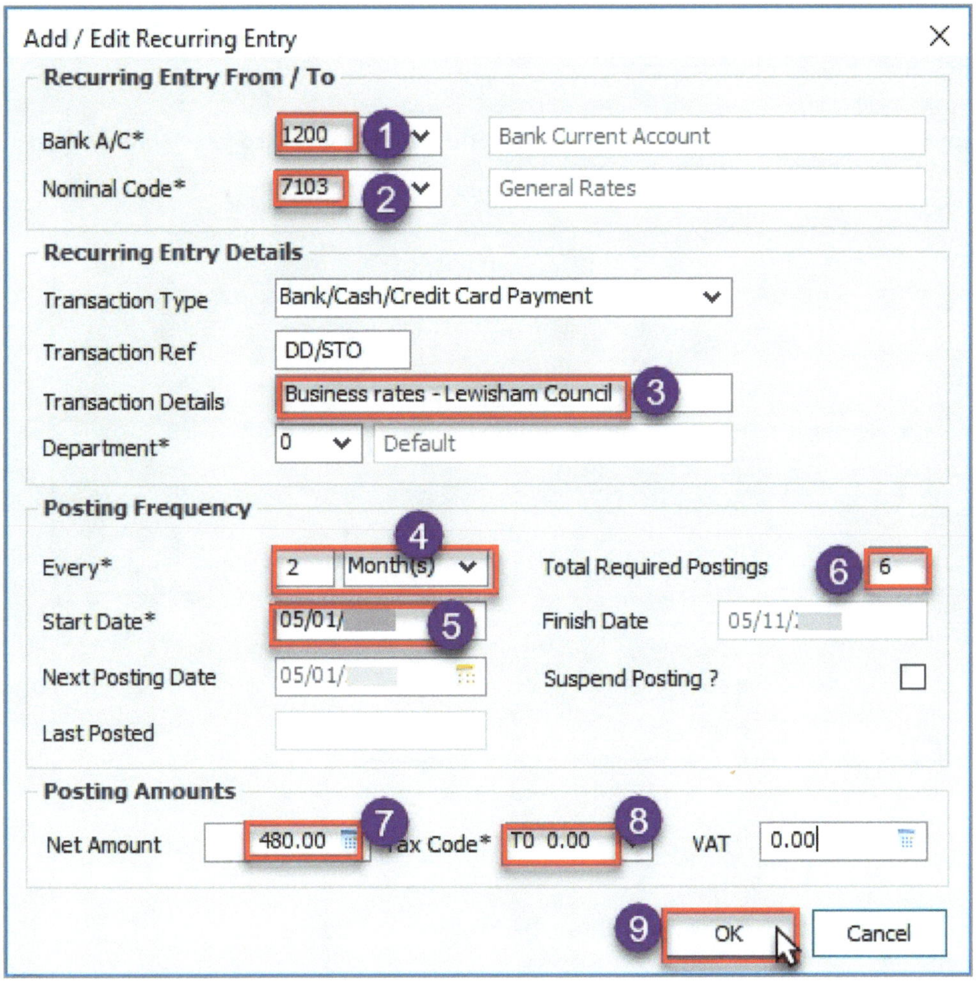

Fig. 161

Steps as illustrated in the figure above

1. Enter in here the account code for the bank account from which this business rate payment will be made from
2. Enter in here the nominal code to be used for business rates
3. Enter appropriate transaction details here
4. Here you record the posting frequency. For example; once, twice, thrice every: day, week, months
5. Enter in here the date when the first transaction should be posted.
6. Enter in here the total number of required postings. Notice that once you enter this number the finish date will automatically be updated with reference to the start date and considering the number of required postings.
7. Here, you enter the net transaction value
8. Since this transaction has no VAT applied to it, choose from the drop-down list the appropriate tax code.
9. Click "Save" to complete the setup of this recurring entry.

Task 6d: How to deal with a finance lease – (fixed asset leased), paid for in part by cash and in part through finance

Before setting up the recurring entries for the Finance lease, please do set up the new Supplier account – BMW dealer 1 and put the default nominal code to be 2310 – Hire purchase. See figure below.

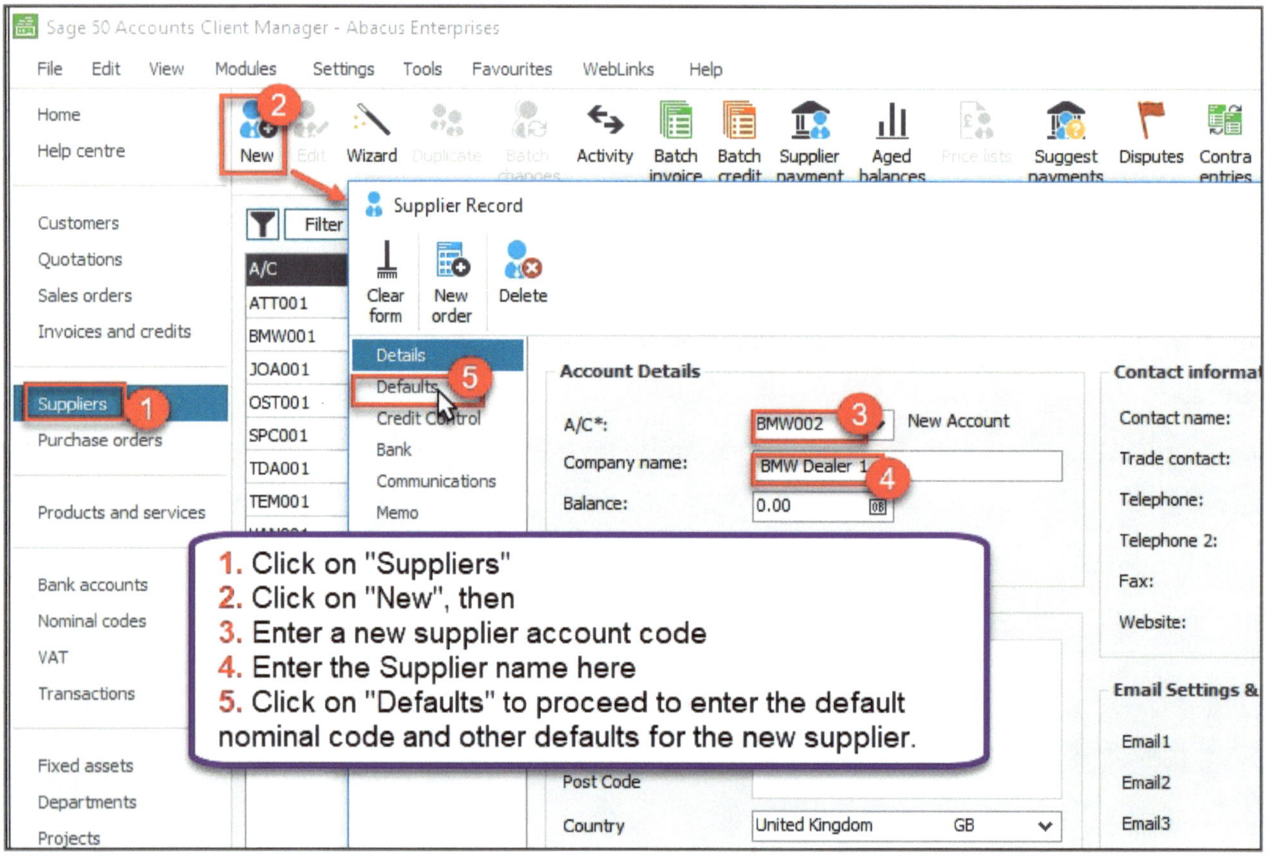

Fig. 162

When you click "Defaults" as illustrated in the figure above, a window similar to the figure 163 on the next page will appear.

This space is for notes

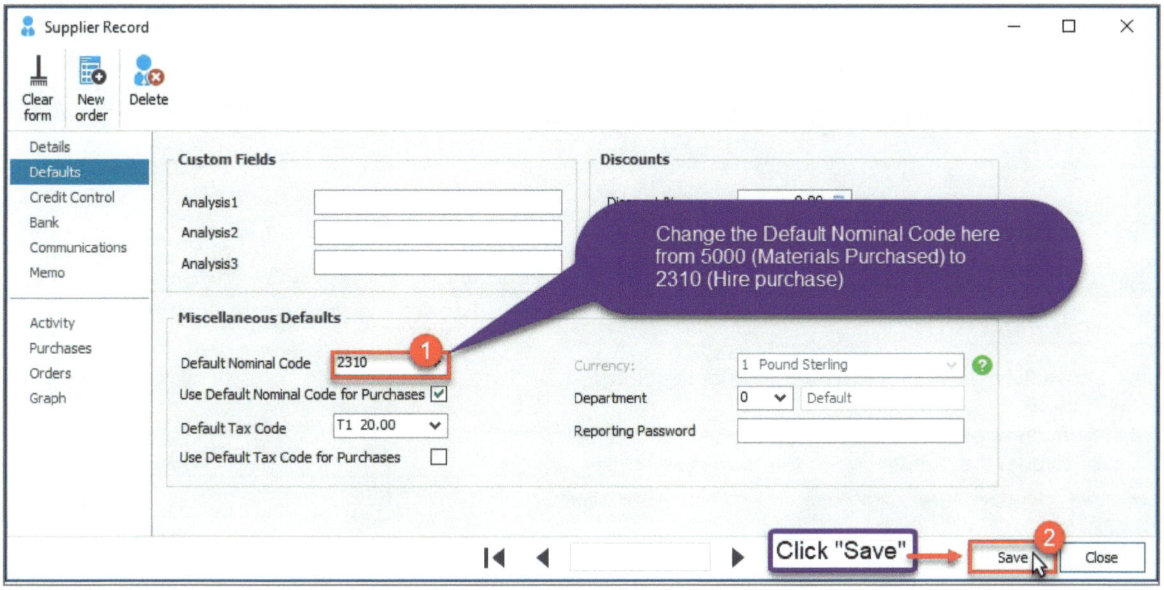

Fig. 163

When an asset is leased (finance lease), the asset will need to be recognised in the balance sheet, and creditor is also created at the same time. There will be a principal payment of the lease amount which will be recorded in the balance sheet and an interest element of the lease amount which will be recorded in profit and loss account.

We have already recorded the lease interest payment setup, now let's record the capitalisation of the fixed asset (motor vehicle – BMW 3 series)

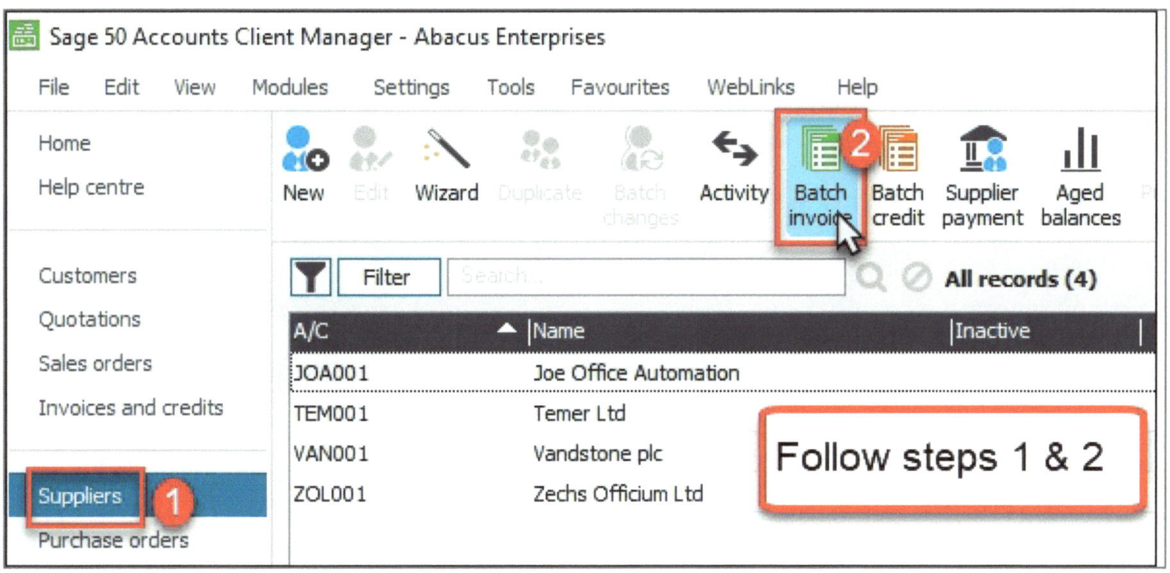

Fig. 164

After step 2 as illustrated in the figure above, a window similar to the figure below will appear.

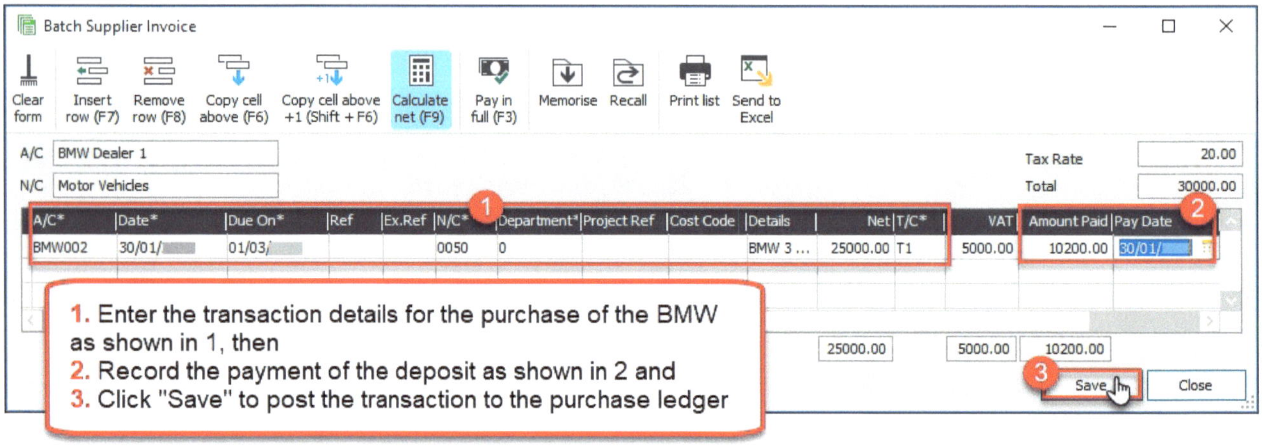

Fig. 165

A note on leases

Leases are classified currently under IAS 17, *Leases*, as finance or operating leases at inception, depending on whether substantially all the risks and rewards of ownership transfer to the lessee. Under a finance lease, the lessee has substantially all of the risks and reward of ownership. Situations that would normally lead to a lease being classified as a finance lease include the following:

- the lease transfers ownership of the asset to the lessee by the end of the lease term
- the lease term is for the major part of the economic life of the asset, even if title is not transferred
- at the inception of the lease, the present value of the minimum lease payments amounts to at least substantially all of the fair value of the leased asset
- the leased assets are of a specialised nature such that only the lessee can use them without major modifications being made
- if the lessee is entitled to cancel the lease, the lessor's losses associated with the cancellation are borne by the lessee
- gains or losses from fluctuations in the fair value of the residual fall to the lessee
- the lessee has the ability to continue to lease for a secondary period at a rent that is substantially lower than market rent

All other leases are operating leases.

Interest on Lease

Since the rest of the lease payments is going to be paid by Direct debit every month, you can set up a recurring entry in Sage 50 Accounts. On the date every month when the transaction is due to be posted, when you login in to Sage 50, there will be an automatic reminder (in the form of a pop up window) for the entry to be posted. What you have to do is click

"Yes" and the transaction posting window will appear with the details of the direct debit transaction ready to be posted for in Sage 50. All you have to do is check those details and if correct, click post, and the transaction will be posted.

Let's set up the Direct debit recurring entry payment for the interest payment to BMW London. For the principal payment, that will have to be recorded every month through the Supplier payment window.

Here is what you need to do to set up the recurring entry.
Click on "Bank accounts" tab, then click on "Recurring items" tab, then click on the "Add" tab – you've already learnt how to set up recurring entries in the previous task.

Once you click "Add" tab illustrated in figure above, a recurring entry set up window will appear, see figure below.

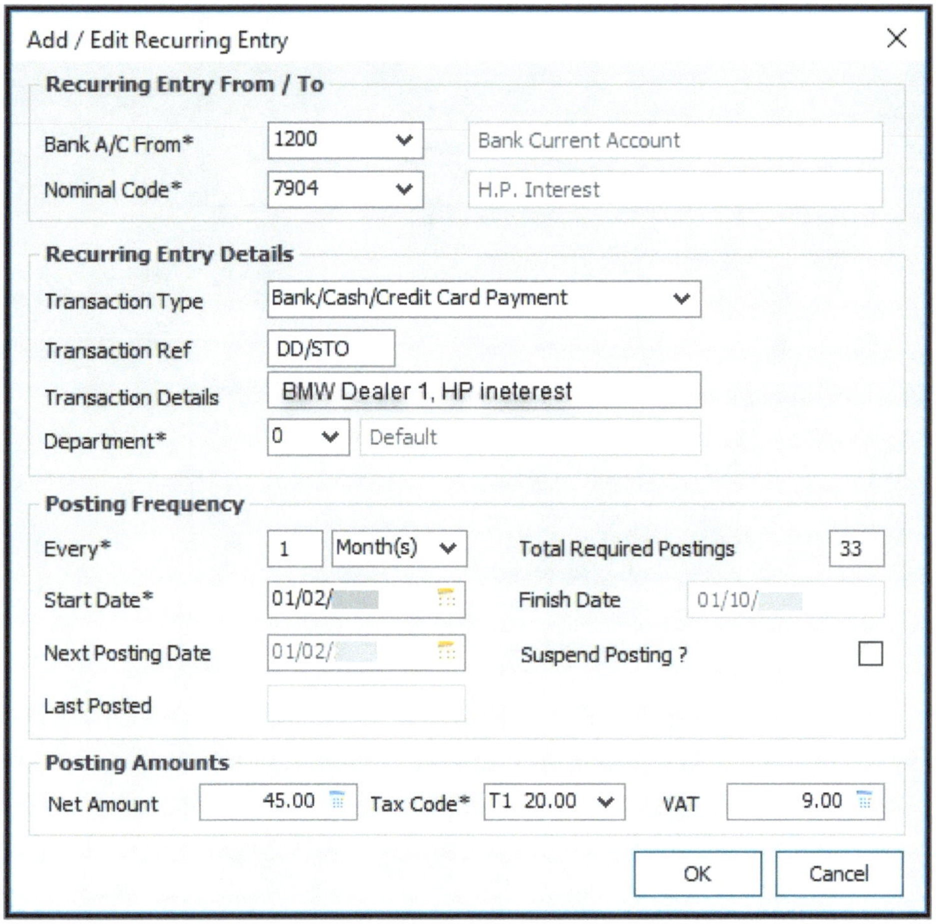

Fig. 166

You are all set now for this recurring entry. So, next time you logon into Sage 50 on the 2nd of every month, a window will pop up saying that there are recurring entries and whether you want to post them. All you have to do is click "Yes" and Sage will automatically have it posted for you. Easy "pizzy", ehh!

Since the 1st payment was due to be processed on the 5th January (Business rates to Lewisham Council), you can go ahead and process it now. See figure 167 below.

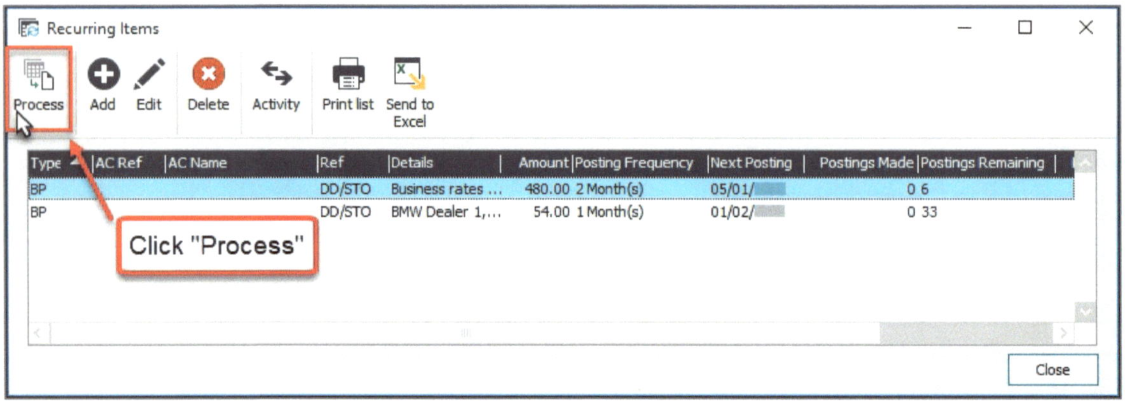

Fig. 167

After step 2 as illustrated in the figure above, a "process recurring items" window appears. See figure below.

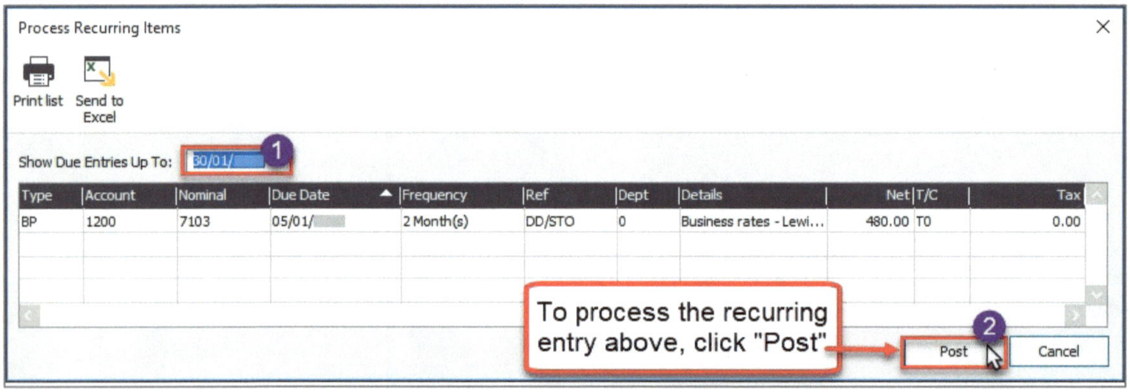

Fig. 168

After clicking post as illustrated in the figure above, your recurring items window will look like the figure below.

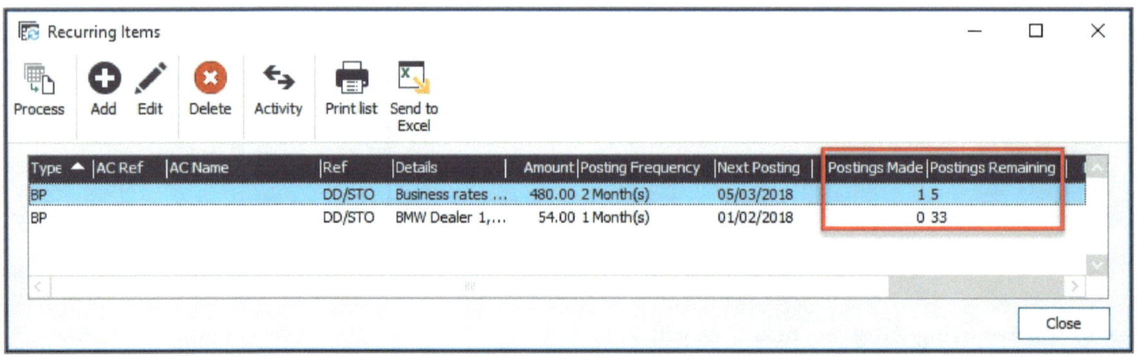

Fig. 169

"The lover of money never has enough money; the lover of luxury never has enough income. this too is pointless" Ecclesiastes 5: 9 CJB

TASK 7: HOW TO PROCESS PETTY CASH

The objective of the petty cash management is to ensure that control is kept over the petty cash tin and that all cash payments are recorded correctly and entered onto the accounting system.

Businesses generally keep small amounts of cash to meet small miscellaneous payments such as entertainment expenses and stationery costs. Such payments are generally handled by a petty cash imprest system whereby an amount of 'Float' is fixed (say £250). This is the maximum amount of cash that can be held at any time, and each time cash level runs low, the petty cash imprest is injected with cash by drawing a cheque.

The amount of reimbursement is equal to the expenses paid through petty cash since the time of last reimbursement. Petty cash balance after reimbursement reverts to back to the level of the float (in this case £250).

For security reasons, the petty cash fund should be locked at all times when it is not in use. Access to petty cash tin is restricted and money cannot be taken out of it without approval.

Any money taken from the petty cash tin should be replaced with a petty cash voucher. This states what the money was taken for and who took it.

The voucher should be signed by the financial accountant or designated signatory.

Whenever a voucher is completed, it is good practice for the custodian to immediately update the petty cash book by adding the amount, type, and date of the expenditure and updating the running cash balance. For example, if you got some refreshments for the office, e.g. some sweets and you need to be reimbursed the amount you spent, you would need to fill out a petty cash voucher with the details of the purchase.

Petty cash tin illustrative picture.

Fig. 170

The Director withdrew some money from the business current account to restore the petty cash to its original float. You should now update the petty cash account with the details of this transaction.

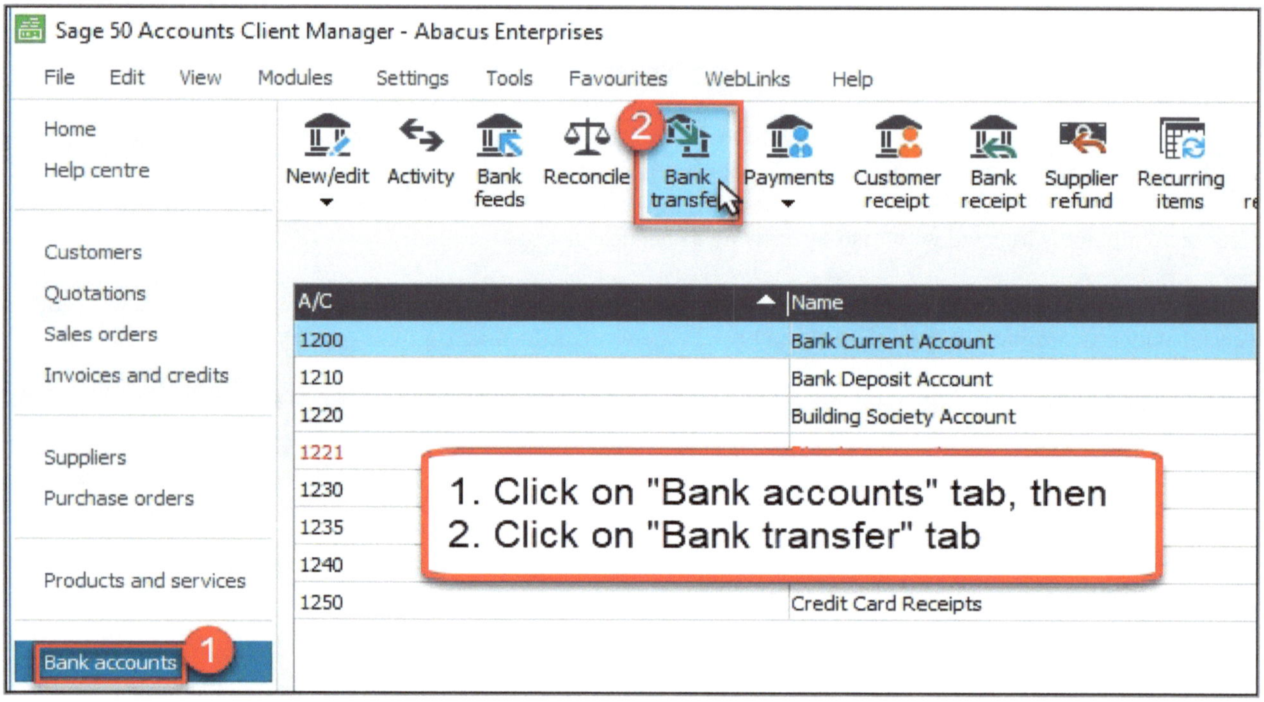

Fig. 171

A bank transfer window appears (figure 172 below) after you have clicked "Bank transfer" as shown in step 2 in the figure above.

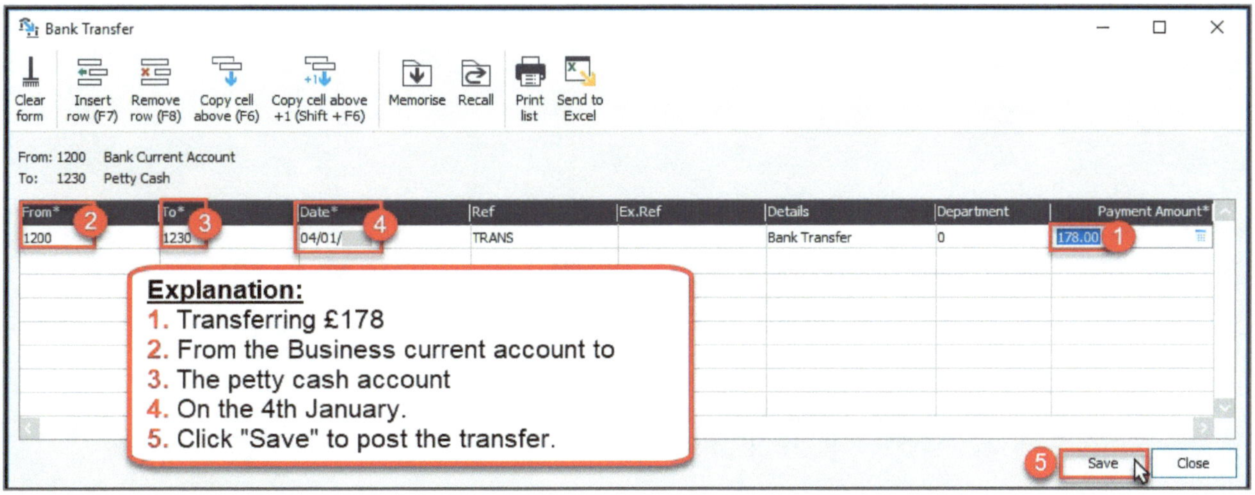

Fig. 172

Some petty cash transactions have occurred, and you are now required to process those transactions.

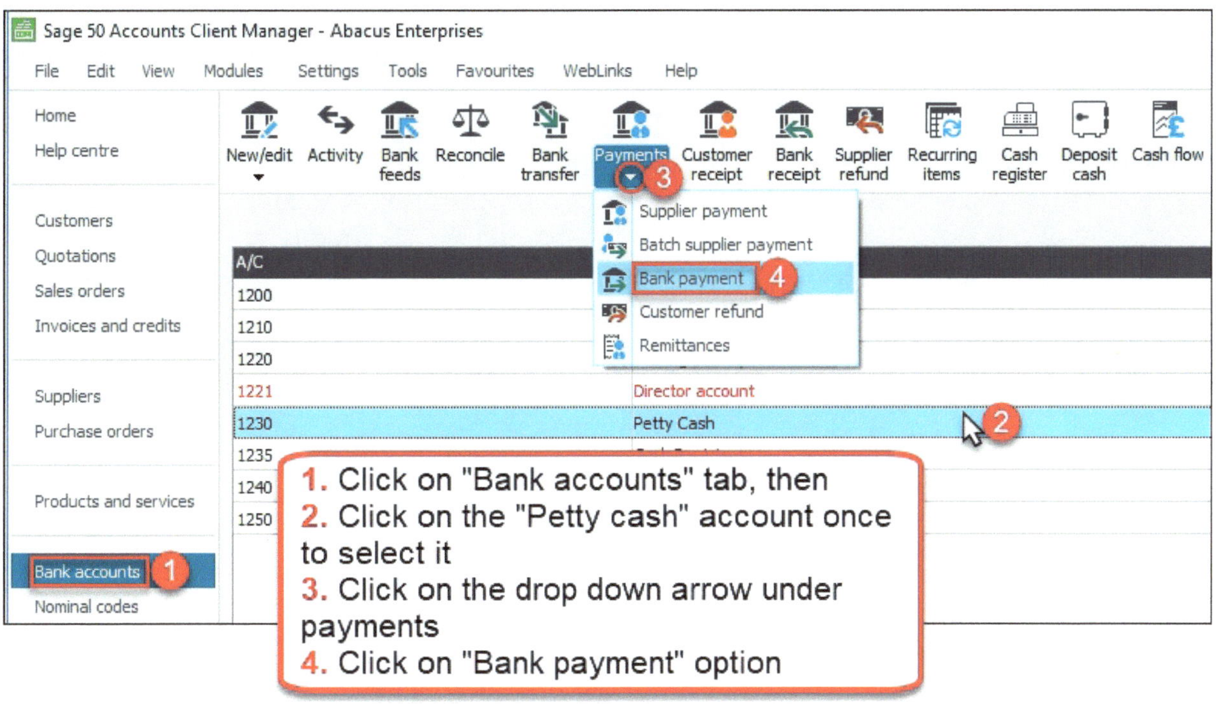

Fig. 173

A bank payment window will appear after step 4 as illustrated in the figure above. Follow the inset steps in figure 174 on the next page to record and post the details of the two petty cash vouchers.

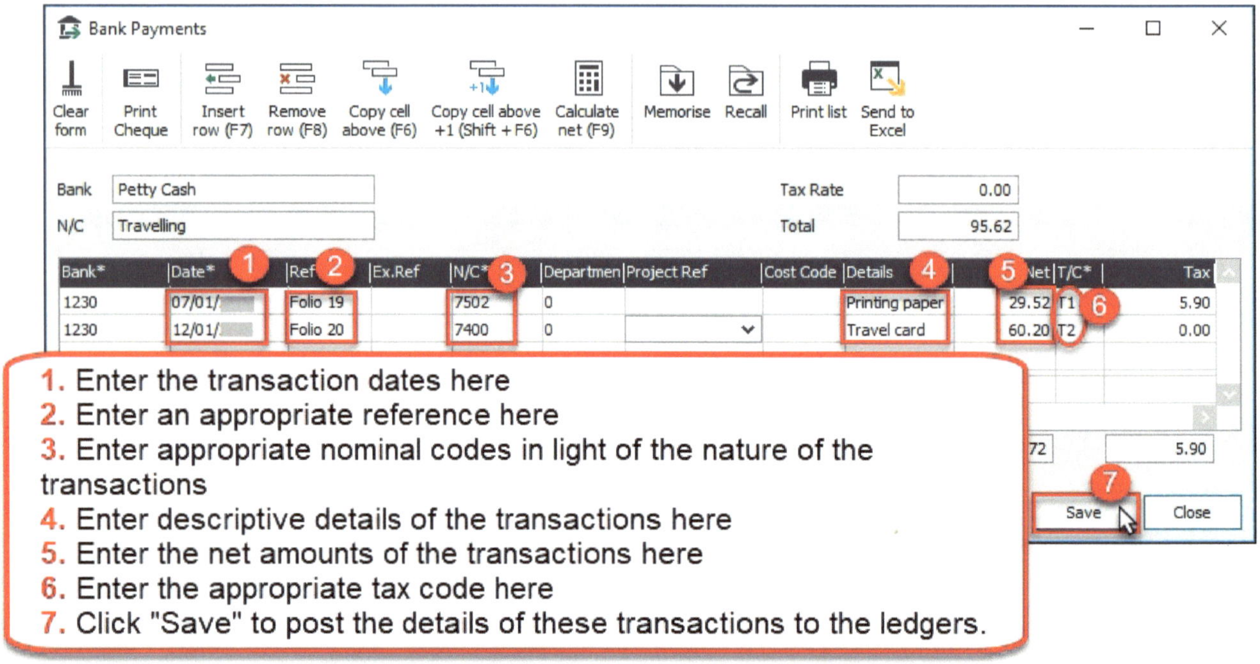

Bank*	Date*	Ref	Ex.Ref	N/C*	Departmen	Project Ref	Cost Code	Details	Net	T/C*	Tax
1230	07/01/	Folio 19		7502	0			Printing paper	29.52	T1	5.90
1230	12/01/	Folio 20		7400	0			Travel card	60.20	T2	0.00

Fig. 174

This space is for notes

"For everything there is a season, a right time for every intention under heaven"
Ecclesiastes 3: 1 CJB

TASK 8: HOW TO RECORD A TRANSACTION FOR THE ISSUE OF ORDINARY SHARES

In the next task - Abacus Enterprises has issued share at a premium and as such the issue costs will be written off against the share premium.

The issue of ordinary share capital creates equity instruments and the entity has no obligation to repay the monies received; rather it has increased the ownership interest in its net assets.

Recording the above transaction in Sage Accounts; you will need to debit the bank account where the share capital money received is deposited then credit the ordinary shares account with the total nominal value of the shares and also credit the share premium account less the issue costs.

Use a journal to record this transaction. But first create a nominal account code for Share premium in Sage Accounts. Click on "Nominal codes" tab then, "New" – See figure 175 on the next page.

> Ordinary Share Capital represents equity of a company and therefore its issuance is recorded as part of the equity reserves in the balance sheet.
> Ordinary Shares are also known as common stock and equity shares.
>
> Company law of many jurisdictions such as USA and UK prohibit public companies from issuing shares to investors before all legal requirements for the issuance of shares have been met (e.g. minimum amount of subscription mentioned in the prospectus must be received). If the requirements for the issue of shares are not met, companies are obliged to return the subscription money received from applicants (subscribers).
>
> To account for the shares issue in such cases, it will be necessary to create a temporary liability account (e.g. Subscription Account) in addition to the 2 accounts discussed above in order to account for the cash advanced in respect of the subscription of shares until the date of issuance of shares or the return of subscription money to applicants.

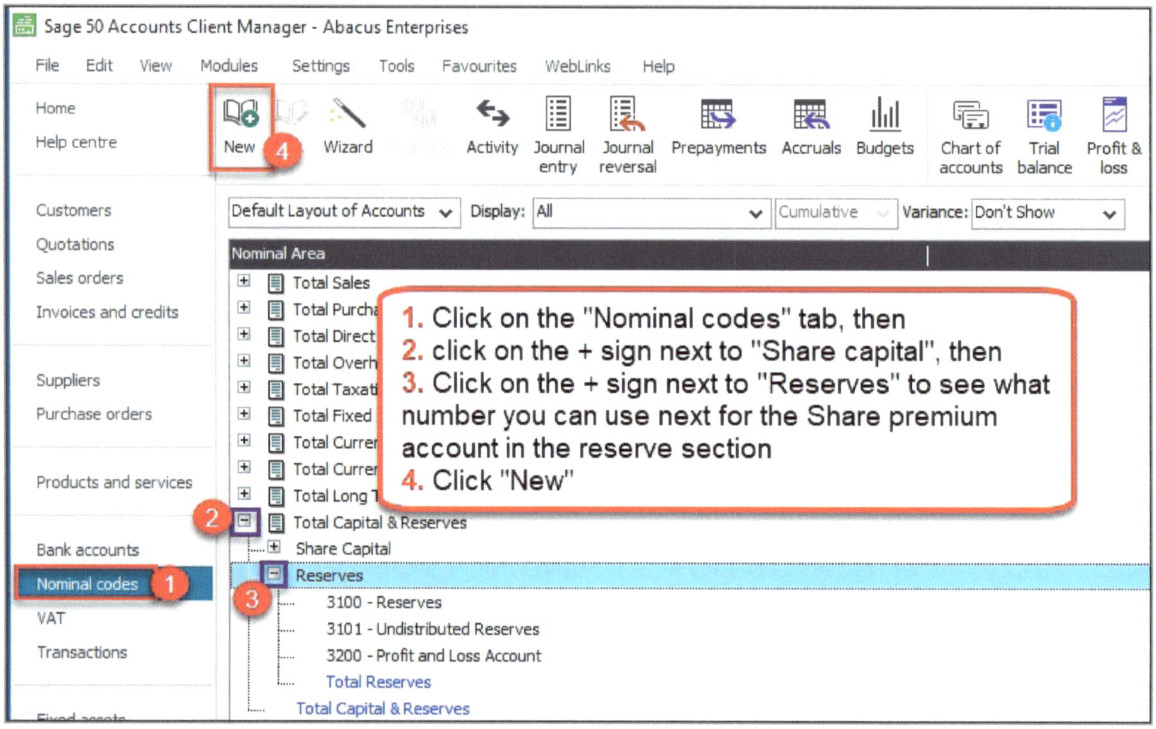

Fig. 175

After step 3 as illustrated in the figure above, a nominal record window appears similar to figure 176. Follow the illustrative inset steps to create the new nominal code.

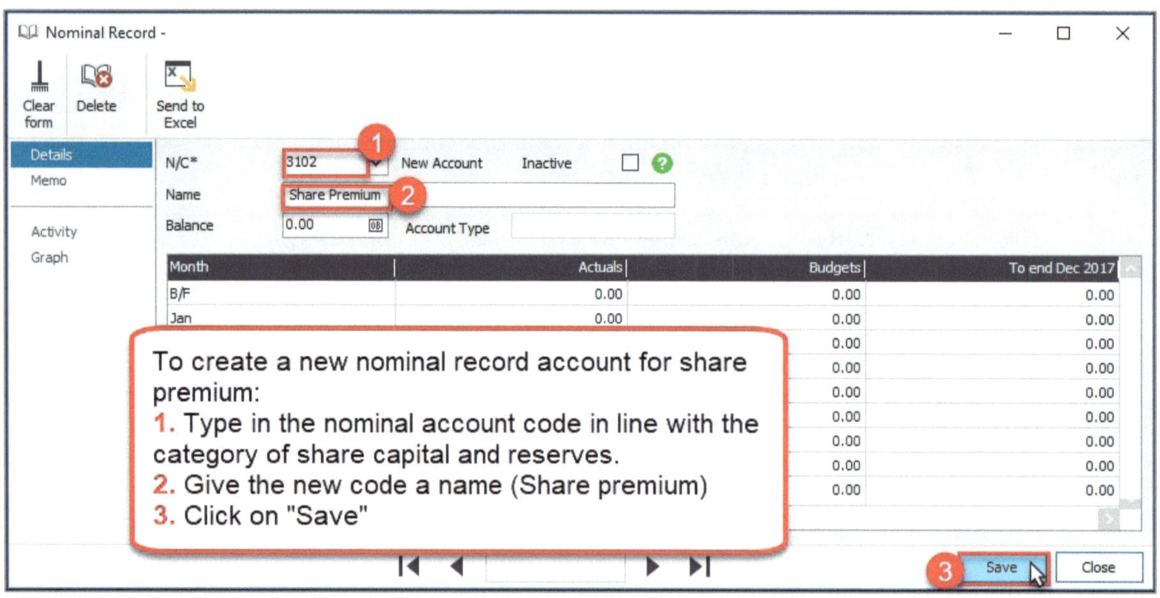

Fig. 176

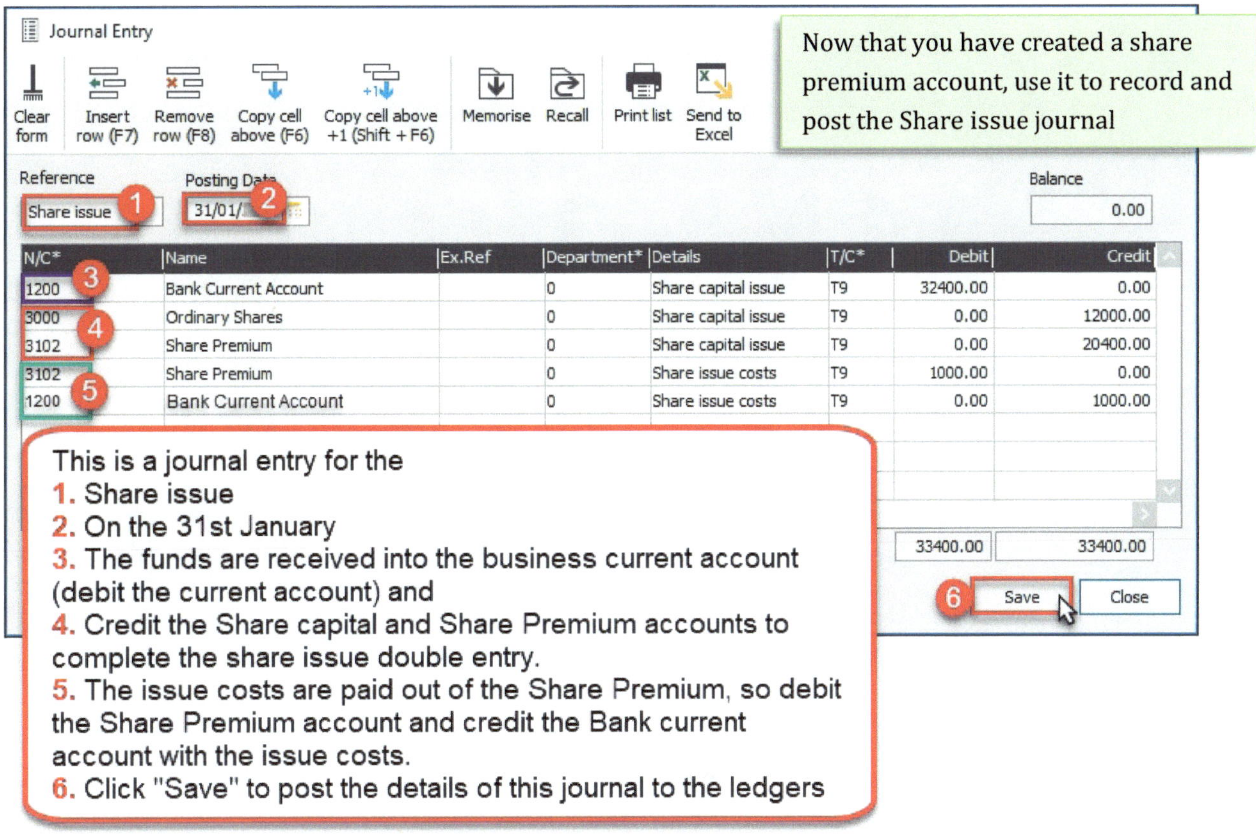

Fig. 177

This space is for notes

"Try not to be a man of success but rather try to become a man of value"

Albert Einstein

"The doors of wisdom are never shut"
Benjamin Franklin.

TASK 9: HOW TO ENSURE SECURITY OF ACCOUNTING DATA

How to change your password in Sage 50 Accounts

In Sage Accounts, you can follow the steps below to change a password while logged in as that user, or while logged in as manager.

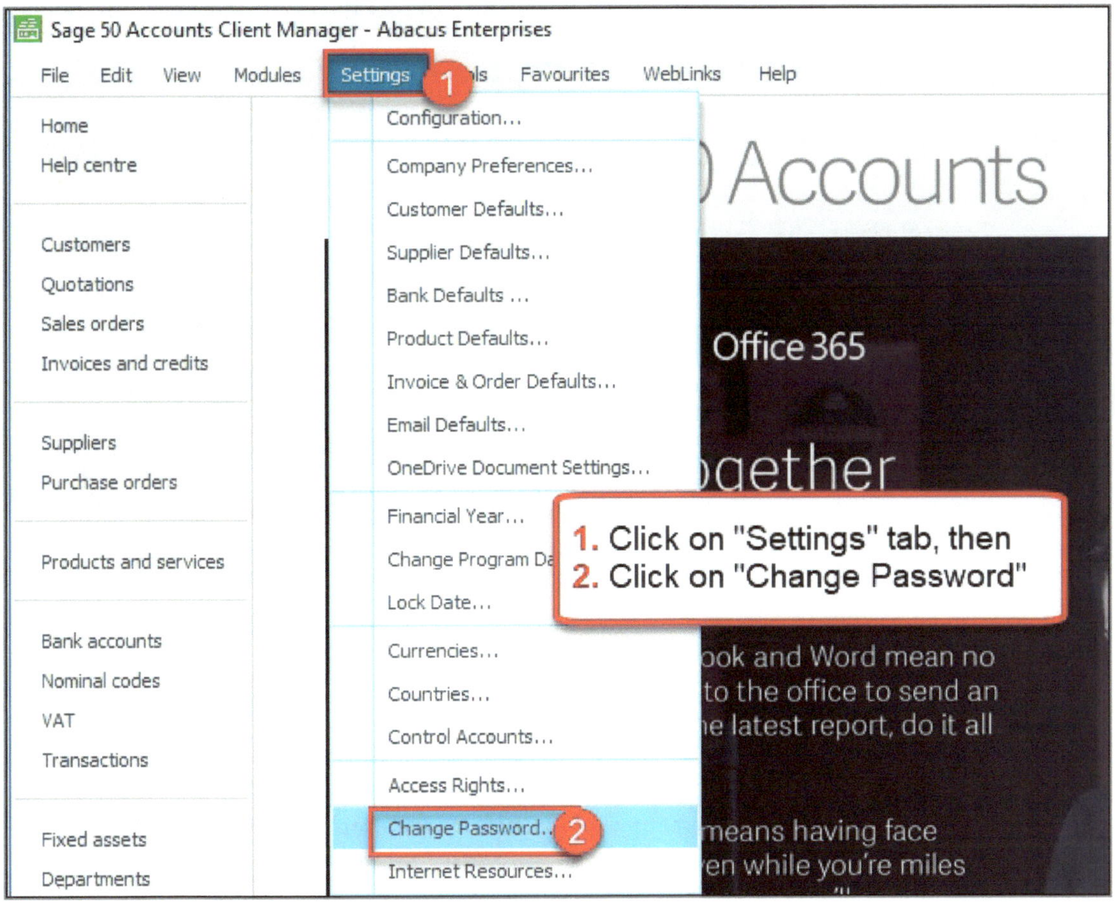

Fig. 178

After step 2 as illustrated in the figure above, the following window appears – see figure 179 & 180 on the next page.

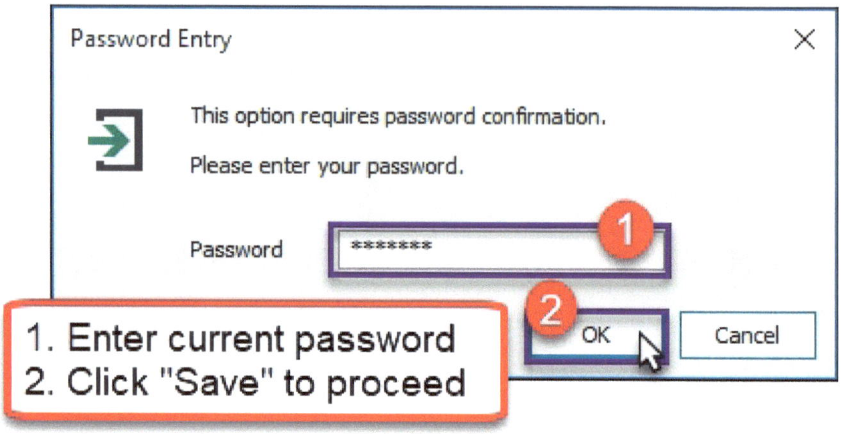

Fig. 179

A change password window appears after step 2 as illustrated in the figure above. Enter the required details accordingly.

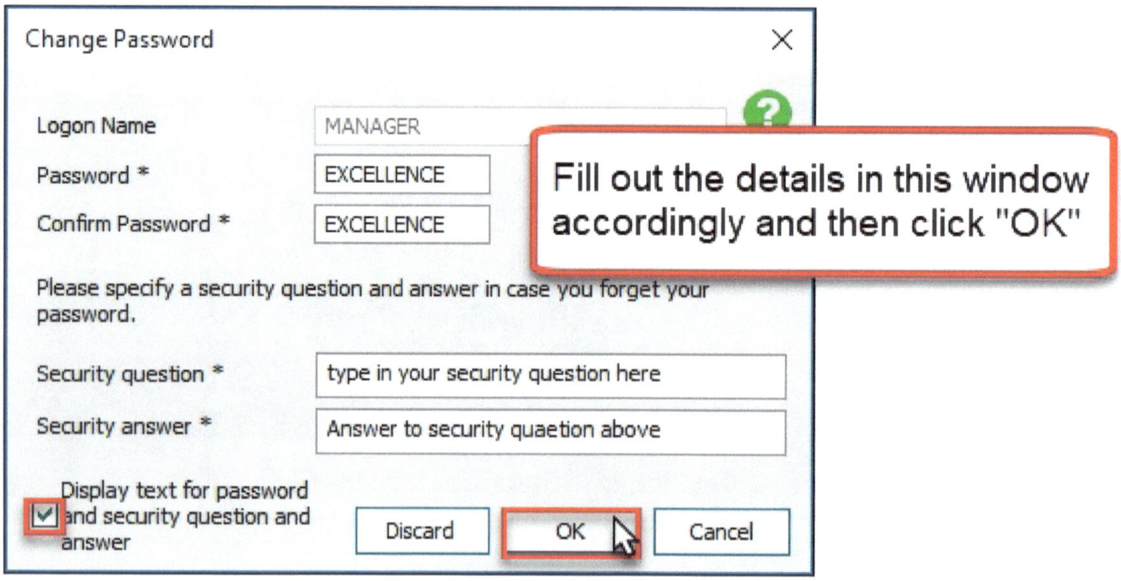

Fig. 180

How to set up a new user in Sage 50 Accounts

You can use the Access Rights option in Sage Accounts to set up logon names and passwords for each person who accesses your software. By doing this you can easily keep track of who's processed information in your accounts and, if required, restrict users to certain areas of the software.

It's recommended that you set up your user access rights before your users start processing in Sage Accounts. This step is essential on network versions of Sage Accounts if more than one person is to process information at the same time

In the task at hand, you are to set up access rights for the assistant you started on the 15th January.

Here is how to set up a new user in Sage 50 Accounts.

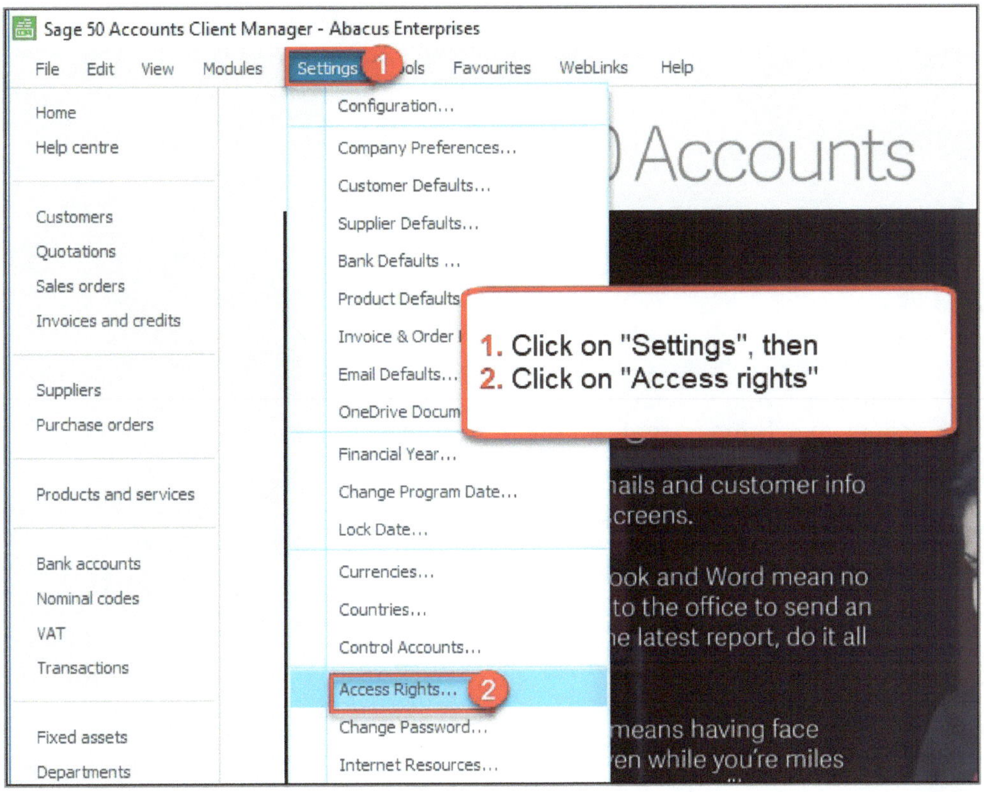

Fig. 181

Once you click Access rights as illustrated in the figure above, a user access rights window appears. See figure below.

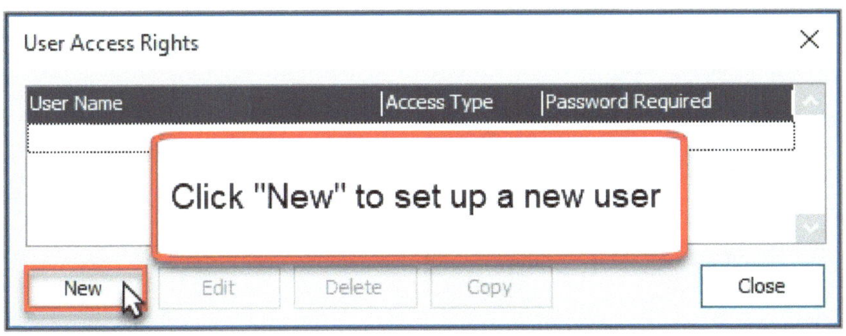

Fig. 182

After clicking "New" create a new user window appears. See figure 183 on the next page.

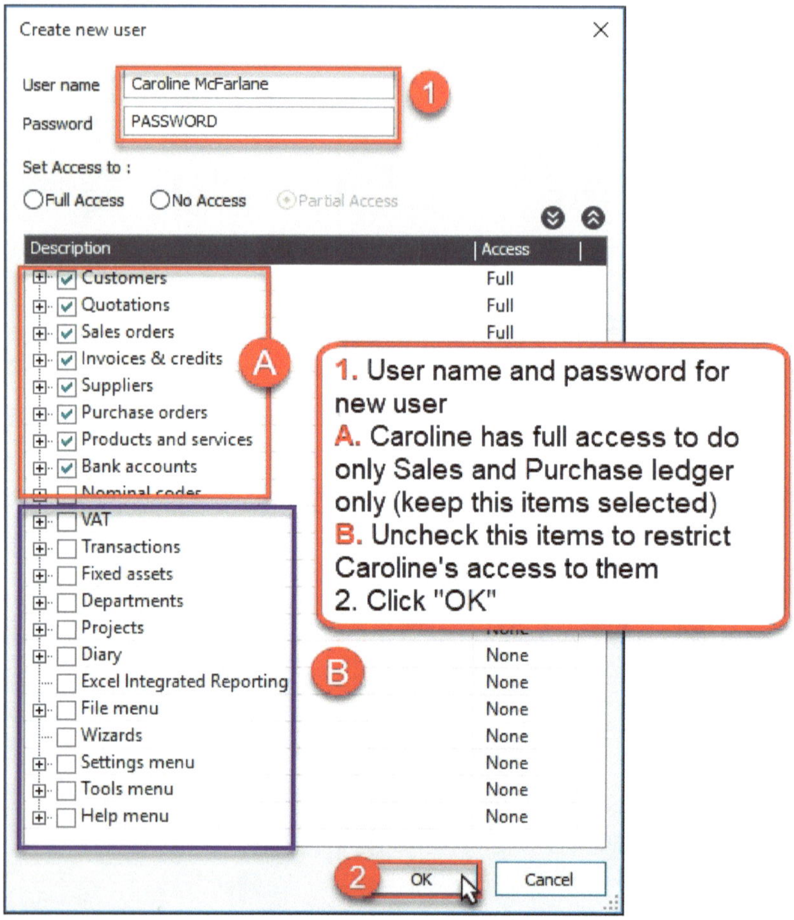

Fig. 183

After step 2 as illustrated in the figure above, a user access rights window appears. See figure below.

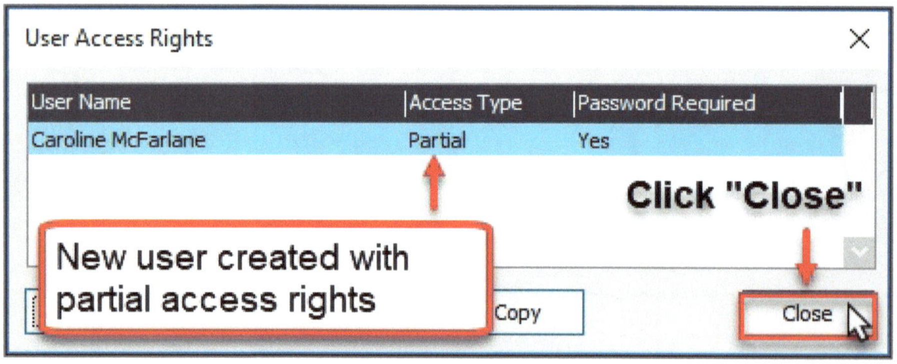

Fig. 184

Fig. 185

This space is for notes

How to back up your data in Sage 50

It's recommended that you take regular backups of your data. How often you do this depends on the number of transactions you enter. If you enter a lot, you may want to back up every day. You should also back up before and after an important accounting process, such as creating a VAT Return or running the year-end routine. If anything happens to your computer, you can simply restore your most recent backup and continue processing where you left off.

Your next task is to back up your work and here is how you do it:

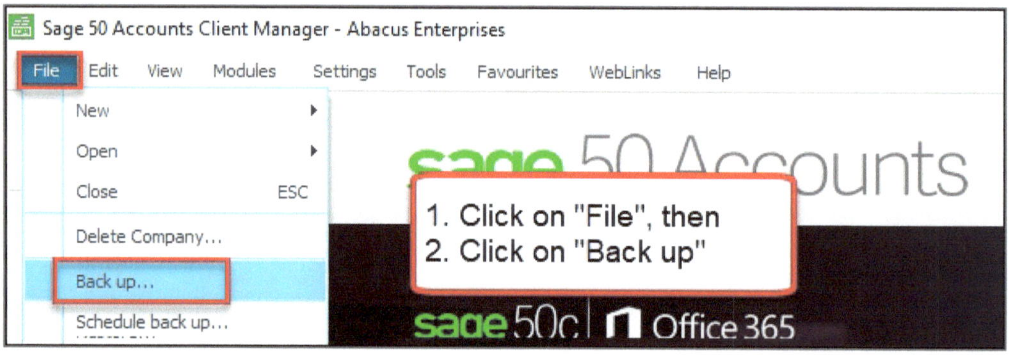

Fig. 186

If this is the first back up you are taking since you opened Sage today, a "confirm" window will appear similar to the figure below.

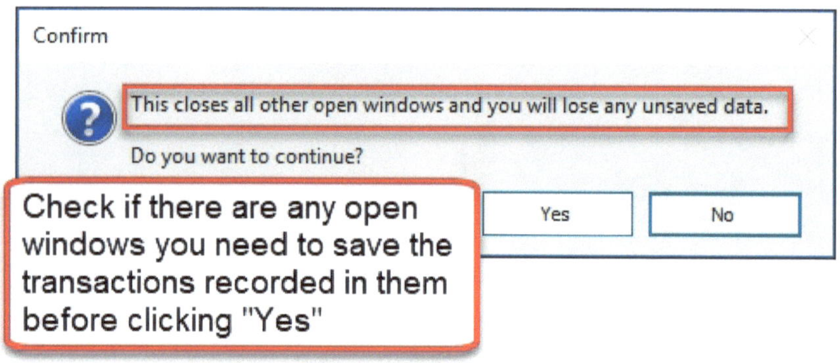

Fig. 187

If you have already taken some backs earlier on since you opened Sage 50 Accounts today, and also after you click "Yes" as illustrated in the figure above, and another "confirm" window will appear. See figure 188 on the next page.

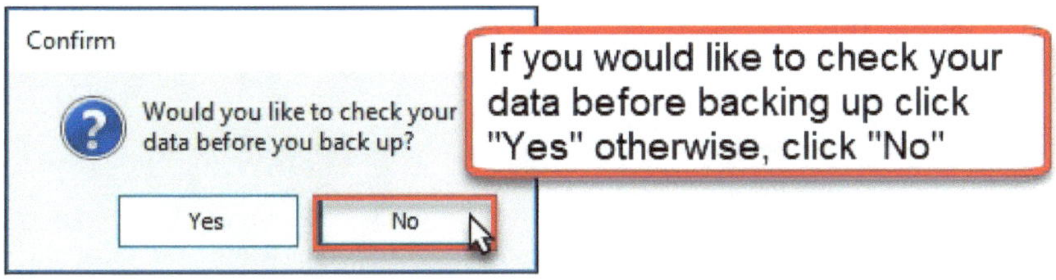

Fig. 188

Once you click "No" as illustrated in the figure above, a backup window will appear. See figure below.

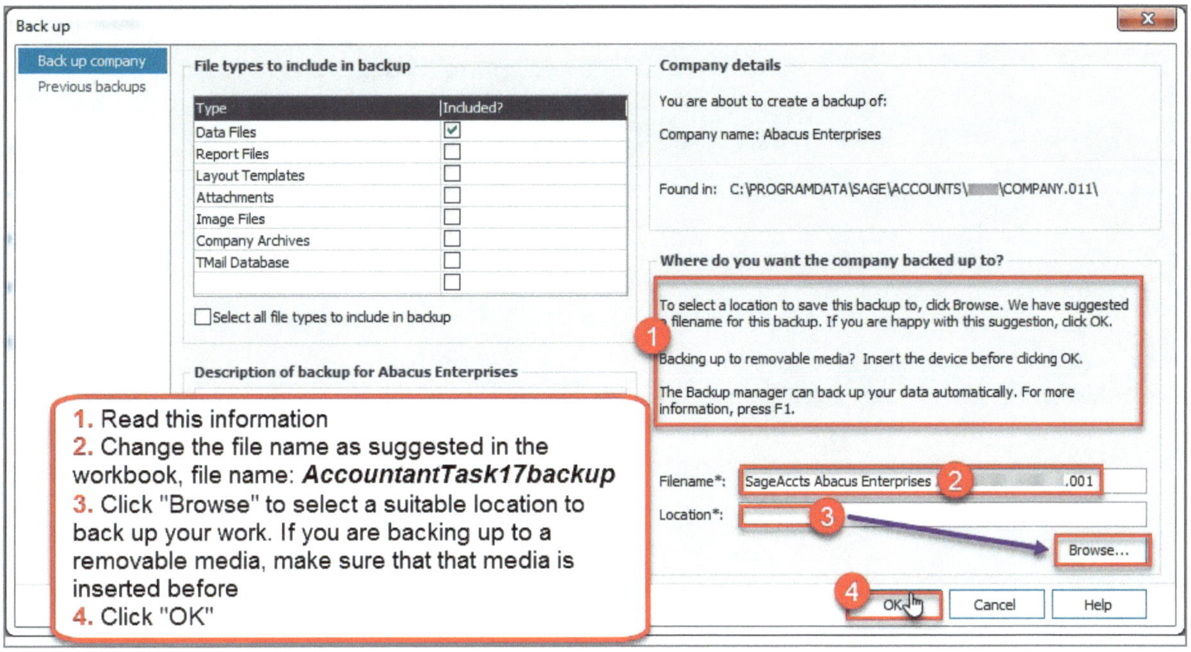

Fig. 189

This space is for notes

After step 5 as illustrated in the figure above, a backup progress window will appear – see figure below

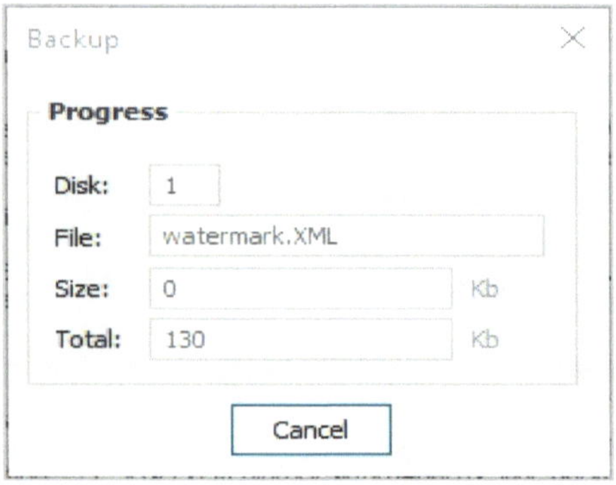

Fig. 190

After the backup progress is complete, a notification window will appear – see figure below

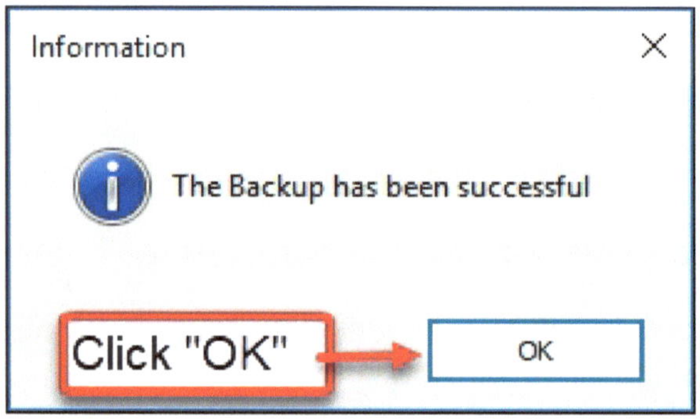

Fig. 191

"ADONAI, in the morning you will hear my voice; in the morning, I lay my needs before you expectantly".

Psalm 5:4 CJB

TASK 10: RECORDING TRANSACTIONS BETWEEN DIRECTOR AND COMPANY

In Sage Accounts, you can use journals to transfer balances between nominal codes without affecting customer or supplier accounts.

Journal transactions are always posted with an equal value in the Debit and Credit columns, with at least one journal debit and one journal credit per journal posting.

Every journal consists of credit and debit values so that every credit must have a debit and vice versa. This does not mean that for every single debit item you must post a single credit item. You can post several debits but one balancing credit, and vice versa. As long as the net difference between your postings is always zero – that is, the total value of credits equals the total value of debits, you can post the journal.

It is important to adhere to strict double-entry bookkeeping principles, when recording journals.

In the task at hand, you have 2 transactions to post to the ledgers. To get started, click on Nominal codes tab then click on Journal entry tab. See figure 192 on the next page.

The directors loan account is simply a record of all transactions between the company and the director/s. You may also hear it being referred to as a Director's Current Account or a DLA. It's the same thing. The amount owed to or from the director. If there are multiple directors in the business, each will have a separate director's loan account in the balance sheet. The DLA is a balance sheet account of course because the balance is either:

- an asset – money owed to the company or,
- a liability – money owed to the director.

DLA's can be made up of:

- monies drawn down by the director
- personal bills paid by the company

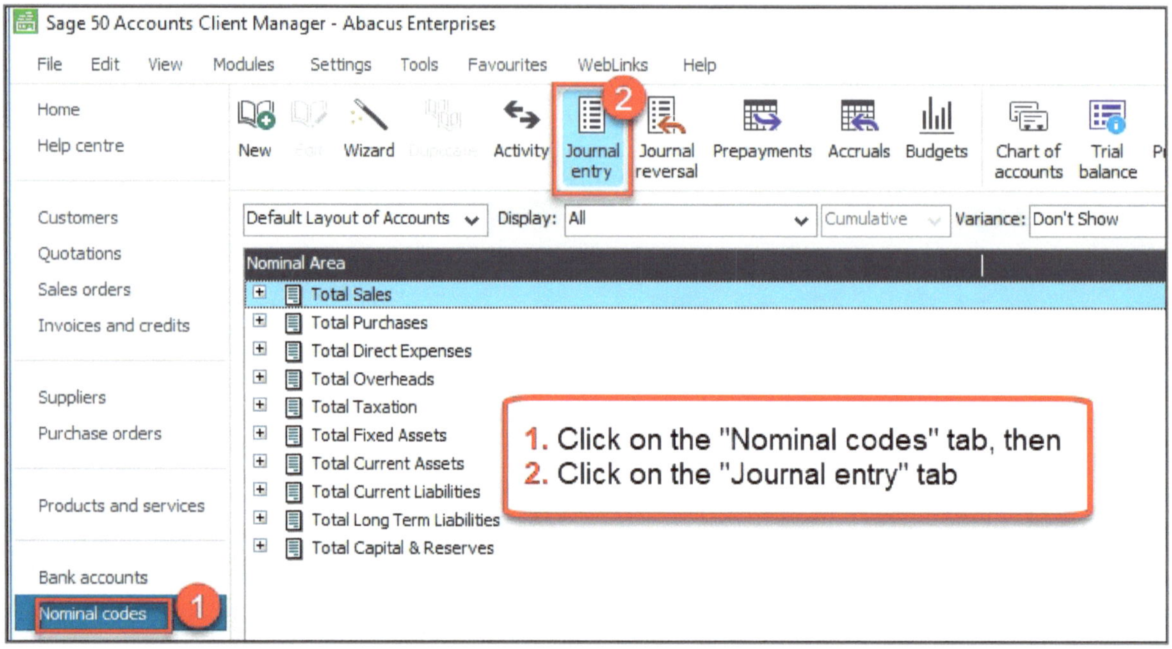

Fig. 192

The journal entry window appears similar to figure 193 below.

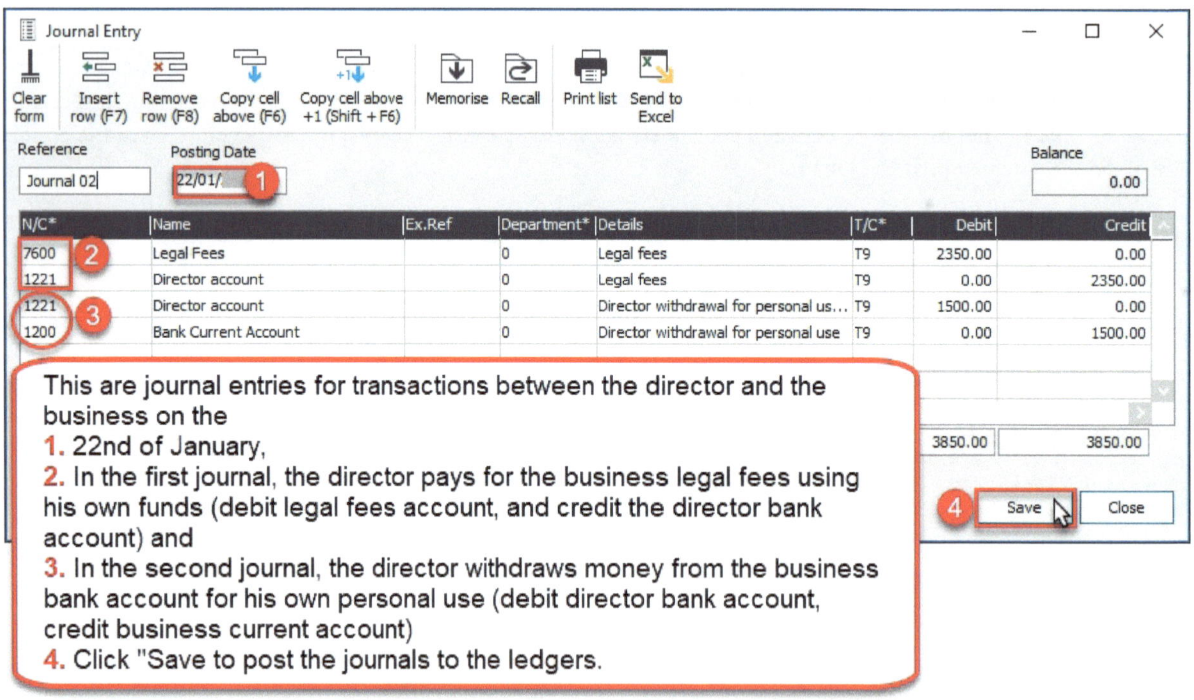

Fig. 193

"Idle/lazy hands bring poverty; diligent hands bring wealth".

Proverbs 104 CJB

TASK 11: HOW TO POST PAYROLL JOURNALS

Terry has decided that effective from the month of January, all staff will be paid in arrears. That means, salary for January will be paid in February, February salary will be paid in March and so on and so forth.

Here is the report form the payroll bureau for January payroll.

Net pay report.

Date : 31st January

Time : 15:19:26

Abacus Enterprises

Payment Summary History Part 1 - By Date

Page : 1 of 1

Employee Reference From : 1 | Payment Period : All | Processing Date From : 06/01/

Employee Reference To : 9999999 | Processing Date To : 05/02/

Process Date: 31/01/ | Tax Week: 43 | Tax Month: 10

E'ee Ref	Employee Name	Gross Pay pre Sacrifice	Gross Pay post Sacrifice	Taxable Gross	P.A.Y.E.	Employee NIC	Employer NIC	Employee Pension	Employer Pension*	Student Loan	SSP	SMP	SPP	SAP	ShPP	Net Pay
1	Z TOMILSON	2,333.33	2,333.33	2,333.33	274.80	198.24	227.98	0.00	0.00	0.00	0.00	0.00	0.00	0.00	0.00	1860.29
2	K PRICHARD	2,083.33	2,083.33	2,083.33	224.80	168.48	193.75	0.00	0.00	0.00	0.00	0.00	0.00	0.00	0.00	1690.05
3	A WILLIAMS	2,083.33	2,083.33	2,083.33	224.80	168.48	193.75	50.00	80.00	0.00	0.00	0.00	0.00	0.00	0.00	1640.05
4	J JONES	2,250.00	2,250.00	2,250.00	0.00	188.64	216.94	50.00	80.00	0.00	0.00	0.00	0.00	0.00	0.00	2011.36
5	C MCFARLANE	1,092.00	1,092.00	1,092.00	218.40	49.44	56.86	0.00	0.00	0.00	0.00	0.00	0.00	0.00	0.00	824.16
	Process Date Total	9,841.99	9,841.99	9,841.99	942.80	773.28	889.28	100.00	160.00	0.00	0.00	0.00	0.00	0.00	0.00	8025.91
	Report Total	9,841.99	9,841.99	9,841.99	942.80	773.28	889.28	100.00	160.00	0.00	0.00	0.00	0.00	0.00	0.00	8025.91

For salary sacrifice pension schemes this is the employer contribution including the amount sacrificed by the employee.

Fig. 178

To record this in Sage 50 Accounts, it would be easier to fill out wages posting document with the figures from the payroll report, then use that posting document to then enter the details to Sage 50 Accounts.

Wages posting document				
		Nominal code (Sage 50)	Debit	Credit
DR	Gross pay due to employees	7000	9,841.99	
DR	Gross pay due to Director	7001	0.00	
DR	Statutory Sick pay	7010	0.00	
DR	Statutory Maternity Pay	7011	0.00	
DR	Employees NI contribution **by the employer**	7006	889.28	
DR	Director's NI contribution **by the employer**	7012	0.00	
DR	Employers pension contribution for employees	7007	160.00	
CR	Net payment to employees	2220		8,025.91
CR	PAYE tax deducted	2210		942.80
CR	National Insurance (NI) – employees	2211		773.28
CR	National Insurance (NI) – employer	2211		889.28
CR	Pension fund liability (employer contribution)	2230		160.00
CR	Pension fund liability (employee contribution)	2230		100.00
		TOTAL	10,891.27	10,891.27

Use this wage posting document to record the journal in Sage 50 Accounts. Click on "Nominal codes" then click on "Journal entry" and a window similar to figure 194 will appear.
Only enter the nominal codes for items that have a value more over 0.

Payroll Accounting Process

Payroll Accounting is the method of accounting for payroll. Payroll is the aggregate expenditure on wages and salaries incurred by a business in an accounting period. It can also refer to a listing of employees giving details of their pay.

Payroll includes the gross pay due to the employee and employer taxes. The gross pay is divided into net pay actually received by the employee and deductions made from the gross pay for employee taxes and other deductions such as pension contributions, healthcare contributions, and union subscriptions.

In payroll accounting it is important to distinguish between **employee** taxes which are deducted from the employees' gross pay and are therefore paid by the employee, and **employer** taxes which are in addition to the gross pay and paid by the employers.

Both payroll taxes are usually collected by the employer and paid over to the relevant tax authority.

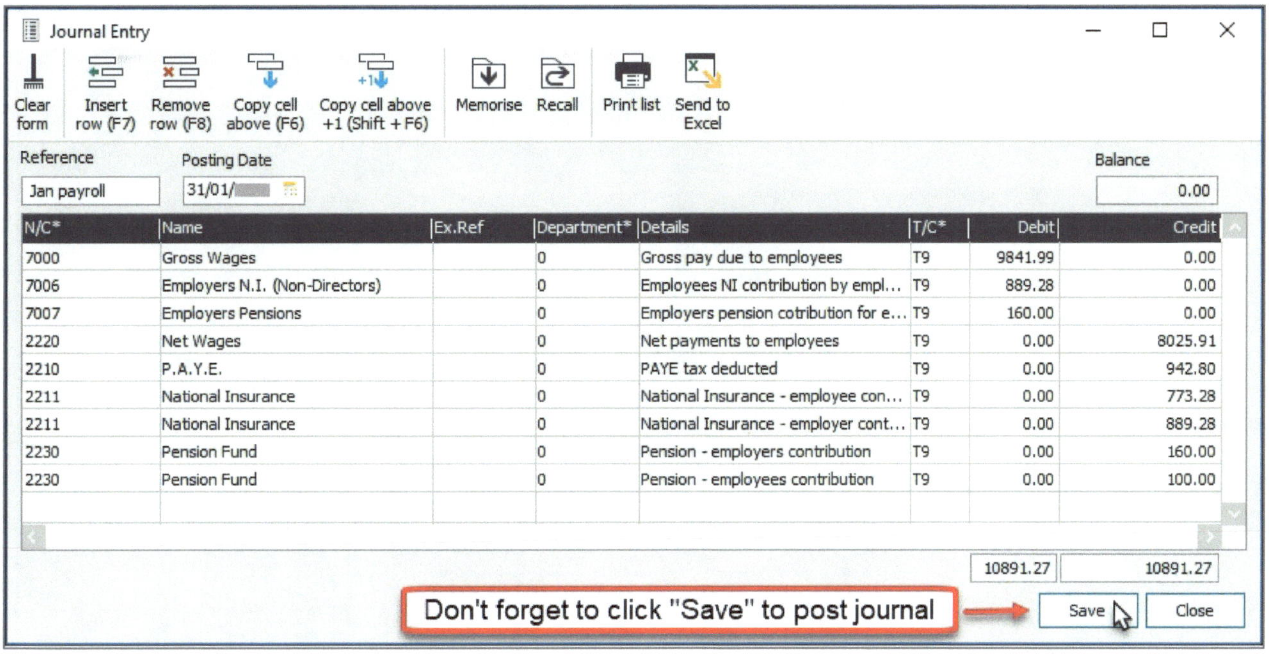

N/C*	Name	Ex.Ref	Department*	Details	T/C*	Debit	Credit
7000	Gross Wages		0	Gross pay due to employees	T9	9841.99	0.00
7006	Employers N.I. (Non-Directors)		0	Employees NI contribution by empl...	T9	889.28	0.00
7007	Employers Pensions		0	Employers pension cotribution for e...	T9	160.00	0.00
2220	Net Wages		0	Net payments to employees	T9	0.00	8025.91
2210	P.A.Y.E.		0	PAYE tax deducted	T9	0.00	942.80
2211	National Insurance		0	National Insurance - employee con...	T9	0.00	773.28
2211	National Insurance		0	National Insurance - employer cont...	T9	0.00	889.28
2230	Pension Fund		0	Pension - employers contribution	T9	0.00	160.00
2230	Pension Fund		0	Pension - employees contribution	T9	0.00	100.00
						10891.27	10891.27

Fig. 194

At the end of each payroll period, you should update your accounts to include any payments relating to the employees, for example wages, national insurance (NI), PAYE and pension contributions. Posting a salary journal to the Nominal ledger ensures that the relevant profit and loss and balance sheet nominal codes are correctly updated.

When you pay your liabilities, posting bank payments to the balance sheet liability nominal codes ensures that the liabilities are cleared and your bank accounts are reduced by the relevant costs.

Common abbreviations

- *SMP – Statutory Maternity Pay*
- *SPP – Statutory Paternity Pay*
- *SAP – Statutory Adoption Pay*
- *SSP – Statutory Sick Pay*
- *PAYE – Pay As You Earn*
- *NI – National Insurance*

This space is for notes

"Always be reconciled to your strengths and not your fears"
Sterling Libs

TASK 12: HOW TO DO BANK RECONCILIATION IN SAGE 50

Reconciling your bank is simply the process of matching your Sage transactions to those that appear on your bank statement.

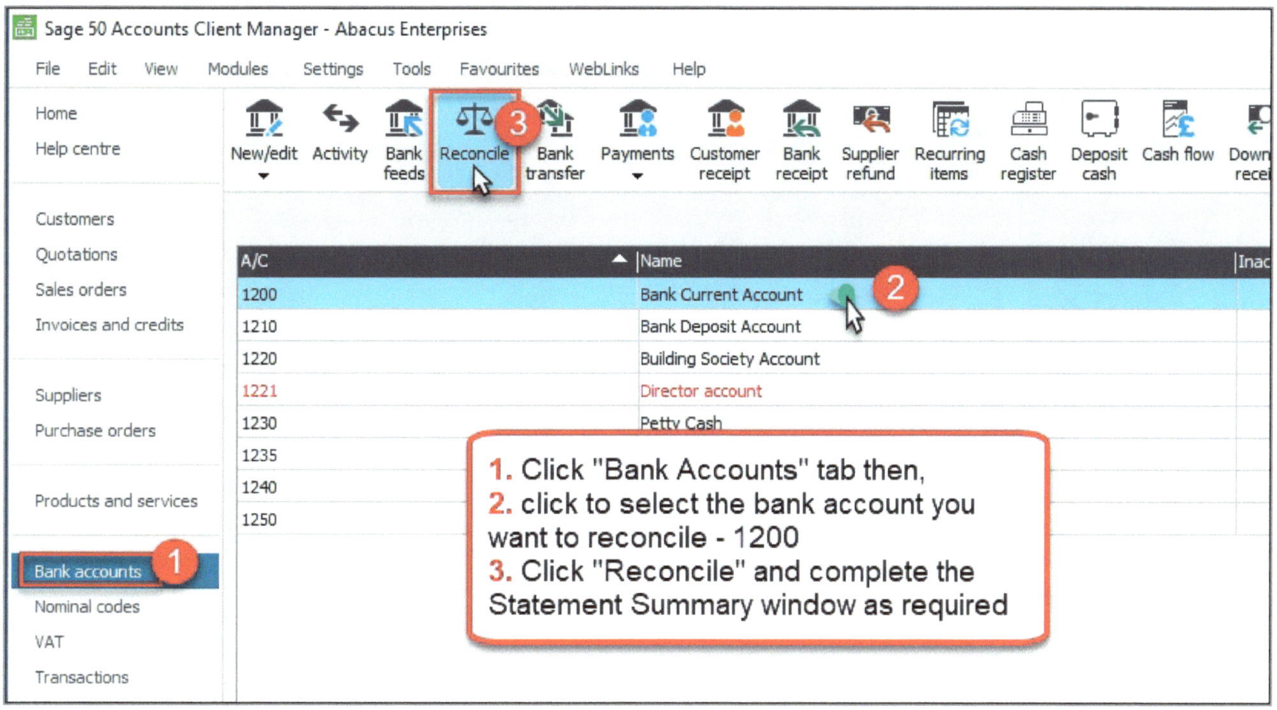

Fig. 195

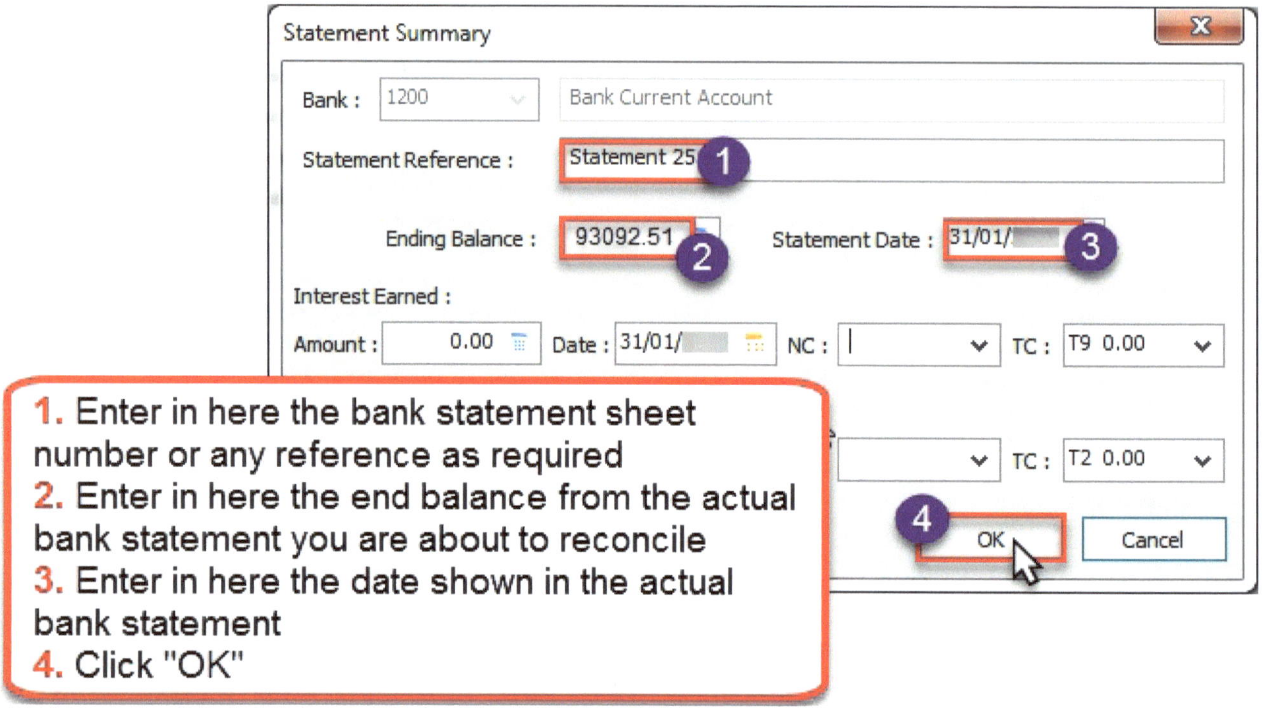

Fig. 196

This space is for notes

"As for those who do have riches in this present world, charge them not to be proud and not to let their hopes rest on the uncertainties of riches but to rest their hopes on God, who richly provides us with all things for our enjoyment. Charge them to do good, to be rich in good deeds, to be generous and ready to share. In this way, they will treasure up for themselves a good foundation for the future, so that they may lay hold of real life"

1 Timothy 6:17-19 CJB

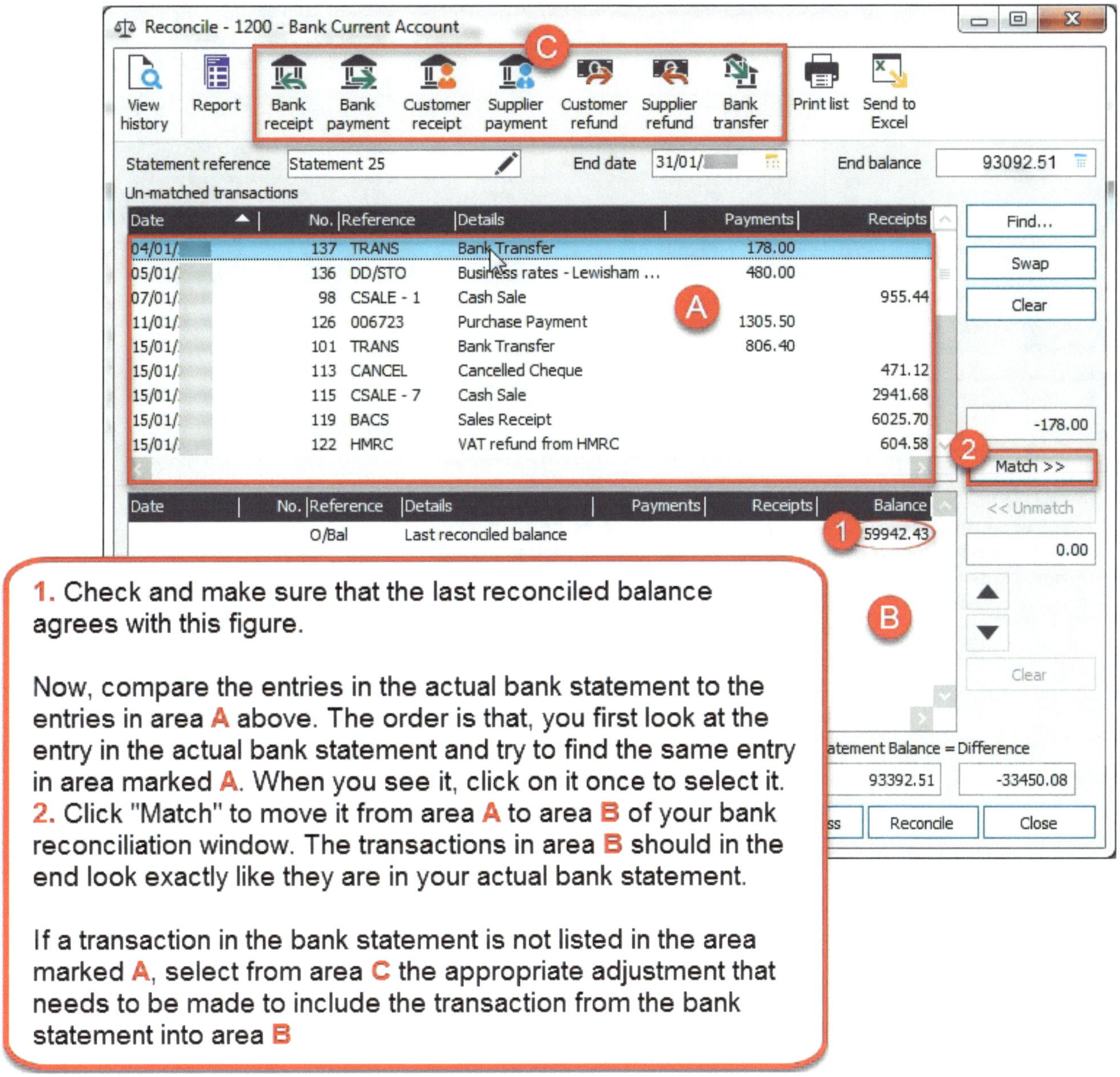

Fig. 197

In this task, **the adjustments you will make during your bank reconciliation process will be for:**

- Bank interest received on the 20th January of £42 *(select bank receipt in the adjustment window)*
- Bank charge on the 25th January for £36 *(select bank payment in the adjustment window)*
- Bank transfer of £300 to the Director bank account in Sage Accounts - Link cash machine withdrawal. *(Select bank transfer in the adjustment window)*

Once complete, check "Matched Balance" and "Statement Balance" are the same, giving a difference of zero. See figure 198 below.

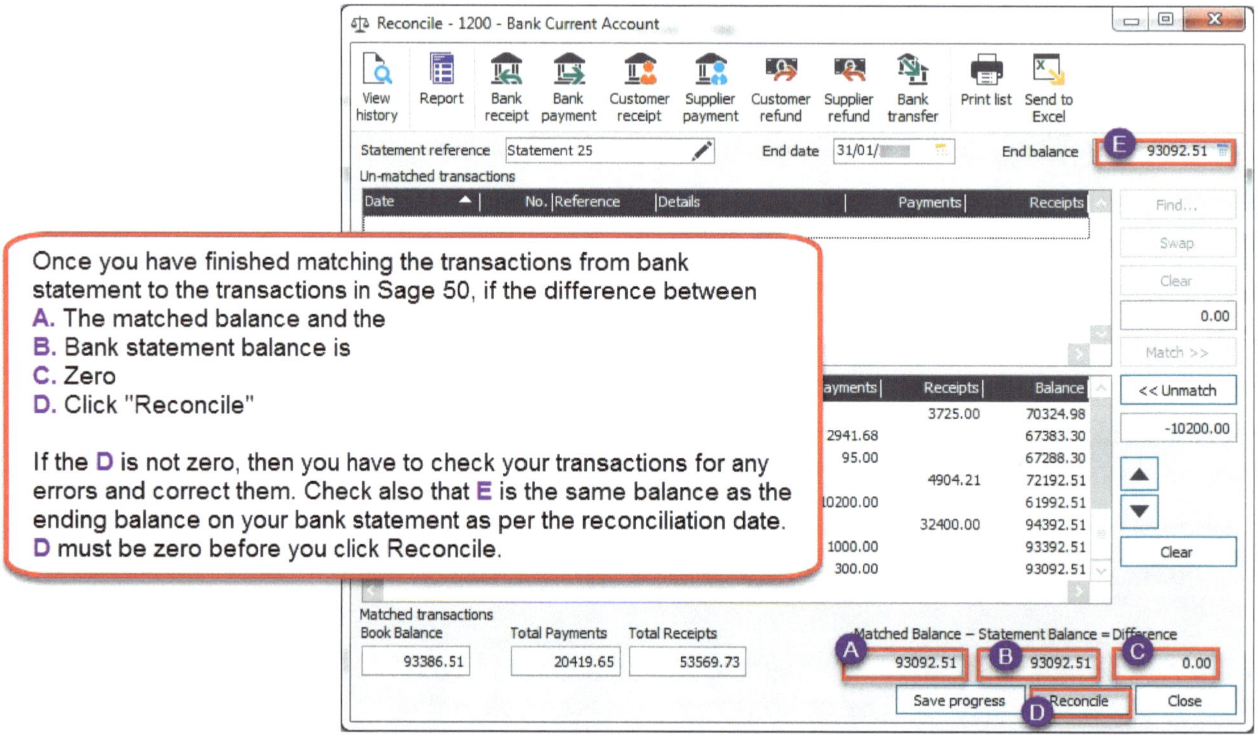

Fig. 198

This space is for notes

"Wealth gotten by worthless means dwindles away, but he who amasses it by hard work will increase it". **Proverbs 13:11**

"Preparation lays a foundation to success"
Sterling Libs

TASK 13: HOW TO PREPARE AND SUBMIT A VAT RETURN IN SAGE 50 ACCOUNTS

When you register for VAT, HMRC will advise you of the VAT periods, you'll submit for. If you submit quarterly your VAT period falls into one of the following staggers:

- March - June - September - December
- April - July - October - January
- May-August - November – February

If necessary, you can apply to have your VAT period end pattern changed to a different pattern, or request to submit monthly or annual VAT Returns.

Calculating the VAT Return doesn't affect your transactions in Sage Accounts, no postings are made to your nominal codes. This means that you can calculate your VAT Return as many times as necessary. However, when you mark your transactions as being reconciled, this prevents them from being automatically included in a future VAT return calculated in Sage Accounts.

You usually submit a VAT Return to HM Revenue and Customs (HMRC) every 3 months (UK). This period of time is known as your 'accounting period.'

The VAT Return records things for the accounting period like:

- ✓ your total sales and purchases
- ✓ the amount of VAT you owe
- ✓ the amount of VAT you can reclaim
- ✓ what your VAT refund from HMRC is

You must submit a VAT Return even if you have no VAT to pay or reclaim.

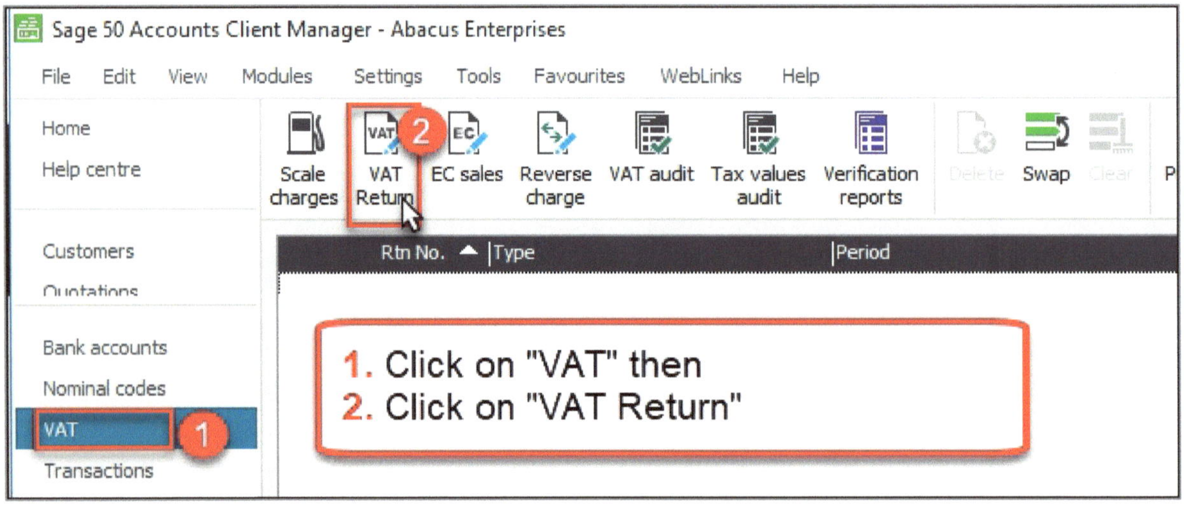

Fig. 199

A VAT Return window appears after step 2 in the figure above. See figure 200 below.

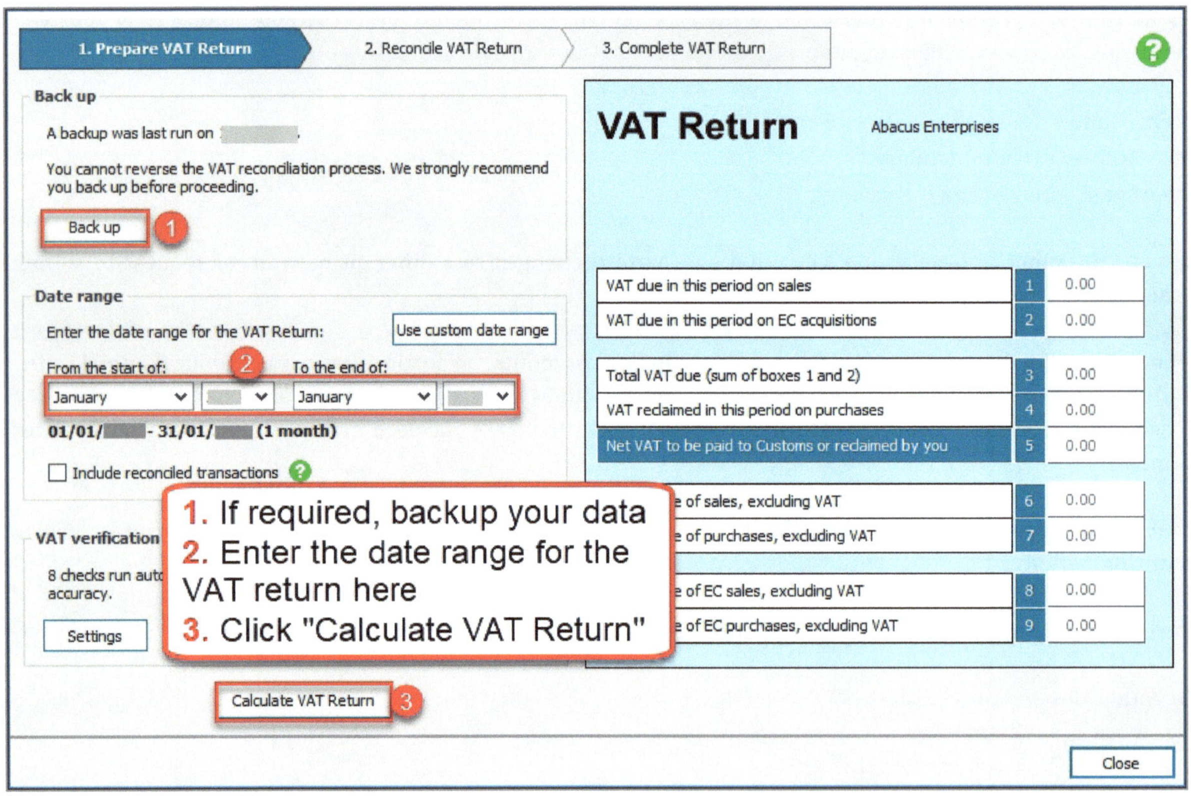

Fig. 200

When you click on "Calculate VAT Return" – step 3 as illustrated in the figure above, if there are any transactions dated before the date range (Step 2 as illustrated in the figure above) which haven't been reconciled, the earlier reconciled transactions window appears.
To include these transactions, click OK, if you don't want to include these transactions, click ignore

If, however there are no transactions dated before the date range selected, a figure similar to the window below will appear.

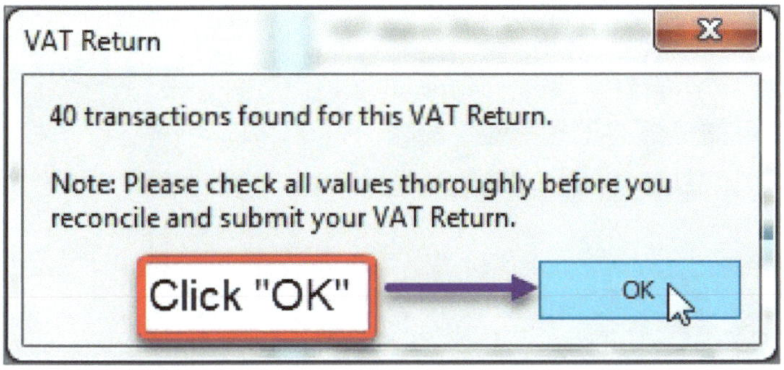

Fig. 201

After you click OK as illustrated in the figure above, you then move to the reconciliation window

Reconciliation:

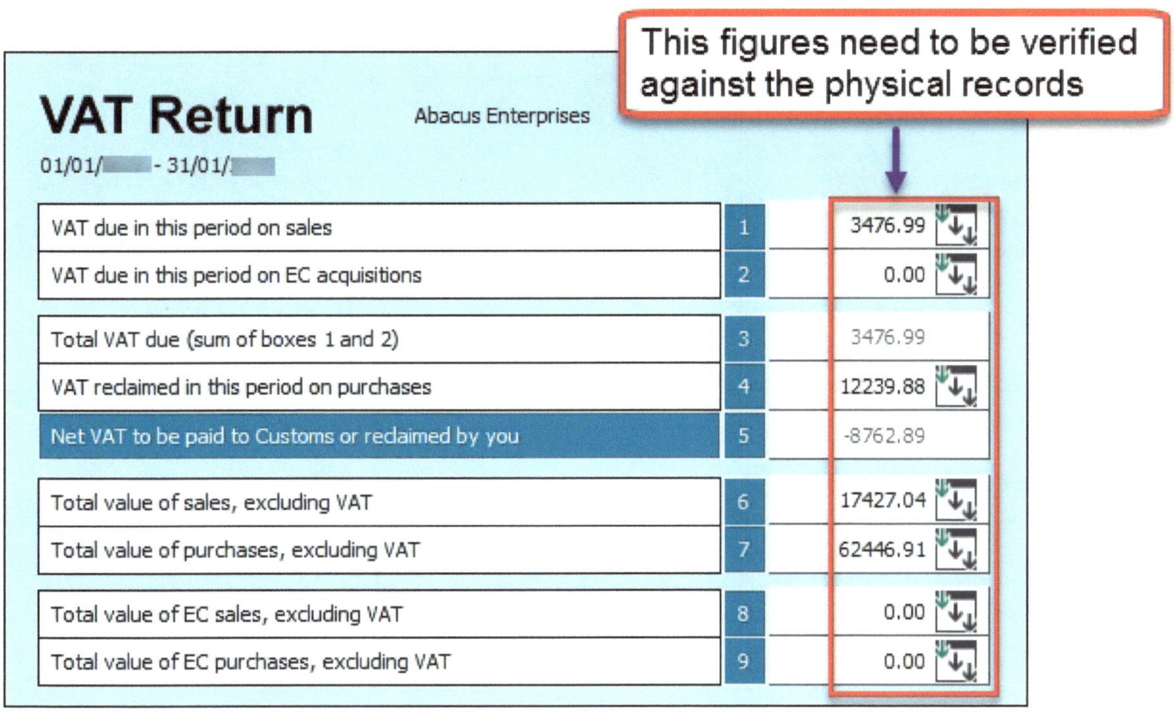

Fig. 202

Reconciling the figures to the source documents:

Click on the three down facing arrows in box 1(at the right of box 1), and a VAT Breakdown window will appear – see figure below

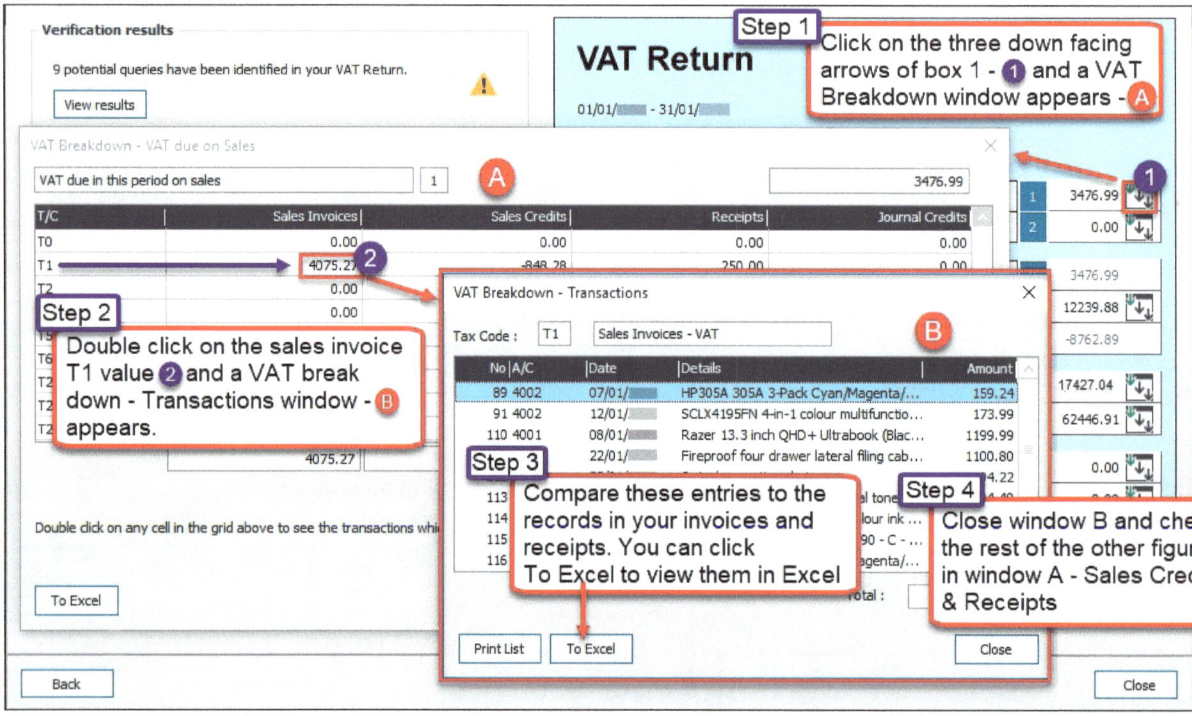

Fig. 203

You will need to check and reconcile all the figures in windows B (as illustrated in the figure above) to the original source documents and do the same for figures in box 4, 6, 7, 8 and 9 of the VAT Return as well.

After checking the figures in each box (1-9) remember to close the excel document, window B and window A.

If you require to make any adjustments to any values of the VAT return, see inset instruction as illustrated in figure 204 on the next page.

Only follow instructions in figure 204 on the next page if you have some adjustments to make otherwise just go to figure 205 for the next steps in the VAT return preparation

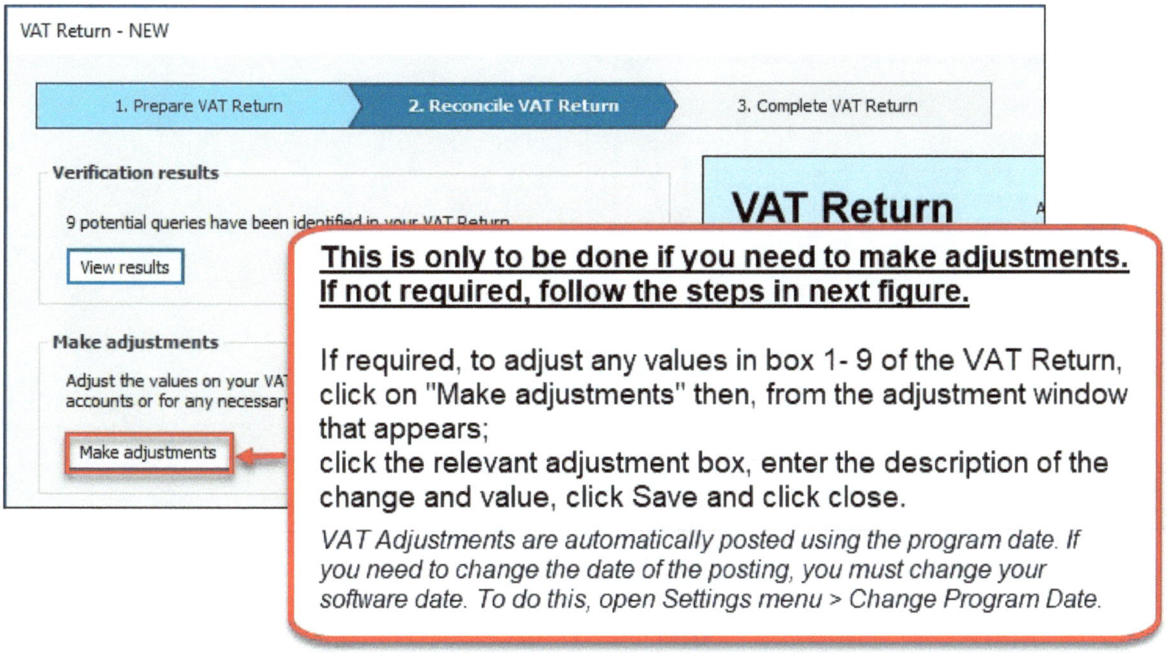

Fig. 204

Final step in Reconciliation:

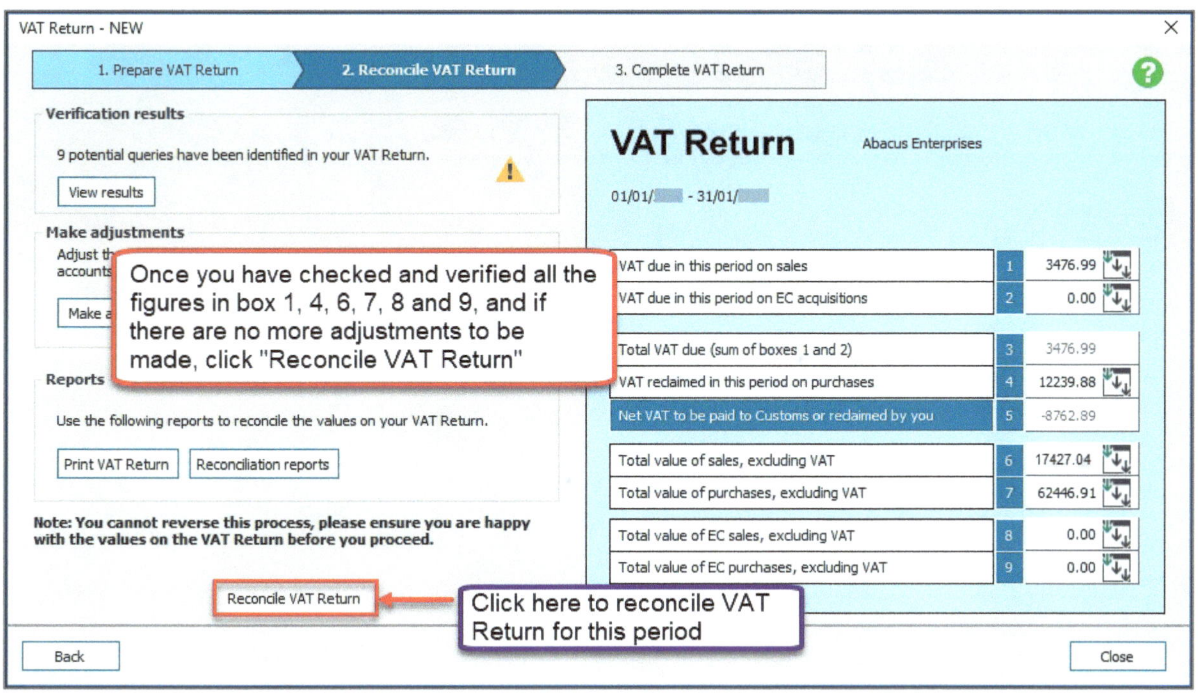

Fig. 205

Once you click on "Reconcile VAT Return" as illustrated in the figure above, a confirmation window appears – see below.

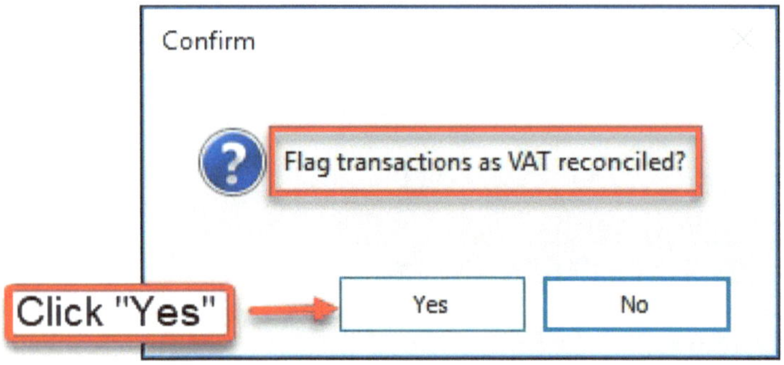

Fig. 206

Once you click Yes as illustrated in the figure above, the reconciliation progress bar appears and the eventually a reconciled VAT return is displayed. See figure below.

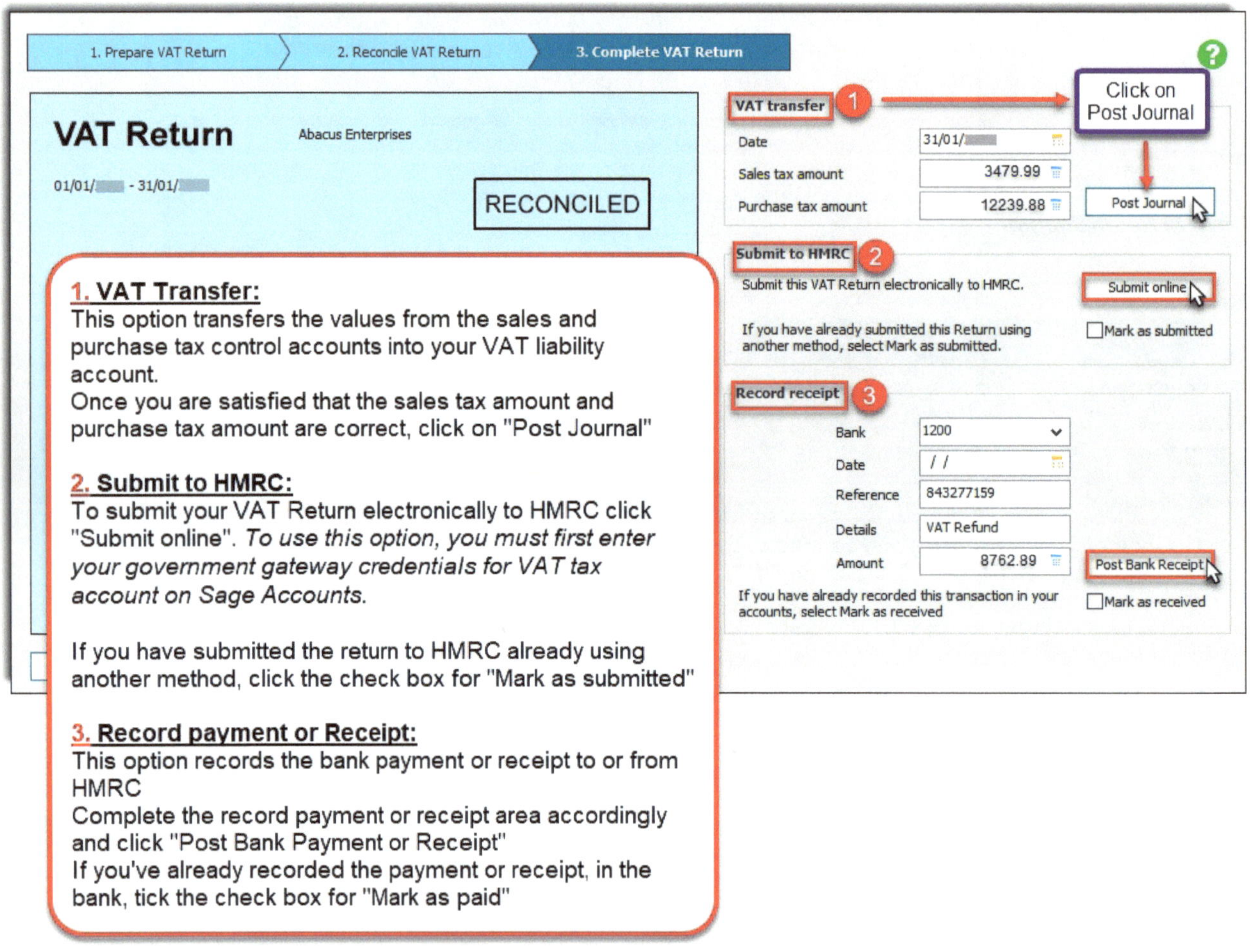

Fig. 207

Printing the VAT reports:

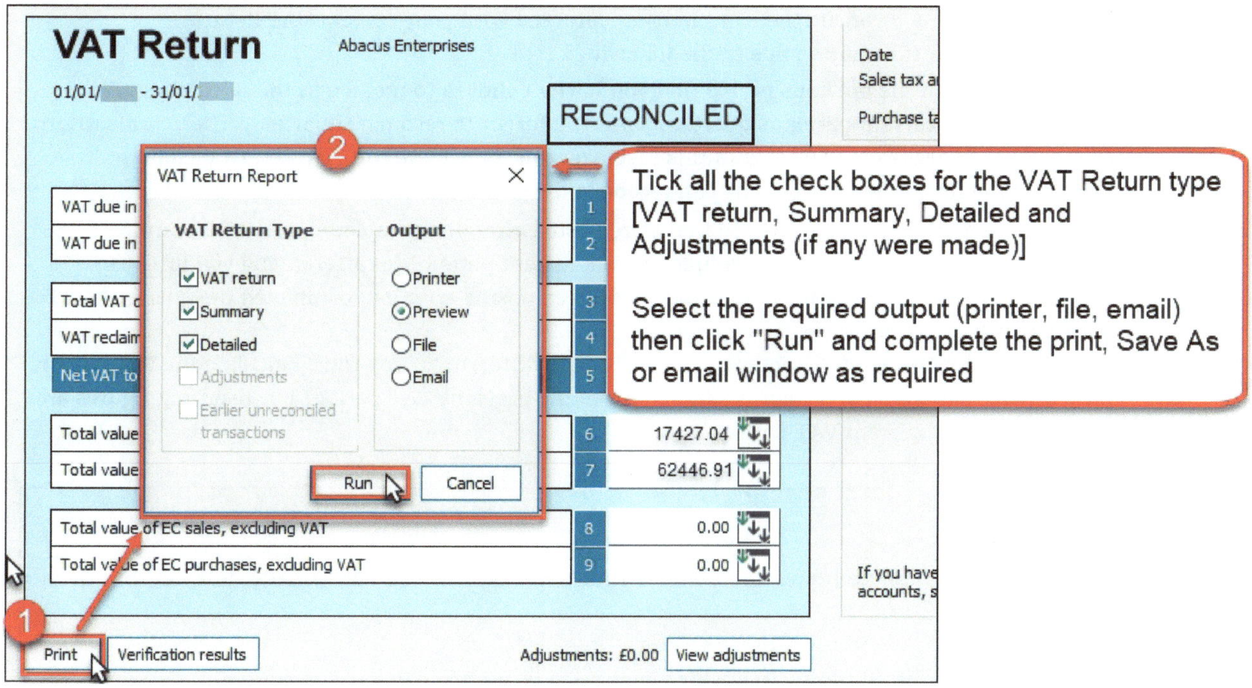

Fig. 208

Please note that once you have reconciled your VAT Return, it isn't possible to undo a VAT reconciliation. To correct this, you need to restore a backup taken before the VAT Return was reconciled.

Brief VAT knowledge base.

What's the difference between zero-rated and exempt items?

Zero-rated items are goods on which the Government charge VAT but the rate is currently set to zero. The goods covered by this classification are items such as children's clothes and footwear, water, basic foods, books and newspapers.

Exempt items are goods on which no VAT is paid or charged, but which still need to be recorded on the VAT Return. The goods covered by this classification are items such as land, postal services, health services, betting and gaming.

I forgot to reconcile my last VAT Return. What should I do?

If you didn't reconcile the transactions on your previous VAT Return, the next time that you calculate your VAT Return a message appears informing you that Sage Accounts has found some unreconciled transactions from before the specified period.

If these transactions relate to a previously unreconciled VAT Return

1. Calculate the VAT Return from the previous period, then check it against the VAT Return that you submitted to HMRC.
2. If the figures are the same > reconcile the transactions > proceed with your current VAT Return.
3. If the figures are different, this may be due to the following:
    - Transactions from the previous period that you haven't chosen to include in the calculation. For example, if your current period is quarter 4, and you forgot to reconcile quarter 3. These transactions may be late entries from quarter 2. In this case, you can recalculate the VAT Return including these figures. If the totals then match, you can reconcile the transactions.
    - Transactions from the current period that were posted after you completed the VAT Return, but are dated in the previous period. For example, if your current period is quarter 4, and you forgot to reconcile quarter 3, these transactions may have been posted after you completed the quarter 3 VAT Return using a quarter 3 date.

      If you don't know which transactions are causing the differences, you must calculate the VAT Return for both VAT periods then deduct the figures from the previous VAT period. The resulting figures are the values for the current VAT period.

Final VAT Returns.

If you cancel your VAT registration, you have to submit a final VAT Return. You can usually do this from most accounting software.

HMRC will send you a paper version to complete if your registration is cancelled due to insolvency.

This space is for notes

"The Kingdom of Heaven is like a treasure hidden in a field. A man found it, hid it again, then in great joy went and sold everything he owned, and bought that field".
Matthew 13:44 CJB

TASK 14: HOW TO DO MONTHEND ACCOUNTING PROCEDURES

Introduction to month end

There are three steps to take to perform the end-of-the-month accounting process successfully. They are:

Description of the key steps	*What to do at each stage (the tasks)*
Key step 1: Checking the general ledger accounts for errors & making the necessary corrections	• *Correct the general ledger account errors including mispostings and inaccuracies.*
Key step 2: Doing Adjustments and Reconciliations	• *Financial adjustments, e.g. interest payments adjustments, prepayments, accruals and depreciation* • *Control account reconciliations: Debtors' control account, Creditors' control account, VAT control account, Bank account, Wages account etc.* • *Balance sheet reconciliation (Reconciliation of the Assets, Liabilities, Equity & Reserves)* • *Calculations of closing balances of the accounts after adjustments & reconciliations*
Key step 3: Reporting to senior management	• *Producing a profit & Loss statement and other various management reports if necessary.*

The accounting process can differ slightly from one business to another based on variances in the chart of accounts, revenue and expense recognition, and cost centre breakdown.

Despite these differences, the overall monthly closing process is the same. Following the same standard procedures to close the books each month will help ensure consistent and accurate reporting.

Let's now have a look at how the month end procedures stated in the table above are performed.

How to make nominal account checks & corrections

At this stage:

- ✓ First, establish a closing date by which all expenses and revenue must be posted.
- ✓ Then communicate the closing date to everyone who has access to modify the ledger and
- ✓ Finally lock the ledgers for the month/period as of the date communicated, prohibiting any further changes to the ledgers for that period.

After that,

- ✓ Produce or generate the trial balance report from your accounting software
- ✓ Review the balances in each of the nominal accounts in the Trial balance report to identify any anomalies from what is expected and correct any errors (arithmetical, principle, etc.)
- ✓ Review the transaction details for any accounts you are uncertain of and note any adjustments that need to be made.

To generate your trial balance in Sage Accounts, click on "Nominal codes" tab, then click on "Trial balance."

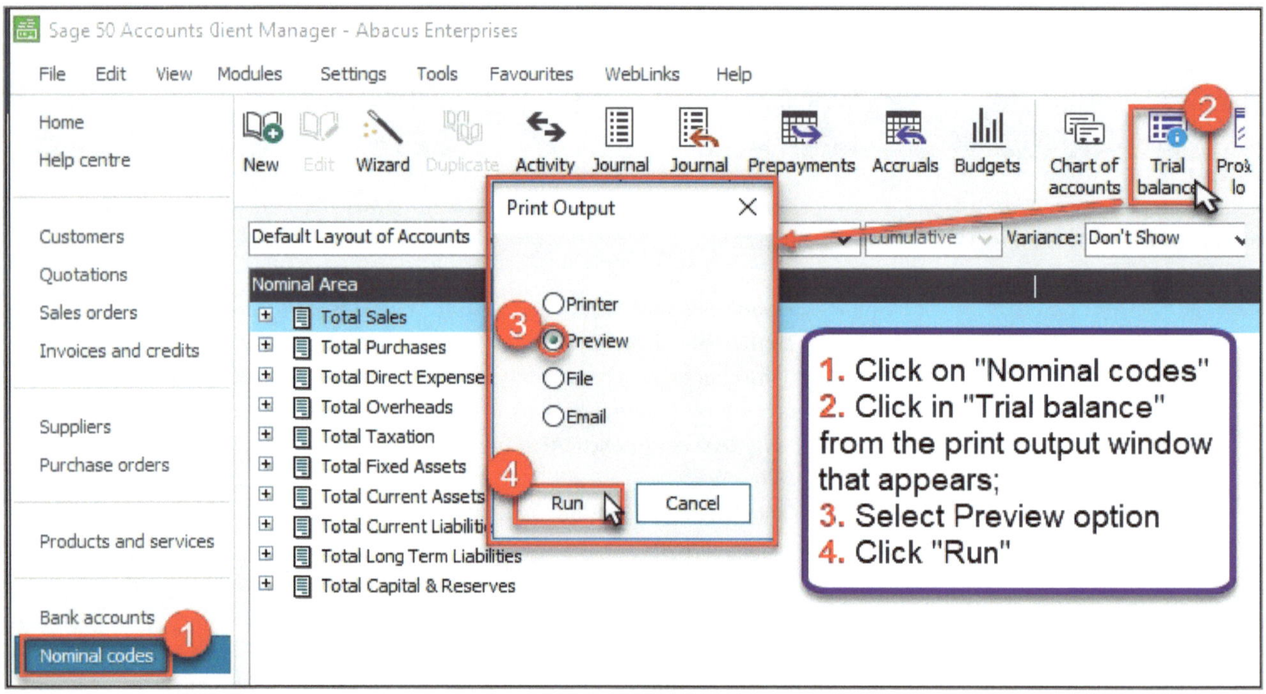

Fig. 209

Click "OK" in the "Criteria for Period Trial Balance" window that appears and the Trial balance report will be generated.

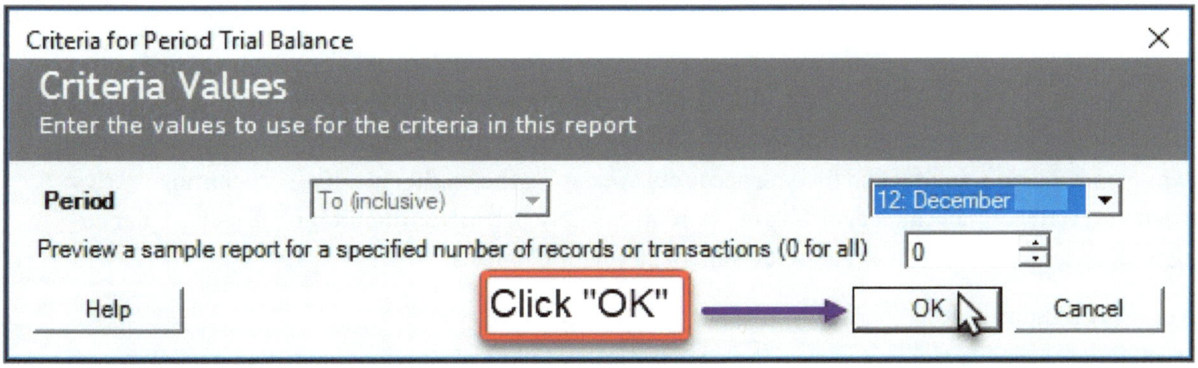

Fig. 210

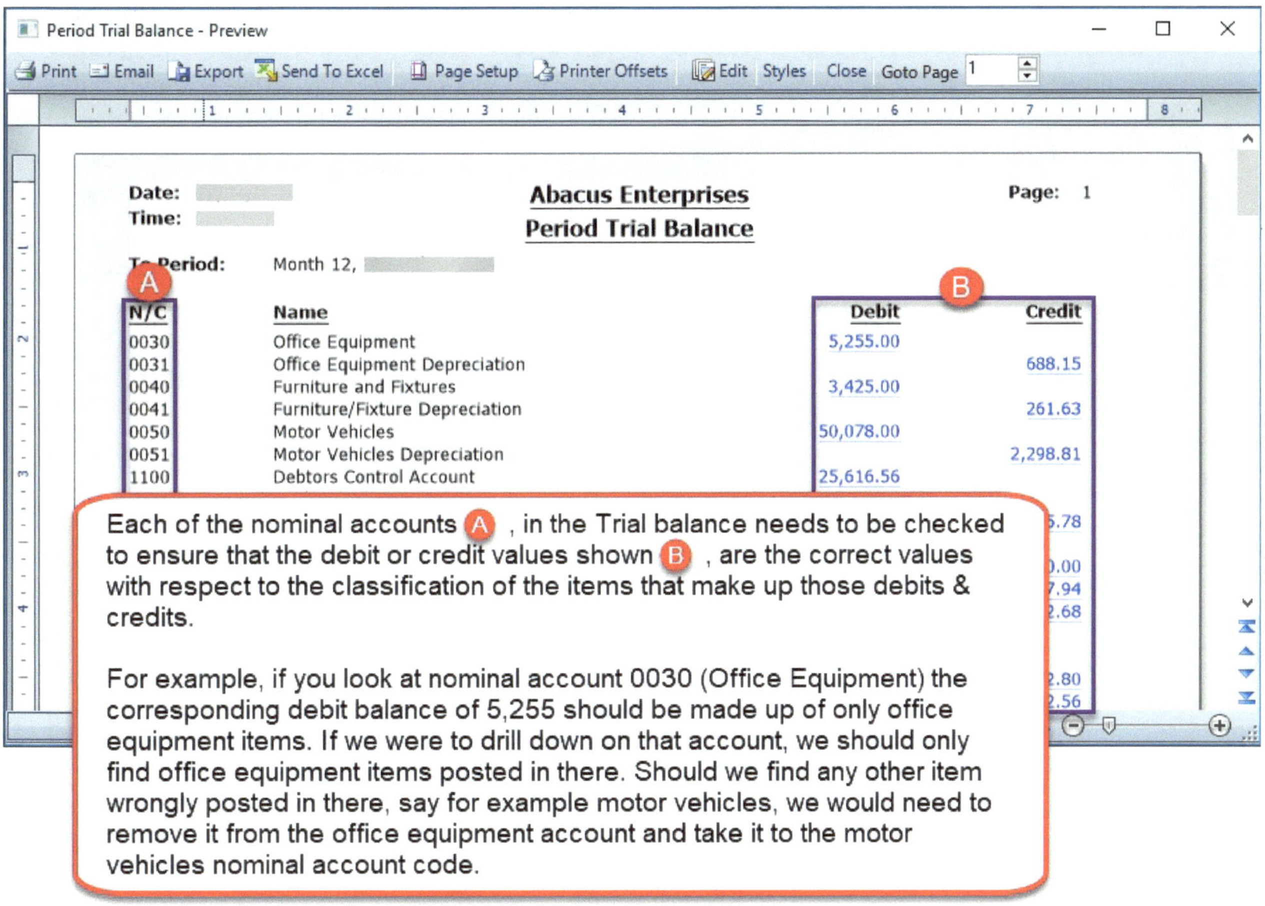

Fig. 211

If you identify any transaction that needs to be corrected or moved to the correct nominal account, make a note of that transaction (get the transaction number) then edit or amend that transaction via transactions. See figure 212 below.

A Trial Balance is a list of closing balances of ledger accounts on a certain date. It is usually prepared at the end of an accounting period to assist in the drafting of financial statements. Ledger balances are segregated into debit balances and credit balances. Asset and expense accounts appear on the debit side of the trial balance whereas liabilities, capital and income accounts appear on the credit side. If all accounting entries are recorded correctly and all the ledger balances are accurately extracted, the total of all debit balances appearing in the trial balance must equal to the sum of all credit balances.

Purpose of a Trial Balance

- Trial Balance acts as the first step in the preparation of financial statements. It is a working paper that accountants use as a basis while preparing financial statements.
- Trial balance ensures that for every debit entry recorded, a corresponding credit entry has been recorded in the books in accordance with the double entry concept of accounting. If the totals of the trial balance do not agree, the differences may be investigated and resolved before financial statements are prepared. Rectifying basic accounting errors can be a much lengthy task after the financial statements have been prepared because of the changes that would be required to correct the financial statements.
- Trial balance ensures that the account balances are accurately extracted from accounting ledgers.
- Trail balance assists in the identification and rectification of errors.

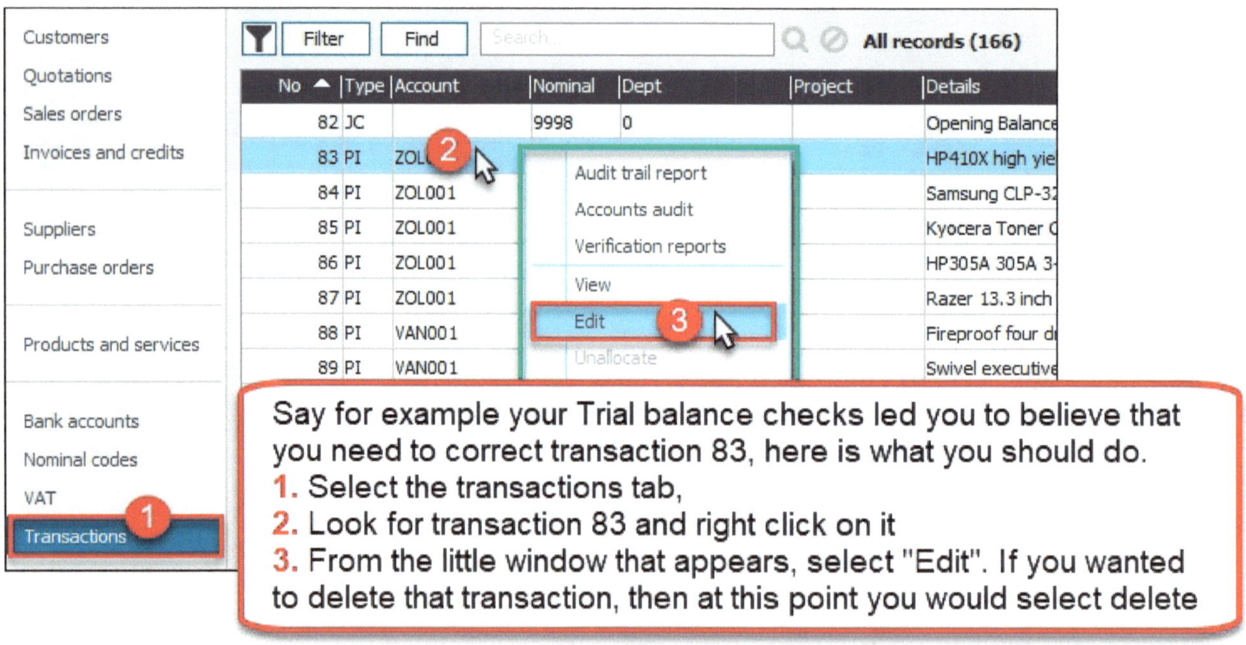

Fig. 212

After step 3 as illustrated in the figure above, a window showing the details of that transaction appears.

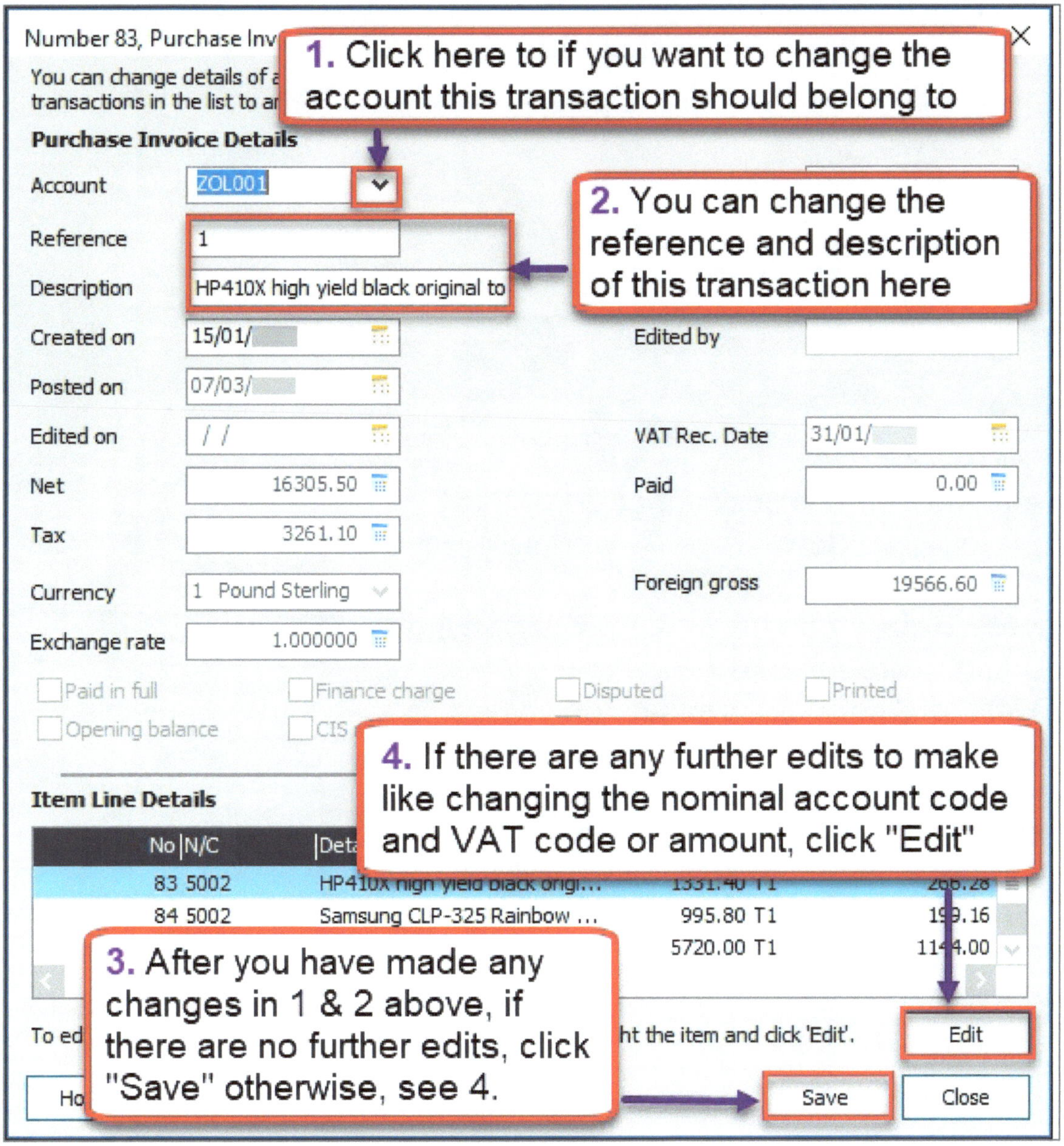

Fig. 213

If you click Edit, an edit window similar to figure 124 on the next page will appear.

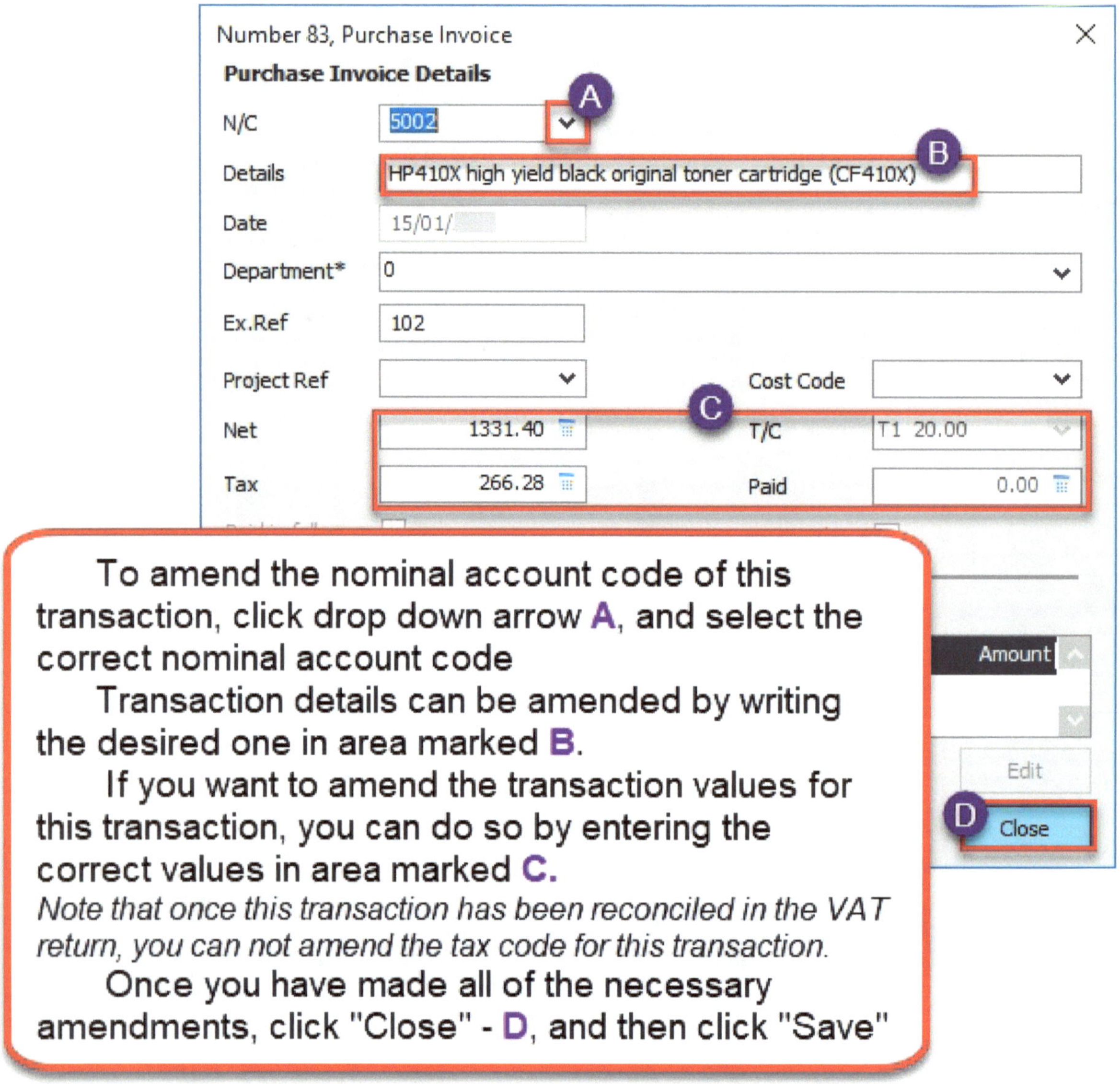

Fig. 214

That's how you amend or move transactions around in Sage Accounts.

This space is for notes

Making adjustments in the accounts

The common adjusting entries that affect the balance sheet are usually; prepayments, accruals, depreciation & amortisation

Let's look at how you should record each of them:

How to adjust Prepayments

A prepaid expense is an advance payment for a future expense that is recorded as an asset at the time of payment, usually within the year or accounting period. All such costs cover a certain period, e.g. a rent purchase invoice is normally billed a quarter in advance. So, any given rent invoice will cover a period of 3 months. Similarly, business rates are billed in advance and cover a period of 12 months.

Given this, we need to calculate and see how much of the overheads relate to the current month/period and how much again relates to the future. If any of the overhead costs that cover future periods have also been posted to the income statement, you should take them out of the income statement for that month/period and post them to the balance sheet as an 'Overhead Prepayment'.

For example, rent invoice from Office Space Today (invoice number 2308-2847 dated 25th January) was paid on the 28th January. This invoice was for the period of February to April. In that case, the payment made on the 28th January is a prepayment, and you now need to make that adjustment for January month end.

Original Entry when invoice was recorded (Rent & internet charges portion):

Nominal Account	Account Type	DEBIT	CREDIT
Rent	Profit & Loss	5,539.55	
Internet Charges	Profit & Loss	180.00	
Purchase Tax (Input VAT)	Balance Sheet	1,143.91	
Office Space Today (Creditor)	Balance Sheet		6,863.46

Original Entry when payment was made:

Nominal Account	Account Type	DEBIT	CREDIT
Office Space Today (Creditor)	Balance Sheet	6,863.46	
Director Bank account	Balance Sheet		6,863.46

Overhead Prepayment Journal to be made on 31 January (prepayment for February to April – 3 months)

N/C	Name	Details	T/C	Debit	Credit
1103	Prepayment	Rent prepayment adjustment	T9	5,539.55	
7100	Rent	Rent prepayment adjustment	T9		5,539.55
1103	Prepayment	Internet Charges prepayment	T9	180.00	
7551	Internet Charges	Internet Charges prepayment	T9		180.00

Post this prepayment using journal – see figure below.

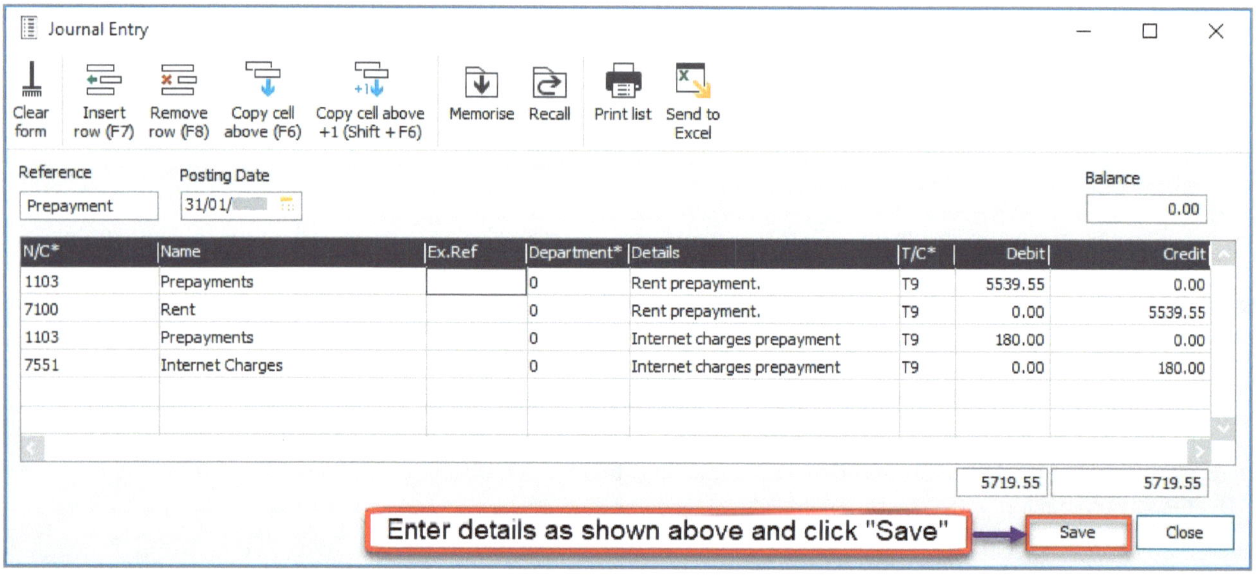

N/C*	Name	Ex.Ref	Department*	Details	T/C*	Debit	Credit
1103	Prepayments		0	Rent prepayment.	T9	5539.55	0.00
7100	Rent		0	Rent prepayment.	T9	0.00	5539.55
1103	Prepayments		0	Internet charges prepayment	T9	180.00	0.00
7551	Internet Charges		0	Internet charges prepayment	T9	0.00	180.00
						5719.55	5719.55

Fig. 215

At the end of February, you will have to reduce the rent prepayment asset by a third (being one month of rent expense incurred). Debit the rent account in the profit and loss and credit the rent prepayment account in the balance sheet

The first adjustment we have looked at is the "Overhead prepayment" adjustment. Let's look at the next adjustment – Accruals.

How to adjust Accruals

The word accrual could mean a transaction in which:

- ✓ Revenue is earned, but no payment has been received – Accrued revenue (an asset), or
- ✓ An expense is incurred, but no payment has been paid – Accrued expense (a liability).

Accrued revenues always create a need to record a new receivable (Debit accounts receivable, and credit revenue/sales).

Let's first of all in this accruals task begin by recording the accrued expense.

In the case of Abacus Enterprises, at the end of January, you realised two issues:

Casual wages for one of the drivers paid on an hourly basis has not yet been paid. His total outstanding hours are 60 hours at an hourly rate of £20 per hour

Post this transaction using a journal – see figure 216 below.

N/C	Name	Details	T/C	Debit	Credit
7005	Casual wages	Casual wages accrual	T9	1,200	
2109	Accruals	Casual wages accrual	T9		1,200

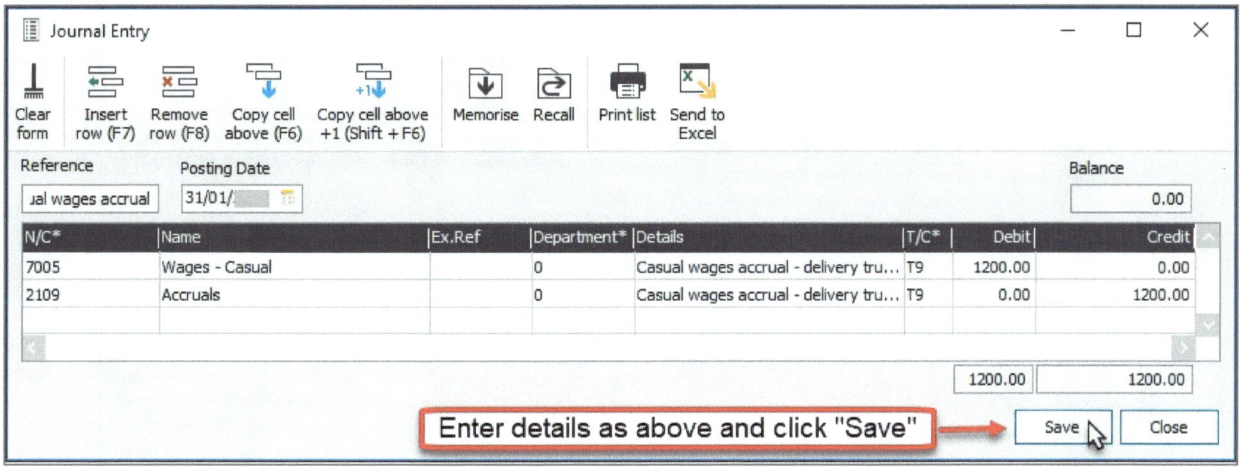

Fig. 216

You also found out that a sale of 2 HP LaserJet printers P2035 to Peacock Interiors on the 23rd January has not been recorded in the books.

Solution: Raise a new invoice to record this transaction. ***Click on "Invoices and Credits" tab>then click on "New invoice">*** then fill out the product invoice window with details as shown in the figure below

This space is for notes

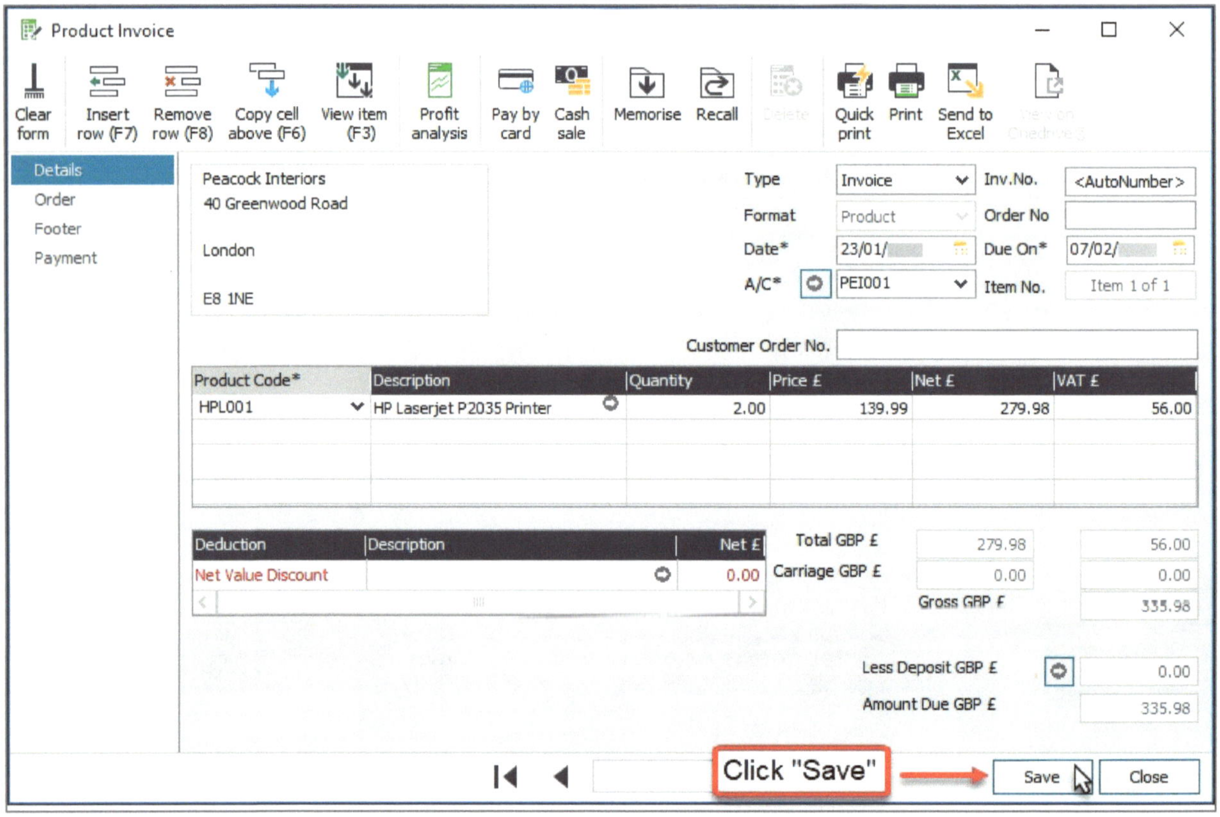

Fig. 217

Remember to click update to post the invoice into the ledgers. *Select the invoice you have just created from the "Invoice and credits" section, then click "Update ledgers".*

How to process an adjustment for Depreciation

Depreciation is the process of allocating the cost of plant and equipment assets into expense, during their estimated useful lives, in a systematic and rational way.

In accounting, depreciation means a process of *matching the expense against revenues.* The purpose is to record how much of the original cost of the asset is being used up each period as the asset helps the business to generate revenue. *This has nothing to do with whatever value an asset could be sold for.*

You have already created the fixed asset register at the beginning of this work experience at the setup stage.
What you do need to do now is add the asset (BMW bought for the sales manager on the 30th January) into the fixed asset register).

Click on "Fixed Assets" then click on "New" – see figure 218 on the next page.

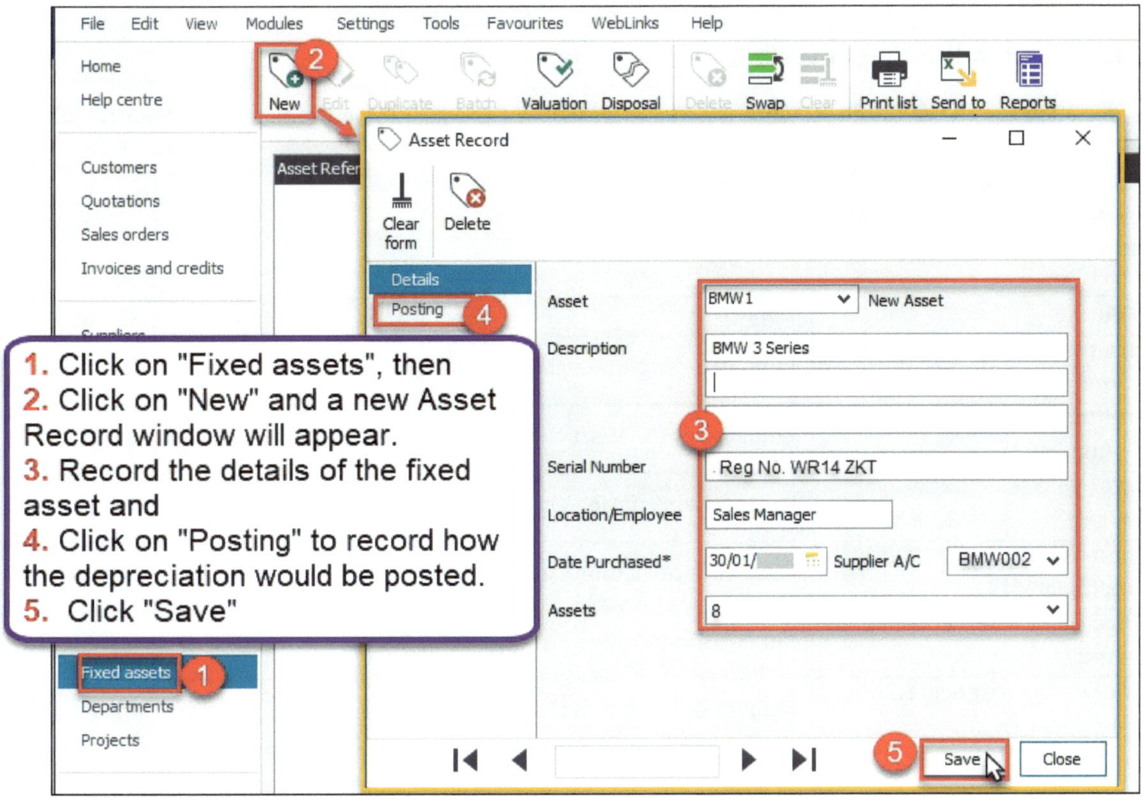

Fig. 218

After step 4 as illustrated in the figure above, the posting section of the Asset record is now ready to be filled.

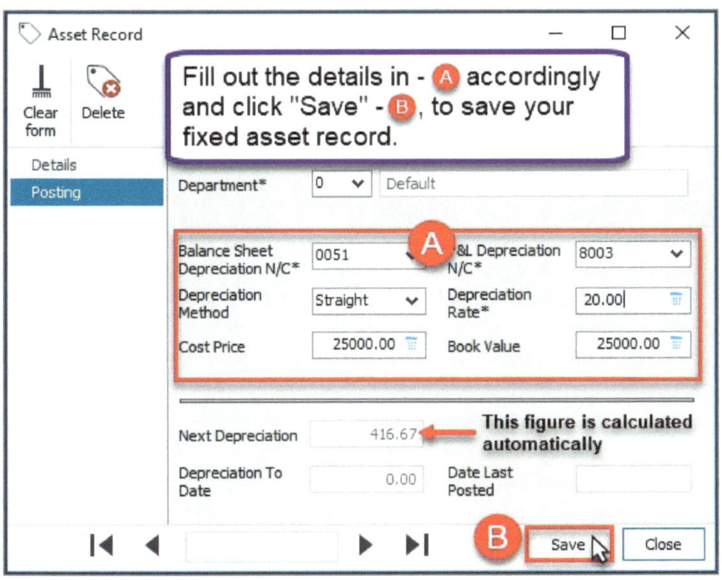

Fig. 219

Making a Depreciation adjusting entry:

Calculate the depreciation for all the fixed assets for the Month of January and post them to the ledgers. Your calculation should yield the following depreciation values:
Furniture and Fixtures: - 40.81
Motor Vehicles: - £208.98
Office Equipment: - £62.63

N/C	Name	Details	T/C	Debit	Credit
8002	Furniture/fittings depreciation charge	January depreciation charge	T9	40.81	
0041	Furniture/fittings depreciation (accumulated)	January depreciation charge	T9		40.81
8003	Motor Vehicle depreciation charge	January depreciation charge	T9	208.98	
0051	Motor Vehicle depreciation (accumulated)	January depreciation charge	T9		208.98
8004	Office equipment depreciation Charge	January depreciation charge	T9	62.63	
0031	Office equipment depreciation (accumulated)	January depreciation charge	T9		62.63

Depreciation expense is a noncash adjustment, and you make the adjustment by Debiting depreciation expense – income statement and crediting accumulated depreciation – balance sheet (you can use a journal entry for this)

Now post these depreciation charges using a journal, here are the journal details:

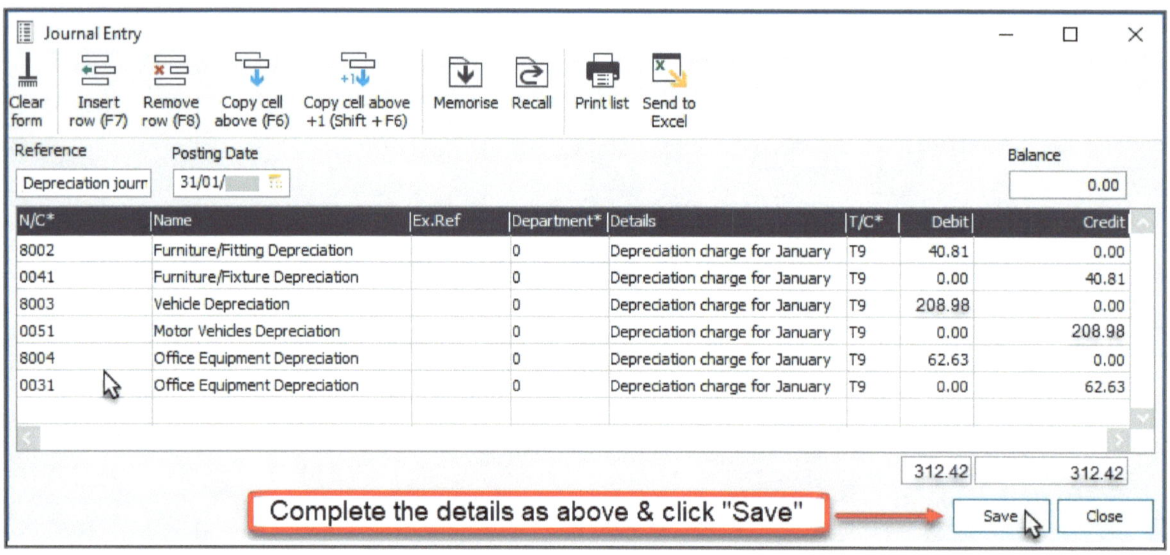

Fig. 220

How to record a sale of a fixed asset (Disposal)

One of the motor vehicles was sold on the 31st January

- A vehicle which was originally purchased for 9,000.
- Depreciation to date is £967.55.
- It was sold for £5,250.

For example, to transfer the original purchase price from the asset nominal code, post the following:

N/C	Name	Details	T/C	Debit	Credit
0050	Motor Vehicle	Disposal	T9		9,000
4200	Sales of Assets	Disposal	T9	9,000	

To transfer the accumulated depreciation to date, post the following:

N/C	Name	Details	T/C	Debit	Credit
0051	Motor Vehicle Depreciation	Disposal	T9	967.50	
4200	Sales of Assets	Disposal	T9		967.50

To record the proceeds from the sale, post the following:

N/C	Name	Details	T/C	Debit	Credit
1200	Bank Current Account	Disposal	T9	5,250	
4200	Sales of Assets	Disposal	T9		5,250

1. Click on Nominal codes, then click on Journal entry.
2. Enter a reference, date and the journal details to record the disposal of the fixed asset.

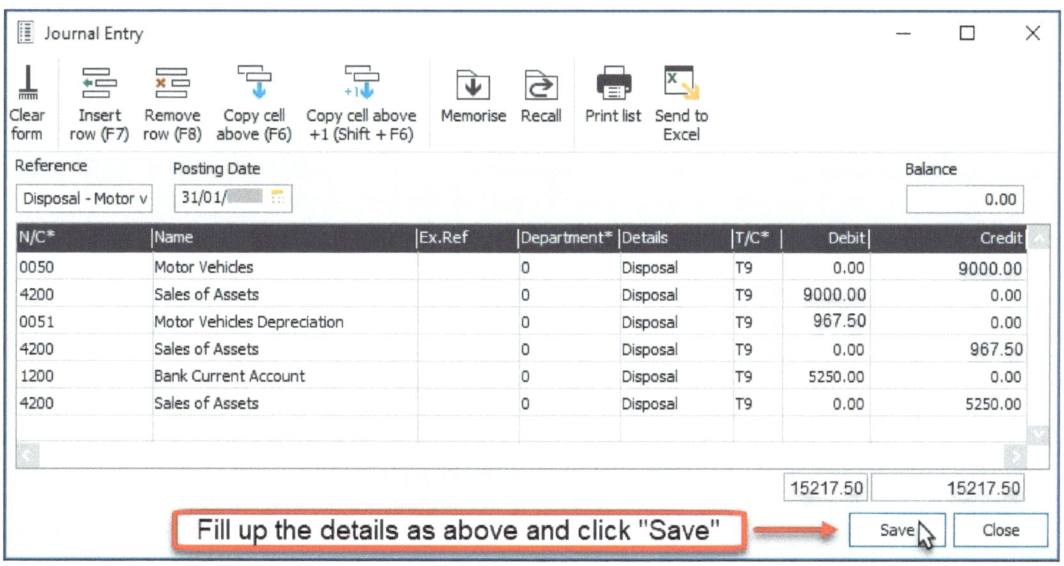

Fig. 221

Note: If you're disposing of an asset and still have an HP (Hire Purchase) loan outstanding, instead of posting the proceeds of the sale to your bank you should post it to the HP loan nominal code, for example, 2310.

You've now posted the journal entries to record the disposal of the asset. As a result of these journals, the balance on the Sales of Assets nominal code is a £2,782.50 debit. This appears as a loss in the profit and loss report.

Bank reconciliation

Bank reconciliation is part of the month end close procedure, and you should do it now. You have done a bank reconciliation before – see figures 195 to 198 on pages 135 to 138

How to adjust Closing stock

Opening and closing stock transactions are posted to adjust the profit and loss calculation, so that the profit figure for a specific period takes into account any unsold stock.
By default, the Profit and Loss report calculates the Gross Profit as:

Gross Profit = Sales – Purchases

However, if you post opening and closing stock transactions the Profit and Loss report calculates the Gross Profit as:

Gross Profit = Sales - Cost of Sales*

*Cost of Sales = Opening Stock + Purchases - Closing Stock

Why you need to post opening and closing stock journals

If you don't post opening and closing stock journals, then the cost of sales on the Profit and Loss report would include the cost of your purchases and not make an allowance for unsold stock.

The Opening and Closing Stock Wizard guides you through the process and posts the relevant journals automatically. The wizard posts 4 journals all on the same date.

This space is for notes

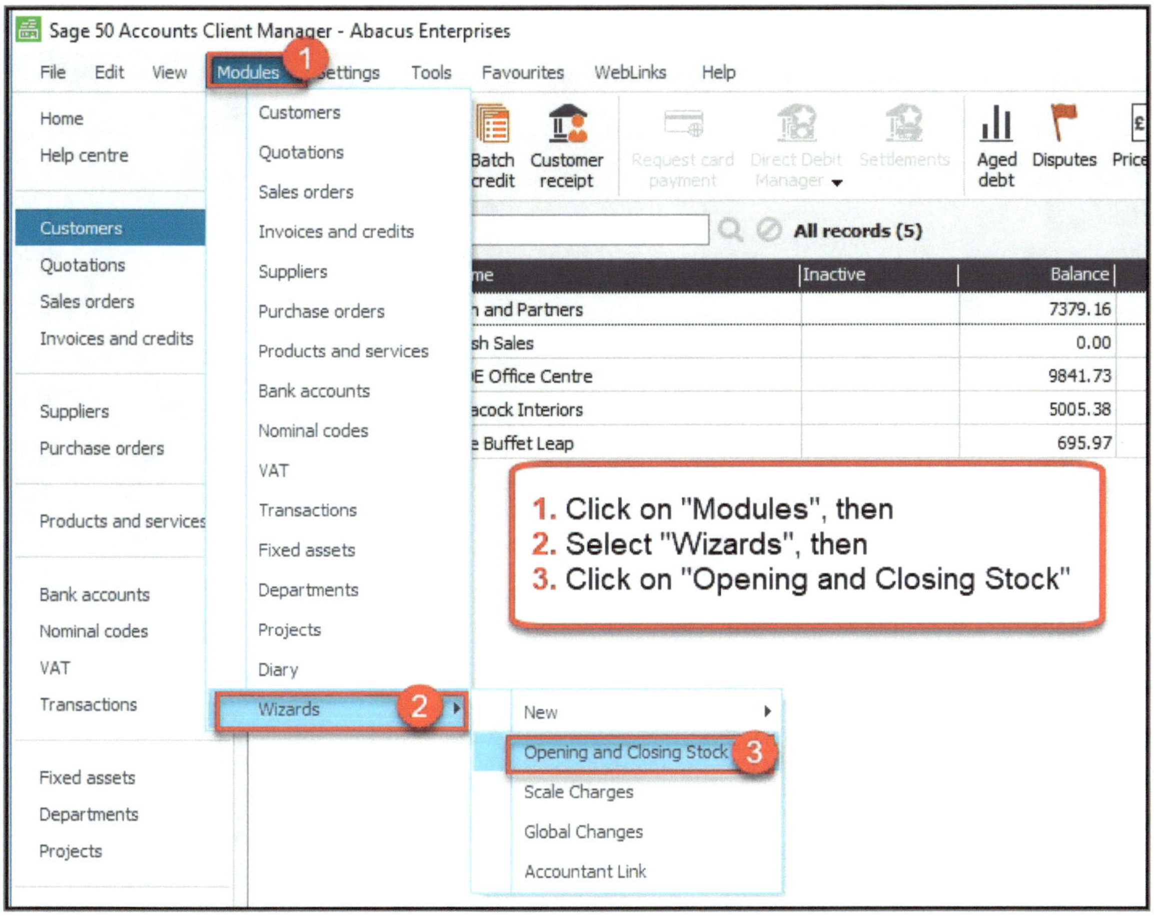

Fig. 222

After clicking opening and closing stock as illustrated in step 3 in the figure above, an opening and closing stock window appears – see figure 223 on the next page.

This space is for notes

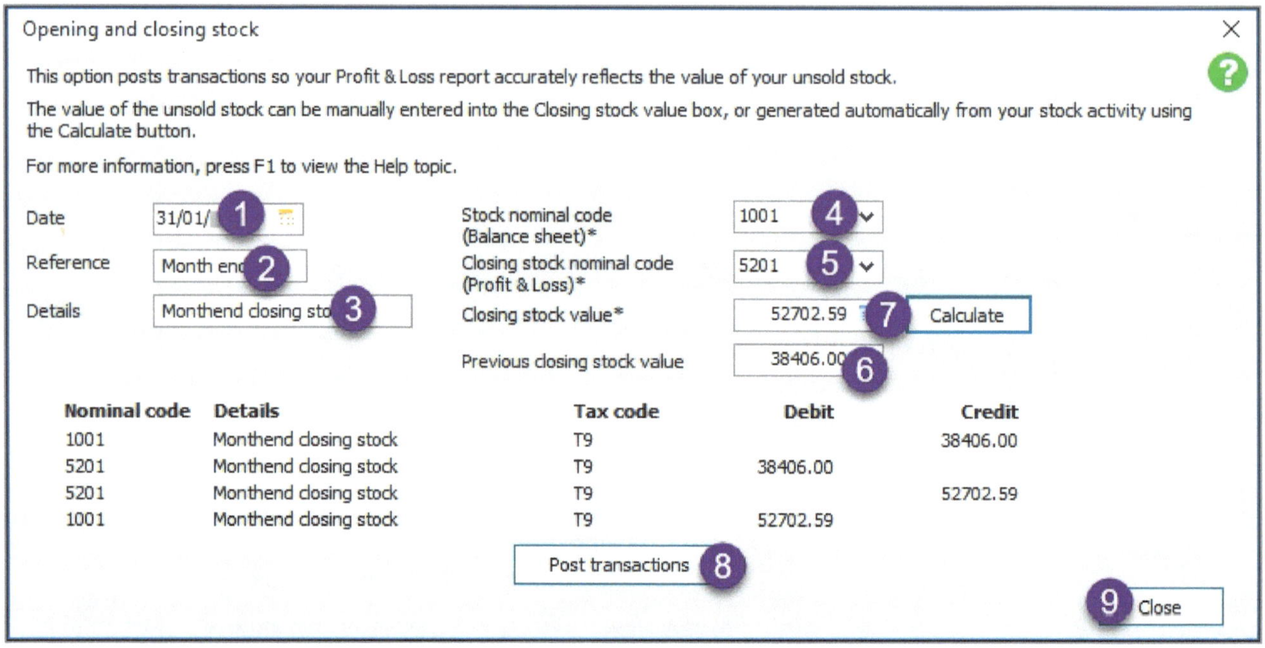

Fig. 223

1.	**Date**	*Enter the required posting date.*
2.	**Reference**	*Enter the required reference.*
3.	**Details**	*Enter the required description, for example, Opening Stock.*
4.	**Stock nominal code (Balance sheet)**	*From the drop-down list, choose the required nominal code. By default, this is 1001.*
5.	**Closing stock nominal code (Profit & Loss)**	*From the drop-down list, choose the required nominal code. By default, this is 5201.*
6.	**Previous closing stock value here.**	*It calculates by multiplying the quantity in stock by the average cost price for every product. In Sage 50 Accounts, you can check this by running the Product Valuation by Stock Category report. This report is not available in Sage Instant Accounts Plus.* ***Note: This valuation is not date specific and is based on all stock transactions that have been posted to date. If required, you can change this value.***
7.	**Closing stock value**	*Enter the closing stock value. Alternatively, to automatically calculate this value, click Calculate.*
8.	**Click "Post Transaction"**	
9.	**Click "Close"**	

How to do Debtors' reconciliation

Let's begin by working out what the debtors balance should be as illustrated in the working below.

	Debit £	Credit £
Debtors at the beginning of the period (Outstanding invoices at the beginning of the period equal to closing balances for previous period)	21,864.88	
Total invoices for the period (Total of sales day book - your list of invoices - gross figure)	20,083.45	
Total receipts for the period (Total from cash book of invoiced income)		14,654.91
***Debtors at the end of period carried forward to the next period* (Balancing figures, which should agree with the prepared list)** →		27,293.42
	41,948.33	41,948.33

Compare this debtors figure with the debtors' figure in the Sage 50 Software; if they match, that's great, move on to do creditors' reconciliation. If they don't match, it might be helpful to go through the checklist below to verify your results and discover any potential errors. Tick the checkboxes on the right of each item as you go along with your checks.

1	Have you listed all your debtors, including invoices only partly paid or outstanding from the beginning of the period, and invoices paid directly after the end of the period, because these receipts would not be in the cash book?	☐
2	Are there any bad debts - invoices you will never receive payment for? These should be entered as a separate credit in your control account.	☐
3	Does your total of invoices in the period include credit notes issued? If not, these must be included on the credit side of the account.	☐
4	Are the receipts from cash book only those that relate to invoiced sales or work done? Exclude any receipts included in the debtors' figure for the sale of a vehicle, loans, refunds etc.	☐
5	Have you included the figure for all un-invoiced sales? - Sales that should have had an invoice raised but by error were not.	☐
6	Have you included as a receipt on the control account any receipts for sales that were not entered into the cash book?	☐
7	Are there any errors of addition of receipts, invoices or debtors' totals, or duplication of invoices, receipts, or debtors in listings?	☐

Once you've gone through the checklist above, start doing your reconciliation with a reconciliation statement that might look something like the following:

	£	Debit £	Credit £
Debtors at the beginning of the period		21,864.88	
Total invoices		20,083.45	
Sales not invoiced in error		0.00	
Credit notes			2,147.98
Total receipts	14,654.91		
Sales of vehicle	0.00		
			14,654.91
Addition error(s)	(0.00)		
Receipts banked in private account			2,559.18
Bad debts write-offs and refunds			0.00
Debtors at the end of the period			**22,586.26**
		41,948.33	41,948.33
Reconciliation			
Original debtors figure per accounting software	23,057.38		
Debtors paid after the period not on the list	0.00		
Bad debt provision	0.00		
Written off invoice/invoice amount included twice	(471.12)		
Reconciled debtors as above	**22,586.26**		

Well, that is how to do a debtors' reconciliation.

How to do Creditors' reconciliation

In a purchase ledger control account, the total outstanding invoices at the beginning of a period and invoices received during that period, less payments made for invoiced supplies, will give a balancing figure of invoices still outstanding at the end of the period - your creditors.

You can compare the figure with your listing of unpaid invoices, and the creditor's value should ideally be the same as that of the purchase ledger control account in the software. If they are not the same, then you will need to reconcile them.

Before reconciliation, this is what you might have worked out – see next page.

This space is for notes

	Debit £	Credit £
Creditors at the beginning of the period (Unpaid invoices at the beginning of period equal to closing balances for previous period)		9,196.40
Total invoices in the period (Total of purchase day book list of invoices - gross figure)		73,847.44
Total payments in the period (Total of purchase cash book for invoiced expenses)	12,583.95	
Creditors at the end of period (Balance figure, which should agree with the prepared list)	70,459.89	
Total	83,043.84	83,043.84

If you now compare the Creditors at the end of the period value of (£74,659.89) with the creditors' value in the software, they should be the same. If they vary, it could be because of some things, use the checklist below to find out.

1	Have you listed all your creditors, including those invoices only partly paid or outstanding from the beginning of the period, and those invoices paid directly after the end of the period, because these payments would not be in the cash book?	☐
2	Does your total of invoices in the period include credit notes received? If not, these must be included on the debit side of the account	☐
3	Check to ensure that payments from cash book should be only those that relate to invoiced expenses, not items such as wages, interest, etc. If included, these figures should be taken off the payments figure in the control account	☐
4	Make sure that purchases, where a discount reduces the payment below the invoiced amount, should have the discount in the control account	☐
5	Those payments for purchases that were not entered into the cash book will have to be included as a payment on the control account	☐
6	Addition errors of payments, invoices, or creditors totals, or duplication of invoices, payments, or creditors in listings should be noted and recorded	☐

The format of your amended purchase ledger reconciliation statement should look as follows.

See next page...

		Debit £	Credit £
Creditors at the beginning of the period			9,196.40
Total invoices			73,847.44
Credit notes		504.77	
Total payments	12,583.95		
Addition error	0.00	12,583.95	
Payments made from the private account		6,937.18	
Discounts received		0.00	
Creditors at the end of the period		**63,017.94**	
		83,043.84	83,043.84
Reconciliation			
Original creditors figure per accounting software	63,017.94		
Creditor paid after a period not on the list	0.00		
Creditor included twice	(0.00)		
Invoice paid short, amount still outstanding	0.00		
Reconciled Creditors as above	**63,017.94**		

At the end of every month or every accounting period, you should work to ensure that the entries in the sales and purchase ledgers (list of individual balances) agree with the entries in the control accounts. The totals in each should be the same, otherwise, follow the above reconciliation steps (debtors & creditor reconciliation steps) to make them the same.

Month end notes:

Posting details of the month end notes given in the workbook

The journal – see next page.

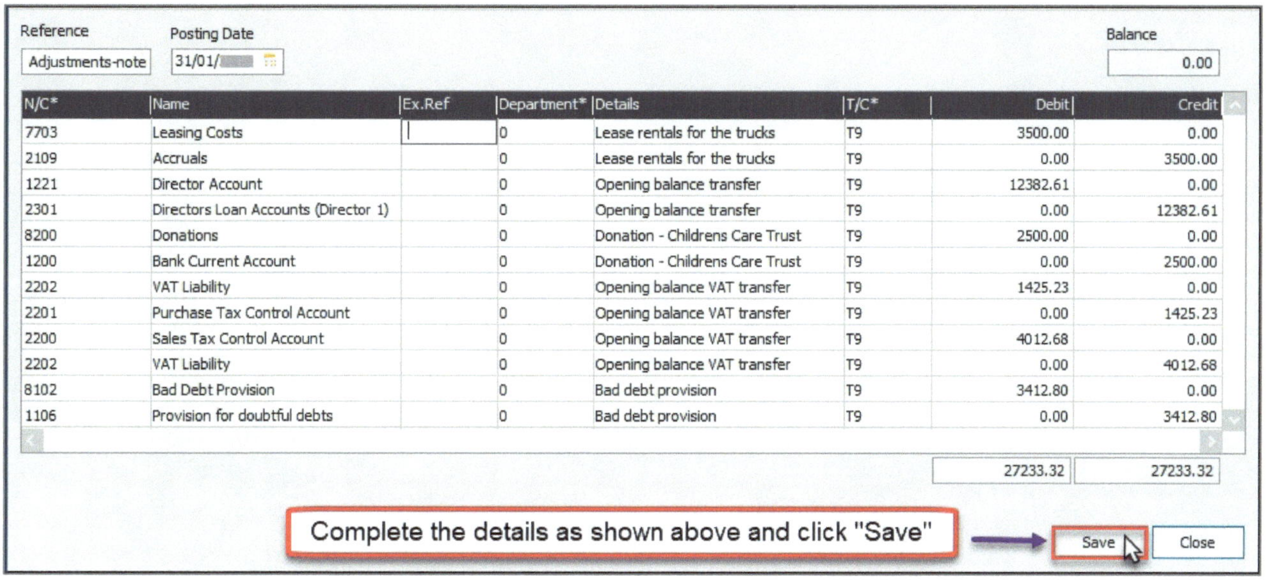

Reference: Adjustments-note | Posting Date: 31/01/ | Balance: 0.00

N/C*	Name	Ex.Ref	Department*	Details	T/C*	Debit	Credit
7703	Leasing Costs		0	Lease rentals for the trucks	T9	3500.00	0.00
2109	Accruals		0	Lease rentals for the trucks	T9	0.00	3500.00
1221	Director Account		0	Opening balance transfer	T9	12382.61	0.00
2301	Directors Loan Accounts (Director 1)		0	Opening balance transfer	T9	0.00	12382.61
8200	Donations		0	Donation - Childrens Care Trust	T9	2500.00	0.00
1200	Bank Current Account		0	Donation - Childrens Care Trust	T9	0.00	2500.00
2202	VAT Liability		0	Opening balance VAT transfer	T9	1425.23	0.00
2201	Purchase Tax Control Account		0	Opening balance VAT transfer	T9	0.00	1425.23
2200	Sales Tax Control Account		0	Opening balance VAT transfer	T9	4012.68	0.00
2202	VAT Liability		0	Opening balance VAT transfer	T9	0.00	4012.68
8102	Bad Debt Provision		0	Bad debt provision	T9	3412.80	0.00
1106	Provision for doubtful debts		0	Bad debt provision	T9	0.00	3412.80
						27233.32	27233.32

Fig. 224

Balance Sheet reconciliation

Balance sheet reconciliations are merely a comparison of the amounts that appear on your balance sheet general ledger accounts to the details that make up those balances while ensuring that any differences between the two are adequately explained and reasonable.

What benefits do Balance Sheet reconciliations provide?

The objective of internal controls is to prevent or detect errors or fraud. Balance sheet reconciliations can highlight issues in three particular ways. Reconciliations can assist in:

i. Detecting missing, duplicated, or untimely transactions.
ii. Monitoring the organisation's activities (e.g. consumption of raw materials, sales, or purchases).
iii. Tracking various regulatory compliance items (e.g. required reserves and allowances or permitted investment holdings).

This space is for notes

"No matter how small and unimportant what we are doing may seem, if we do it well, it may soon become the step that will lead us to better things"

Channing Pollock

"Do not spread false reports. Do not help guilty person by being a malicious witness".

Exodus 23:1

TASK 15: HOW TO PRODUCE ACCOUNTING REPORTS

There are three key fundamental stages in practical accounting; First you analyse the financial documents. Secondly, you record the details in the financial documents into your accounting system, thirdly you produce financial reports after correcting any errors of the analysis and recording stages and also after making some crucial adjustments to the accounts.

Accounting reports are compilations of financial information that are derived from the accounting records of a business. These can be brief, custom-made reports that are intended for specific purposes, such as a detailed analysis of sales by region, or the profitability of a specific product line. More commonly, accounting reports are considered to be equivalent to the financial statements. These statements include the following reports:

- *Income statement*. States the revenues earned during a period, less expenses, to arrive at a profit or loss. This is the most commonly used accounting report, since it is used to judge the performance of a business.
- *Balance sheet*. Shows the ending asset, liability, and equity balances as of the balance sheet date. It is used to judge the liquidity and financial reserves of a business.
- *Statement of cash flows*. Shows the sources and uses of cash related to operations, financing, and investments. Can be the most accurate source of information regarding the cash-generating ability of an entity.

A number of disclosures may accompany the financial statements, in the form of footnotes. This is more likely to be the case when the financial statements have been audited.

The next task is about producing accounting reports.

i. Trial balance report

A trial balance is a list of all the general ledger accounts (both revenue and capital) contained in the ledger of a business. This list will contain the name of each nominal ledger account and the value of that nominal ledger balance.

Each nominal ledger account will hold either a debit balance or a credit balance. The debit balance values will be listed in the debit column of the trial balance, and the credit value balance will be listed in the credit column. The trading profit and loss statement and balance sheet and other financial reports can then be produced using the ledger accounts listed on the trial balance.

To produce a trial balance in Sage 50 Accounts is really easy, click on "Nominal codes" tab, then click on Trial balance – see figure 225 below & 226 on the next page.

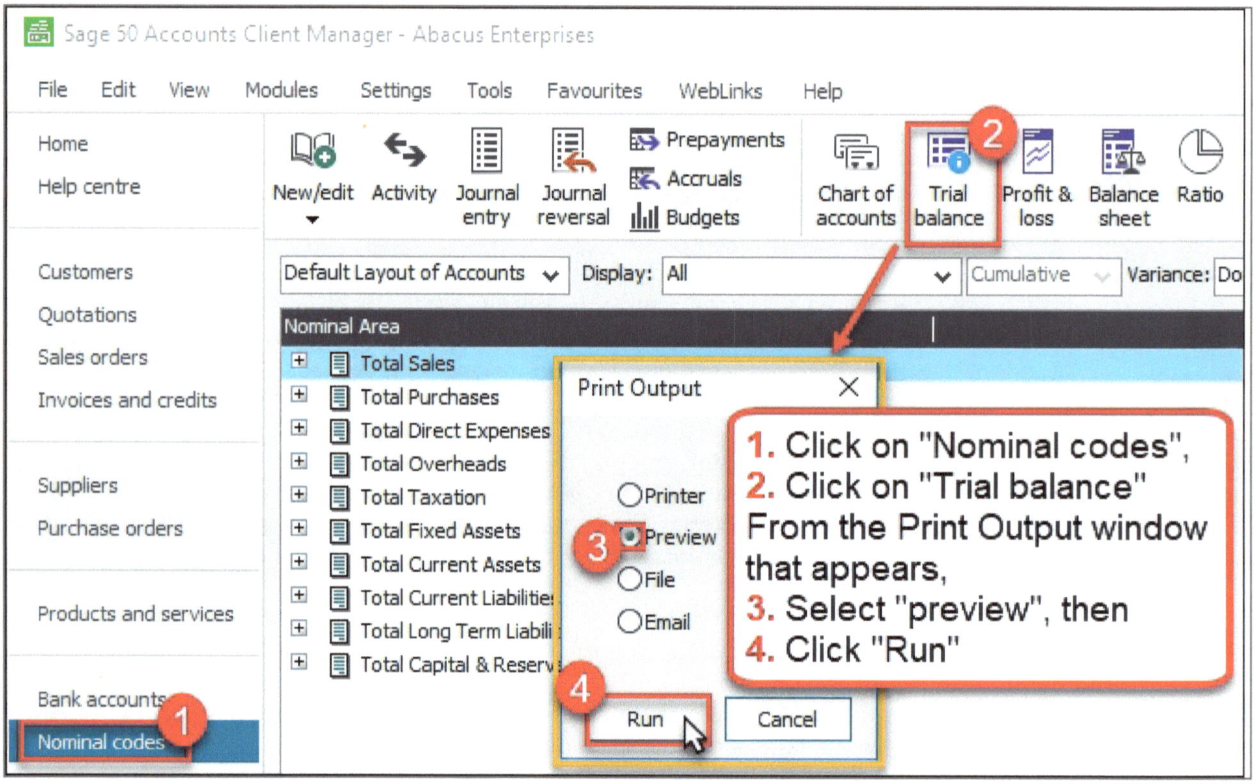

Fig. 225

After clicking "Run" as illustrated in step 4 of the figure above, a "criteria for period trial balance" window will appear. See figure 226 on the next page.

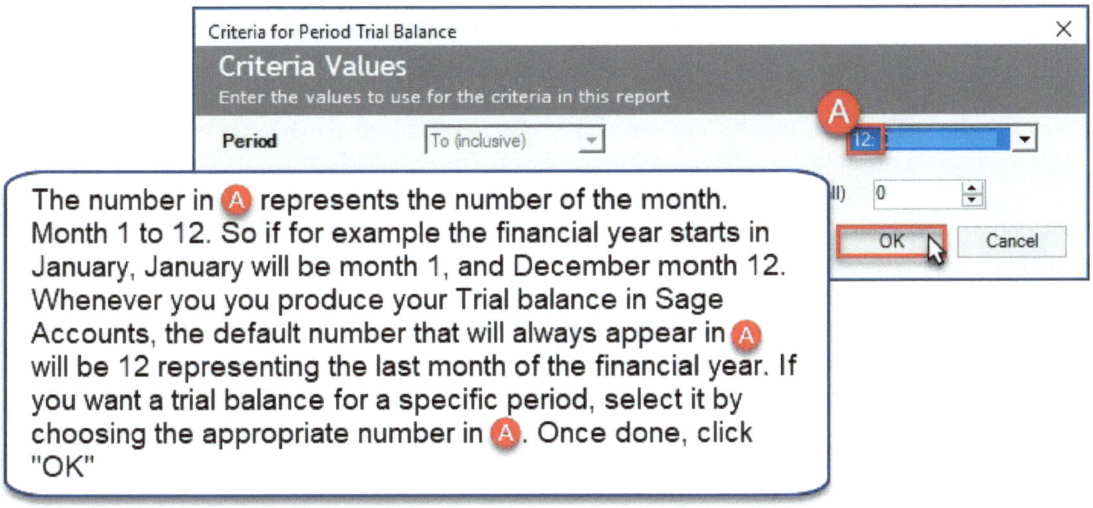

Fig. 226

After clicking "OK" as illustrated in the figure above, your trial balance will be generated, and here is how it looks like – see figure below.

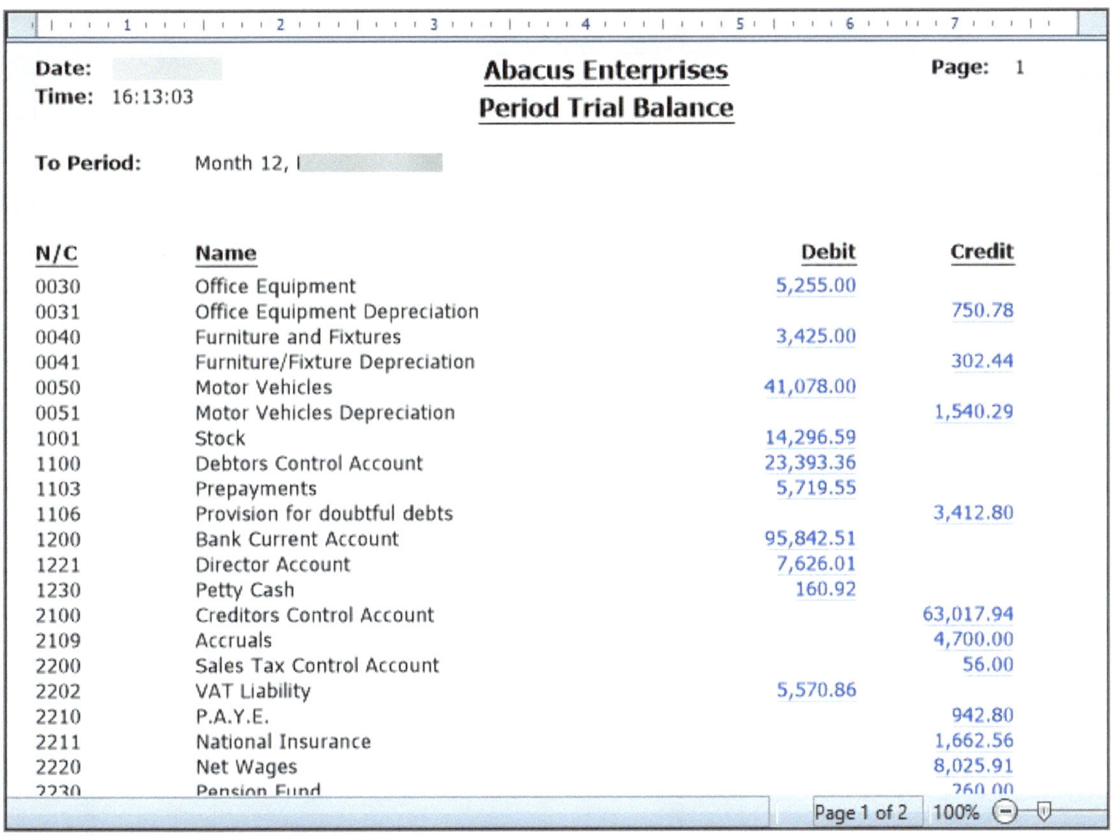

Date:

Time: 16:13:03

Abacus Enterprises

Period Trial Balance

Page: 1

To Period: Month 12,

N/C	Name	Debit	Credit
0030	Office Equipment	5,255.00	
0031	Office Equipment Depreciation		750.78
0040	Furniture and Fixtures	3,425.00	
0041	Furniture/Fixture Depreciation		302.44
0050	Motor Vehicles	41,078.00	
0051	Motor Vehicles Depreciation		1,540.29
1001	Stock	14,296.59	
1100	Debtors Control Account	23,393.36	
1103	Prepayments	5,719.55	
1106	Provision for doubtful debts		3,412.80
1200	Bank Current Account	95,842.51	
1221	Director Account	7,626.01	
1230	Petty Cash	160.92	
2100	Creditors Control Account		63,017.94
2109	Accruals		4,700.00
2200	Sales Tax Control Account		56.00
2202	VAT Liability	5,570.86	
2210	P.A.Y.E.		942.80
2211	National Insurance		1,662.56
2220	Net Wages		8,025.91
2230	Pension Fund		260.00

Page 1 of 2 100%

Fig. 227

ii. Income statement – also known as Profit and Loss account report

A profit and loss statement (P&L) is a financial statement that summarises the revenues, costs and expenses incurred during a specific period of time, usually a fiscal quarter or year. These records provide information about a company's ability – or lack thereof – to generate profit by increasing revenue, reducing costs, or both.

The P&L statement is also referred to as "statement of profit and loss", "income statement," "statement of operations," and "income and expense statement."

1. To produce a profit and loss report in Sage 50 Accounts is incredibly easy, just click on **Nominal codes** tab then
2. Click **Profit & loss** then click **Preview** then click **Run.**
3. Select the required **Period** and **Chart of Accounts**, then click **OK.**

The Profit and Loss report appears.

4. To **Print**, **Email** or **Export**, choose the relevant option and follow the on-screen instructions.

And here is your profit and loss account – see figure below.

Date:
Time: 16:21:19

Abacus Enterprises
Profit and Loss

e: 1

From: Month 1, December
To: Month 12, November

Chart of Accounts: Default Layout of Accounts

	Period		Year to Date	
Sales				
Product Sales	142,535.99		142,535.99	
Sales of Assets	(2,782.50)		(2,782.50)	
Other Sales	167.00		167.00	
		139,920.49		139,920.49
Purchases				
Purchases	27,117.06		27,117.06	
Stock	(14,296.59)		(14,296.59)	
		12,820.47		12,820.47
Direct Expenses				
Sales Promotion	10,783.22		10,783.22	
		10,783.22		10,783.22
Gross Profit/(Loss):		116,316.80		116,316.80
Overheads				
Gross Wages	48,554.54		48,554.54	
Rent and Rates	1,345.54		1,345.54	
Heat, Light and Power	325.44		325.44	
Motor Expenses	25.00		25.00	
Travelling and Entertainment	4,573.82		4,573.82	
Printing and Stationery	80.24		80.24	
Telephone and Computer charges	267.23		267.23	
Professional Fees	6,135.85		6,135.85	
Equipment Hire and Rental	10,500.00		10,500.00	
Maintenance	875.00		875.00	

Fig. 228

What the Income Statement is useful for

Analysts use the income statement for data to calculate financial ratios such as return on equity (ROE), return on assets (ROA), gross profit, operating profit, earnings before interest and taxes (EBIT), and earnings before interest taxes and amortisation (EBITDA). The income statement is often presented in a common-sized format, which provides each line item on the income statement as a percent of sales. In this way, analysts can easily see which expenses make up the largest portion of sales. Analysts also use the income statement to compare year-over-year (YOY) and quarter-over-quarter (QOQ) performance.

The income statement typically provides two to three years of historical data for comparison.

After you have established the trading profit, you now need to get the profit chargeable to corporation tax.

How to Calculate corporation tax.

Profit/(loss) before interest and taxation	34,010.61
Add back disallowable expenses	
Entertainment	0.00
Legal & professional fees	0.00
Late Filing Fee	0.00
Donations	0.00
Depreciation and (profit)/loss on sale of assets	709.06
Less:	
Capital allowances	0.00
Add back dividends payable on non-equity shares included in interest payable	0.00
Deduct non-trading income	
Interest receivable	0.00
Property income	0.00
Franked investment income	0.00
Other income not taxable	0.00
Taxable profit/(loss)	34,719.67

Days in accounting period falling in each tax year

Tax year	Days falling in tax year	Days in year
Prior Year	122	
Current Year	243	
	365	365

Corporation tax payable

Tax year	Taxable profit	Tax rate	Corp Tax
Prior Year	11,604.93	20%	2,320.99
Current Year	23,114.74	20%	4,622.95
	34,719.67		
Corporation tax payable			**6,943.94**

You now need to post this tax figure to the accounting software using a journal – see below.

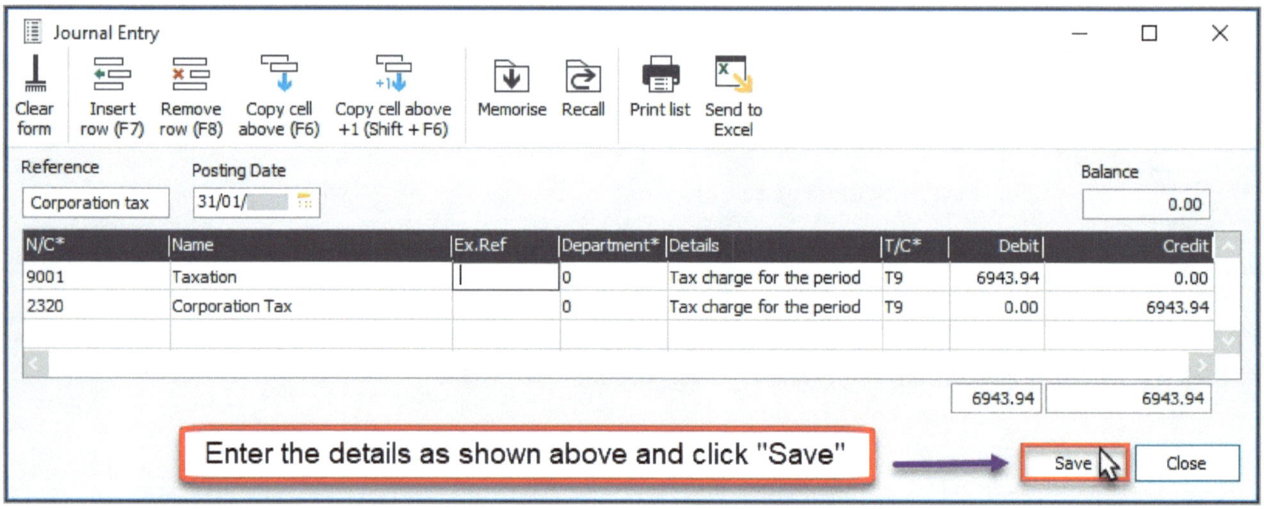

Fig. 229

iii. Balance Sheet

A balance sheet is a financial statement that summarizes a company's assets, liabilities and shareholders' equity at a specific point in time. These three balance sheet segments give investors an idea as to what the company owns and owes, as well as the amount invested by shareholders.

All accounts in your General Ledger are categorized as an asset, a liability, or equity. The relationship between them is expressed in this equation: **Assets = Liabilities + Equity**

1. To produce a Balance sheet report in Sage 50 Accounts is incredibly easy, just click on **Nominal codes** tab then
2. Click **Balance Sheet** then click **Preview** then click **Run**.
3. Select the required **Period** and **Chart of Accounts**, then click **OK**.

The Balance Sheet report appears.

4. To **Print**, **Email** or **Export**, choose the relevant option and follow the on-screen instructions.

And here is your Balance Sheet - See below.

Date:
Time: 16:39:20

Abacus Enterprises
Balance Sheet

Page: 1

From: Month 1, December
To: Month 12, November

Chart of Accounts: Default Layout of Accounts

	Period		Year to Date	
Fixed Assets				
Office Equipment	4,504.22		4,504.22	
Furniture and Fixtures	3,122.56		3,122.56	
Motor Vehicles	39,537.71		39,537.71	
		47,164.49		47,164.49
Current Assets				
Stock	14,296.59		14,296.59	
Debtors	25,700.11		25,700.11	
Deposits and Cash	7,786.93		7,786.93	
Bank Account	95,842.51		95,842.51	
VAT Liability	5,514.86		5,514.86	
		149,141.00		149,141.00
Current Liabilities				
Creditors : Short Term	67,717.94		67,717.94	
Payroll Taxation	2,605.36		2,605.36	
Wages	8,285.91		8,285.91	
		78,609.21		78,609.21
Current Assets less Current Liabilities:		70,531.79		70,531.79
Total Assets less Current Liabilities:		117,696.28		117,696.28
Long Term Liabilities				
Creditors : Long Term	6,943.94		6,943.94	
		6,943.94		6,943.94
Total Assets less Total Liabilities:		110,752.34		110,752.34
Capital & Reserves				
Share Capital	47,250.00		47,250.00	

Fig. 230

Make sure that each of the title headings in the balance sheet like Office equipment's, deposits & cash, etc. and the corresponding figures are correctly reconciled to the general ledger (GL) accounts.

iv. Aged trade payables report

See below for the steps in producing this report in Sage 50 Accounts:

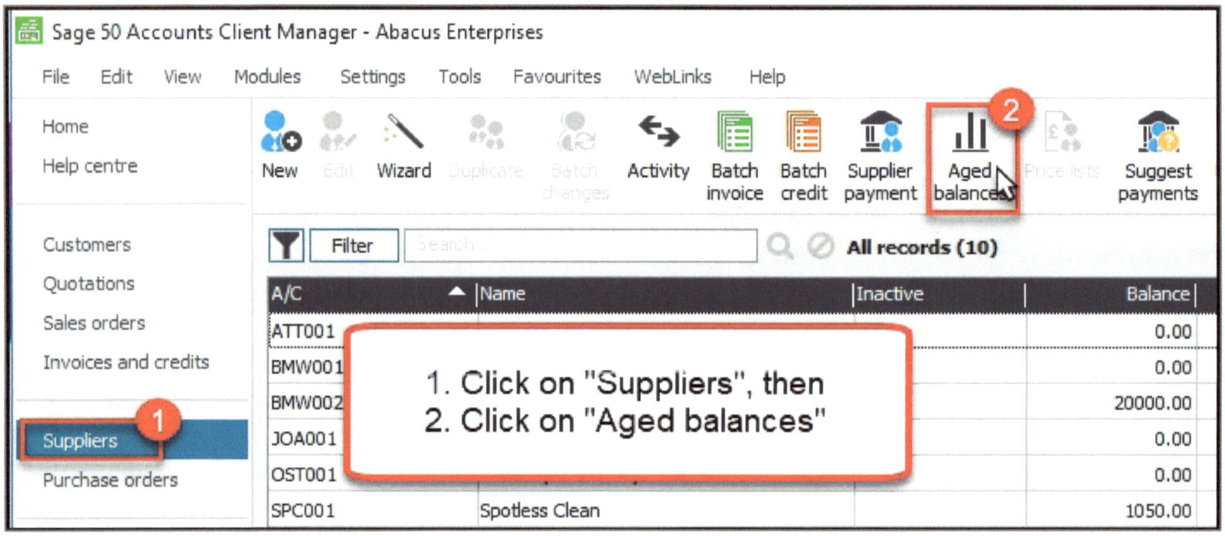

Fig. 231

After step 2 as illustrated in the figure above, an aged balances report appears – see below.

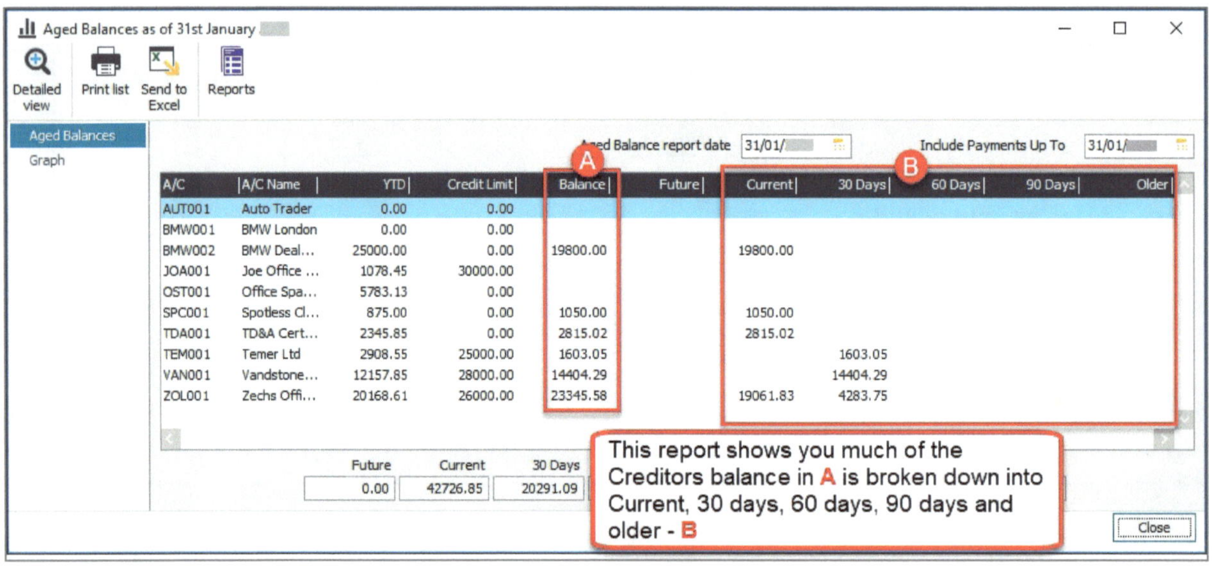

Fig. 232

If you want to find out the detailed breakdown of which invoices constitute a specific aged balance, you can do that by looking at a specific supplier activity report to identify those invoices.

v. Aged trade receivables report

See below the steps to take to produce the aged trade receivables report:

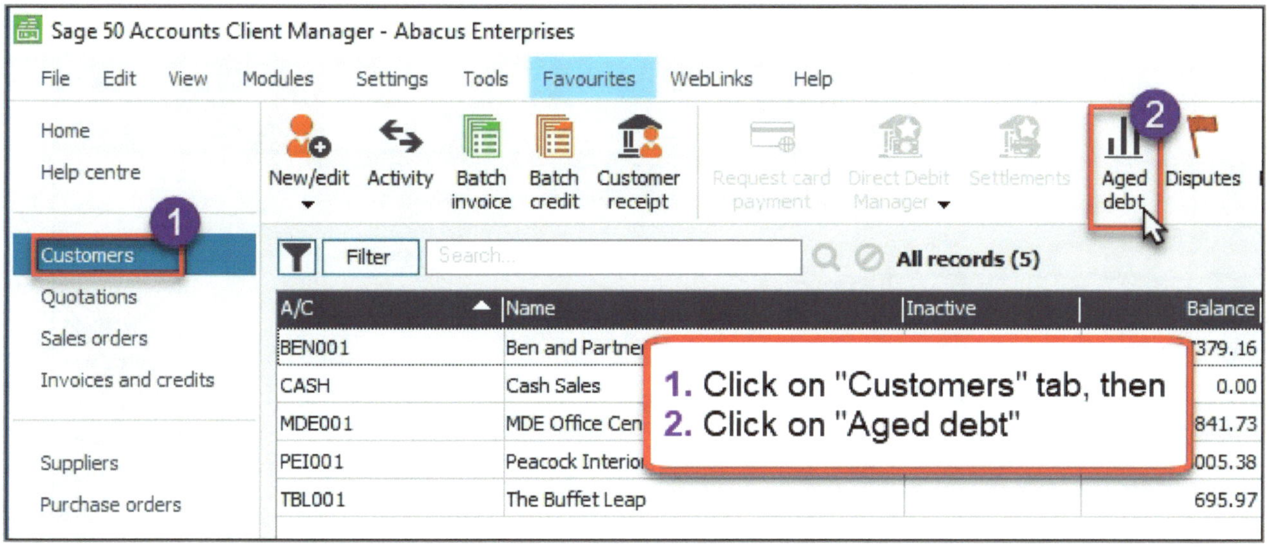

Fig. 233

After step 2 as illustrated in the figure above, an aged balances report appears. See below.

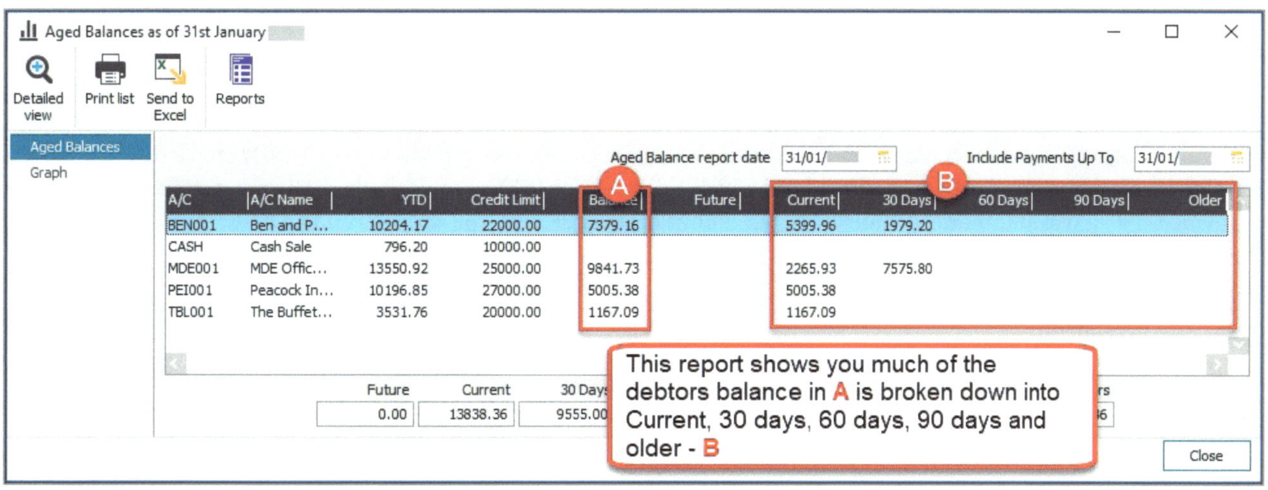

Fig. 234

vi. Audit trail report

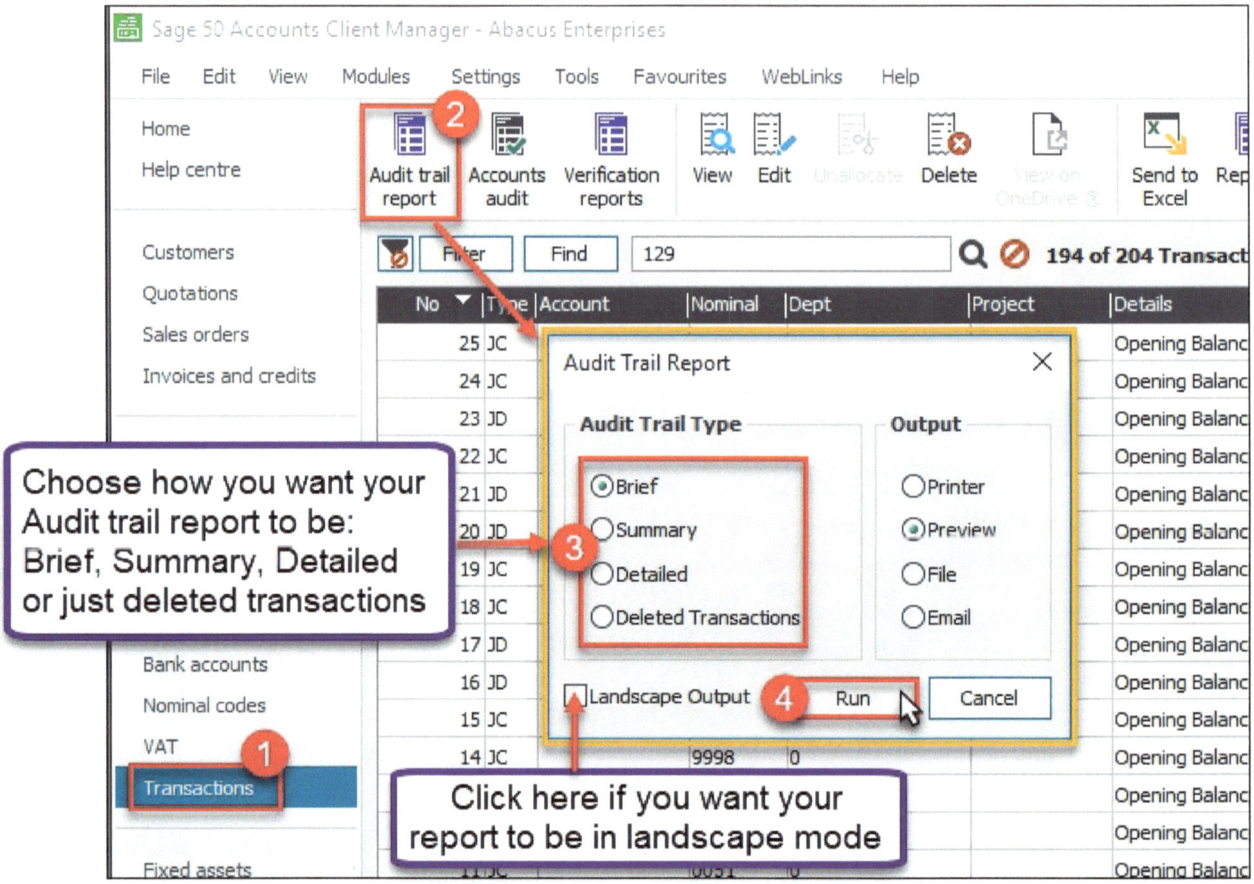

Fig. 235

Note: The Audit Trail Detailed report prints in landscape or Portrait format (depending on which output you specify) and shows detailed information for each transaction. For example, if you are viewing a sales invoice (SI) transaction, the details of the sales invoice appear as well as the details of which sales receipt (SR) or sales credit (SC) transactions are allocated to the invoice. To view a summarised audit trail, without allocation details, you should run the Audit Trail (Summary) or Audit Trail (Summary, Landscape/portrait) report.

This space is for notes

Management accounting reports.

i. **Profit and loss variance analysis report (Actual vs prior periods)**
ii. **Monthly profit & Loss account report and Company performance report**

To generate this reports in Sage 50 Accounts is easy. Click on "Nominal codes" tab, then click on "Reports" tab – at the top right-hand side in Sage 50 Accounts software.
The Nominal code report window will appear – see below.

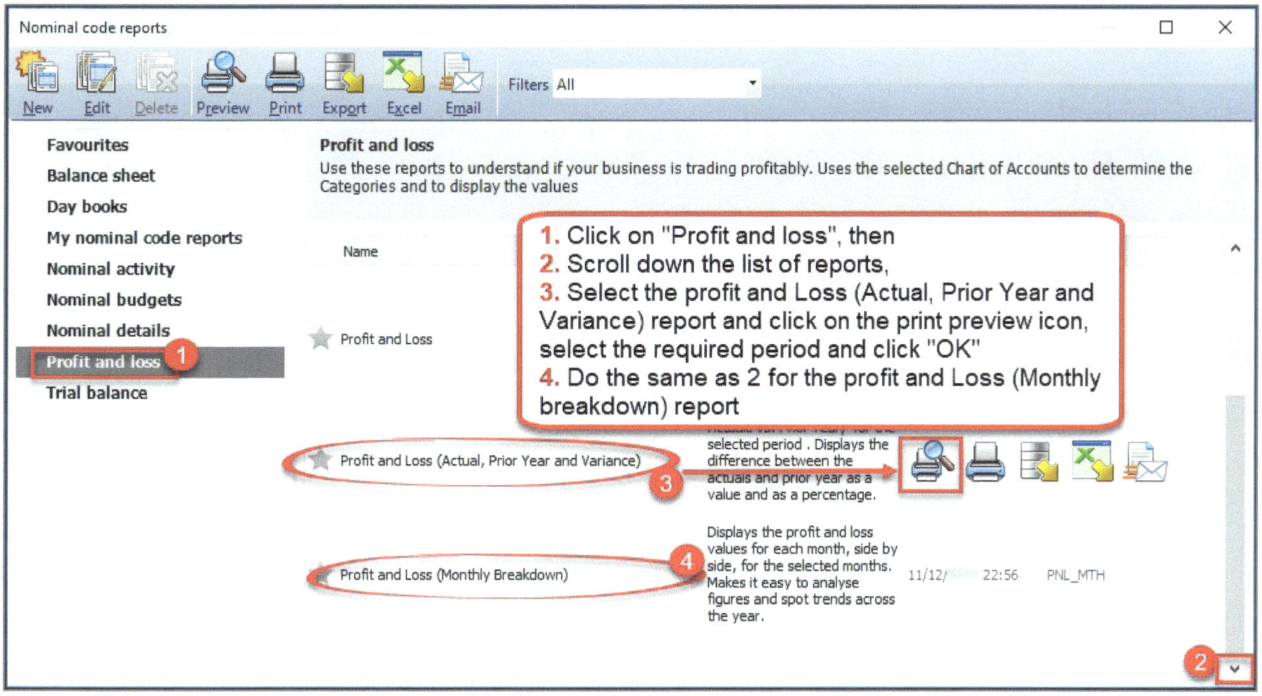

Fig. 236

This space is for notes

iii. Key ratio analysis report

Ratio Analysis - Key Ratios	Prior Year	Current year
Balance Sheet		
Cash	55,250	96,003
Accounts receivable, net	16,100	19,509
Total current assets	120,512	149,141
Total long-term assets	17,150	47,164
Total current liabilities	65,180	78,609
Total long-term liabilities	1,601	6,944
Total shareholders' equity	98,286	110,752
Income Statement		
Total sales	119,142	139,920
Gross profit	87,254	116,317
Total operating expenses	79,250	82,306
Income (loss) before taxes	8,004	34,011
Net income (loss)	6,403	27,067
KEY RATIOS		
Profitability Ratios		
Return on equity	7%	24%
Return on assets	5%	14%
Return on sales	5%	19%
Gross profit margin	73%	83%
Asset turnover ratio	87%	71%
Leverage and Liquidity Ratios		
Current ratio	1.85	1.90
Quick or acid test ratio	1.09	1.47
Long-term debt to asset ratio	0.012	0.035
Debt to equity ratio	0.679	0.772

Ratio analysis

What is ratio analysis?

Ratio Analysis is a form of financial statement analysis that is used to obtain a quick indication of financial performance of a business in several key areas.

The ratios are categorised as:

- ✓ Short-term Solvency Ratios, e.g. *Current ratio and Quick or acid test ratio.*
- ✓ Debt Management Ratios, e.g. *Debt to equity ratio*
- ✓ Asset Management Ratios, e.g. *Receivables turnover*
- ✓ Profitability Ratios, and
- ✓ Market Value Ratios. E.g. *Price earnings ratio*

Return on Equity and Return on Assets

The Return on Assets Ratio indicates the pound (£) in income earned by the company on its assets and the Return on Equity Ratio indicates the pounds (£) of income earned by the company on its shareholders' equity. It is important to remember that these ratios are based on accounting book values and not on market values. Thus, it is not appropriate to compare these ratios with market rates of return such as the interest rate on Treasury bonds or the return earned on an investment in a stock.

Formula

$$\text{Return on Assets (ROA)} = \frac{\text{Net income}}{\text{Total Assets}}$$

$$\text{Return on Equity (ROE)} = \frac{\text{Net income}}{\text{Total Owners' Equity}}$$

Return on Sales:

Return on sales, often called the operating profit margin, is a financial ratio that calculates how efficiently a company is at generating profits from its revenue. In other words, it measures a company's performance by analysing what percentage of total company revenues are actually converted into company profits.

$$\text{Return on Sales (ROS)} = \frac{\text{Operating profit}}{\text{Net Sales}}$$

Analysis

You can think of ROS as both an efficiency and profitability ratio because it is an indicator of both metrics. It measures how efficiently a company uses its resources to convert sales into profits. For instance, a company that generates £1,000,000 in net sales and requires £900,000 of resources to do so is not nearly as efficient as a company that can generate the same about of revenues by only using £500,000 of operating expenses. The more efficient management is cutting expenses, the higher the ratio.

Investors tend to use this iteration of the formula to calculate growth projects and forecasts. For example, based on a certain percentage, investors could calculate the potential profits if revenues doubled or tripled.

Gross profit margin

Gross profit margin is a profitability ratio that calculates the percentage of sales that exceed the cost of goods sold. In other words, it measures how efficiently a company uses its materials and labor to produce and sell products profitably.

The gross profit ratio is important because it shows management and investors how profitable the core business activities are without taking into consideration the indirect costs. In other words, it shows how efficiently a company can produce and sell its products. This gives investors a key insight into how healthy the company actually is. For instance, a company with a seemingly healthy net income on the bottom line could actually be dying. The gross profit percentage could be negative, and the net income could be coming from other one-time operations. The company could be losing money on every product they produce but staying afloat because of a one-time insurance pay-out.

That is why it is almost always listed on front page of the income statement in one form or another. Let's take a look at how to calculate gross profit and what it's used for.

Formula

$$\text{Gross Profit Margin} = \frac{\text{Total Sales} - \text{Cost of goods sold}}{\text{Total Sales}}$$

Analysis

The gross profit method is an important concept because it shows management and investors how efficiently the business can produce and sell products. In other words, it shows how profitable a product is.

The concept of GP is particularly important to cost accountants and management because it allows them to create budgets and forecast future activities. For instance, Abacus GP was £113,892. This means if Abacus wants to be profitable for the year, all of her other costs must be less than £113,892. Conversely, Abacus Enterprises can also view the £113,892 as the amount of money that can be put toward other business expenses or expansion into new markets.

Investors/management can also use a gross profit margin calculator to measure scalability. Abacus' investors can run different models with her margins to see how profitable the company would be at different sales levels. For instance, they could measure the profits if 100,000 units were sold or 500,000 units were sold by multiplying the potential number of units sold by the sales price and the GP margin.

Asset Turnover Ratio

The asset turnover ratio is an efficiency ratio that measures a company's ability to generate sales from its assets by comparing net sales with average total assets. In other words, this ratio shows how efficiently a company can use its assets to generate sales.

The total asset turnover ratio calculates net sales as a percentage of assets to show how many sales are generated from each pound/dollar of company assets. For instance, a ratio of .5 means that each pound/dollar of assets generates 50 pence/cents of sales.

Formula

$$\text{Gross Profit Margin} = \frac{\text{Net Sales}}{\text{Average total assets}}$$

Net sales, found on the income statement, are used to calculate this ratio returns and refunds must be backed out of total sales to measure the truly measure the firm's assets' ability to generate sales.

Average total assets are usually calculated by adding the beginning and ending total asset balances together and dividing by two. This is just a simple average based on a two-year balance sheet. A more in-depth, weighted average calculation can be used, but it is not necessary.

Analysis:
This ratio measures how efficiently a firm uses its assets to generate sales, so a higher ratio is always more favourable. Higher turnover ratios mean the company is using its assets more efficiently. Lower ratios mean that the company isn't using its assets efficiently and most likely have management or production problems.

Like with most ratios, the asset turnover ratio is based on industry standards. Some industries use assets more efficiently than others. To get a true sense of how well a company's assets are being used, it must be compared to other companies in its industry.
The total asset turnover ratio is a general efficiency ratio that measures how efficiently a company uses all of its assets. This gives investors and creditors an idea of how a company is managed and uses its assets to produce products and sales.

Current ratio

The current ratio is a liquidity and efficiency ratio that measures a firm's ability to pay off its short-term liabilities with its current assets. The current ratio is an important measure of liquidity because short-term liabilities are due within the next year.

This means that a company has a limited amount of time in order to raise the funds to pay for these liabilities. Current assets like cash, cash equivalents, and marketable securities can easily be converted into cash in the short term. This means that companies with larger amounts of current assets will more easily be able to pay off current liabilities when they become due without having to sell off long-term, revenue generating assets.

Formula

$$\text{Current ratio} = \frac{\text{Current Assets}}{\text{Current Liabilities}}$$

Analysis:
A higher current ratio is always more favourable than a lower current ratio because it shows the company can more easily make current debt payments.

If a company has to sell of fixed assets to pay for its current liabilities, this usually means the company isn't making enough from operations to support activities. In other words, the company is losing money. Sometimes this is the result of poor collections of accounts receivable.

The current ratio also sheds light on the overall debt burden of the company. If a company is weighted down with a current debt, its cash flow will suffer.

Quick or acid test ratio

The quick ratio or acid test ratio is a liquidity ratio that measures the ability of a company to pay its current liabilities when they come due with only quick assets. Quick assets are current assets that can be converted to cash within 90 days or in the short-term. Cash, cash equivalents, short-term investments or marketable securities, and current accounts receivable are considered quick assets.

Formula

$$\text{Quick ratio} = \frac{\text{Cash + Cash Equivalents + Short term investments + Current receivables}}{\text{Current Liabilities}}$$

Sometimes company financial statements don't give a breakdown of quick assets on the balance sheet. In this case, you can still calculate the quick ratio even if some of the quick asset totals are unknown. Simply subtract inventory and any current prepaid assets from the current asset total for the numerator. Here is an example.

$$\text{Quick ratio} = \frac{\text{Current Assets} - \text{Inventory} - \text{Prepaid Expenses}}{\text{Current Liabilities}}$$

Long term debt ratio

A company can build assets by raising debt or equity capital. The ratio of long-term debt to total assets provides a sense of what percentage of the total assets is financed via long-term debt. A higher percentage ratio means that the company is more leveraged and owns less of the assets on balance sheet. In other words, it would need to sell more assets to eliminate its debt in the event of a bankruptcy. The company would also have to generate strong revenue and cash flow for a long period in the future to be able to repay the debt.
This ratio provides a sense of financial stability and overall riskiness of a company. Investors are wary of a high ratio, as it signifies management has less free cash flow and less ability to finance new operations. Management typically uses this financial metric to determine the amount of debt the company can sustain and manage the overall capital structure of the firm.

Formula

$$\text{Long Term Debt Ratio} = \frac{\text{Long term debt}}{\text{Total Assets}}$$

It's also important to look at off-balance sheet items like operating lease and pension obligations. These items are not presented in the long-term liabilities section of the balance sheet, but they are liabilities nonetheless. If you don't include these in your calculation, your estimates will not be completely correct.

Keep in mind that this ratio should be used with several other leverage ratios in order to get a proper understanding of the financial riskiness of a company. Some of other relevant ratios that you can use are the Total debt to total assets ratio, Total debt to Equity ratio, and the LT debt to Equity ratio.

That's how you can use the LT-debt ratio to measure a company's financial leverage and calculate its overall risk. Used properly while considering all the loopholes, this metric can be an important tool to initiate constructive discussion with the management about the future of the company.

Debt to Equity ratio

The debt to equity ratio is a financial, liquidity ratio that compares a company's total debt to total equity. The debt to equity ratio shows the percentage of company financing that comes from creditors and investors. A higher debt to equity ratio indicates that more creditor financing (bank loans) is used than investor financing (shareholders).

Formula

$$\text{Debt to Equity Ratio} = \frac{\text{Total Liabilities}}{\text{Total Equity}}$$

Analysis

A lower debt to equity ratio usually implies a more financially stable business. Companies with a higher debt to equity ratio are considered riskier to creditors and investors than companies with a lower ratio. Unlike equity financing, debt must be repaid to the lender. Since debt financing also requires debt servicing or regular interest payments, debt can be a far more expensive form of financing than equity financing. Companies leveraging large amounts of debt might not be able to make the payments.

Creditors view a higher debt to equity ratio as risky because it shows that the investors haven't funded the operations as much as creditors have. This could mean that investors don't want to fund the business operations because the company isn't performing well. Lack of performance might also be the reason why the company is seeking out extra debt financing.

"Victory is not won in miles but in inches. Win a little now, hold your ground, and later win a little more"

Louis L'Amour

"It's often a good idea to have a backup plan for the just in case times"
Sterling Libs

HOW TO RESTORE A BACKUP FILE ONTO SAGE 50 ACCOUNTS

There are several reasons why you might want to restore a backup, for example:

- Because you bought a new computer and want to transfer your data.
- You made a mistake and want to start processing from before the mistake was made.
- You have a reports or layouts backup and you want to copy them to another installation of accounts.

Tip: If you backed up using this computer in the past, you can find a list of your previous backup on the Previous backups tab. You can't restore a backup from more recent versions into earlier versions. For example, you can't restore a backup from Sage 50 Accounts v22 into v21 or below.

You can restore a backup in just a few quick steps.

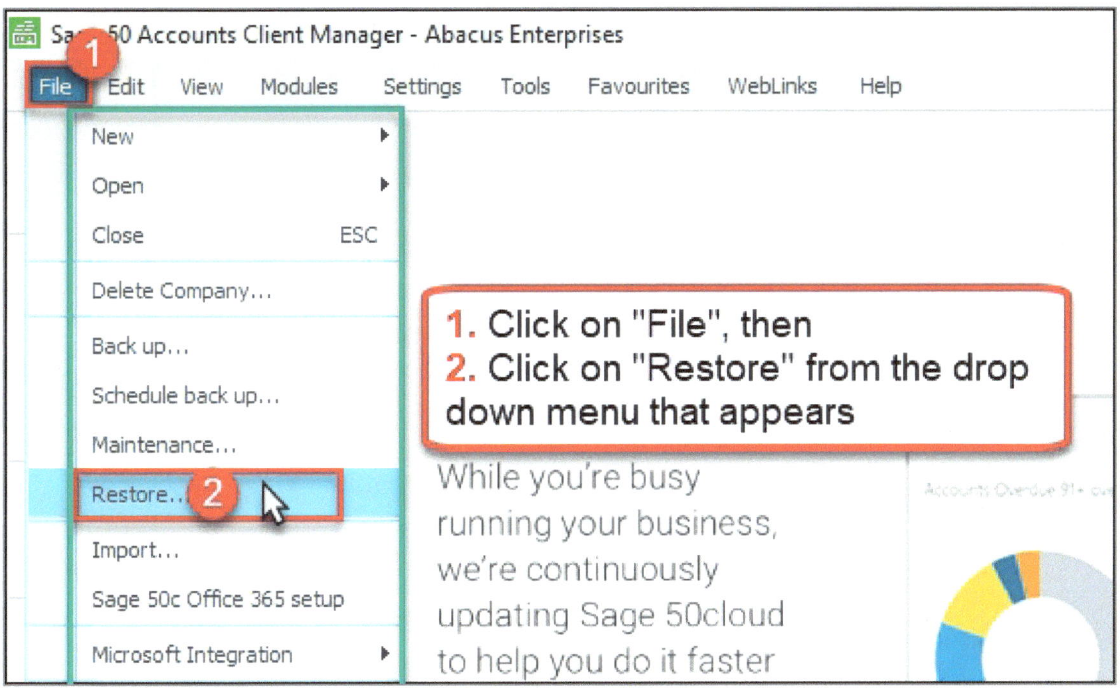

Fig. 237

Next, locate the file to restore.

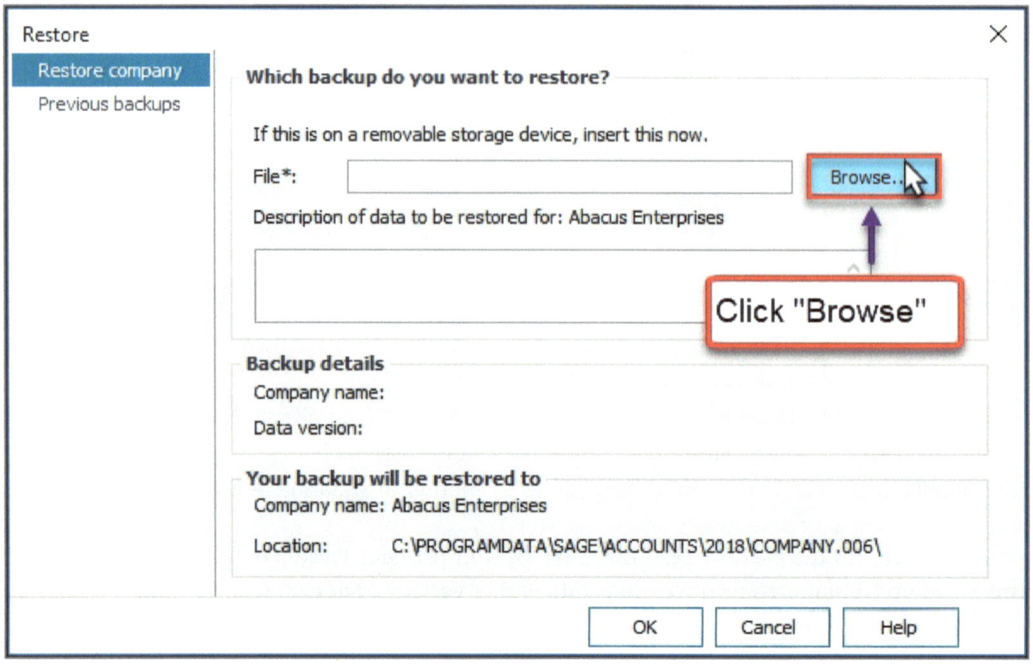

Fig. 238

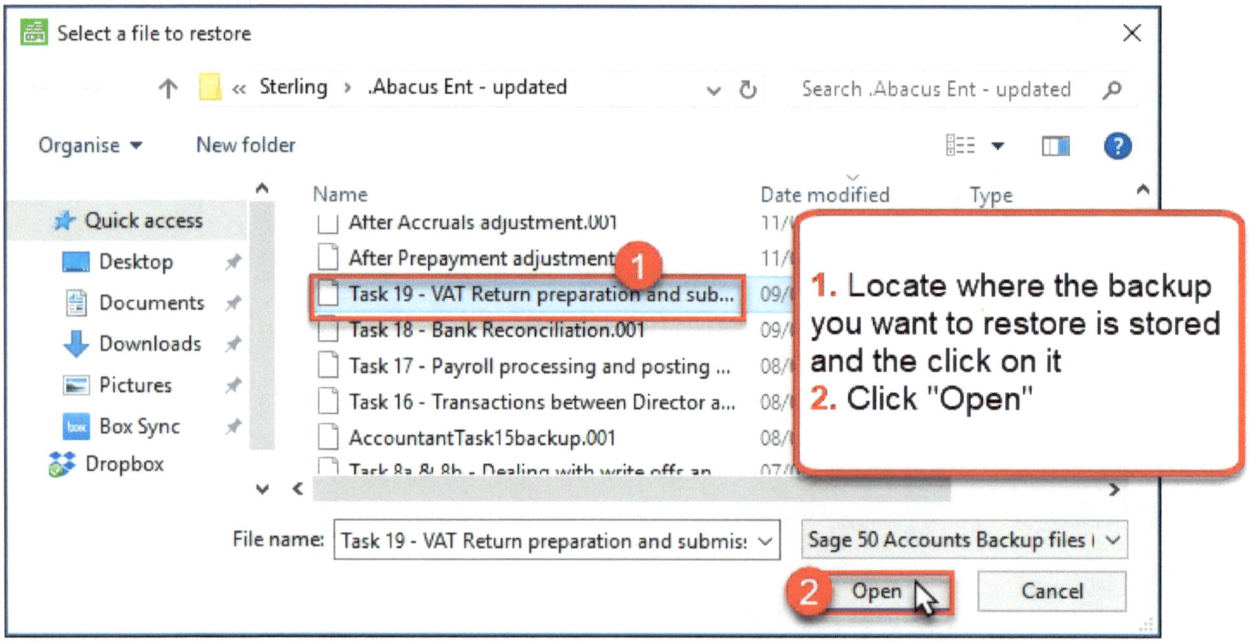

Fig. 239

The backup file will now be uploaded onto the restore window – see figure 240 on the next page.

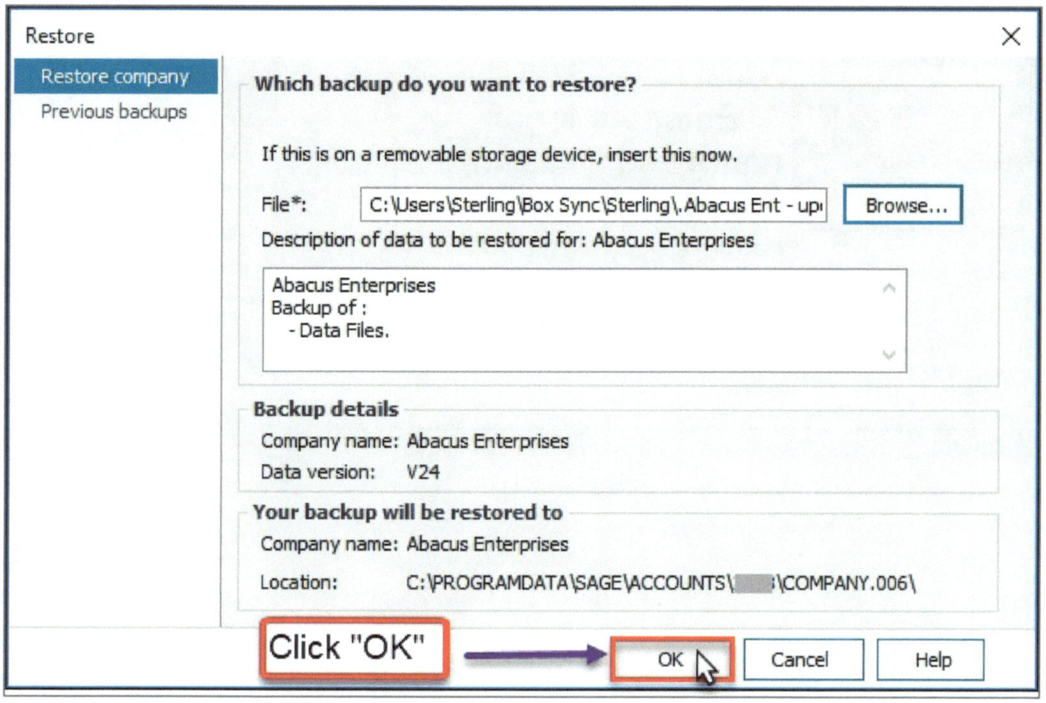

Fig. 240

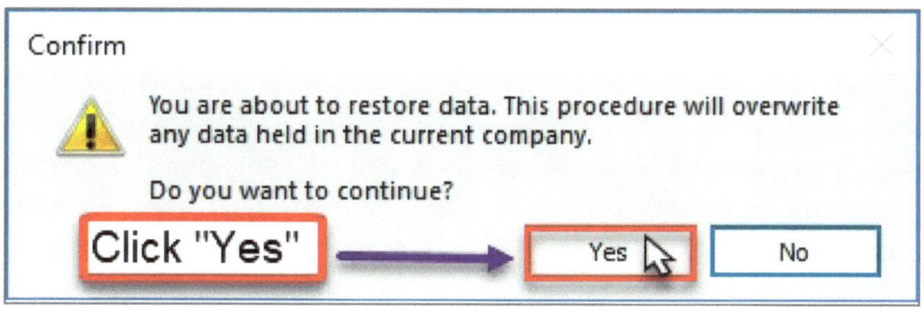

Fig. 241

Next, the restore process begins.

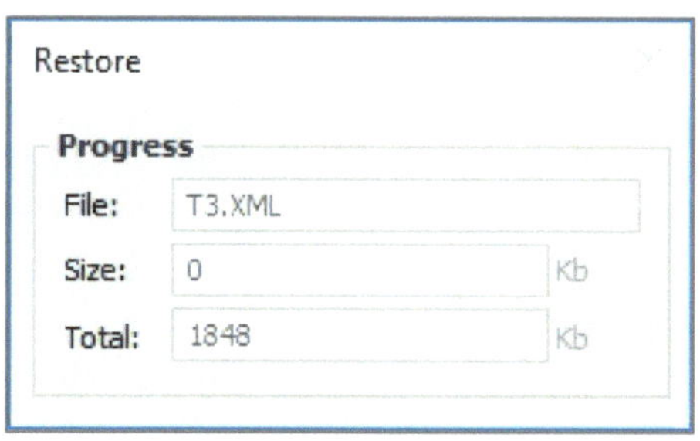

Fig. 242

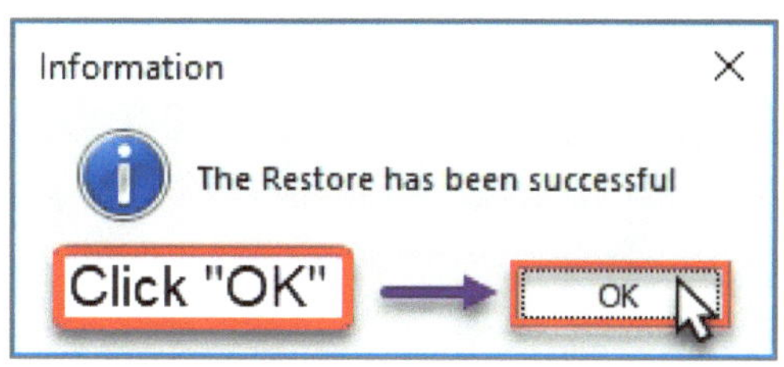

Fig. 243

Next, enter the logon name and password.

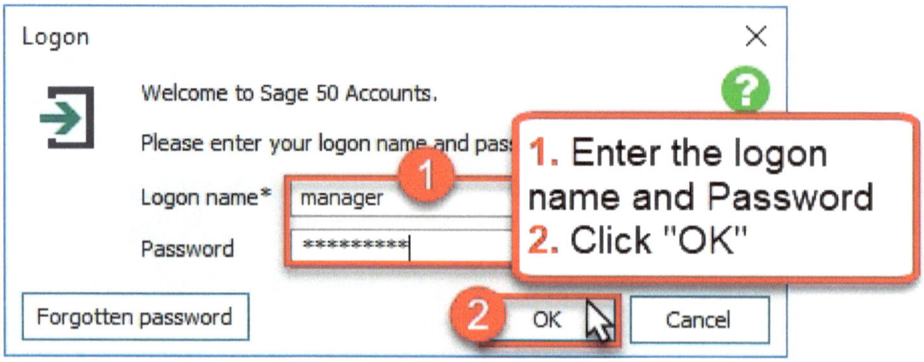

Fig. 244

This space is for notes

How to do Cash flow budget projection

Monthly cash flow projection: February to April

Abacus Enterprises

	February		**March**		**April**	
	Budget	Actual	Budget	Actual	Budget	Actual
1. CASH ON THE PREMISES [Beginning of month]						
2. INCOME						
(a) Cash sales						
(b) Collections from credit accounts						
(c) Loan or other cash injection						
3. TOTAL CASH RECEIPTS [2a + 2b + 2c=3]						
4. TOTAL CASH AVAILABLE [Before cash out] (1 + 3)						
5. OUTGOINGS						
(a) Purchases (merchandise)						
(b) Gross wages (excludes withdrawals)						
(c) Payroll expenses (taxes, etc.)						
(d) Outside services						
(e) Supplies (office and operating)						
(f) Repairs and maintenance						
(g) Advertising						
(h) Travel expenses (including deliveries)						
(i) Accounting and legal						
(j) Rent						
(k) Telephone						
(l) Utilities						
(m) Insurance						
(n) Taxes (real estate, etc.)						
(o) Interest						
(p) Other expenses [specify each]						
(r) Subtotal						
(s) Loan principal payment						
(t) Capital purchases [specify]						
(u) Other start-up costs						
(v) Reserve and/or escrow [specify]						
(w) Owner's withdrawal						
6. TOTAL CASH PAID OUT [Total from 5a to 5w]						
7. CASH POSITION [End of month] (4 minus 6)						

Look at the performance of Abacus Enterprises so far and complete the budget section of this cash flow projection according to what you think might realistically be the cash position of the company.

After each month, you should complete the "Actual" section with the figures of what actually was reflected in the accounts.

Do a variance analysis thereafter with possible explanations for the variances

"On your way to success, you will meet with many obstacles that will tend to undermine you; you will be tested sometimes more severely. if you persist and not give up, you will be rewarded in a big way."

Sterling Libs

"Knowing is not enough; we must apply. Wishing is not enough; we must do".
Johann Von Goethe

TASK 16: HOW TO FILE ACCOUNTS TO COMPANIES HOUSE & HMRC

From: https://www.gov.uk/guidance/corporation-tax-use-hmrcs-free-filing-software

You can use the HMRC online service to file your company, charity or association's:

- Company Tax Return (CT600) for Corporation Tax
- supplementary return pages CT600A, CT600E and CT600J
- statutory company accounts
- Corporation Tax computations
- other attachments (in PDF format) to support your return

The service will:

- help you work out your profit or loss adjusted for tax purposes
- automatically complete most of the form CT600 Company Tax Return for you

You'll be able to report:

- gross income from property up to £5,200 (expenses should not be greater than income)
- income up to £1,000 that does not come from your organisation's main trade
- capital allowances and balancing charges for plant and machinery in the main pool
- Annual Investment Allowance (AIA)
- low emission cars
- trading losses brought forward, set against profits in the same period or carried back from a later period
- share dividends

Companies that can file a Company Tax Return with the HMRC online service

You can use the service if:

- you're a charity and your turnover is up to £6.5 million per year
- a company whose turnover is up to £632,000 per year and are either a:
    - limited company
    - community amateur sports club
    - members club or other unincorporated organisation
    - community interest company

You must:

- have income from the profits of a single UK trade
- only need to make adjustments for:
    - depreciation
    - disallowable entertaining
    - donations
    - legal and professional fees
    - net losses on the sale of fixed assets
    - penalties and fines
    - unpaid employees' remuneration

Companies that cannot use the service

You cannot use the service if your company is:

- in liquidation or receivership
- not registered in the UK
- part of a group
- an insurance company, not including independent insurance brokers
- an investment company
- a credit union
- a commercial property management company

You also cannot use the service if your company has had more than 12 company directors at any one time in the return period, or:

- your accounts need an audit or have been audited
- the Corporation Tax accounting period for the return is covered by more than one set of statutory accounts
- your company pays its Corporation Tax in instalments
- you need to claim a repayment of a loan to a participator (for example, a director's loan) more than 9 months after the end of the accounting period
- you need to report:
    - adjustments for something reported in a previous year

- called up share capital not paid
- capital allowances (except for specific plant and machinery, AIA and low emission cars)
- chargeable gains or losses
- complex loan-relationship entries
- contingent assets
- financial instruments
- foreign currency transactions
- foreign trade income
- income or expenditure from investment assets
- leased cars
- non-trading income (except interest received)
- research and development costs
- restructuring costs
- share-based payments
- share premium

If you cannot file a Company Tax Return using the HMRC online service

If you cannot use the HMRC online service you can send your Company Tax Return online using commercial software.

The process of filing the accounts using HMRC online software

This task assumes that you will be using HMRC online software as opposed to third-party commercial software to file your accounts and tax return.

Here is what you'll need before you start:

a) Your Accounts (Profit and Loss account, Balance sheet & Trial Balance) prepared using your accounting software.
b) Your Government Gateway user ID and password - register for a HMRC online account if you don't have one by visiting this web address: *https://online.hmrc.gov.uk/registration/newbusiness*
c) Your Companies House password and authentication code if you're filing your accounts with Companies House at the same time - register online with Companies House if you haven't already by visiting this web address: *https://ewf.companieshouse.gov.uk/runpage?page=webfilingRegister*

Once you have those details handy (a, b and c), type *https://www.gov.uk/file-your-company-accounts-and-tax-return* to a web browser.

Here is what you will see once that page loads up – see figure 245 on the next page.

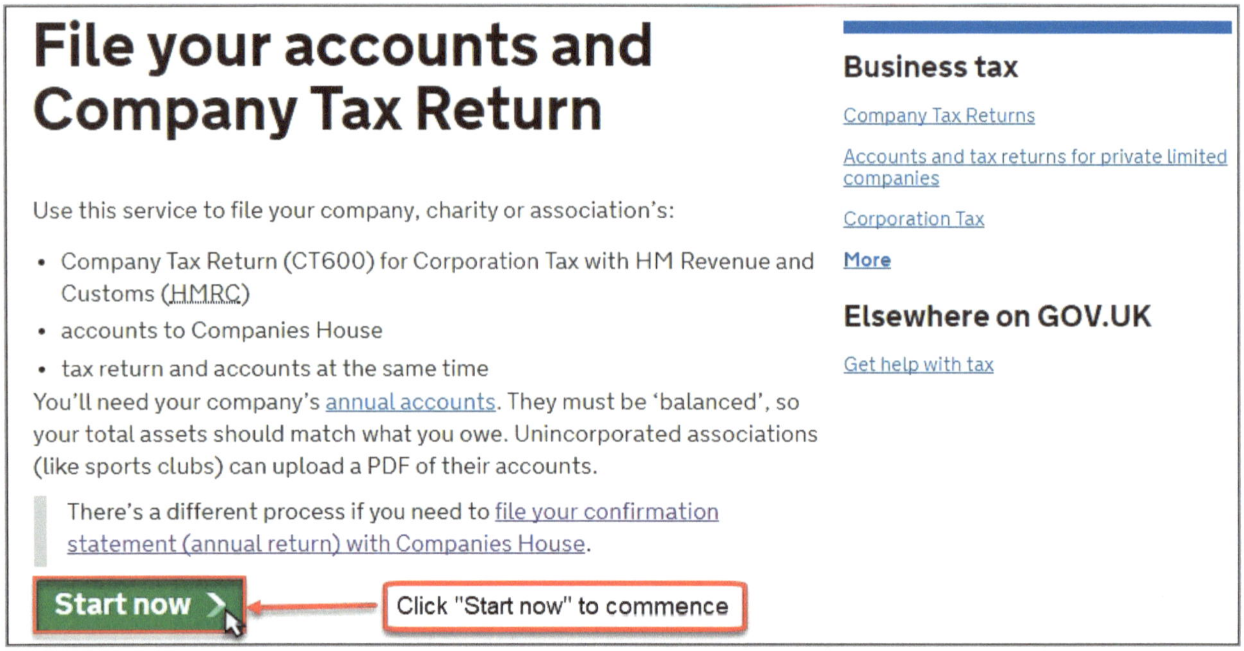

Fig. 245

Once you click start now as illustrated in the figure above, you will be directed to the sign in page.

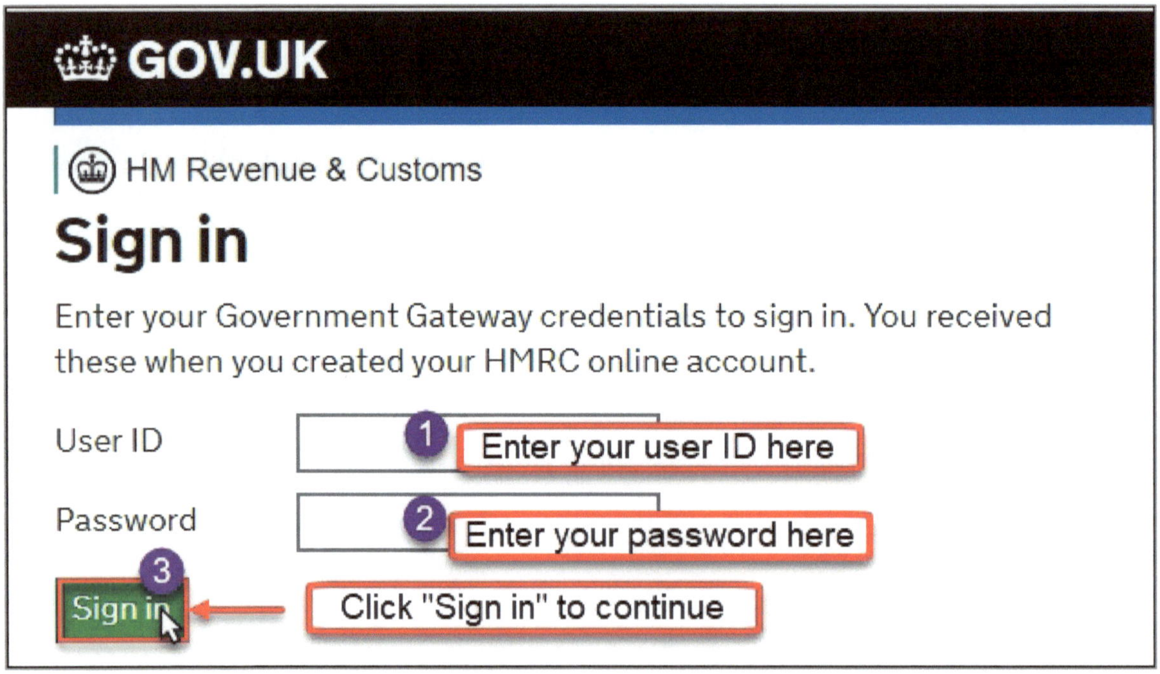

Fig. 246

For security reason, once you have signed in an access code will be sent to the mobile phone number you have registered for this purpose.

Fig. 247

You will then be directed to set up security back up – see figure on the next page.

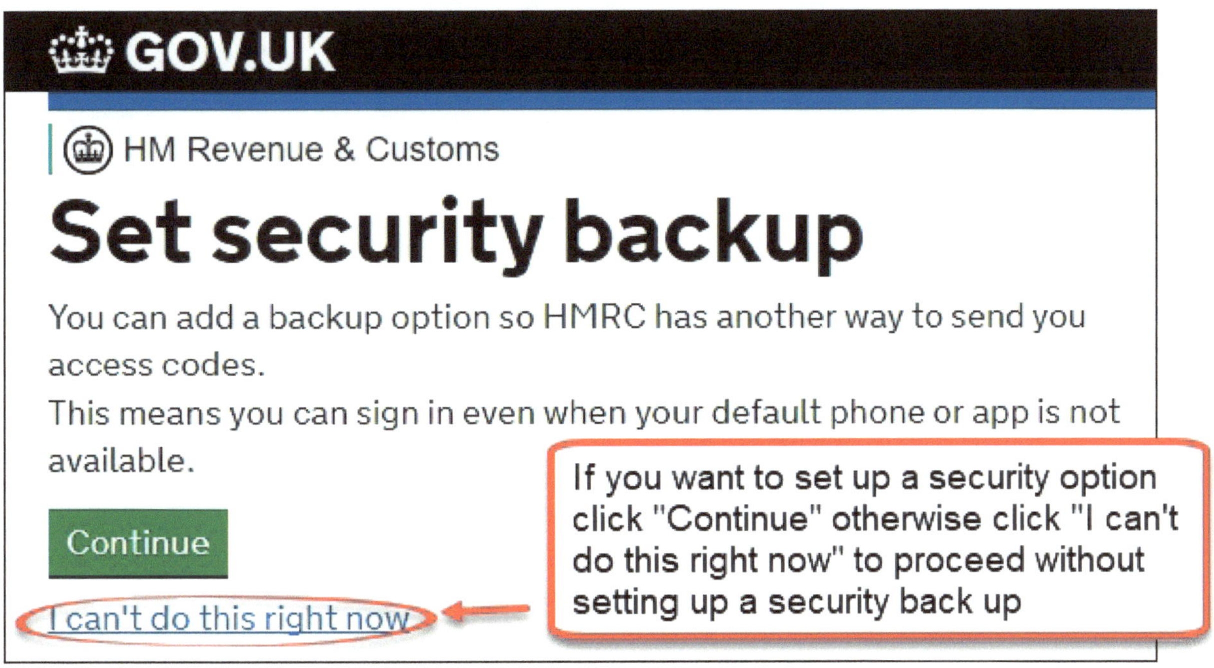

Fig. 248

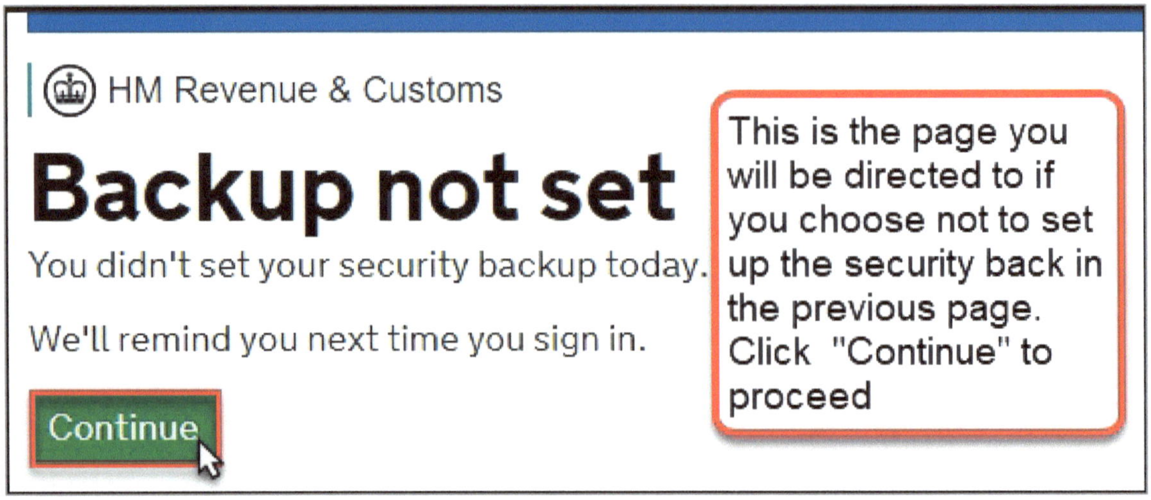

Fig. 249

You will then be directed to the dashboard of your tax account when you click continue.

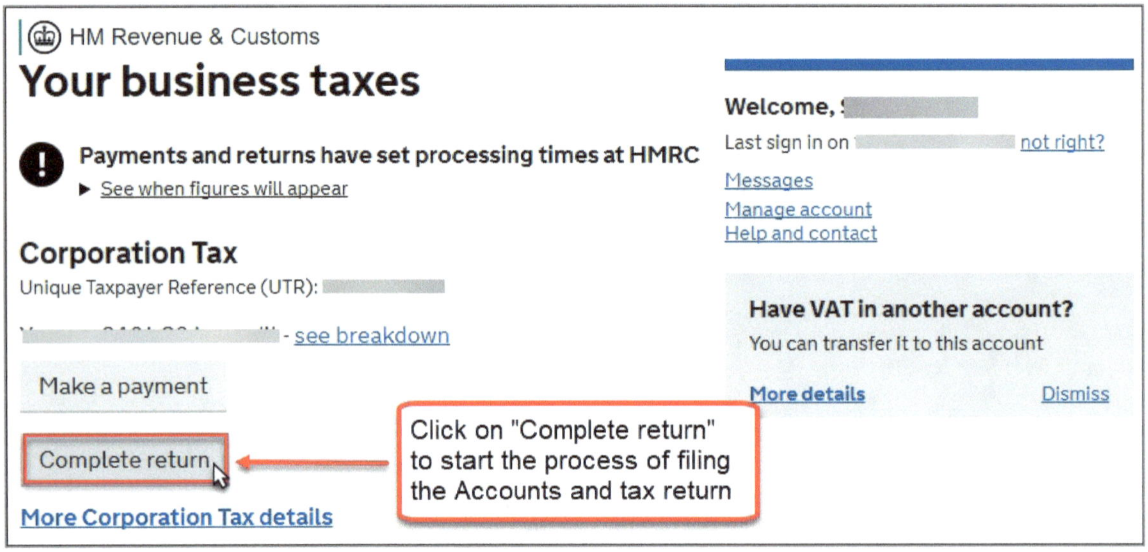

Fig. 250

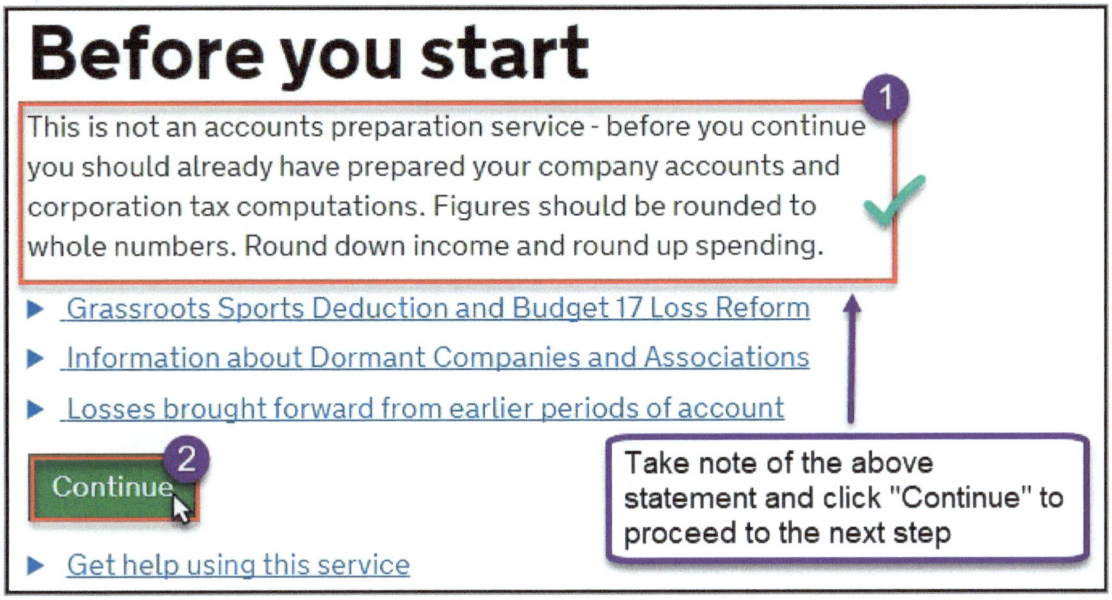

Fig. 251

Having got your accounts (Trial balance, Profit and Loss account and Balance sheet) ready and handy, when you click continue as illustrated in the figure above, you will then be led through a series of questions requiring mostly yes or no answers.

Once you have answered the questions accordingly, you will come to the profit & loss and balance sheet pages where you will then be able to use the figures of the profit & Loss, Trial balance and balance sheet produced from your accounting system to complete the profit & Loss and Balance sheet details within HMRC software and eventually once you have completed filling in the profit & Loss account details and the balance sheet, you will then be directed to a page where you can submit the accounts and tax return to Companies House & HMRC.

This space is for notes

"In the long run, you hit only what you aim at. Therefore, though you should fail, immediately you had better aim at something high."

Henry David Thoreau

"Be transformed by the renewing of your mind"
Romans 12:2

THE KEY SKILLS THAT CAN HELP YOU GET AND KEEP AN ACCOUNTING JOB

Identifying the skills that lead to success in accounting will not only increase your job satisfaction, but also make it easier for you to build your long-term career goals.

No matter how big a company ever gets, the need for an accounts department persists. Perhaps that focus is on auditing, maybe management or tax and finance related. Chances are, you will start in one of two career paths – technical or commercial.

Accounting requires certain hard skills, such as mathematics and expertise with accounting software. A thorough knowledge of relevant laws and regulations is necessary in many positions, too.
However, accounting also requires a number of soft skills that you might not learn in school but will definitely help you land and keep a job.

Here is a list of six accounting skills that employers are looking for in CV's/resumes, cover letters, job applications and interviews. It will serve you well to be in possession of this skills in increasing measure as you progress in your accounting career.

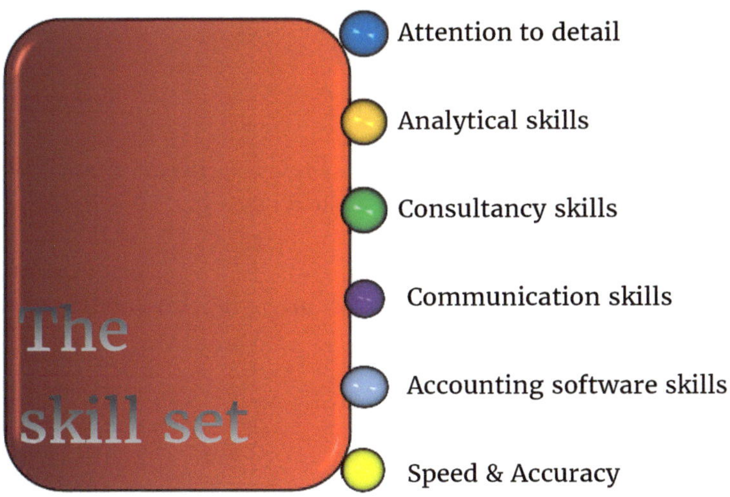

staying current with technology is perhaps the greatest pressure you will constantly face in your accounting and finance career. As technology impacts on the way you do your job as accountant, make sure you stay abreast of the changes and train and retrain to keep your skills up to date.

And here is the professional code of ethics you are required to abide by as an accountant.

Under the Code of Professional Ethics, as an accountant, you must follow these five principles:

1. **Integrity.**

You must be straightforward and honest in all professional and business relationships.

2. **Objectivity.**

You must not compromise professional or business judgment because of bias, conflict of interest or the undue influence of others.

3. **Professional competence and due care.**

You must maintain professional knowledge and skill (in practice, legislation and techniques) to ensure that a client or employer receives competent professional service.

4. **Confidentiality.**

You must not disclose confidential professional or business information or use it to your personal advantage, unless you have explicit permission to disclose it, or a legal or professional right or duty to disclose it.

5. **Professional behaviour.**

You must comply with relevant laws and regulations and avoid any action that may bring disrepute to the profession.

ABOUT THE AUTHOR

Sterling Libs has trained over one thousand people in his accounting firm and mentored many of them who eventually went on to get jobs in the accounting industry.

Sterling trained as a Chartered Accountant and has written several practical accounting books that have helped many accounting students and graduates in their accounting career journeys to getting accounting jobs. He studied and qualified for his professional accountancy career in London England. He currently lives and works in London.

He has been very instrumental in training many accounting students, and graduates in gaining work-based practical accounting experience and many of his trainees have been able to get accounting jobs in the UK and abroad. He loves mentoring individuals to discover, develop and deploy their talents and gifts to make the world a better place for all.

He is passionate about inspiring confidence for work, and life in general, among all those he meets and interacts with.

More on Sterling Libs

To have Sterling Libs speak to your organisation or train your staff on the principles and strategies found in *this book* or any other productivity insights, email sterling@sterlinglibs.com

For more information about Sterling, visit www.sterlinglibs.com

STERLING LIBS

www.ingramcontent.com/pod-product-compliance
Lightning Source LLC
LaVergne TN
LVHW070935210926
848482LV00003B/247
* 9 7 8 1 9 1 1 0 3 7 1 8 7 *